D0288345

Mistrusting Refugees

Mistrusting Refugees

EDITED BY

E. Valentine Daniel and John Chr. Knudsen

BOWLING GREEN STATE UNIVERSITY DISCARDED LIBRARY

UNIVERSITY OF CALIFORNIA PRESS

Berkeley   Los Angeles   London

BOWLING GREEN STATE UNIVERSITY LIBRARIES

University of California Press
Berkeley and Los Angeles, California

University of California Press
London, England

Copyright © 1995 by The Regents of the University of California

Library of Congress Cataloging-in-Publication Data

Mistrusting refugees / edited by E. Valentine Daniel and John Chr.
Knudsen.
    p.   cm.
   Includes bibliographical references and index.
   ISBN 0-520-08898-0 (c : alk paper).—ISBN 0-520-08899-9 (p :
alk. paper)
    1. Refugees—Psychology. 2. Trust (Psychology) I. Daniel, E.
Valentine. II. Knudsen, John Chr.
HV640.M57 1995
362.87′019—dc20   95-18975
                                               CIP

Printed in the United States of America

1 2 3 4 5 6 7 8 9

The paper used in this publication meets the minimum requirements of American National
Standard for Information Sciences—Permanence of Paper for Printed Library Materials,
ANSI Z39.48-1984 ⊗

CONTENTS

FOREWORD
Lal Jayawardena / *vii*

ACKNOWLEDGMENTS / *xi*

Introduction
E. Valentine Daniel and John Chr. Knudsen / *1*

1. When Trust Is on Trial: Negotiating Refugee Narratives
John Chr. Knudsen / *13*

2. Trust, Abuse of Trust, and Mistrust among Cambodian Refugee Women:
A Cultural Interpretation
Marjorie A. Muecke / *36*

3. Torture, Refuge, and Trust
Stuart Turner / *56*

4. (Mis)Trusting Narratives: Refugee Stories of Post-1922 Greece
and Post-1974 Cyprus
Mary N. Layoun / *73*

5. On Ropes of Memory: Narrating the Palestinian Refugees
Muhammad Siddiq / *87*

6. Refugees as Foreigners: The Problem of Becoming German and Finding Home
Jeffrey M. Peck / *102*

7. Starting Over: How, What, and for Whom Does One Write about Refugees?
The Poetics and Politics of Refugee Film as Ethnographic Access
in a Media-saturated World
Michael M. J. Fischer / *126*

8. Fostering Trust in a Climate of Fear
Beatriz Manz   /   151

9. Transforming Trust: Dispossession and Empowerment among Palestinian Refugees
Julie M. Peteet   /   168

10. Afghanistan's Muhajirin (Muslim "Refugee-Warriors"): Politics of Mistrust
and Distrust of Politics
M. Nazif Shahrani   /   187

11. In Search of the Locus of Trust: The Social World of the Refugee Camp
Eftihia Voutira and Barbara E. Harrell-Bond   /   207

12. Forms, Formations, and Transformations of the Tamil Refugee
E. Valentine Daniel and Yuvaraj Thangaraj   /   225

13. State-centered Refugee Law: From Resettlement to Containment
T. Alexander Aleinikoff   /   257

CONTRIBUTORS   /   *279*
INDEX   /   *281*

FOREWORD

The world is awash with refugees. According to the United Nations High Commissioner for Refugees (UNHCR), in 1970, there were 2.5 million refugees in the world. Ten years ago, this number increased to 11 million. In early 1994, it reached 20 million. The *New York Times* of 8 August 1994 puts the number at 23 million. To this subtotal must be added an additional 25 million who are displaced within their own countries in their attempt to escape violence. This gives a rough total of 45 to 48 million people who have been forced from their homes. The numbers continue to increase.[1] The collapse of the former Yugoslavia alone has displaced 3.8 million people (UNHCR 1993b). The more recent horrors of Rwanda and Burundi make counting itself a heartless activity. Civil wars in the name of blood, ethnic purity, the nation, religion, and language that have the potential of escalating across national boundaries are being fought in all continents, with the possible exception of Australia. And the refugees from war fail to include those millions who are displaced from their homes as a result of poverty, persecution, and a whole array of other widespread violations of human rights. The high commissioner of the UNHCR, Sadako Ogata, has correctly observed that "the subject of refugees and displaced people is high on the list of international concerns today not only because of its humanitarian significance, but also of its impact on peace, security and stability. The world cannot reach a new order without effectively addressing the problem of human displacement" (1993a: iii).

Alas, the increasingly reactive response of nations of the developed world is not the provision of refuge or the restoration of security in the homes and homelands of those who flee but the securing of their own national boundaries against what is described with the terrifying images of tides, floods, and inundation. What is wrong with these images are not that they are not true but that they are inappropriate for describing the trickle of refugees into Europe and North America. Europe, for example, is on the verge of turning its territory into a *Festnung*. Ironically, the brunt of the economic burden[2] of refugees is not borne by nations of the developed world but by nations such as Malawi, Pakistan, Ethiopia, Tanzania, Sudan, Iran, Zaire, Burundi, Kenya, Uganda, and Bangladesh, to name but the top eleven.[3]

Among the conditions that have made this apparently never-ending crisis of refugees possible are colonial and postcolonial politics and geographies, the rise of the nation-state as a reality, the rise of industrial capitalism and industrial socialism with the accompanying development and spread of arms, and finally, cold war and post–cold war politics. It is true that the United Nations as well as individual nation-states have faced and continue to "deal with" the problem of refugees. Unfortunately, this problem is not seen as one until it is also perceived as a "crisis." And when it is thus perceived, there are two courses of action that are resorted to. The first is the self-protective reaction of nation-states. The action generated in this domain is mainly political, aimed primarily at protecting the borders and "integrities" of nation-states, nation-states that are but historical bantlings but are imagined by its citizens as being ancient. Economic action, in this course, is but a subsidiary of the political. The second course of action is crisis management that is triggered by UNHCR and other humanitarian aid-giving agencies. When these two courses of action do meet—and their meetings are always practical and almost never ideological—their encounters are frustrating at best and confrontational at worst.

Mistrusting Refugees addresses the "refugee problem," not merely as a crisis, but as something diffuse and enduring, something that ought to be seen if not as fundamentally human, then at least as being fundamental to the human condition of the late twentieth century and, in all likelihood, of the twenty-first century as well. The refugee is as real as the nation-state is real. What is both diffuse and enduring in this reality is a pervasive cultural and psychological attitude, an attitude that is grounded on what the editors of this volume have called mistrust. The cure—if that is the word—that the authors of this volume suggest is nothing dramatic or drastic. Such a cure is called for only when crises are perceived and when only what is perceived are crises. Even though the authors of this collection do not deny that the refugee problem has begun reaching the crisis stage with increasing frequency in the closing years of this century, their focus is not on the refugee *crisis* per se but on the pervasive attitude of cultured human beings that makes these crises possible. By identifying "trust" or the lack thereof as being one of the central and chronic attitudinal—cultural as well as psychological—conditions that provide the ground that spawns refugees, the cure they do suggest is also a gradual and, in the long run, more effective, one. Continuing our medicalizing metaphor, we may say that the treatment is more homeopathic than allopathic. Crisis management through the repeated administration of allopathic antibiotics seems to have run its course of usefulness and has even created a newer, drug-resistant strain.

This collection of essays, written by fifteen individuals who have worked with refugees and their problems at the theoretical as well as practical levels, is both timely and deserving of the serious attention not only of those who are intimately engaged in refugee studies or refugee work but of every thinking citizen. For who in this world is not either a potential refugee or a potential host to one?

Lal Jayawardena
Founding Director,
World Institute for Development
and Economics Research

NOTES

1. The numbers presented here are taken from a recent book compiled by the UNHCR: *The State of the World's Refugees: The Challenge of Protection* (UNHCR 1993*a*).

2. As a ratio of refugee population to gross national product per capita (see UNHCR 1993*a*: Annex I.3, 155).

3. These figures do not include Bosnia and Herzegovina, which had an estimated 810,000 internally displaced people as of 31 December 1992 (ibid.).

REFERENCES

UNHCR

1993*a*   *The State of the World's Refugees: The Challenge of Protection.* Penguin: London.
1993*b*   *Information Notes on Former Yugoslavia.* No. 12/93. Geneva.

ACKNOWLEDGMENTS

The editors wish to express their thanks to the World Institute for Development and Economics Research for funding the conference "Trust and the Refugee Experience," where most of the papers published in this volume originated. This conference, which was held in June 1991, was hosted in Bergen, Norway, by the Department of Anthropology of the University of Bergen, to whom we extend our thanks. The editors also thank Margaret Hoey-Daniel for copy editing an early draft of the volume, and Stephanie Hoelscher, Ellen Moodie, and Veve Lele for final preparation of the manuscript. And finally, we owe a special debt of gratitude to Michelle Nordon of the University of California Press for her guidance. Would that all authors could have an editor as patient as she.

Introduction

E. Valentine Daniel and John Chr. Knudsen

From its inception the experience of a refugee puts trust on trial. The refugee mistrusts and is mistrusted. In a profound sense, one becomes a refugee even before fleeing the society in which one lives and continues to be a refugee even after one receives asylum in a new place among a new people. The process of the breakdown of trust may range from a breach of faith between ethnic communities in a multiethnic nation that were once committed to upholding a multiethnic democratic state in the abstract as in Sri Lanka (see Daniel and Thangaraj this volume) to events far more immediate, as when a Cambodian girl unwittingly betrays her grandmother to the Khmer Rouge by telling her captors that she had read stories to her, revealing thereby her grandmother's literacy and, ergo, making her into an "enemy" of the people, deserving extermination (Sheehy 1987). The event or set of events that triggers a person's decision to become a refugee is the radical disjunction between this person's familiar *way-of-being* in the world and a new reality of the sociopolitical circumstances that not only threatens that way-of-being but also forces one to *see* the world differently. The crisis that precipitates the refugee status is at once personal and social, and therefore it is a crisis that pursues the refugee well into his or her life in the country in which he or she seeks asylum. Such crises of being are invariably accompanied by the erosion of trust.

By "trust," we do not intend a largely conscious state of awareness, something akin to belief, but rather its opposite: something more akin to what the French anthropologist Pierre Bourdieu called "habitus" or what Martin Heidegger called "being-in-the-world." In the best of all possible worlds, at the point of a refugee's reincorporation into a new culture and society, trust is reconstituted, if not restored. The real world, however, is not the best of all possible worlds. And in the real world, whether one is a refugee or not, trust will—no, it must—coexist with mistrust. Unlike life under "ordinary" circumstances, or more correctly, under circumstances over which one exercises a certain measure of control, in the life of a refugee, trust is overwhelmed by mistrust, besieged by suspicion, and relentlessly undermined by caprice. One may ask why "mistrust" too, like trust, is not part of a habitus, an aspect of being-in-the-world. Indeed, as Eftihia Voutira and Barbara Harrell-Bond point out, mistrust is a cultural value in many societies. But there is a difference. The distinction lies, we believe, in the measure of mistrust's magnitude in the experience of a refugee: not only does mistrust push itself onto the surface of a quickened consciousness but the agitated state of awareness that it creates bars it from settling back into a state of comfortable and largely unconscious comportment with the surroundings of its world. By contrast, where mistrust is a cultural value, available for invocation into conscious ideology or normative recitation, such a comportment is commonplace.

Furthermore, the capacity to trust needs to be underwritten by the capacity to tame chance, especially the chance of being hurt. This capacity is not an individual matter but a gift that a cultured society[1] gives a person. In refugee experience it is this capacity that is rendered powerless; individuals and groups have little else to do than to flee. It is this escape from violence that Aristide R. Zolberg, Astri Suhrke, and Sergio Aguayo (1989) have constructed as the central feature of the refugee experience. As political scientists, their study has highlighted violence emerging from the abuse of power, mainly state-centered power. In our more anthropological collection, we attempt to look at the consequences of the abuse of power from another aspect, the aspect of the collapse of culturally constituted trust.

TRUST AND THE SEMIOTICS OF CULTURE

We hold with Marjorie A. Muecke (1987:274) that "the experience of the political refugee is profoundly cultural because it compels refugees as individuals and as collective victims/survivors of massive chaos to resolve what Max Weber ([1915] 1958) identified as the problem of meaning, the need to affirm "the ultimate explicableness of experience." By culture, we do not intend to refer to something essential and fixed but rather to a creative activity of symbol making and symbol sharing. Culture is fundamentally dialogic, that is, a logic that bridges the gap of understanding that exists between individuals or groups. That culture, by definition, entails more than one individual goes without saying. But a dialogue involving two individuals is only a metonymic moment in culture. Cultural dialogic in its unlimited sense entails symbolic worlds in communicative interaction with each other. The logic in question is not a perfectly systematized one but rather contains within it both a certain measure of redundancy (ergo, systematicity and predictability) and a certain measure of the uncertain, the indeterminate, the novel, and the creative. Culture entails active agreement and disagreement. As the Russian semiotician Mikhail Bakhtin (1986:142) observed, this "stimulates and deepens understanding, makes the other's word (and world) more resilient and true to itself, and precludes mutual dissolution and confusion." Culture, in other words, is a process: it is forever emergent. This process can flourish or it can be stifled. When it flourishes, it yields meaning. When it is stifled, it is stifled by one of two processes, which may be formally defined in terms of hyperinformation, on the one hand, and hyperredundancy, on the other.

Meaning, Information, and Hyperredundancy

In the technical sense derived from communication theory, information and redundancy occupy the poles in a continuum. In structural linguistics, absolute information is absolutely syntagmatic. For example, an ever-unfolding series of numbers that defies all predictability as to what number will turn up next is such a purely syntagmatic chain. Where information cannot be related to something pre-existing (i.e., made into at least a partially redundant form) meaning cannot exist. Such common experiences described in ordinary language as "culture shock" or "sensory overstimulation" are states entailing hyperinformation devoid of redundancy, making one sigh in exasperation, "What next!" In accounts of initial experiences in concentration camps and other such settings of extreme uncertainty and unpredictability, we see humans caught in such a state of hyperinformation, unable to give meaning to their experiences. Primo Levi's description of the newcomers' first traumatic experiences of arriving in Auschwitz and their inability to create a decipherable world serves as an apt example of such a state. He remarks,

> In conformity to that simple model which we atavistically carry within us—"we" inside and the enemy outside, separated by a sharply defined geographic frontier— . . . one entered hoping at least for the solidarity of one's companions in misfortune. But the hoped-for allies, except in special cases, were not there; there were instead a thousand sealed-off monads, and between them a desperate hidden and continuous struggle. (1988:23–24)

When each monad presents itself as distinct and unpredictable we have a total collapse of meaning as a result of hyperinformation. But these same monadic formations that emerge in camps are also capable of destroying meaning from the opposite end. On this extreme, meaning is negated when predictability becomes absolute and no information is forthcoming: one monad becomes just like another. In a thoroughly regimented camp (not unusual in refugee experiences), where blueprints for behavior are offered and enforced by well-meaning caseworkers, a state of hyperredundancy is created. In keeping with such a hyperredundant context is the belief of refugee relief organizations and workers that all refugees, merely by being "refugees," are to be treated as "equal" (read, "identical") regardless of their vast variations in personal background, motives for leaving, reasons for escape, and plans for the future. That is, individual identities and continuities, sustained by unique biographies, are systematically neutralized, once again making for meaningless existence.

If caseworkers present highly systematized, rule-governed, and therefore hyperredundant social orders into which refugees are expected to be socialized, many refugees imagine, either independently or in reaction to the ones presented by the caseworkers, social orders of their past in equally frozen and unreal terms. The freedom to change, modify, and equivocate is the very sign that the work of culture is functioning freely. The petrified social orders mandated by caseworkers or imagined by refugees under conditions of confinement signify a crisis in culture wherein past and present remain as rigid as they are disparate, connected only by a chasm of despair.

Meaning (and, therefore, culture) is sustained by bringing about an optimal balance between the extremes of redundancy and information. Where meaning prevails, culture flourishes. Meaning links what is traditional with what is new and the past with the future. As noted by Bruno Bettelheim (1986) and Levi (1988), the most successful survivors in the Nazi camps were those able to link their present to the past as well as to the future. This was as true of Communists as it was of the deeply religious Jehovah's Witnesses. "Sorrow, in them or around them, was decipherable, and therefore did not overflow into despair" (Levi 1988:118)—decipherability itself being dependent on continuity and continuity dependent on a certain measure of redundancy. The various stages in the refugee's life cycle, which threaten life with radical discontinuity, are stages in which "trust" is placed on trial. The vindication of trust depends on the creation of meaning and the survival of the cultural process. For this to happen, the refugee must be free to seek information when hyperredundancy has made life meaningless and to seek redundancy when hyperinformation has made life equally meaningless.

A refugee must be free to choose to provide information and must feel assured that the information provided will not be given a meaning that could be used against him or her. In refugee camps, rehabilitation centers, and countries of settlement, refugees feel that they have no control over how caseworkers, government organizations, or strangers use the information they have provided. Much of the success of caseworkers as well as government policies regarding refugees pivots on this fulcrum of trust. Psychosocial workers who probe and obtain information that is likely to be quite dear and personal receive along with this information the added responsibility of not turning it into a weapon of oppression. For a simple act such as assigning a psychiatric label to a set of behaviors and recording it on a refugee's chart (without regard to the cultural embeddedness of the label in question and its inappropriateness to the culture of the refugee at hand) could turn out to be precisely the kind of weapon that justifies the refugee's mistrust. It could lead to the postponement of an individual's date of release or even the denial of asylum. In the case of the former, the logic underlying the labeling deems that those demonstrating signs of severe personal problems should remain in the camp until they are better prepared for life in the country of asylum—a reasoning that may be more the cause of the problem than the cure (see Knudsen 1988:122–141).

To be sure, caseworkers do not constitute a monolithic lot. The reasons that make them choose their vocation are complex. Some are impelled by impeccable altruism and a desire to help, some find fulfillment in wielding power over the lives of helpless others, and some consider themselves servants of the countries of asylum they represent. And sadly, the demands of states and state interests—even when channeled through the United Nations—exert a stronger force on the daily duties of the average caseworker than do humanitarian interests. Add to the burden of the caseworkers who are overwhelmed by their case loads the myriad national and international bureaucratic microstructures that, once again, are primarily beholden to states' interests, and one ends up with caseworkers who are reduced to information-gathering and information-dispensing functionaries. They become men and women who have no real opinions of their own, and the information they gather does not inform them.

Information provided by a refugee must not only *not* be used to oppress but if trust is to be restored, it must also be rendered meaningful. Transit camps and locations of resettlement are contexts wherein the need to create meaning and recover the cultural process becomes acute for refugee and "stranger" (whether a caseworker or a native of the new country). The meaning-making process is not one that can be brought about by the refugee or the "stranger" in isolation; it is the product of collaboration between the two. In particular, the refugee needs to be a full participant in the formulation and reformulation of culture in this context. The question that confronts us then is, how is this collaborative venture of making meaning and enhancing the cultural process to be facilitated?

Several anthropologists working with refugees have found that one of the important components in the recovery of meaning, the making of culture, and the reestablishment of trust is the need and the freedom to construct a normative picture of one's past within which "who one was" can be securely established to the satisfaction of the refugee. The refugee's self-identity is anchored more to who she or he was than what she or he has become. In the context of rehabilitation in Western countries, as an extension of the valorization of an egalitarian ideology, agents of the host country seek to level down each refugee to a common denominator, an ideal-typical refugee, and neutralize differences so as to provide each refugee not only with a fresh start but also with an equal one. "Individualities" constructed in oral autobiographies are deemed irrelevant by many caseworkers, whereas for the refugee this is the foundation on which a meaningful world may be rebuilt.

Adverse forces that beat on the self-identity of refugees come also from fellow refugees, from "one's companions in misfortune" (Levi 1988:23). Ironically, fellow refugees are more capable of and effective in making one's past irrelevant and dubitable than are social workers. What are the interests served by such actions on the part of refugees themselves, and what are their effects? How do these processes figure into the refugee experience of trust and the loss of culture? These are questions that several chapters in this collection, especially John Chr. Knudsen's, address.

Refugees and the "National Order of Things"

The appeal for research that sheds light on the cultural dimension of the refugee problem is not intended to make a case for a romantic preservation or restoration of a lost way of life. The understanding of culture as a process precludes such romanticism. On the contrary, the cultural argument does recognize that the refugee has to live in a world of new social, political, linguistic, economic, and other realities. No understanding of or prescription for the refugee problem will be sound without the recognition of this fact. But these are realities to the construction of which the refugee is fully capable of contributing—and contributing richly, as history has shown only too well. But there is one reality that merits interrogating and therefore relaxing. This is the reality that Liisa Malkki (1992) calls the "national order of things." With far-reaching implications for rethinking identity, Malkki exposes the irony of our contemporary world: awash with refugees, on the one hand, and shackled to the national order of things, on the other. If the two are ironically linked, they are also complementary, the one phenomenon sustaining the other. Refugee and host are equal believers in national identities. The rub is that the host's nation and national identity are perceived as being intact and the refugee's in tatters. And there are myraid ways in which the haves lord it over the have-nots in this particular context, creating a state of affairs hardly conducive to fostering trust. There is a way for the host to meet the refugee halfway. This would be to realize that "identity [including the host's] is always mobile and processual, partly self-construction, partly categorization by others, partly a condition, a status, a label, a weapon, a shield, a fund of memories, . . . a creolized aggregate" (37). One's national identity is no less creolized. Such a realization is a significant step toward putting the refugee at ease, the first step toward what will and must come in its own time and way, the denationalization of the refugee's identity. The halfway meeting calls for the corresponding denationalization of the host's own smug nationalized identity. This is a theme that T. Alexander Aleinikoff and E. Valentine Daniel and Yuvaraj Thangaraj pick up, albeit on different registers, in their chapters in this volume.

THE ESSAYS

In the collection of essays that follows, anthropologists, literary critics, a psychiatrist, a geographer, a philosopher, and a legal scholar discuss the idea contained in the title of this volume, relating it to their own work with, among, or on refugees. In his opening chapter, John Knudsen describes the Vietnamese crisis of refuge, brought to international attention by the "boat people." In the boats, in transit camps, and later in countries of asylum we find these refugees making strategic adjustments to cope with profound uncertainties about life, culture, and trust. He argues that with the radical breakdown of relationships of trust, culture—in its dynamic everydayness—yields to anxiously calculated adjustments to rapidly and unpredictably changing realities, on the one hand, and to the memorializing of a past moral order and a tradition represented in "still-life" images, on the other. In short, when a community has little to put its trust in in the present and the future, an essentialized (but lost) "culture" is summoned to compensate for the absence of a trust-driven cultural life. While members of the older generation are the most zealous in trying to "retrieve" such a culture in their narratives, it is the younger ones who are most torn between the need to get on with life in a new world of trust and culture making and the need of their parents to hold onto an essentialized cultural past—a past that the young can only ambivalently imagine and suspiciously narrate. Knudsen wonders further about the propriety of the researcher's part in the making and breaking of the narratives in question.

Marjorie Muecke has worked closely for many years with Cambodian (Buddhist) refugees in Seattle. Her chapter shows us how "trust" is both gendered and culturally inflected. Besides being a moving account of the almost impossible burden that women, especially young nubile women, have to bear in proving their trustworthiness throughout the brutal travails of being a refugee and later, it is a telling indictment on refugee studies in general, which have failed to appreciate the distinctive experience of women refugees. "Being a refugee," Muecke tells us, "puts Khmer women at risk of self-mistrust on two accounts: first, the impossibility, when outside the traditional cultural bounds of Khmer society, of upholding the womanly ideal of being 'virtuous,' and second, their separation from children." Neither of these applies to men.

Stuart Turner has done extensive work with refugees who are victims of torture. On their bodies and psyches torture victims carry the insignia of state violence. Paradoxically, in their flight from violence, it is to another state, albeit a new one, that they must turn for refuge. Unfortunately, these states, especially those of the first world, meet the refugee with further displays of state power and violence, even if the latter takes on only bureaucratic and judicial forms. Turner laments the fact that in some first world countries refugee organizations offer help only to those who have already obtained legal status. Does the sufferer have to be legalized in order for his or her pain to be recognized as such? He further comments that as long as therapeutic work is directed to the individual, ignoring the wider context of community, state, and broader social issues, the likelihood of restoring trust is minimized. This sober advice, especially since it comes from someone whose professional ideology is individual centered, cannot be taken lightly.

The authors of the next four chapters are literary critics who remind us not only that those interested in expressive culture, including the literary critic, have invaluable insights into the refugee experience but also that the enormity of the problem imposes on a much wider set of professionals and scholars the burden of having to critically reflect on its nature and alleviation. Mary N. Layoun leads with an analysis of refugee narratives with a special focus on the novels of the Greek writer Dido Soteriou. Layoun finds in refugee narratives, not so much a nostalgia for a past when all was well and a trust-driven story prevailed, but a claim to "having known better even then" that the master story was suspect. What is both more threatening and more promising is the creation of a "critical community" through these narratives whereby a "moral claim" is made as to what the future "should or perhaps would be if the story (and its telling) were different." For in these narratives one finds not only the prefiguring of a future for the refugees but also the potential of "a radicalizing force on the indigenous population."

Muhammad Siddiq observes that with the establishment of the state of Israel, "Palestinians became a 'refugee nation' " and every Palestinian's individual life became a token of the collective historical experience of the Palestinian people. It was left to the poet and the novelist to reinscribe through the metaphor of individual lives in Palestinian narratives "national allegories." Siddiq reminds us that most of these narratives are carried forth in an oral tradition and most that are committed to writing are written in Arabic. It is in this context that Siddiq finds it painfully ironic that in a comment on Edward Said's book, *After the Last Sky: Palestinian Lives,* Richard Poirier writes, "It is Said's great accomplishment that thanks to this book, Palestinians will never be lost to history." To believe that only that which is written will survive is bad enough but to predicate the survival of an entire people's history on a book written in English, the colonialists' language, is elevated cheek. Siddiq's contribution belongs to a new genre of scholarship committed to revealing through translation a far richer corpus that is lost to translation, enticing thereby an indifferent world to step into a richer world—resilient, resourceful, and heroic—of which we know so little. This chapter also serves two more general functions. First, it makes us reflect on our ignorance of the lives and histories and cultures of refugees other than the Palestinians of whom we know even less. Second, it speaks to the refugee in all of us, the stranger within. We do not have to accept all the formulations of a postmodernist theoretician and cultural commentator such as Jean Baudrillard to realize that at the turning of this century, each one of us is vulnerable to becoming a construct, a work of inference, a statistic and an artifact of so-called information, a simulacrum;[2] just like a refugee.

Jeffrey M. Peck looks at the new Germany and its struggle with old prejudices that persist in its popular and commodity cultures. German exclusionary logic constructs fine gradations of differences and foreignness whereby a place for the "true" German can be secured and preserved. From his chapter, not only do we learn about Germany or Germans but we also learn about a certain xenophobia that is lodged in the soul of all European nations. Germany becomes the exemplar of this xenophobia because it, more than any other European nation, has had to come to terms with its recent history in which such dark fears had had even darker consequences and has had to atone for these consequences by instituting the most liberal immigration laws of any nation in Europe.

Michael M. J. Fischer brings this set of chapters to a close by making a case for "starting all over again"—for looking at refugees not as an archaically fixed category but one that has itself been caught in the new kinds of population shuffles

that characterize our postmodern world, for taking into account how refugees represent themselves, especially in and through the media whenever they have access to it. The medium that is Fischer's primary interest is film; his secondary interest, the novel. In both instances he invites us—by introducing several well-analyzed examples—to take note of the difference between these representations of refugees and those of the dominant media such as television newscasts. Fischer helps us appreciate refugees not only as victims but also as human beings with admirable resilience who leave to the generations that follow not merely a sense of passivity and dysfunction but in and through their expressive forms, a sense of identity and purpose.

The title of Beatriz Manz's chapter, "Fostering Trust in a Climate of Fear," is, if anything, an understatement of the enormity of the problem as well as of the hope contained in the experience of Guatemalan Indians. Even though the twentieth century is marred by violence of unprecedented scale, this century's other characteristic, change, again unprecedented in its rapidity, gives us the illusion that everything, even violent events, will pass. A side effect of this illusion is inaction and apathy. This is why Manz's account of five hundred years of suffering endured by Mayan Indians, brought closer to home in the late twentieth century by those known as Guatemalan refugees, is so profoundly disturbing. Where "punishment is arbitrary, irregular, and often fatal" and where "the rule of law is nonexistent," Manz writes, "there does not have to be a radical moment of disjunction . . . but rather a deepening of the lack of trust and estrangement."

If the challenge faced by Guatemalan refugees is to get the world to pay attention to an atrocity that has lasted almost five hundred years, the Palestinians' challenge is to prevent the world from forgetting an atrocity that has lasted almost fifty years. Nearly 2.5 million Palestinians—almost 50 percent of their population—live in camps in Lebanon and elsewhere. In her chapter, which is the most acute analysis of the sociocultural geography of trust in this collection, Julie M. Peteet finds that the Palestinians were displaced from a place where they felt they belonged to a space that was alien and alienating. The place and space in question pertain at once to both an exterior and an interior landscape. Place, in this usage emphasizes a way-of-being in the world and space, a way of seeing the world Being signifies a mode of surrender to a field of forces—political or sentimental—that one basically trusts and therefore can let be and get on with the act of livir It allows the suspension of ever-anxious vigilance. Seeing signifies its opposite: a ing against the grain, a refusal to lose sight of the conditions of one's existenc resistance to being called a "refugee." The generation that actually remem the homeland and "the year of the disaster"—the name given to 1948—is l replaced by the children who know only the camps. But the new gener; through the rich memorialization by narrative, literature, and action, has r the total conversion of space into place. Empowered by this resistance, h recovery is nurtured.

The refusal of the label "refugee" is even more pronounced in the ca;

Afghans who have lived in camps in Pakistan since 1982. Their self-definition as muhajirin—"those who leave their homes in the cause of Allah"—rather than as refugees found recognition among their Pakistani, fellow Muslim, hosts. The muhajirin leave only to return to triumph over the enemy who had "temporarily" displaced the believers from their rightful home. M. Nazif Shahrani argues that the Prophet Muhammad's *hijrah*—"the migration from the Domain of Disbelief to the Domain of Faith" only to return to reestablish the Faith—serves as a potent paradigm shared by Pakistanis and Afghans and that it is this sharing that has made the long sojourn of Afghans in Pakistan one of the more successful stories of refugee accommodation in the world. Beyond this, it is also a reminder that, despite the first world nations' mixture of self-righteousness and anxious hand-wringing about the "waves," "droves," and "tides" of refugees, the bulk of the "burden" in providing refuge for those escaping violence is borne by nations of the third world without the help and interference of hysterical headlines so frequently found in the Western press. Based on figures available for 1992, the burden shared by the developed and the underdeveloped countries was heavily weighted against the latter. In a list of the top fifty countries ranked according to the ratio of refugee population to the total population, only the following ten developed countries figure: Sweden (12), Canada (19), Denmark (30), Germany (33), Norway (36), Austria (39), Luxembourg (42), New Zealand (44), and Switzerland (49). In terms of the number of refugees ranked according to the ratio of refugee population to gross national product per capita, the only first world nations that figure in the top fifty are Germany with 827,000 refugees (ranked 42) and the United States with 473,000 refugees (ranked 49). The total number of refugees in the top twenty-six industrialized countries adds up to only 3,747,100. This leaves the countries of the developing world to bear the burden of more than 38 million refugees. Such is the magnitude of the imbalance of burden-sharing.[3]

Eftihia Voutira and Barbara E. Harrell-Bond open their chapter by questioning the assumption in the "founding document" of the conference from which this volume has emerged, the assumption that trust is basic to being human. Based on work in refugee camps in Africa and an understanding of societies and cultures of Africa among which the authors have carried out field research, they submit a thesis that appears to run against the grain of most of the other chapters in the volume. We shall leave it to the reader to work through the narrower understanding of trust critiqued by Voutira and Harrell-Bond and the broader conceptualization of trust as presented in the editors' introduction and the penultimate chapter by Daniel and Thangaraj and take what is valuable from this juxtaposition. This chapter is, however, more than an argument about the place of trust and mistrust in society. It opens a window into the complex factors and interactions that go into the making of a refugee camp: its multicultural and multiethnic composition; its inherent structures of power, hierarchy, and suspicion; and the magnitude of the task faced by helpers and helping agencies as well as the insensitivity with which they try to get the job done.

Daniel and Thangaraj begin with the thesis that (wo)man is a representation or a sign, or even more correctly, a locus of complex sign activity or semiosis. But to be fully human, they argue, is to be able to partake of a culture, where culture is seen as yet another domain of sign activity but a domain that is public, shared, and quasi-conventional. This public domain in which individuals find their place and through which they define their being-in-the-world must be sustained by a certain measure of trust. From this prolegomenon they go on to illustrate through a detailed case study of Sri Lankan Tamil refugees in Sri Lanka and in London how structures of trust are constantly undermined and the means these refugees employ to prevent the erosion of trust, culture, and their humanness.

In the chapter we have chosen to conclude this volume, Alex Aleinikoff clearly spells out what all the other contributors hint at: not merely a big part but an increasingly big part of the refugee problem results from an international regime of refugee law that owes its primary allegiance not to refugees but to states. Even if expressed in humanitarian terms, the bias of refugee law and policies toward controlling the source rather than toward the provision of asylum ends up being "more about 'containment' of migration than about improved protection of refugees." Aleinikoff's radical proposal to remedy this situation is as original as it is timely, and most important, it is not the product of pie-in-the-sky humanitarianism but of years of firsthand knowledge of the legal aspect of asylum seekers' plight. In this the late twentieth century, when nation-states are being ripped apart by internal contradictions, no one can afford not to seriously contemplate the analyses and proposals presented in this chapter of far-reaching consequences. It is a veritable new beginning.

NOTES

1. We emphasize "culture" here so as to distinguish human society from the society of social animals, which is not our concern here.

2. A simulacrum is a construct or a model that has no referent or ground in any "reality" except its own. "A simulation is different from a fiction or a lie in that it not only presents an absence as a presence, the imaginary as the real, it also undermines any contrast to the real, absorbing the real within itself" (poster in Baudrillard [1988:6]).

3. UNHCR, *The State of the World's Refugees 1993: The Challenge of Protection* (New York: Penguin, 1993).

REFERENCES

Bakhtin, M. M.
    1986   *Speech Genres and Other Late Essays*. Trans. Verne W. McGee, ed. C. Emerson and M. Holquist. Austin: University of Texas Press.
Bettelheim, Bruno
    1986   *The Informed Heart: A Study of the Psychological Consequences of Living under Extreme Fear and Terror*. Old Saybrook, Conn.: Peregrine Books.

Baudrillard, Jean
    1988   *Selected Writing.* Ed. Mark Poster. Stanford: Stanford University Press.
Knudsen, John Chr.
    1988   *Vietnamese Survivors: Processes Involved in Refugee Coping and Adaptation.* Bergen:
                University of Bergen, Department of Anthropology.
Levi, Primo
    1988   *The Drowned and the Saved.* Philadelphia: Abacus.
Malkki, Liisa
    1992   "National Geographic: The Rooting of Peoples and the Territorialization
                of National Identity among Scholars and Refugees." *Cultural Anthropology* 7
                (1):24–44.
Muecke, Marjorie
    1987   "Resettled Refugees' Reconstruction of Identity: Lao in Seattle." *Urban
                Anthropology* 6(3):273–290.
Sheehy, Gail P.
    1987   *Spirit of Survival.* New York: Bantam Books.
Weber, Max
    [1915] 1958 "The Social Psychology of World Religions." In *From Max Weber,* ed. H. H.
                Gerth and C. Wright Mills, 267–301. New York: Oxford University Press.
Zolberg, Aristide R., Astri Suhrke, and Sergio Aguayo, eds.
    1989   *Escape from Violence: Conflict and the Refugee Crisis in the Developing World.*
                Oxford: Oxford University Press.

ONE

When Trust Is on Trial:
Negotiating Refugee Narratives

John Chr. Knudsen

Trust is central to Vietnamese culture. Ideally, family solidarity, harmony, and a supportive kin network are foregrounded and friends are considered close allies, whereas strangers are different and dangerous until their actions—not mere words—prove them trustworthy. Postwar Vietnam and its attempts to remodel person and society have only deepened this distinction. Now, trust is on trial even within the family, the most basic social unit of society. Contradictions have arisen between ideals like trust, love, and harmony, on the one hand, and the reality of authoritarianism and the use of coercive means of control, on the other. Such contradictions, however strongly felt, are never expressed, either within the family or to strangers; individuals learn to adapt, carefully composing their stories as they move from one context to another.

When refugees were forced out of Vietnam, the transit camp became a threatening maze en route to their goal, a country of asylum. In these camps the refugee met strangers playing the role of helpers, whom, through a process of camp socialization, the refugee had to relearn to trust while keeping them at a safe, preferably controllable, distance. In this environment, attempts were made to keep social or emotional problems within the family or even within oneself, in the hope of being able to deal with them when finally in exile.

Once in exile, when children, men, and women all experienced new freedoms as well as new constraints, socialization turned out to be even more complicated. Ultimately, for the Vietnamese refugee, in settings in which "who I have become" presents a threat to the concept of self, "in whom I trust" is irrevocably linked to "who I am."

I. STILL-LIFE IMAGES

The Historical Background

The fall of Saigon on April 30, 1975, marked the end of the virtually constant state of war that began with the partitioning of Vietnam in 1954. The beginning of the "Vietnam war" is often dated from the landing of the first American troops at Da Nang, March 8, 1965, yet the conflict and the military, economic, and political engagement of the United States had actually begun ten years earlier.[1]

For much of her history, Vietnam had suffered from disturbing and destructive internal forces interspersed with foreign invasions and occupations. The Chinese were there the longest, from 111 B.C. to 939. Vietnam's recent history has also been characterized by extensive processes of change as a result of its colonization by the French (1862–1940) and the concomitant breakdown of traditional Confucian society based on family, village, and state; occupation by the Japanese during World War II; recolonization by the French (1945–1954); the partitioning of Vietnam between the Ho Chi Minh regime in the North and the regime of Ngo Dinh Diem (1954–April 1963) in the South and later the direct involvement of the United States through supporters such as Nguyen Van Thieu and Nguyen Cao Ky.

From 1954 on, life in Vietnam began to be characterized by the effects of war: refugees, flight from villages and war zones to larger cities, and the breakup of families. These problems were exacerbated by processes of urbanization and Westernization, although with iron-willed determination and great flexibility, large parts of the urban population managed to exploit niches in the wartime economy. The violent and ruthless competition that emerged resulted in people carefully protecting their own while keeping strangers at a safe distance. Many of those who would later become postwar refugees had already fled from North to South Vietnam when the country was partitioned in 1954. At that time, almost a million people fled to the South to escape brutally imposed land reforms, reprisals, and religious persecution.

After the Fall

The initial wave of postwar escapees was made up of the classic ancien régime, including large numbers of the 1954 North-to-South refugees. Of the later refugees, the majority fled following experiences of political and/or religious persecution under the new regime. In addition, they lived in constant fear of being accused of having been members or employees of the previous regime. From 1975 to 1991, Norway received about ten thousand Vietnamese refugees, the majority of whom were "boat people." By mid-1978, another distinct social group began to leave, among whom were large numbers of ethnic urban Chinese who had more or less tacit permission to do so, particularly after the border conflict with China. Few of the ancien régime or the ethnic Chinese ended up in Norway, however.[2]

The new regime not only wished to get rid of political opponents but also to purge the private economy, since these two were considered to be the main obstacles to the socialist transformation of society. Many who had once supported the regime gradually found they had no reason to expect any benefits. On the contrary, they had great problems adapting to the changes that the new regime forced through from 1976 to 1980. The new rulers ignored the advice of their earlier allies in the South, the National Liberation Front (NLF) and the Provisional Revolutionary Government of South Vietnam (PRG), who had warned against forcing on the region a North Vietnamese model that had functioned only because of the enormous flow of capital and materials from China, the USSR, and other allies (Truong 1986). The new regime sought to put the country back on its feet again as quickly as possible after the long war. In the former South Vietnam, heavy taxes had already been imposed on the peasants, who were also ordered to deliver most of their surplus harvest to the state for a fixed price. This price was so low that many peasants produced no more than what was required for their own consumption. Likewise, the attempts at collectivizing met with strong resistance, and within a year the production teams established in 1979 had broken down. Nor were the New Economic Zones (NEZ) a success. An estimated 400,000 Vietnamese were sent from Saigon to settle in these areas from 1975 to 1976. The aim was both to increase agricultural production and to reduce the unnaturally high urban population resulting from the war. Within a few months, however, nearly 60 percent of these settlers had returned to the city.[3]

Vietnamese refugees often point out another objective in establishing the NEZ: the areas constituted an important link in the government's attempt to control the uncertain situation in the former South Vietnam. Fearing that they and their families would be forced to live in the NEZ, many of the former officers and other government employees under the deposed regime who had been interned after the change in power went underground when released. Others succeeded in joining their relatives or returning to their previous homes in the villages or on the coast, to anxiously await the first opportunity to flee the country.[4]

Among the internees of the NEZ and the "reeducation" camps were many who had supported the fight against the previous regime in the South. Not satisfied with eliminating the NLF and the PRG, the new rulers began to arrest any individual whom they considered to be a real or potential threat. The authorities promised a short internment during which the "volunteers" would go through a program of "reeducation" and "self-criticism." In reality, for more than ten years thousands remained imprisoned and humiliated (Amnesty International 1987).[5] Once free, they chose to join the close to one million refugees who had been forced into exile.

The fundamental problems encountered in implementing the original plans for a united Vietnam led the regime to initiate strict security measures. Rigid control was exercised through a refined system of betrayal. Schoolteachers encouraged children to report what their parents talked about at home, what plans they had, who visited them, what they thought of the new regime, what they ate, and so forth. Many lived in fear of being arrested one night and taken away, perhaps never to return. For refugees from rural areas these raids came as no surprise, for life in the country had constantly been a delicate balancing act of trying to avoid the stigma of being denounced as an enemy either of the Viet Cong or the Army of the Republic of Vietnam (ARVN). The former, in particular, had exploited children as their reporters.[6]

One of the strongest rebellions against the new regime stemmed precisely from what the refugees describe as the rulers' attempts to divide and destroy the family. In the past, children had been taught that teachers had great authority and had to be respected. Traditionally, the teacher's position was above that of the parents and second only to the emperor. Thus the children found themselves in conflict: torn between loyalty to the school, and hence indirectly to the party, on the one hand, and to their parents, if they disagreed with the regime, on the other. The situation was further aggravated when children's own experiences of the conflict did not correspond with that of their parents', heightening the tension within the family. In the past, parents left their children to the teachers and the school, safe in the knowledge that the socialization at school corresponded. As the role of the school changed, this confidence was destroyed.

Certainty about the new regime's antagonistic attitude toward the family constituted one major reason for the flight from Vietnam. The wars had already divided families, leaving family members as opponents in battles defined by international politics. Mass migration scattered victims and survivors into "safer areas," mainly close to the larger cities, and in the process changed the very fabric of society. The refugees felt that the basis of society was on the verge of destruction. They saw their children transformed by the school system and youth brigades, the latter being viewed as "police forces," whose aim was to report the thoughts and actions of parents, neighbors, and strangers.

Vietnam is still under the control of the North. The authorities have now perceived the problems in the economic realm and have taken a more liberal line *(doi moi)*, which encourages the production of surplus for sale on the private market as well as to the state. In addition, a system of individual payment for production has been introduced. Nevertheless, fundamental problems remain as a result of the withdrawal of economic support not only from the United States but also from China following the Vietnamese invasion of Cambodia and the 1979 border war with China. While the 1989 withdrawal from Cambodia may have brought Vietnam closer to the international community, an enigma lingers on. The country became once more the victim of external events in 1991. The war in the Persian Gulf, orchestrated by the United States (which claimed victory over Vietnam—in Iraq!), was followed by the collapse of the USSR, a collapse having ramifications in Vietnam, as the circle goes, accelerating the already sharp loss of aid and preferential trade terms with the Soviet Union *(FEER, 31 January 1991)*. Having paid the price of thirty years of continuous war, many Vietnamese find it difficult to accept "the austerity of relative peace" as a reward (Zolberg, Suhrke, and Aguayo 1989:165).

Socialization in Vietnam

Growing up in a place like Vietnam teaches the child to be ever watchful. Compared to the exile setting, where several avenues compete for attention, I have been told that in Vietnam alternative role models were few. My questions about childhood triggered deeply emotional responses as parents remembered these complicated years. When I discussed with young Vietnamese the differences between the exile setting and Vietnam, even deeper frustrations emerged, differences they admit to seldom discussing with their parents.

Similar contentions are reported in research from inside Vietnam. Here, conflicting values are often ascribed to the following irony: in spite of the high value placed on being careful and flexible, most Vietnamese remember their childhood as a period of rigid socialization, in which they were taught stylized forms of role playing with little room for individuality. In these narratives, the primary sense of personal identity seems inseparable from that of the family, leaving the person with few alternative role models and no real alternatives outside the family. Vietnamese socialization is described by others (e.g., Forrest 1971, 1982; Slote 1972) as a balance between extreme indulgence and permissiveness, especially during the first few years of life, and the strong imposition of parental authority and control, in particular in later years. The person is defined within a society rooted in a religious-philosophical system of Confucianism-Taoism-Buddhism (Hickey 1967; Keyes 1977; Marr 1981).

Let me focus on other details of this very general portrait of the Vietnamese. An individual secure in the knowledge of his or her position vis-à-vis parents and community is able to take on almost any situation, David Forrest and Walter Slote tell us. This same security is not without its difficulties, however. The parent-child relationship itself has been described as a difficult balance between role playing and genuine affection. This is particularly problematic when parental affection is experienced as a means parents employ to exert economic and emotional control over their children. Vietnamese sometimes admit that they remember their parents as excessively restrictive and the demands for loyalty and expectations of filial piety bereft of love. In most cases, the dethronement of the firstborn from the mother's solicitude by subsequent births is used to illustrate this emotional problem (Forrest 1971, 1982; Slote 1972). This dethronement is further accentuated by the hierarchy of siblings and the accepted, or rather, enforced, subordination of younger to elder siblings who, in return, are made responsible for the younger siblings' behavior. It may be a source of hostility between siblings, a disturbing relationship meant to serve, paradoxically, as a primary model for harmony and trust within Vietnamese culture. It is a relationship often described as a paradigm for cooperation as well as for ambivalence within Vietnamese kinship, as reflected in several key myths.[7]

Various versions of such ambivalence emerge in my conversations with the Vietnamese. The messages are less static than those described by Forrest and

Slote, however. Told in fragments, they express anxiety and sadness. These mixed emotions are hidden not only from strangers but also from oneself, concealed by feelings of guilt. Having learned to suppress hostile feelings through the idealization of their parents, many children become tethered to constructed memorials to and of the past and are estranged from their inner emotional lives. Typically, personal problems "belong" to the family and, on a deeper level, to the person. Such problems are almost uncommunicable. The child matures knowing that no one will intervene in "family problems." Relations with strangers are less rigidly defined and less emotionally loaded than are the more intimate relationships, whether hierarchical (e.g., with parents, elder siblings, or spouse) or egalitarian (e.g., among friends).

Familial relational forms emerge even in the nonfamilial domains of social life.[8] The development of self as a relational entity is anchored to the central relationships and principles of family life.[9] The Vietnamese learn to defend this unit and to thereby reduce uncertainty. A family member expects and demands support and solidarity from patrilineal and matrilineal kin. The ideal settlement pattern was for married sons to establish independent households close to their parents and their ancestral land. The youngest son (in South Vietnam) continued to live in his parents' house and was responsible for their welfare. Traditionally, the worst punishment for a Vietnamese was to be expelled from the family—and thus the land. To be alone was (and is) considered to be socially dead—in essence, to be a stranger.

The stranger is not an unfamiliar category, however. Rather, people are normatively warned against readily trusting strangers. The very real fear generated by life under the ever-watchful eye of competing forces, the secret police, and the elaborate system of surveillance taught Vietnamese to be careful and adaptive where strangers are involved. Vietnamese in Norway often stress that the brutality of the wars has engendered suspicion, individuality, and distrust rather than forthrightness, cooperation, and trust. Hence even daily communication is described as more indirect than direct and often accomplished through intermediaries. When strangers are involved, a suitable identity is appropriated through a process of negotiation and strategic self-presentation. As Slote notes (1972:119–120), the individual may decide on a role and create a personal mythos, selectively disregarding factual events that do not fit into the life history constructed and presented. This act of construction draws on appropriate cultural stereotypes, Slote argues. I shall argue that added to this are, for refugees, more general strategies of coping.

II. IMAGES IN PLAY

The next two stages in the refugee's career are to be found in the settings of transit and exile, stages in which moments from Vietnam reemerge. In the camps, refugees enter a limbo state as they carefully attempt to prove their right to asylum. Whom to trust is as much a problem at this stage as it was during the preceding flight. The past is memorialized as if it were a retrievable moral order, filled with still-life images refusing to yield. These images are invoked to "explain" and "explain away" problems—all cast as a battle between Vietnamese and Norwegian culture(s).

The Flight

Escape represented a fundamental break with a social and cognitive system founded on "safe" relationships. The flights of Vietnamese refugees were often dramatic. The composition of a boat team was often haphazard, and strangers were forced into close proximity. Preexisting internal rivalries and personal conflicts that may have arisen while planning the flight intensified the tension. The paying passengers, often members of the urban middle class, resented the owners, mere fishermen, who often charged so much for a seat that it was impossible for the passengers to bring their families. In such extreme circumstances, the question of trust became pivotal.

For those who survived, the moment of rescue was crucial. Those rescued by foreign ships in international waters were granted political asylum in the country of the rescuing ship, on the condition that this country had already agreed to such a procedure. Some refugees had close relatives or other valid reasons for being resettled in a country ranked higher on their list of preferences.[10] The majority of Vietnamese sailed directly to Hong Kong, the Philippines, Thailand, Malaysia, or Indonesia, where they had no right to resettlement. In their attempt to reach a country likely to offer them at least temporary asylum, these refugees often suffered enormous hardships, such as exposure, death of family members, pirate attacks, rape, and the possibility of having a government tow their boat back to sea. Fortunate indeed were those whose flight was numbered in days. The less fortunate drifted for months. Children were sometimes placed on these boats alone or with a distant relative and most often were not even informed about the flight. Why is this happening to me? they wondered

Those who survived generally waited in uncertainty to be selected and eventually granted asylum in a third country. Others were rejected and kept under camp arrest. Most hoped to gain access to one of the countries ranked highest on their list of preferences, the most popular being the United States, Canada, France, or Australia.

Trust in an Environment of Distrust

Arrival in a camp represents the next important step en route to freedom. Once safe, survival, emotional as well as material, depends on their ability to put such experiences behind them. Conflicts within a boat team or a family, between enemies, or even within a person must not be expressed until one is in a safer environment. Exhausted, these survivors have to learn to deal with transitory life under the control of yet another new set of strangers. The camps vary greatly in location, standard, and size, as well as in the assistance offered to residents. At one extreme is Hong Kong, where the closed camps are appropriately called "detention centers," administered by the prison regime. Here Vietnamese are caged like animals behind several-meter-high fences topped with barbed wire, all blessed by the internationally saluted principle of "the human deterrence policy."[11] At the other extreme is Bataan, in the Philippines, where the camp is called a "processing center," where refugees are prepared for resettlement in Norway or the United States—the two countries having programs in the camp—by the administration of six months of "training" in language and "culture." In spite of these variations, some disturbing patterns seem common.[12]

Most Vietnamese spend time in more than one camp, sometimes as much as ten years or more. Vietnamese not rescued in international waters are in particularly difficult situations as they have no links with any potential country of asylum. Many are rejected before the battle for resettlement even starts. Not having been able to prove their case, they are screened out as "illegal immigrants" or "economic migrants." Denied refugee status, they are de facto kept on hold for an indefinite sojourn or, as in Hong Kong, designated for "voluntary repatriation" back to Vietnam.[13] Those fortunate enough to be granted refugee status enter a new period of waiting and screening, this time for resettlement. Each individual's position is unique, since the right to resettlement is governed by possible links to a third country or to ascribed resettlement potential. Receiving countries rank individuals according to elaborate systems of classification,[14] their destinies being determined by stranger-helpers, gatekeepers to their future. Camp administrators, as well as relief workers, are perceived as both opponents and allies, with the power to determine whether and to which country one may leave. To be allowed to depart, the refugees have to operate not only within the rigid rules of the camp but also within the parameters peculiar to this hybrid helper-controller.[15]

Camp life represents a tightrope walk between exposure, necessary if one is to be recognized and granted the right to depart the camp, and a low profile, necessary if one is to avoid camp arrest through rejection. Success depends on not being categorized as "a problem" in any medical (somatic or mental) or criminal sense.[16] In transit camps, refugees may find themselves in a safe but extremely uncertain and vulnerable situation. Left with few, if any, of their significant others, they are often alone for the first time. Newcomers soon learn to weigh the need for contacts among settled sojourners—their teachers in camp socialization—against the need to remain anonymous. The enforced association of persons from extremely diverse backgrounds results in attempts to seek out camp dwellers with whom one can identify. Therefore, in the construction of social networks, even amorous friendships founded on similarity of circumstances in Vietnam may ripen, in spite of the knowledge that lovers may be resettled in different countries. Although newlyweds with camp-born children are sometimes granted altered status that allows them to leave as one family, many are left on their own. For the young singles in particular, some of whom spend most of their adolescence behind bars, the camp

sojourn represents a brutal dislocation as they find themselves in a marginal position with few reliable alliance partners.[17]

In this environment of distrust, the person gradually discovers that there is little
to be gained from discussing problems even with compatriots who share similar
experiences (Nhat et al. 1981). At the same time, there is a gradual shift in preoccupation from those relating to life in their shared transit situation to those associated with the individual's life course. To battle frustration and hopelessness, the
focus often shifts from the limitations of camp life to a simple goal: the shortening
of the waiting period and the uncertainty of the future.

The Refugee–Relief Worker Relationship

To decrease the stress associated with camp life, refugees fall back on strategies of
proven efficacy, and this is typically reflected in the relationship between refugees
and relief workers. As demonstrated elsewhere (Knudsen 1991), relief workers'
therapeutic strategies, while decreasing their own stress, may serve to intensify that
of the refugees. Camps with the most complex relief systems often leave residents
with little control over their own lives, making them into recipients of imposed
aid, which serves to satisfy more the needs of workers than those of the refugees.[18]
Paradoxically, various sets of professionals may be seen by refugees as adversaries,
since their therapeutic interventions are yoked to the screening process. The
refugees have to carefully balance their need to trust against the dangers of being
betrayed. Complicated relief systems, intended to help the refugees manage camp
life, cannot provide the care and help previously offered by family and friends. On
the contrary, the camp organization itself serves to increase the feelings of uncertainty and insecurity. To deal with these feelings, camp dwellers resort to a strict
dichotomization of "us," Vietnamese, versus "them," the management, which
includes relief workers.

Relief programs reduce the Vietnamese to a single category: "refugee." Once
this identity is forced on them, the camp dwellers are assigned a standardized set of
rights and duties. Frustrations increase when this collective identity is reinforced by
the professionals' lack of concern for the camp dwellers' self-ascribed (personal)
identities and their own view of their social reality. These are overruled in the
name of equality.[19]

In fact, therapeutic projects often serve to solidify the distance separating camp
dwellers and relief workers. Fearing sanctions, the camp dwellers try to avoid confrontations and exposure. They withdraw into personal networks and confine crit-
icisms of relief workers and "the system" to private jokes and ridicule. A model of
a "community of refugees" may be "good to think," in Claude Lévi-Strauss's (1963)
phrase, insofar as it creates cognitive order for the professionals. However, for the
camp dwellers the effects are negative, contributing to their stress by adding fuel to
internal conflicts that would otherwise have been ameliorated by class and status
differences.

Although the camp dwellers may express a desire for professional assistance, the opposition between the two parties clearly limits the possible therapeutic role of relief workers. Even in cases in which an individual is striving to live through the suffering generated by traumatic experiences and is alone or only marginally linked to a social network, he or she may continue to consider strategic self-presentation, choosing silence and withdrawal, as a safer strategy than talk and self-revelation. As in Vietnam, problems are either suppressed or discussed with persons with whom one feels safe, principally relatives and/or friends. Moreover, since mental problems have been stigmatized, the importance of self-control becomes quintessential; at stake is not only the integrity of the person and the honor and face of the family but also the right to asylum.

Paradoxically, silence provides the camp dwellers with a greater feeling of safety than revealing personal problems does. They fear being put on "medical hold," and they know that information concerning somatic and psychological problems may be used to evaluate their ability to adapt to the camp and to a future homeland. As long as the countries accepting refugees can choose whom they accept, the slightest symptom of a possible pathology represents a serious danger to the refugee. The implications of diagnosis and treatment for the individual's life course or even destiny convince the refugees that personal problems are best kept private. Thus help can be seen as a threat to one's future.

The camp offers little opportunity for the restoration of trust, as camp dwellers perceive both the content and the form of most therapeutic encounters as threatening. On arrival, they go through a series of routine interviews. They soon learn that a carefully crafted life history is a ticket for an early camp departure while a mismanaged one could be a cause for camp arrest. Any incongruity between interviews has serious consequences if judged to be a deliberate deception intended to advance one's position in the departure queue. Inconsistencies must, therefore, be minimized, not only in the personal data reported but also in the life history presented. Many pursue this strategy—the crafting of content-sensitive narratives—without manifest problems in identity management. This would be so especially if their personal identities are supported by compatriots who share their background and experiences from home. Problems arise, however, when the borderline between fiction and fact is erased and when one has invested so much in the official version that one starts to believe one "is" the story presented (Chan and Loveridge 1987). Thus two battles are fought at the same time; one for recognition as a refugee and one for recognition as a person.

Those refugees who are offered permanent asylum in a third country sometimes seem to have been more successful getting out of the camps than in finding ways to manage exile. While in transit, the need to restore the microcommunity of trust is such that problems inherent in these community structures, especially that of the family, are repressed or ignored. To have done otherwise would have, among other things, run the risk of drawing the attention of the authorities to "pathologies" that may have disqualified their exit. Quite another setting awaits them in exile. The difference between life in the country of resettlement and life in Vietnam may turn out to be greater than the difference between life in Vietnam and that in transit camps. Trying to replicate the tightly woven networks of kinship and friendship in the resettlement countries may be more difficult than expected, particularly when forced together into vulnerably small and fluid exile communities like those found in Norway. With greater freedom also comes the greater possibility of these very ties of friendship and kinship being loosened or broken. In addition, many family stories are not all that sweet.

Exile— Negotiating Narratives in Fluid Settings

Life in exile represents a new situation in which refugees must once again balance between exposure and withdrawal. The newcomers have to devise strategies that enable them to deal with three sets of strangers: the relief workers responsible for their integration; the old-timers, that is, already settled compatriots; and the host population in general. Vietnamese relationships once again turn out to be the most critical for the social and emotional survival of the person. Let us, however, start by examining the relationship vis-à-vis the relief workers.

On arrival in Norway, the refugees are greeted by new relief workers and a new round of interviews. Once again, they find that information provided earlier in camp interviews is checked and rechecked—by the police as well as relief workers—in separate interviews and often with different interpreters. The fact that they are encouraged to correct any inaccurate information is not necessarily reassuring. On the contrary, having just arrived, this focus on misinformation seems threatening. As mentioned, personal data may have undergone modification not merely as a strategy to secure their right to asylum but also as a strategy for identity management vis-à-vis the compatriots one is forced to associate with. Hence the first interviews are experienced as confrontations rather than as exchanges based on trust.[20]

Certain parallels in the organization of life in transit and in exile characterize, in part, the refugees' world. Once again, they are confronted with relief programs based on the idea that adaptation requires specially designed reeducation; that is, as newcomers, they have to be taught how to function in a "Western" society. As in the camps, the relief measures are based on a model that ascribes to all refugees a common identity, without reference to their backgrounds or needs. The new professionals perform ambiguous roles similar to the refugee workers in the camps: they offer help (material, social, and emotional) and, simultaneously, represent authority. Their mandate strengthens the professionals' tendency to focus on the more immediate problems: each day has to be organized, whether within the reception centers or the private apartments. However, this focus on the present hardly matches the refugees' focus on the future and, at the same time, the past.

The role of helper versus client ceases. Both parties are feeling guilty and inadequate at being unable to break out of this framework, with the result that they become increasingly cautious and withdrawn. The equality enforced on the refugees does not ensure impartiality and equal treatment, however. The formal rules (at the state level) leave room for interpretation (at the level of the municipality) by the relief worker. Refugees report considerable variation in cash assistance as well as in the relief workers' personal styles. Furthermore, the principle of equality is not only external to the refugee's need for identity confirmation and feelings of personal worth but also contradictory to the kind of cooperation necessary for trust to be established in the first place. When the individual is treated not as a person but rather as a pawn in a therapeutic game, the counterstrategy applied in the camps is revived and the helper is placed in an equally clear category: the impersonal bureaucrat (i.e., one who is paid to help), set in opposition to friends, who volunteer their services. In Vietnam, different strategies would be devised for dealing with representatives of these two categories; for example, one might try to bribe a bureaucrat, while payment would be inappropriate for the relatives and friends to whom one brought personal problems, whether social, economic, or emotional. Other roles encountered in diaspora such as those of teacher, guard, or supervisor are not generally subject to similar conflicts, since these roles remain familiar and clear.

According to Diego Gambetta (1988:217), "When we say we trust someone or that someone is trustworthy, we implicitly mean that the probability that he will perform an action that is beneficial or at least not detrimental to us is high enough for us to consider engaging in some form of cooperation with him." The refugees have no real basis for engaging in cooperation if they come to distrust the relief workers in this manner. For if camp life is any precedent, they expect to be more likely hurt than helped if they lay their needs before the relief workers. Trying to deal with uncertainties, the individual has to carefully balance the very basic need for support against the risk of being let down.

In Quest of Anonymous Safety

Once independent of refugee assistance, however, less is at stake. Now, stories are cast around the hard fact of being left with the freedom to choose whether to enter into, maintain, or withdraw from a relationship, a freedom that gives the individual a feeling of having at least some control over his or her life course. But the battle for safe positions continues through negotiations and strategic maneuverings. They attempt to deal with their loss and sorrow by clinging to familiar patterns in unfamiliar settings. Newcomers and their settled compatriots are strangers to each other, left to prove anew their place and worth. Beneath their shared battle as refugees, they are individuals engaged in their very personal struggles.

As noted, each refugee seeks recognition of his or her personal identity as established in the hierarchy of positions from Vietnam, positions supported by the family and/or friends. Recognition of the enforced, and ascribed, position of "refugee" is neither sought after nor desired. It only serves as a reminder of the recent past and the repression experienced under the transit camp authorities. Forced association with persons with whom one does not identify accentuates the tendency to withdraw into secure personal networks and, on a deeper level, into the family or even oneself.

The quest for familiar structures based on kinship and friendship seems to be particularly important for persons from middle and higher classes who seek the recognition of merit and age. To secure a positive feeling of self ("who I am") through identity management, the individual often tries to negotiate on the basis of past, now lost, positions ("who I was") rather than present positions ("who I have become"). Central to these processes of negotiation, as well as the disputes arising from them, is the strategic presentation of self through life histories. Being "Vietnamese" is painted once again with colors from the still-life figures mentioned above, while problems within the family, and the person, continue to be played down.

Compatriots may either support or threaten an individual's attempts to recover his or her position and self-esteem. Within the exile communities, statements are easily misconstrued and rumors easily started. Clearly, the opportunity to choose with whom one would like to associate or to avoid is not as free as it should be. The cultural predilection to include and exclude remains and even becomes a central part of local (Vietnamese) discourse, which piles ridicule on the excluded. Public ascription arrests a person in one role, as for instance, when a professor from Vietnam is kept in one position even when he wants to escape into a more anonymous one. Not only he, but his family, may be belittled ("see who they have become"), thus making him even more eager to escape into the private life of his family. A downfall from an earlier position (i.e., from a professor to a janitor) hurts all the more if compatriots of more modest backgrounds declare their own success climbing the economic ladder (i.e., from a peasant to a janitor). As a counterstrategy, former middle-class and higher-ranking persons may claim that upwardly mobile peasants or fishermen reveal their true selves through their material display, for example, by driving expensive cars and buying expensive furniture, stereos, and so forth. According to this former elite, status should be earned, an achieved position granting the incumbent the respect due in view of his or her knowledge and inner quality (duc). The middle-class attempts at identity confirmation on the basis of past position/rank are typically made vis-à-vis others from similar backgrounds. If past positions are disputed in the broader community, these positions are underplayed in general interaction, and anonymity is sought.

As a hedge against exposure and the consequent adverse transformation of one's self-identity in public discourse, refugees retain their strategy of withdrawal and restricted conversation. As in the camps, talk is not expected to relieve pain. Rather, silence continues to be held as the basic way of handling deeper feelings of bereavement and loss. When events of the past are recalled, whether from Vietnam, the flight, or the camp, they are recounted in very general terms, told in detached or depersonalized ways, with the most painful episodes skimmed over.[21]

Self-identity beyond the family level is, as we have seen, mainly defined according to perceptions of former rank and position in Vietnam. The gap between self-ascribed identity and that ascribed by compatriots is more fundamental than between that of relief workers and refugees. The Vietnamese can hardly escape being assigned positions that may not coincide with self-ascribed identities and may be questioned, or even worse, publicly rejected. Typically, such discourse revolves around the carefully constructed life histories in which individuals seek to integrate elements from the past and the present into projections for the future.[22] The general lack of contact with Norwegians, as well as the low expectations regarding the benefits from such contact, makes the Vietnamese less vulnerable to criticism from natives than to criticism from compatriots. Relationships with the natives remain superficial, based on limited contact and mutual stereotypes. The possible hurt from natives' stereotypes is not as significant as that stemming from attack by compatriots, especially from persons considered to be friends or, even worse, close relatives. Over time, the isolation felt vis-à-vis the natives *(tach biet)* seems easier to handle than the strong feelings of loneliness *(co don)* experienced vis-à-vis compatriots.

Negotiating Trust within the Family and the Person

Trust is related to cooperation and the freedom to choose whether to enter into, maintain, or withdraw from a relationship, as mentioned. In carefully weighing the very basic need to trust someone against the risk of being hurt, the individual may exert some control over his or her life course. But insofar as this capacity to control is a limited one, we may say that a situation prevails in which trust is on trial at all stages in the refugee's career. The question about the destruction and possible restoration of trust has to be addressed from the semiotic of refugee narratives, keeping in mind that beliefs are not necessarily held in common. Furthermore, uncertainties about the likelihood of receiving the desired response are accentuated when "the other"—whether stranger, friend, or relative—is obliged to cross loyalties. In situations of uncertainty, withdrawal is a safer strategy than exposure and silence a better language of control.[23] The kind of conversation appropriate to the therapeutic encounter in a therapist's office is not merely inappropriate but could be quite dangerous, and many refugees continue to fear that information divulged may be used against them at a later moment.[24] When a person finds the need to express her or his feelings, however, another problem remains: that of finding a confidant.

Many refugees feel that their problems have gradually changed from being shared ones to becoming private. The former is considered "normal" (even by refugees), the latter as personal defeat and loss of face (Muecke 1983). When an individual is no longer able to gain the necessary support from close relatives and friends and when even the family has proved incapable of living up to its expected therapeutic potential—a healing capacity highly anchored in the ideal of kinship mentioned earlier—the individual is alone in a new and heightened sense.

Some young refugees in Norway portray their childhood in Vietnam as a time of great frustration, of having been moved around separated from parents. Some share stories they never told before as there simply was no one there to listen. These stories are about not having been loved, of suffering under strict fathers, of feeling rejected to such an extreme that they were no longer certain whether the decision to send them from Vietnam was an act of love or banishment (tradition- ally, banishment is the strongest sanction applied toward a family member in Viet- nam). Thus some of these stories repeat the problems of socialization in Vietnam, leaving the child bewildered as she or he tries to live up to expectations that are either taken for granted or described as undisputable. Most have tried to forget, they tell me. But their memories haunt them. How to decipher love from control? Was I betrayed? they wonder. Or did I betray them by leaving my family in a difficult situation?[25] Why were my siblings treated differently? Feelings of resent- ment are exacerbated by feelings of guilt and unfulfilled obligations. Even within one and the same family, individuals' perceptions of the world vary considerably. The parents, representing first-generation refugees, belong to a universe of dis- course rooted in shared experiences and memories of Vietnam. Their world remains theoretical to many children. Other children remember glimpses of what appears to be a world lost, partly mythical and partly theoretical.

Each person's involvement with the natives varies as well, the children being much more active than their parents. Family roles are often reversed, with the children suddenly becoming brokers and spokespersons on behalf of their parents, so the latter, especially the elderly, suffer further loss, left in passive isolation in their apartments. For the older generation, exile may be experienced as deeply frustrating when the flexibility they might have displayed in Vietnam, or even in the camps, is removed by the realities of exile.

Because of the fluid nature of the local exile communities in Norway, the refugees feel vulnerable. Though physically safe, they continue to fight for social and emotional safety. Within this community, trust is complicitous with loyalty, on the one hand, and face-saving strategies, on the other. Within the family, the strict patterns of socialization from Vietnam reappear. In separate conversations with parents and children, contrasting views on such familiar "still-life" virtues as trust, love, and harmony starkly appear. In the experience of children, these same virtues are seen as means of control and authority. Some youngsters note that fam- ily life is like a theater with a fixed audience that has exacting expectations, cementing each person in her or his role. When strangers join the audience, the stage relaxes somewhat, and strict rules get underplayed as the harmony of roles imposes itself as the main organizing principle. When they leave, however, the sit- uation reverts to its previous disharmonic rigidity. The parents' reading of the play does not necessarily match that of the children.

The parents' withdrawal to the safety of the family or circle of friends, so as to secure their position, becomes a significant feature of the socialization of children as well. Compared to Norwegian children of a similar age, Vietnamese children spend more time with their families. As they mature, they claim to feel more secure in their Vietnamese identity than in their identity as Norwegians. There is a high price to be paid, however. The demands placed on them may be extreme and unrealistic. Some parents try to deal with, and compensate for, their own losses through ambitious plans for their children. From their lonely position, these parents trust that their children will restore the family honor, a tough task within the Norwegian educational system. In Vietnam, the parents' place was secure, and the love shown their children was accompanied by economic control. In Norway, the situation is very different. Security is government sponsored and administered by relief workers and the school system. Norwegian parents use varied and individualized methods of parenting. To Vietnamese parents, especially to those who have little or no contact with the natives, this Norwegian multiplicity represents an uncomfortable and threatening level of chaos. To them, the Norwegian parents are without economic and emotional control over their children, as demonstrated by the children's lack of respect. Furthermore, the Norwegian divorce rate is high, and divorce itself is a threat, as women are generally left not only with the house but even with custody over the children. These sterotypical perceptions of Norwegians only convince the Vietnamese that they should reinforce their traditional family patterns.

When Vietnamese culture is planted in this soil, Norwegian culture appears as an intruder capable of choking out the Vietnameseness so dramatically portrayed in the still-life images, and the oral tradition is summoned to defend against this threat. But under these circumstances, Vietnamese culture runs the danger of becoming even more essentialized and, thus, even more unreal. The children's perception of their world complicates this binary opposition. They are like *bricoleurs,* trying to integrate the new with the old, often a difficult venture in a homogeneous white society such as Norway. They simply resist being victims of culture—whether Vietnamese or Norwegian. Parents are worried. "If this had been in Vietnam," they tell me, "our children, as well as you, could just look out the window. Then you would know, you would see what we try to explain. Even your questions wouldn't have been necessary. In Vietnam everything was normal. Things happened because they happened. Words were not necessary. We knew, and the children knew. Every little thing has to be explained in Norway. Words become so important. Everything is a problem. We are tired."

Battles of this kind are fought within many families. Problems remain extremely private and can be glimpsed only in flashes of communication. Youngsters, like their parents, give ambiguous sets of answers, knowing that I, a non-Vietnamese, am an outsider when it concerns the circulation of rumors, but also a partial insider insofar as they know that I appreciate the stakes involved. Some youngsters who arrived alone or together with distant relatives struggle with guilt mixed with sorrow, because family reunion creates a new set of problems. Others are all alone, left completely to themselves, forced into isolation. Inside some families, a member may feel particularly lonely, unable to locate the one person she or he might trust, the friend with whom she or he shared experiences. Sometimes, the parents remain remote and inflexible and the gap is impossible to close without violating the expected loyalty. The strongest feelings of loneliness are reported by youngsters who suffer behind closed bedroom doors, beyond the love (or rather, control) of their parents, who think they are doing their homework.

Negotiating Researchers

Given its situationally constructed nature, a life history is not a story of a life but rather a conscious, or even unconscious, strategy for self-presentation, a legitimization of moves and countermoves and of projections for the future. The concomitant theoretical and methodological, as well as ethical, problems relate to the question of how one interprets a life history (perhaps more accurately, interprets the elements that have been linked together as a story) when the articulated versions are selected remnants that cannot be verified (since the researcher cannot go back in time and check) or questioned (since even to raise the question of falsification would signal distrust in the subject's presentation and thus destroy the necessary basis for receiving information or performing therapy).

I argue that these problems pertain not only to the actual editing, interpreting, and directing of narratives but also to the use of qualitative methods in general. (This is not to deny the prejudices of quantitative methods either. But that is a different matter.) Already before the first researchers ask their questions, refugees have passed through several interviews and conversations with various categories of "helpers." When the researchers finally arrive, the situation is redefined once more, and the conversation changes. This redefinition may be seen as a survival strategy, an attempt to have as much influence on the definition of self and situation as possible. Like many "helpers," the researcher becomes upset and frustrated if met with strategic self-presentation, silence, and withdrawal. The two parties are cast as opponents: the ones asked, in their presentations, the others doing the asking, in their frantic search for valid data. The result may be a folie à deux, a double illusion.

Yet another ethical question must be asked concerning the research design appropriate for studying persons in vulnerable situations in which strategic self-presentation is very much a matter of life and death. Why should the refugee trust the researcher—a person whose questions and, even more dangerously, whose interpretations may represent a threat to their future? As researchers, we have to understand our roles as gatekeepers to landscapes of emotions. In particular, our roles may become complicated if a person is attempting to deal with unprocessed trauma through silence, withdrawal, and protection of his or her innermost private feelings. If we, as researchers, open the door to such landscapes, are our professional and personal abilities adequate to deal with this information? Are we prepared and willing to accept the ethical responsibility to function therapeutically—if necessary? Our role is not to penetrate what may seem to be fiction and thus expose the person to further loss but to assist the refugees in their attempts to remake their world. We can speak against hegemonic discourses that attempt to cut people down to size, whether they come from a screening officer, a scientist, a therapist, a father, or a mother.

NOTES

Most of the data presented come from conversations with refugees in Southeast Asian camps (1982 and 1991) and in Norway (1981–1992). I want to thank E. Valentine Daniel, Michael Fischer, and Moslih Kanaaneh for their comments on an earlier draft of this chapter. Also, my thanks to the workshop participants for their comments.

1. See, e.g., Doan and Chanoff 1986a, 1986b; Fitzgerald 1973; Freeman 1989; Hayslip 1990; Hickey 1967; Karnow 1984; Lewy 1978; Marr 1981; Truong 1986; Wiesner 1988.

2. The majority being ethnic Vietnamese from the former South Vietnam. Before they finally succeeded after the change of power in 1975, some had attempted to flee their country several times.

3. See *Far Eastern Economic Review (FEER)*, 2 May 1985; UNHCR 1985.

4. See, e.g., Bousquet 1991; Doan and Chanoff 1986a, 1986b; Freeman 1989; Hawthorne 1982; Hitchcox 1990; Nguyen 1982; Truong 1986.

5. According to a report made by Vietnamese refugees (Que Me 1985), the numbers in the camps were close to 500,000. *FEER* (6 August 1982:32) estimates the numbers to lie between 20,000 and 200,000, divided among at least 50 camps, each with 500 to 5,000 prisoners. The aim of the imprisonment was to "reeducate" the inhabitants "into men useful to the country and to their families" (*Asia 1981 Yearbook*, 263—quoted from President Nguyen Huu Tho).

6. See, e.g., Hayslip 1990; Hitchcox 1990; Nguyen 1982; Que Me 1985.

7. See, e.g., "The Betel and the Areca Tree," discussed in Forrest 1971, 1982.

8. From the political arena, Ho Chi Minh, born Nguyen That Thanh, also called Nguyen Ai Quoc, is famous for his use of the referent *bac* (uncle Ho) to create an intimate, yet authoritative, relationship toward his compatriots.

9. The five most central relationships *(ngu luan)* in society have always been those of ruler/subject, father/son, husband/wife, elder brother/younger brother, and friend/friend. The essence of the first two relationships was personal loyalty of the subject to the ruler *(trung)* and filial piety *(hieu)*. The first three were known as the basic elements of social ethics. "Ethical cement for this structure was supplied by a set of cardinal virtues . . .: benevolence *(nhan)*, righteousness *(nghia)*, ritual *(le)*, knowledge *(tri)*, and sincerity *(tin)*" (Marr 1981:58). The five relationships served to define a society based on personalistic connections, and "a father, or an elder brother was supposed to rule primarily by example, by cultivating and projecting the inner quality of virtue *(duc)*, not by promulgating an outer system of laws and institutions" (ibid.). See also Luong (1981, 1984) for a detailed analysis of the Vietnamese system of person reference.

10. Other refugees had no other alternative than to leave for a northern shore like Nor-

way. Up until 1988, approximately 60 percent of those who qualified later came to Norway. The rest found more desirable solutions (Knudsen 1988).

11. The horror of these prison camps is described in Hitchcox 1991 and Knudsen 1992. See also Bale 1990; Chan 1990.

12. For a comparison of various camps and detention centers in Southeast Asia, see Hitchcox 1990; Knudsen 1988.

13. Camp policies, repatriation, and international law are discussed in, e.g., Helton 1990. See also Aleinikoff, this volume.

14. Most refugees claim the criteria for acceptance to be shifting and fluid. Smaller families with upper-middle-class backgrounds and higher education from the cities would stand a better chance than large families with less education from rural areas. However, if a person can deliver sensitive information, to, for example, the United States authorities, the chances would increase. A homosexual Communist will have a hard time if the United States is his number-one priority.

15. These helpers too are kept under control by the gatekeepers at much higher levels. One proof of this conspiracy is the famous June 16, 1988, decision. Ten years after the international resolution to grant admit status automatically to Vietnamese refugees arriving in Hong Kong, a new decision reversed the whole issue. From that time, each person had to prove his or her right to asylum. Overnight, the Vietnamese had turned from "refugees" (fleeing communism, which was fine at the time) to "asylum seekers" and, if screened out, "illegal immigrants." To be rescued here is perhaps less the individual refugee than the nation-state in its almost xenophobic dislike of strangers, whether in the shape of foreigners, aliens, or simply others. See also Kristeva's (1991) investigation of the history of foreigners in Europe and Malkki's (1992) discussion of the analytical consequences of rooting "people" and "cultures" in soil and metaphysics.

16. This virtual deselection of people is described in Hitchcox 1990; Knudsen 1988, 1991, 1992; Rangaraj 1988.

17. Being without the support and control of a family unit, these youngsters are considered a threat to the young women in general and to unaccompanied women in particular. In Chi Ma Wan Detention Center, Hong Kong, for example, the women were singled out for protection and unmarried male residents above 21 years old were moved to other prison camps, including those who left younger sisters behind.

18. See also Harrell-Bond 1986; Hitchcox 1990; Malkki 1992; and Voutira and Harrell-Bond, this volume.

19. The Vietnamese may also give the position "refugee" a positive connotation, perceived as a fight for human and political rights denied to them by the screening process in Hong Kong, for example. The same is true for the battle for human, and other, rights when safe in exile, as we shall see.

20. Similar experiences were reported by unaccompanied children who arrived in Norway as asylum seekers—from Eritrea, Somalia, and Iran (Knudsen 1990*b*).

21. A more general process is invoked here. Levi (1988:11) wonderfully, as always, calls human memory a "marvellous but fallacious instrument," pinning down the often forgotten fact that it is more important that memories seem real than that they are real. Levi goes on: "It has been noted, for instance, that many survivors of wars and other complex and traumatic experiences tend unconsciously to filter their memory: summoning them up among themselves, or telling them to third persons, they prefer to dwell on moments of

respite, on grotesque, strange or relaxed intermezzos, and to skim over the most painful episodes which are not called up willingly from the reservoir of memory, and therefore with time tend to mist over, lost their contours" (ibid., 19). See also Layoun's discussion of memory and retelling in this volume.

22. See, e.g., Chan and Lam 1987; Chan and Loveridge 1987; Freeman 1989; Knudsen 1990*a*; Longva 1987; Luong 1981, 1984.

23. See also Bettelheim 1986; Knudsen 1992; Levi 1987, 1988. Daniel (1992) and Scarry (1985) remind us about the severe problems of restoring trust that has been deliberately attacked as an essential part of torture. See also Manz, this volume.

24. For a discussion of alternative therapeutic approaches to "talk," see Turner and Muecke, this volume.

25. Similar sentiments are reported by Freeman (1989) among Vietnamese in the United States.

REFERENCES

Amnesty International
    1987   *Amnesty International Annual Report.* London: Amnesty International Publications.
    1989   *Amnesty International Annual Report.* London: Amnesty International Publications.
Asia 1981 Yearbook
    1981   Hong Kong: FEER.
Bale, Chris
    1990   "Vietnamese Boat People." In *The Other Hong Kong Report*, 159–174. Hong Kong.
Bettelheim, Bruno
    1986   *The Informed Heart: A Study of the Psychological Consequences of Living under Extreme Fear and Terror.* Barclay: Penguin.
Bousquet, Gisèle L.
    1991   *Behind the Bamboo Hedge: The Impact of Homeland Politics in the Parisian Vietnamese Community.* Ann Arbor: University of Michigan Press.
Chan, Kwok B.
    1990   "Hong Kong's Response to the Vietnamese Refugees: A Study in Humanitarianism, Ambivalence and Hostility." *Southeast Asian Journal of Social Studies* 18 (1): 94–110.
Chan, Kwok B., and Lawrence Lam
    1987   "Psychological Problems of Chinese Vietnamese Refugees Resettling in Quebec." In *Uprooting, Loss and Adaptation: The Resettlement of Indochinese Refugees in Canada*, ed. Kwok B. Chan and Doreen Indra, 27–41. Ontario: Canadian Public Health Association.
Chan, Kwok B., and David Loveridge
    1987   "Refugees 'in Transit': Vietnamese in a Refugee Camp in Hong Kong." *International Migration Review* 21 (3): 745–759.
Daniel, E. Valentine
    1994   "The Individual in Terror." In *Embodiment and Experience: The Existential*

Ground of Culture and Self, ed. Tom Csordas, 229–247. Cambridge: Cambridge University Press.

Doan Van Toai and David Chanoff
    1986*a*   *The Vietnamese Gulag.* New York: Simon and Schuster.
    1986*b*   *Portrait of the Enemy.* New York: Random House.

Far Eastern Economic Review (FEER)
    6 August 1982; 2 May 1985; 31 January 1991.
        Hong Kong. Asia 1981 Yearbook.

Fitzgerald, Frances
    1973   *Fire in the Lake: The Vietnamese and the Americans in Vietnam.* New York: Random House/Vintage Books.

Forrest, David
    1971   "Vietnamese Maturation: The Lost Land of Bliss." *Psychiatry* 31 (May): 111–138.
    1982   "The Eye in the Heart: Psychoanalytical Keys to Vietnam." *Journal of Psychoanalytical Anthropology* 5 (3): 259–299.

Freeman, James
    1989   *Hearts of Sorrow: Vietnamese-American Lives.* Stanford: Stanford University Press.

Gambetta, Diego
    1988   "Can We Trust Trust?" In *Trust: Making and Breaking Cooperative Relations,* ed. Diego Gambetta, 213–237. Cambridge: Cambridge University Press.

Grant, Bruce
    1979   *The Boat People: An "Age" Investigation.* Barclay: Penguin.

Harrell-Bond, Barbara
    1986   *Imposing Aid: Emergency Assistance to Refugees.* Oxford: Oxford University Press.

Hawthorne, Lesleyanne
    1982   *Refugee: The Vietnamese Experience.* Oxford: Oxford University Press.

Hayslip, Le Ly
    1990   *When Heaven and Earth Changed Places.* New York: Plume.

Helton, Arthur C.
    1990   "What Is Refugee Protection?" *International Journal of Refugee Law,* Special Issue (September): 119–120.

Hickey, Gerald
    1967   *Village in Vietnam.* New Haven: Yale University Press.

Hitchcox, Linda
    1990   *Vietnamese Refugees in Southeast Asian Camps.* London: Macmillan.
    1991   "Preliminary Notes on the Circumstances of Vietnamese Asylum Seekers in Hong Kong." MS. Institute of Anthropology, St. Antony's College.

Hoskins, Marilyn, and Eleanor Shepherd
    1966   *Life in a Vietnamese Urban Quarter.* Center for Vietnamese Studies, Southern Illinois University, Carbondale. Monograph Series, no. 1.

Karnow, Stanley
    1984   *Vietnam: A History.* Barclay: Penguin.

Keyes, Charles F.
    1977   *The Golden Peninsula: Culture and Adaptation in Mainland Southeast Asia.* New York: Macmillan.

Knudsen, John Chr.
    1988   "Vietnamese Survivors: Processes Involved in Refugee Coping and Adaptation." Department of Social Anthropology, University of Bergen.
    1990*a*   "Cognitive models in life histories." *Anthropological Quarterly* 63 (3): 122–134.
    1990*b*   *De trodde jeg var fattig: Om asylsøkerbarn i Norge.* Bergen: MiCo Forlag.
    1991   "Therapeutic Strategies and Strategies for Refugee Coping." *Journal of Refugee Studies* 3 (4): 21–38.
    1992   *Chickenwings: Refugee Stories from a Concrete Hell.* Bergen: Magnat Forlag.

Kristeva, Julia
    1991   *Strangers to Ourselves.* New York: Columbia University Press.

Levi, Primo
    1987   *If This Is a Man* and *The Truce.* London: Abacus.
    1988   *The Drowned and the Saved.* London: Abacus.

Lévi-Strauss, Claude
    1963   *Totemism.* Boston: Beacon Press.

Lewy, Guenter
    1978   *America in Vietnam.* Oxford: Oxford University Press.

Lin, Keh-Ming et al.
    1982   "Adaptational Problems of Vietnamese Refugees." Pt. III. "Case Studies in Clinic and Field: Adaptive and Maladaptive." *Psychiatric Journal of the University of Ottawa* 7 (3): 173–183.

Longva, Ahn Nga
    1987   "Coping with Refugeeness: Intra-Ethnic Backstage and the Management of Self-Image among the Vietnamese." Thesis for the Magister Artium in Social Anthropology, University of Oslo.

Luong Van Hy
    1981   "The Vietnamese System of Person Reference: A Study of Rules, Structural Contradictions, and Action." Ph. D. dissertation, Department of Anthropology, Harvard University.
    1984   " 'Brother' and 'Uncle': An Analysis of Rules, Structural Contradictions and Meaning in Vietnamese Kinship." *American Anthropologist* 86:290–315.

Malkki, Liisa
    1992   "National Geographic: The Rooting of Peoples and the Territorialization of National Identity among Scholars and Refugees." *Cultural Anthropology* 7 (1):24–44.

Marr, David
    1981   *Vietnamese Tradition on Trial, 1920–1945.* Berkeley, Los Angeles, and London: University of California Press.

Muecke, Marjorie
    1983   "Caring for Southeast Asian Patients in the U.S.A." *American Journal of Public Health* 73 (4):431–437.

Nguyen Ngoc Ngan
    1982   *The Will of Heaven: A Story of One Vietnamese and the End of His World.* New York: E. P. Dutton.

Nhat Tien et al.
  1981   *The Pirates on the Gulf of Siam: Report from the Vietnamese Boat People Living in the Refugee Camp in Songkla, Thailand.* San Diego: Boat People S. O. S. Committee.

Que Me
  1985   *Vietnam Today.* Paris: Vietnam Committee for Human Rights, France.

Rangaraj, A. G.
  1988   "The Health Status of Refugees in South East Asia." In *Refugees: The Trauma of Exile,* ed. Diana Miserez, 39–44. Dordrecht: Martinus Nijhoff.

Scarry, Elaine
  1985   *The Body in Pain: The Making and Unmaking of the World.* New York: Oxford University Press.

Slote, Walter
  1972   "Psychodynamic Structures in Vietnamese Personality." *Transcultural Research in Mental Health,* University of Hawaii.

Truong Nhu Tang
  1986   *A Viet Cong Memoir: An Inside Account of the Vietnam War and Its Aftermath.* New York: Vintage Books.

United Nations High Commissioner for Refugees (UNHCR)
  1985   "Refugees," no. 17. Geneva: UNHCR.

Wiesner, Louis A.
  1988   *Victims and Survivors: Displaced Persons and Other War Victims in Vietnam, 1954–1975.* New York: Greenwood Press.

Zolberg, Aristide R., Astri Suhrke, and Sergio Aguayo, eds.
  1989   *Escape from Violence: Conflict and the Refugee Crisis in the Developing World.* Oxford: Oxford University Press.

TWO

Trust, Abuse of Trust, and Mistrust among Cambodian Refugee Women: A Cultural Interpretation

Marjorie A. Muecke

Because "trust is basic to being human" (Daniel and Knudsen 1991:5), it is cultur-ally constructed. Following Clifford Geertz's (1973a:87–125) view of religion as a cultural system, religion is important both as a source of conceptions about life and the self and as a paradigm for interpreting social relationships and psycholog-ical events. In this chapter, I demonstrate that trust among Cambodian women who survived the Khmer Rouge regime and the Vietnamese invasion of 1979, later to resettle in border holding areas or in the United States, is informed both by Buddhist doctrine and by Khmer folklore; that the implications of these cultural texts for trusting are gendered and therefore that responses to the traumas should be explained not only in terms of a universalist human psychology but also in terms of a more or less implicit cultural heritage. I conclude with comments on how Khmer cultural heritage is being modified to provide new directions for work-ing with traumatized Khmer women.

THE CULTURAL CONSTRUCTION OF TRUST BY THERAVADA BUDDHISM

Understandings about trust in the plains societies of mainland Southeast Asia are informed by Theravada Buddhist thought (Keyes and Daniel 1983). The Four Noble Truths of Buddhism begin with the Truths that there is suffering *(dukka)* and that the cause of suffering is attachment *(upaathaan)*. The third Noble Truth is the cessation of suffering and the fourth, detachment as the way to the cessation of suffering or the way to truth. Since trust signifies attachment to worldly affairs, according to Theravada Buddhist orthodoxy and folk belief, it causes suffering. Truth, in contrast, is the cessation of suffering: nirvana. Thus Buddhism makes trust incompatible with truth and disvalues trust for the suffering it incurs through attachment.

Buddhist tradition and folk interpretation position women in the world differ-ently from men, situating women more irretrievably in a context of human attach-ments by virtue of their reproductive function. The bearing and succoring of chil-dren bind women more than men to human relationships and to the worldly material necessary for their support (Muecke 1992). The contrasting sociocultural role for men—being ordained as a monk—provides men with the positive sanction to detach themselves from human relationships, specifically, from primary kin—spouse, parents, and children—the relationships to which culture and biology bind women. The different social spheres of the sex-linked roles, mother and monk, invest women with closer primary human attachments than they do men. The biosociocultural position of women confronts them more than men with trust as an issue in human relationships and with suffering when the bonds of trust are broken or abused.[1]

KHMER DEFINITIONS OF TRUST

The root of the Khmer terms for trust, *jat*, translates as "heart." The term *tuk jat* (to put and keep in the heart) is used to describe secular relationships, while *ja jat* (believe [from] the heart) signifies an emotional and spiritual depth associated with faith in a superhuman or supernatural order. Some close kin relationships, par-ticularly parent-child and sometimes wife-husband, are said to express karmic bonds between the two people. This grounds trust between primary kin in a meta-physical domain. Similarly, Khmer monarchs and persons of high rank have been believed to have accrued their privilege by moral order: trust in them presupposes trust in the moral order they represent.

The notion of karma includes the understanding that life events have causes but are not predictable. This notion contrasts with Euro-American notions that trust is associated with predictability. Erik Erikson (1963:247), for example, saw the person who is trusted as "an inner certainty as well as an outer predictability." Aaron Antonovsky (1979) has proposed that health originates in having a sense of coherence about the world, in having a sense that the world outside oneself is pre-dictable.[2] The Theravada Buddhist acceptance of the capriciousness of fate con-trasts with the expectation of lawful predictability in Euro-American thought. The Khmer Buddhist notion of trust is associated less with predictability and more with kinship and status roles than in Euro-America.

TRUST/MISTRUST AS A REFUGEE ISSUE

The international lawyer Atle Grahl-Madsen (1966:78) has said that it is charac-teristic of the refugee that "in his [sic] relations with [his home] government, fear has taken the place of trust, and hatred the place of loyalty." While many people may lack trust in their governments and be afraid of them without becoming refugees, or may lose trust in their government long before they flee it to become refugees, refugees by definition fear rather than trust their home government. In mistrusting the authorities, refugees lack a "serene belief" that those in control of society have legitimate power and act in their interests (Keller 1975:196). Mistrust of the government from which a refugee flees is consistent with the United Nations High Commissioner for Refugees (UNHCR) definition of refugees as politically motivated.

By fleeing their government and country, refugees also cut loose, however unintentionally, from what Geertz (1973b:259–269) has called "primordial attachments" as well. Primordial attachments are those bonds of belonging and identity that stem from the "givens" of an individual's social existence. Four of the five grounds for persecution that are specified in the 1967 United Nations Protocol as defining refugee status—race, religion, nationality, and membership of a particular social group—are "givens," identities into which a person is born. Although sex is a given and refugee women are at special and often high risk of sexual abuse, the Protocol does not include a person's sex as grounds for persecution.[3,4]

The experience of massive trauma undermines the ability to trust largely because it proves the givens of one's identity as grounds for being defined as wrong or evil. Twenty-four years ago the psychiatrist Henry Krystal found "distrust and fear of man" common among Nazi concentration camp survivors and ascribed their high degree of "social pathology" to it.

> Their basic trust in the beneficence of God, reasonable behavior of man, and causality in general has been destroyed. This trust is an essential ingredient in that minimum of optimistic faith in the future without which men are not able to plan effectively and live in constant worry and apprehension. The destruction of the feeling of man's basic goodness . . . places the survivor in a world of chaos and danger. He suspects every one and trusts no one, including himself. (Krystal and Petty 1968:325)

TRUST AS A KHMER ISSUE

While genocide was perpetrated against Krystal's Jews in World War II, as a people the survivors emerged with a renewed sense of ethnic/religious pride as a primordial attachment. Cambodian survivors of the Khmer Rouge killings, in contrast, have emerged with a new and profound ambivalence about their ethnic/religious identity that compounds their experience of massive trauma. The challenge for them to regain trust is perhaps extreme since in their experience of genocide, compatriots tortured and killed each other, children killed adults, and the selection of those to be murdered seemed capricious and arbitrary. All Cambodians, not just a stigmatized group—even Khmer Rouge elite themselves (Kiernan and Boua 1982)—were at risk of being murdered. Today the question of political authority in Cambodia remains contentious and threatens redestabilization leading to a takeover by the Khmer Rouge. Under these tenuous conditions, mistrust of the government and of would-be governing regimes remains an appropriate and widespread strategy for survival. As will be discussed later, Cambodians' mistrust of their worlds often extends to include the religious ideology associated with the past orderliness that has forsaken them.

I discuss below two aspects of Cambodian culture that, combined with the historical events of the U.S. bombings prior to 1975, the 1975–1979 Khmer Rouge totalitarian reign of oppression, and the 1979 takeover by the enemy Vietnamese, influence the meaning of trust among Cambodian refugee women in asylum and in the United States: the Theravada Buddhist tradition and the notion of the ideal Khmer woman.

Khmer Buddhist Tradition

The Buddhist tradition still informs the meaning of suffering among Cambodians, despite the systematic destruction of organized religion under the Khmer Rouge.[5] Those born before 1975 (except the Muslim Cham and a few hill groups) were socialized by Buddhist tradition. The Buddhist heritage still informs their worldview and shapes the avenues they see available for reconciling the pain of their losses (Boehnlein 1987; Eisenbruch 1984).

Those born since 1975 were bereft of that tradition in childhood since organized religion, including its monks, architecture, art, and paraphernalia, was systematically destroyed by the Khmer Rouge. The wholesale murder of religious leaders and the destruction and appropriation of temples for purposes of indoctrination in Khmer Rouge ideology seem to have precluded a bond of shared religious sentiment between the two generations of Khmer refugees, those born prior to 1975 and those born after 1975. Although there is evidence that Buddhist sentiment is reemerging in Cambodian refugee and indigenous communities, until recently, without the common interpretive discourse that religion provides, communication and trust between the generations has floundered.[6]

For the adult generation and some children in third country resettlement, Buddhist interpretations remain relevant. Central among Buddhist tenets is the concept of karma. While attachment is understood as the cause of suffering in this life, one's general condition in this life is attributed to karma as the effects of one's acts of volition in previous lives. Each successive reincarnation reflects a person's merit store, or karma, that has accrued through the accumulation of merit or demerit in past lives. Karma determines major characteristics of one's life such as sex, wealth, prestige, intelligence, social status, health, happiness, age at death, and naturalness of death. Buddhist doctrine thus looks to the unverifiable past, the past of another life, to explain the quirks of birth and the major parameters of an individual's life circumstances.

As an explanation of the Cambodian holocaust of the 1970s, karmic theory would say that Cambodians, both those who died and those who survived, perpetrated unspeakably horrid deeds in their past lives and that those misdeeds brought on the suffering they have endured over the past twenty years. Which group, the deceased or the survivors, suffered more is a question still posed by survivors. The notion that one is responsible for such horrors is unacceptable to normal human comprehension, so many Cambodians have drifted away from karma and in so drifting, both reflected and contributed to the disintegration of traditional Cambodian culture.

In an attempt to comprehend the heinousness of the mass persecution of Cambodians in the late 1970s, many Cambodians have raised the possibility that Cambodian culture itself had a bad karma. Belief in a karmic explanation of their misery could enable Cambodians to sustain the legitimacy of Buddhism and to rebuild their confidence in their future by virtue of having now expiated their karmic demerit through their massive sufferings. But belief in a karmic explanation could also justify a belief in the imminence of Armageddon. Fear of extinction is not new among the Khmer. Stephen Heder (1978:8) writes,

> Practically every analysis of Kampuchean history or commentary on modern Kampuchean politics written by a Kampuchean repeatedly and ominously raises the specter of the disappearance of the Kampuchean race, culture and nation. There is frequent [for example,] reference to the fate of the Kingdom of Champa, which once ruled most of the peninsular Southeast Asia but ceased to function as a coherent political entity in the 15th century, leaving its people, the Chams,[7] at the mercy of foreign states.

Fear of extinction is often expressed among educated Khmer communities in the United States. They attribute rumors of impending doom to monks' sermons heard as early as the Lon Nol regime (1970–1975), when the United States was bombing the Cambodian countryside. The rumors became rife as the oppression of the Khmer Rouge regime intensified into terrorism (1975–1979). Cambodians now resettled in Madison, Wisconsin (Smith 1989:19), and in Seattle, Washington, report that such predictions *(put tumniay)* were widespread among the victim laborers of the Khmer Rouge, who were afraid that the doom was karmically determined. The predictions included the dreaded ultimate catastrophe: the land drenched in blood and the death of all Khmer except the handful that could be protected by the shade of a single sugar palm tree. Religion itself predicted its own demise. The ensuing sense of moral and political anarchy and of mistrust of government, of Cambodians, and even of self survives inside Cambodia (AID 1991; Cambodia 1990; Muecke 1989; Muskie 1990). It also survives among those Cambodians in holding camps at the Thai border (French 1990; Mollica and Jalbert 1989; Mollica et al. 1989) and among Khmer in resettlement countries (Mollica 1990; Mollica, Wyshak, and Lavelle 1987).

In most major sociopolitical crises, alternatives to the precrisis belief systems emerge, such as new religions, elaborations of certain aspects of the old religion, or radical revisions of the old religion. Cambodians have experienced periods of massive destruction before, and Buddhism has survived them. The historian David Chandler (1975) writes of the 1800–1850 era as the "dark ages" of violence that resemble the brutal destruction and dangers of the 1970s. It may be too early to tell how religion will reemerge now (June 1992), as the threat that the Khmer Rouge will return to power remains real. The challenge to Buddhism is greater now, because even though there is a memory of a past in which the enemy left "people cowering in the forest," as did the Khmer Rouge, and in which villagers died in fear in forests or survived in foreign lands of refuge, as they have since 1979 (Chandler 1982:66, 69), the enemies of the early eighteenth century were not Khmer; they were Khmer enemies, Vietnamese and Siamese. And, contrary to Khmer Rouge strategy, the people killed in earlier periods of widespread destruction were largely peasants and slaves, rather than all the monks, elite, and leaders. For example, the Faculty of Medicine at Phnom Penh University (Samedy 1989:29) reported the following percentages of health care providers who had died between April 1, 1975, and the Vietnamese invasion in 1979.

Health Care Role	% Died	No. in April 1975
Medical and pharmacy faculty	100	19
Rural midwives	94	941
Laboratory technicians	93	120
Physicians	91	444
Sanitarians	89	472
Pharmacists	83	123

Female Virtue

The erosion of trust in religion has been compounded by the erosion of cultural identity and of family for Cambodian women. The ideal Khmer woman historically was a goddess, or *apsara:* she embodied the virtue and purity of the kingdom or state as well as of the family. The apsara remains the symbol of serenity and control (Catlin 1987). Judy Ledgerwood (1988) has made the insightful argument that prior to the Pol Pot era, there was an ideal of the perfectly virtuous woman *(sri grap lakkhana)*. This ideal was reiterated in proverbs, folktales, and novels and believed achievable. According to the ideal, the unmarried woman was sexually naive, timid around men, a virgin; the married woman was a passive accepting partner to her husband but never to another man. She respected her husband with deference no matter his behavior and met all his domestic needs quietly and dutifully. She was considered totally trustworthy by her husband, parents, and community.

Khmer who are now in border camps and in third country resettlement have been displaced from the historical context of Khmer society where it was conceivable that a woman could be virtuous according to the ideal. There is a general sentiment among resettled Khmer that the anonymity and numerous opportunities for transgression in places of resettlement make it impossible for any woman to be virtuous. Loss of life under the Khmer Rouge, subsequent guerrilla war conditions at the Thai-Cambodian border, and resettlement in the pluralistic societies of the West have all contributed to the unprecedented situations in which young nubile women are not always protected by the mindful eye of parents and are exposed to myriad opportunities for contacts with men. New opportunity coupled with the increased absence of society's traditional supports for women's virtue—parents, elders, and husbands—make it no longer plausible that a woman can be virtuous in the Khmer sense of the term.

Nevertheless, the ideal of female virtue remains, as does the association of family honor with the daughter's virtue. Nancy Smith-Hefner (1991) reports from her intensive interviews with Khmer in Boston that parents retain control over their daughter's sexuality through arranged marriages and the practice of bride-price. Higher bride-prices are due the more virtuous women. The price has inflated as rapidly as the opportunity for sexual transgression has multiplied by the resettlement in urban U.S. society. With current bride-prices ranging between three and six thousand dollars, the daughter has been a source of tension in the community. The young women stand at the impossible interface of traditional ideals held by parents and contemporary expectations expressed by peers, a stand that is shrouded with violence. Some young women attempt suicide as an exit (Blanchard, McAlpine, and Yao 1986; Nolan, Elarth, and Barr 1988); others are beaten by father or husband for their rumored liaisons.

A Khmer woman who is known to have been sexually active prior to or outside marriage, even if by sexual abuse, is marked as a moral and aesthetic discredit to her people. Even if extreme conditions reduced her to accept a trade of sex with the enemy for food for her children, she and Khmer society believe that her violation was her fault. She has failed the ideal of the perfect Khmer woman. The Khmer woman therefore must suffer her humiliation in silence to maintain membership in her family and community. If her sexual violation were known, her husband would have the right to leave her, and when he did, she would be ineligible for remarriage.

The ideal of the virtuous woman punishes today's Cambodian women for not being able to achieve it. Most of all the ideal demeans female unaccompanied minors because they do not have the parental constraint that could keep them from harm's way. It also stigmatizes widows since they belong to no man yet are already "deflowered," so sullied (Catlin 1987; Williams 1990). Both sets of "unprotected" women, unmarried and widowed, are troubled and troubling to Khmer traditions. At the border camps, women have said,

> It is difficult for the women who live alone: . . . men want to come into their houses and attack them while they sleep alone. Young Cambodian women who are living along the border are always looked down upon if there are no men in their families. . . . But if we have a father, we feel secure and there is no one who dares to look down on us. No one dares to flirt with us or speak disrespectfully to us. (French, Man, and Wuthy 1990)

Cambodian refugee women who were widowed as young mothers were in a culturally anomalous position and particularly vulnerable to sexploitation. Their proven loss of virginity made them undesirable as wives, but their youth made them sexually attractive; their status as widows has left them socially unprotected and exploitable by other men.

Unattached women's loss of social and moral value has had observable clinical effects. Richard Mollica and colleagues have reported finding that Cambodian refugee women without spouses and widows have presented more serious psychiatric and social impairments than all other Indochinese patient groups attending his Boston clinic. After several years of continuous supportive therapy, some of Mollica's women clients have revealed their histories of sexual abuse. Elsewhere it has been reported that female-specific tortures were carried out in Tuole Sleng prison in Phnom Penh: these included subjecting women to sexually sadistic brutality and to watching their children being slowly tortured (Becker 1986). Slowly emerging clinical evidence indicates that some (proportions and numbers unknown) women were raped and sexually brutalized by Khmer Rouge cadres. The horrors of their experiences could alone explain why the literature is replete with comments that Southeast Asian women refugees rarely and reluctantly admit to experiences of sexual abuse (Burton 1983; Truong 1989).

There is one recent report of some Cambodian women having an unconscious refusal to see as well as to talk about horrible memories (Rozee-Koker 1987).[8] Fifty-four Cambodian women over age forty presented with psychosomatic blindness at a Los Angeles eye clinic over a three-year period. While the best predictor of poor subjective visual acuity among them was the number of years they were in enforced labor and starvation under the Khmer Rouge plus the number of years in border refugee camps, the majority (79%) had also lost at least three members of their families, often in their presence and often to arbitrary killings. Most of the women also reported severe beatings to their heads and shoulders, and many attributed their blindness to these. It makes sense that a response to having witnessed and experienced such totalizing brutalities over a prolonged period of time might include a person's closing out the possibility of continued witness through the loss of the capacity to see it.

Although we have too little understanding of how people react to sexual violence, recent psychiatric evidence compiled by R. Ramsay and colleagues suggests that avoidance symptoms are significantly associated with sexual torture (Ramsay, Gorst-Unsworth, and Turner 1993). Krystal (1978:113) has described a syndrome, "catastrophic trauma," whereby the traumatized person has a "numbing of self-reflective functions, followed by a paralysis of all cognitive and self-preserving mental functions." This syndrome explains the silence of the traumatized as a culture-free human response to overwhelming intrusions. Therapists as well as survivor clients tend to avoid the topic of sexual violence. Yael Danieli (1985) has proposed that a "conspiracy of silence" between torture survivor and psychiatrist arose because the survivors' Holocaust accounts were too horrifying for anyone to listen to and comprehend. Similarly, O. Rasmussen (1990) has suggested that avoidance of sexual torture even in the therapy of torture survivors is associated with the therapist's avoidance behavior.

Mollica and team have reported finding that few Indochinese women revealed their rape experiences even after years of therapy "if they believe[d] that other staff members, their family (including their husband), and/or their community [would] find out about it" (Mollica 1988*a*). But once they felt secure that their stories would be kept confidential from their families and Cambodian communities, some have told their stories, including experiences of forced marriage and repeated rape (Mollica 1988*b*, 1990; Thompson 1991).

The silence of most Khmer women about their experiences of sexual abuse should be seen not only as a human response to profoundly intimate trauma but also as an implicit cultural strategy for survival in their communities, for face-saving of their families, and for honoring lost parents. Their silence should not be reduced to repression, denial, or some similar defense mechanism. From a psychiatric perspective, the silence of Khmer women makes it impossible for them to mourn the losses of their womanly integrity and of their cultural identity as virtuous persons. In their silence, Khmer women learn to trust themselves only in the negative, by excluding awareness of their feelings. From a cultural perspective, by trying to ignore the sexual violations of their past, they serve the Cambodian cultural mandate to appear virtuous. They give the semblance of control but without the serenity of the ideal Khmer woman.

Unmotherly Khmer Wives: Two Case Examples

Being a refugee puts Khmer women at risk of self-mistrust on two accounts, neither of which apply to Khmer men: first, the impossibility, when outside the traditional cultural bounds of Khmer society, of upholding the womanly ideal of being "virtuous," and second, separation from their children. Both are breaches of fundamental Khmer ideals for women.

There is a Khmer folktale, *koun look* (child of the world), that portrays a woman's desertion of her children as the ultimate betrayal, the paramount breach of human trust and of blood ties (Chandler 1982). In the story, a young widow deserted her children in the wilderness so as to take a lover; the gods rescued the children. Later when the mother returned to the edge of the forest to find her children, they had been transformed into birds; they rejected her overtures at reunion and mocked her, the human mother. She died for her wrongdoing. The tale can be seen as a metaphor for the situation of young mothers who also find the roles of wife and mother incompatible in the limbo of the Thai-Cambodian holding areas.

Border area health staff have reported[9] that some women have induced abortion in order to give the fetus to their husband or lover as a most powerful protective amulet. They and their men view the act as a desperate survival attempt that is committed to protect their men as they return to battle in land mine and malaria-ridden zones. To protect the life of their husband and children's father, the women commit the ultimate betrayal of taking the life of their own unborn child. Here is a cultural solution of the absurd kind, yet it demonstrates the complexity, flexibility, and durability of culture against the severest constraints. In this instance, culture serves function. A woman's inducing abortion to salvage the fetus as a protective amulet recasts the myth of the spirit child to bring hope to an otherwise hopeless situation.

The tradition of salvaging fetuses as auspicious protective amulets probably is long-standing. In the "normal" past, Khmer (and Thai) sorcerers and exorcists have exhumed the corpses of women who died in childbirth and excised the fetus to salvage the power of its karma for black magic.[10] Fetuses are thought to have potent and good karmas because they had accumulated sufficient merit to be reborn as human beings. Once the fetus was obtained, it was dried and given to "parents" to "raise" on the expectation that it had the karmic power to bring its "parents" extremely good fortune. The "parents" kept the fetus in the home and fed, dressed, and doted on as if it were a human child. In the desperate guerrilla conditions of the Thai-Cambodian border area and in an asylum society depleted of material resources, a woman's gift of her dead fetus has come, for at least some, to represent her ultimate gift rather than the ultimate betrayal of human bonds. The reenactment of the *koun look* myth at the Thai-Cambodian border represents some women's desperate attempt to gain hope for their families. When women induce abortions to obtain the dead fetus, they do so at the triple costs of undergoing the self-imposed trauma, of losing a potential child, and of the threat of their own ultimate demise as wretched persons. These are brave women in a despicable world.

The absurdities of border life have twisted motherhood in yet other ways. The following example is the unintended outcome of nongovernmental organizations' (NGO) food distribution policy in the Thai-Cambodian border area. For a period, women have been given access to food and other essentials that men were not; men were excluded from the handouts to prevent the Thai government from appearing to support Cambodian military in exile. Being so cut off from direct receipt of food, many Cambodian men augmented their indirect access to food by taking more than one wife, with severe unintended consequences for their families.

Despite the impossibility of preserving pre–Pol Pot kinship norms, some Khmer kinship traditions persist. Prior to the 1970s, if a young widow remarried, she would usually give her children by her first husband to a barren sister or to her own mother to raise. In the partial families of asylum, the kinship resources of peacetime are not always available. In border camps, when some women discovered their husbands' polygyny, they took a new husband. Some chose to abandon their children by the first husband to an NGO nursery to protect the children while being a good wife to the new husband. A vicious cycle was started: if the first husband returned from fighting inside Cambodia, a woman might take him back in order also to reclaim her children by him. When he returned to battle and her second husband returned from the border, she would leave the children to the nursery again. Nursery staff have reported that some children were abandoned and reclaimed several times by the age of three years.[11]

These two patterns, a woman taking the life of her own fetus and a woman abandoning her young children to nonkin, are horrible inversions, but permutations no less, of traditional Cambodian culture. They depict the creative modification of culture to address the overwhelming dilemmas of group survival in tenuous asylum.

INTERVENTIONS TO REGENERATE TRUST

Both Western psychotherapeutic efforts and Khmer healers have revised their respective traditions in efforts to support traumatized Cambodian survivors. Generally, Western practitioners have found that supportive therapy with the same persons, provided in familiar, socially supportive environments, has been prerequisite for any sense of healing. Among Cambodians in the United States, women seek clinical care more than men: the majority of the women clients are thirty to fifty years of age, withdrawn, and clinically depressed. It appears from both the literature and clinical experience that long-term supportive group work (rather than psychotherapeutic, individual work) in which the women are slowly encouraged to tell their stories has enabled some Cambodian women to address their pain in healing ways (Mollica 1988*b*). Until the "trauma story" is told, the Mollica team has found that it is "desperately concealed from others" yet "usually reviewed nightly in the patient's nightmares." Telling the trauma story is "the first step in the construction of a new story," in the women's turning from a fixation on hopelessness to a new story about survival, recovery, dignity, and virtue. By being guided to emphasize the strength of the survivor in her telling of her story, she is assisted to construct a more positive story of and for herself and her future (Mollica 1990). That is, she permits and then gradually accepts a cultural redefinition of herself and of those like her as decent women and human beings.

Others have modified Buddhist ritual and messages to encourage Khmer survivors to forget the past and to focus on living in the present and on building a better future. It is to these attempts that I now turn because of their role in the rapid process of creating culture among the Khmer survivors and their children.

Buddhist Revision

Among recent attempts to promote healing are efforts to resurrect Buddhist ideology at some border holding camps. There has been an attempt to reestablish a *sanga,* or order of ordained monks, and in some camps, an order of lay devotee nuns. The monks, however, have almost all been youth who are untutored in Buddhism, so perceived by the refugee community as not wholly qualified and prepared to redress their needs (Gyallay-Pap 1990). The nuns, in contrast, have been mostly older women who were raised in a Buddhist society but who have had little leadership potential because of traditional cultural interpretations of their sex, religious role, and widowhood. The border temples have therefore played a marginal role at best in the daily life of the border refugees (ibid.).

Inside Cambodia, Ka Sunbaunat, M.D., of the Faculty of Medicine, Pharmacy, and Dentistry in Phnom Penh, is perhaps the only physician focusing his practice on the mental health needs of Cambodians inside their country. He says neither he nor others use "talk therapy" in their practices. Instead, in addition to medicine, he uses the Buddhist message that one can make merit in this life in order to be happy in the next life as a therapeutic to loosen the bind of depression on his patients and to motivate them with renewed hope. He stresses to them that Buddhist doctrine affords each person the opportunity to be what she or he wants or deserves in the next life and that Buddha will save all who practice his teachings. He expects that, by giving transcendent meaning to his patients' current actions, their capacity to hope, and to trust in themselves and their futures, might be rekindled. He finds that those few who do believe that Buddhism will save Cambodia were raised as Buddhists prior to 1970; only they observe the Precepts, as did the elderly in pre–Pol Pot times.[12]

Dr. Ka has created an unorthodox interpretation of Buddhist thought in the interests of healing. He strategically ignores the problem that Buddhism considers suffering in this life as an outcome of poor karma. Instead, he preserves the karma principle as the moral core of Theravada Buddhism by revising karmic theory to shift focus from the past to the present. Past causes of current consequences are ignored, and current actions as causes of desired future effects are emphasized.

Dr. Ka is not alone in espousing a Buddhistically informed therapeutic. Monks in Seattle also attempt to revive the utility of Buddhism as an explanatory and motivating belief system for their followers. Like Dr. Ka, they exhort their community to make merit for the future in order to revive their ability to trust in and hope for a better life. They help their followers refocus the cause-effect paradigm of karma away from the past and onto the future. They consciously and purposefully legitimize forgetting the past and sanction Cambodians' silent response to the unspeakably bad memories associated with it.

Those who support the temples in resettlement, however, are, as they were in pre-1975 Cambodia, primarily the elderly, widows, and well-to-do. In resettlement, the economically more successful communities have reconstructed their lives and temples in relative peace. They are the only ones to have had sufficient resources to build and support Buddhist monasteries and to import career monks. Yet still the temple is more of a peripheral option for the community than its epicenter. Religious sentiment is hard to revive among many segments of the community, particularly among youth, since their experience with Buddhism is limited to seeing monks murdered and temples desecrated inside Cambodia, or to knowing untutored and variably disciplined "instant monks" in border holding camps.

Nevertheless, the reenactment of Khmer Buddhist ritual has been effectively implemented to facilitate grief work and to develop Cambodians' readiness to focus on the present and future. This indicates again the persistence and flexibility of culture. At a program for unaccompanied refugee children in Tacoma, Washington,[13] Dr. Julianne Duncan worked with the Cambodian community to develop a cultural ritual cycle of three ceremonies for each child: *Ban Skol*, a memorial for absent family members, was performed by Buddhist monks in the child's foster home soon after the child's arrival in the United States; Pratchun Ban, an annual family reunion of living and deceased relatives, was held each September; and a religious observance for absent family members was held in conjunction with the celebration of the Cambodian new year in April. Observance of the rituals appeared to be associated with reduction of nightmares, disturbing dreams of absent family members, and visits by unknown hostile spirits (Duncan 1984).

These examples indicate that both Western therapy and Buddhist healing with Khmer refugee women have been changing to emphasize empowering, positive, and future-oriented perspectives.

Ongoing Violence

However, much as they try, many Cambodians cannot forget, many cannot trust. The therapeutic efforts referred to above are promising and useful but not enough. The violence in the homes and neighborhoods inside Cambodia, in border asylum, and in resettlement raises new threats while perpetuating past horrors by stimulating recall of persistent disturbing memories. For example, a recent study by Mollica and colleagues (1991) of a random sample of approximately one thousand Khmer families in asylum at Site Two at the Thai-Cambodian border in 1990 found that during the year prior to the survey, serious injury, grenade attacks, armed robbery, knifing and axing, torture, imprisonment, brainwashing, and sexual violence were still problems. Linked to these traumas as well as to the violence experienced and witnessed between 1975 and 1979, among the adults, 71 percent had nightmares, 46 percent reported recurrent thoughts or memories of traumatic events, and 35 percent felt that a terrifying event was recurring (flashbacks). Field experience with Cambodian women in Seattle corroborates the findings of the Refugee Women in Development, Inc. (RefWID) group that domestic violence directed at women is widespread among resettled refugee communities (Richie 1988; Wali 1990:5). The continuous reliving of violence in one's external and internal environments makes a sense of trust in the world inappropriate, belief in the former religion difficult, and the imperative for intervention beyond the psychotherapeutic immediate.

CONCLUSION

I have argued that while trust may be universally experienced, its significance varies because it is sociopolitically and culturally constituted. I have shown that trust in the contexts of refugees and Khmer Buddhists is gendered, with special implications for women. In traditional Khmer society, young nubile women were the least trustworthy, a source of suspicion, and married mothers, the most trustworthy, the refuge of trust. The Khmer Rouge ordeal and its transformation of survivors into refugees have created two new groups of highly vulnerable and therefore untrustable women: unaccompanied minors and young widows. These women have been most subject to sexploitation because they lack proper parental or husbandly protection. Cambodian women who have been sexually violated typically have attempted to live up to their cultural image of a trustable woman by denying their feelings and memories associated with violation. Denial has enabled the women to regain a sense of dignity as Cambodian women. Denial, thereby, has preserved an ideology of virtuous women as an ethnic marker of the Khmer in resettlement countries.

NOTES

1. The cultural nature of this distinction between mother and monk is evidenced in the parallelism of the rites of passage to adult maturity for women and men: lying by the fire after her first delivery has been interpreted in Lévi-Straussian terms as "cooking" a woman, making her a full-fledged adult of Theravadin Buddhist society, just as a man's first ordination as a monk "cooks" him into adult status (Ebihara 1974: 305–347; Hanks 1963; Muecke 1976).

2. "The sense of coherence is a global orientation that expresses the extent to which one has a pervasive, enduring though dynamic feeling of confidence that 1) the stimuli deriving from one's internal and external environments in the course of living are structured, predictable, and explicable; 2) the resources are available to one to meet the demands posed by these stimuli; and 3) these demands are challenges, worthy of investment and engagement" (Antonovsky 1987:19).

3. There is a growing groundswell of opinion that because of their sex-linked oppression and exploitation, refugee women should be considered "a particular group" to whom the UN Protocol definition of refugees applies. In the past few years, the Executive Committee of the UNHCR has issued a number of *Conclusions on the International Protection of Refugees* that prescribe special measures to protect refugee women from assault, support their rights equal to refugee men, provide for the care of abused women, and enable them to participate in decision making regarding how they lead their lives. (UNHCR 1985, 1989, 1990).

4. It is also argued that rape of refugee women is not only an instance of individual oppression but also represents persecution based on the group characteristics of refugee women. Intergroup rape indicates mistrust among juxtaposed or intermixed groups. Anecdotal evidence from the Thai-Cambodian border suggests that intergroup rape is associ-

ated with the placement of opposing political factions in close proximity to each other and with the monitoring of camps by ambivalent host government military or other officials. Although intergroup rape targets women as victims, it also has the effect of humiliating the violated women's husbands, fathers, and brothers. The power-driven assault demonstrates the men's ineffectiveness in protecting their own kin and kind (Greatbatch 1989; Mulligan 1990).

5. For example, the highly revered monk-in-exile, Maha Ghosananda, returned to Cambodia in 1992 by leading some hundreds (at departure) to one thousand (on arrival) on a "walk for reconciliation" from the border holding camp area of Aranyaprathet, Thailand, to Phnom Penh. It is implied in Bernstein and Moser's (1992) account that most of the Khmer participating in the demonstration were over age 50.

6. For example, Khmer parents in Seattle commonly report feeling mystified by their children's disobedience and inhibited from disciplining their children. They know that by reporting being hit at home, a schoolchild can get her or his parents reported to Child Protective Services and perhaps taken to courts, thus putting the parents in opposition to the very state to which they had fled for refuge. With the option of physical punishment as a form of discipline closed, many parents are at a loss about how to discipline their children. They are then stupefied when children show them disrespect, a flagrant violation of Buddhist codes for social relationships.

7. The Chams, a Muslim people most densely settled in southeastern Cambodia, with some in central-southern Vietnam, were singled out for even more murder than other groups in Cambodia. Kiernan (1988:30) estimates that about 90,000 Cham "perished at the hands of the Pol Pot regime." In 1970, there were some 200,000 Cham in Cambodia (ibid.).

8. One woman said, "My family was killed in 1975 and I cried for four years. And when I stopped crying, I was blind" (Rozee-Koker 1987).

9. Pers. com., field trip June 1986.

10. In the 1950s in northeastern Thailand (adjacent to Cambodia) the anthropologist Robert Textor described the dried fetus amulets as having been stillborn, but the details vary from my field notes. This variation probably reflects the flexibility and responsiveness of culture to contextual contingencies (1974:263–278).

11. Pers. com., field trips December 1982, June 1986.

12. Personal interview, 7 March 1991, Seattle, Wash.

13. The Cambodian Children's Project.

REFERENCES

Agency for International Development (AID)
  1991   *Report to Congress: Cambodia: Humanitarian and Development Assistance Priorities.* Washington, D.C.: U.S. Department of State.
Ang Choulean
  1986   *Les Êtres Surnataurels Dans la Religion Populaire Khmère.* Collection Bibliotèque Khmère, Série Travaux et Recherches. Paris: Cdeoreck.
Antonovsky, Aaron
  1979   *Health, Stress and Coping.* San Francisco: Jossey-Bass.
  1987   *Unraveling the Mystery of Health: How People Manage Stress and Stay Well.* San Francisco: Jossey-Bass.

Becker, Elizabeth
  1986   *When the War Was Over: The Voices of Cambodia's Revolution and Its People.* New
              York: Simon and Schuster.
Bernstein, Elizabeth, and Yeshua Moser
  1992   "Washing Away the Blood." Manuscript, 23 June.
Blanchard, P. D., Donald McAlpine, and Joseph D. C. Yao
  1986   "Isoniazid Overdose in the Cambodian Population of Olmstead County,
              Minnesota." *Journal of the American Medical Association* 256:3131–3133.
Boehnlein, James K.
  1987   "Clinical Relevance of Grief and Mourning among Cambodian
              Refugees." *Social Science and Medicine* 25(7):765–772.
Burton, Eve
  1983   "Surviving the Flight of Horror: The Story of Refugee Women." *Indochina
              Issues* 34 (February): 1–7.
Cambodia 1990
  1990   *Cultural Survival Quarterly* 14(3).
Catlin, Amy
  1987   *Apsara: The Feminine in Cambodian Art, An Exhibition.* Los Angeles: Woman's
              Building.
Chandler, David Porter
  1975   "Cambodia before the French: Politics in a Tributary Kingdom,
              1794–1848." Ph.D. dissertation, Department of History, University of
              Michigan, 1973. Ann Arbor: University Microfilms 1975.
  1982   "Songs at the Edge of the Forest: Perceptions of Order in Three Cambo-
              dian Texts." In *Moral Order and the Question of Change: Essays on Southeast Asian
              Thought,* ed. David K. Wyatt and Alexander Woodside, 53–77. Monograph
              Series no. 24, Yale University SE Asia Studies.
Daniel, E. Valentine, and John Chr. Knudsen
  1991   "Trust and the Refugee Experience: A Proposal for a Workshop at the
              United Nations University, World Institute for Development Economics
              Research " Helsinki.
Danieli, Yael
  1985   "The Treatment and Prevention of Long-Term Effects and Intergenera-
              tional Transmission of Victimization: A Lesson from Holocaust Survivors
              and Their Children." In *Trauma and Its Wake: The Study and Treatment of Post-
              Traumatic Stress Disorder,* ed. C. R. Figley, 295–313. New York: Brun-
              ner/Mazel.
Duncan, Julianne
  1984   "Use of Traditional Cambodian Culture as a Mental Health Program to
              Help Children Cope with Separation and Loss." Paper presented at the
              National Unaccompanied Minors Conference, Washington D.C., 15
              November.
Ebihara, May
  1974   "Khmer Village Women in Cambodia: A Happy Balance." In *Many Sisters:
              Women in Cross-Cultural Perspective,* ed. Carolyn J. Matthiason, 305–347. New
              York: Free Press.

Eisenbruch, Maurice
  1984   "Cross-Cultural Aspects of Bereavement. I: A Conceptual Framework for Comparative Analysis." *Culture, Medicine and Psychiatry* 8:283–309.
Erikson, Erik H.
  1963   *Childhood and Society.* New York: Norton.
French, Lindsay, ed.
  1990   *Displaced Lives: Stories of Life and Culture from the Khmer in Site II.* Bangkok: International Rescue Committee.
French, Lindsay, Barnabas Man, and Tith Wuthy, eds.
  1990   *Displaced Lives: Stories of Life and Culture from the Khmer in Site II.* Bangkok: International Rescue Committee.
Geertz, Clifford
  1973*a*   "Religion as a Cultural System." In *The Interpretation of Cultures: Selected Essays,* ed. Clifford Geertz, 87–125. New York: Basic Books.
  1973*b*   "The Integrative Revolution: Primordial Sentiments and Civil Politics in the New States." In *The Interpretation of Cultures: Selected Essays,* ed. Clifford Geertz, 255–310. New York: Basic Books.
Grahl-Madsen, Atle
  1966   *The Status of Refugees in International Law.* Vol. 1. Leyden: A. W. Sijthoft.
Greatbatch, J.
  1989   "The Gender Difference: Feminist Critiques of Refugee Discourse." *International Journal of Refugee Law* 1(4):518–527.
Gyallay-Pap, Peter
  1990   *Khmer Monk Education in the Thai Border Camps.* Bangkok, Thailand, and Amherst, Mass.: Khmer-Buddhist Educational Assistance Project (KEAP).
Hanks, Jane Richardson
  1963   "Maternity and Its Rituals in Bang Chan." Southeast Asia Program Data Paper no. 51. Ithaca: Cornell University.
Heder, Stephen R.
  1978   "Origins of the Conflict." *Southeast Asia Chronicle* 64:8.
Keller, Stephen L.
  1975   *Uprooting and Social Change: The Role of Refugees in Development.* Delhi: Manohar Book Service.
Keyes, Charles F., and E. Valentine Daniel
  1983   *Karma: An Anthropological Inquiry.* Berkeley, Los Angeles, and London: University of California Press.
Kiernan, Ben
  1988   "Orphans of Genocide: The Cham Muslims of Kampuchea under Pol Pot." *Bulletin of Concerned Asian Scholars* 20(4):2–33.
Kiernan, Ben, and Chanthou Boua, eds.
  1982   *Peasants and Politics in Kampuchea 1942–1981.* Armonk, N.Y.: M. E. Sharpe.
Krystal, H.
  1978   "Trauma and Affects." *Psychoanalytic Study of the Child* 33:81–116.
Krystal, Henry, and T. A. Petty
  1968   "The Psychological Complications of Convalescence." In *Massive Psychic*

Trauma, ed. Henry Krystal, 277–326. New York: International Universities Press.

Ledgerwood, Judy
  1988   "Sri Grap Lakkhana: Khmer Images of the Perfect Woman." Paper presented at the annual meeting of the American Anthropological Association, Phoenix, Ariz.

Mollica, Richard F.
  1988*a*   "Southeast Asian refugees." In *Clinical Guidelines in Cross-Cultural Mental Health,* ed. L. Comas-Diaz and E. E. H. Griffith, 262–304. New York: John Wiley & Sons.
  1988*b*   "The Trauma Story: The Psychiatric Care of Refugee Survivors of Violence and Torture." In *Post-Traumatic Therapy and Victims of Violence,* ed. F. M. Ochberg, 295–314. New York: Brunner/Mazel.
  1990   "The Social World Destroyed: The Psychiatric Care of the Refugee Trauma Survivor." In *Health Services for the Treatment of Torture and Trauma Survivors,* ed. J. Gruschow and K. Hannibal, 15–33. Washington, D.C.: American Association for the Advancement of Science.

Mollica, Richard F., and Russell R. Jalbert
  1989   *Community of Confinement: The Mental Health Crisis in Site Two (Displaced Persons Camps on the Thai-Kampuchean Border). Committee on Refugees and Migrants.* World Federation for Mental Health.

Mollica, Richard F., Grace Wyshak, and James Lavelle
  1987   "The Psychological Impact of War Trauma and Torture on Southeast Asian Refugees." *American Journal of Psychiatry* 144(12):1567–1572.

Mollica, Richard F., James Lavelle, Svang Tor, and Christopher Elias
  1989   *Turning Point in Khmer Mental Health: Immediate Steps to Resolve the Mental Health Crisis in the Khmer Border Camps. Committee on Refugees and Migrants.* World Federation for Mental Health, 1 December.

Mollica, Richard F., Karen Donelan, Svang Tor, James Lavelle, Christopher Elias, Robert J. Blendon, Martin Frankel, and Douglas Bennett
  1991   *Repatriation and Disability: A Community Study of Health, Mental Health and Social Functioning of the Khmer Residents of Site Two. Vol. 1, Khmer Adults.* Harvard School of Public Health and the World Federation for Mental Health.

Muecke, Marjorie A.
  1976   "Health Care Systems as Socializing Agents: Childbearing the North Thai and Western Ways." *Social Science and Medicine* 10(8–9):377–383.
  1989   "Cambodia Trip Report, 22–29 Dec." Seattle: University of Washington.
  1992   "Mother Sold Food, Daughter Sells Her Body: The Cultural Continuity of Prostitution in Thailand." *Social Science and Medicine* 35(7):891–901.

Mulligan, M.
  1990   "Obtaining Political Asylum: Classifying Rape as a Well-Founded Fear of Persecution on Account of Political Opinion." *Boston College Third World Law Journal* 10(2):355–380.

Muskie, Edmund S.
  1990   *Exploring Cambodia: Issues and Reality in a Time of Transition.* Washington, D.C.: Center for National Policy.

Nolan, Charles M., Anna M. Elarth, and Heather W. Barr
    1988   "Intentional Isoniazid Overdosage in Young Southeast Asian Refugee Women." *Chest* 93(4):803–806.
Ramsay, Rosalind, Caroline Gorst-Unsworth, and S. W. Turner
    1993   "Psychological Morbidity in Survivors of Organized State Violence including Torture: A Retrospective Series." *British Journal of Psychiatry* 160:55–59.
Rasmussen, O. V.
    1990   "Medical Aspects of Torture." *Danish Medical Bulletin* 37(Suppl. 1):1–88.
Richie, Beth
    1988   *Understanding Family Violence within U.S. Refugee Communities: A Training Manual.* Washington, D.C.: Refugee Women in Development (RefWID).
Rozee-Koker, Patricia
    1987   "The Psychological Effects of Abuse on Older Cambodian Refugee Women." Paper presented at the annual meeting of the Association for Women in Psychology, Denver, Colo.
Samedy, My
    1989   "Crimes et repercussions dans le domaine de la sante publique sous le regime genocidal de Pol Pot." Ieng Sary, Kheiey Samphan, Faculty of Medicine, Phnom Pehn, 20 July.
Smith, Frank
    1989   "Interpretive Accounts of the Khmer Rouge Years: Personal Experience in Cambodian Peasant World View." *Wisconsin Papers on Southeast Asia, Occasional Paper* no. 18. Madison: University of Wisconsin.
Smith-Hefner, Nancy
    1991   "Education, Gender and Generational Conflict among Khmer Refugees." Paper presented at the annual meeting of the Association for Asian Studies, New Orleans, La., 14 April.
Textor, Robert
    1974   "An Inventory of Non-Buddhist Supernatural Objects in a Central Thai Village." Ph.D. dissertation, Cornell University. Ann Arbor: University Microfilms.
Thompson, Janice L.
    1991   "Exploring Gender and Culture with Khmer Refugee Women: Reflections on Participatory Feminist Research." *Advances in Nursing Science* 13(3):30–48.
Truong Thi Dieu De
    1989   *Vietnamese Women and Sexual* [sic] *Violence.* Rijswijk, The Netherlands: Refugee Health Care Centre, Ministry of Welfare, Health and Cultural Affairs, March.
United Nations Convention on the Elimination of All Forms of Discrimination Against Women. Document A/AC.96/754. Geneva.
United Nations High Commissioner for Refugees (UNHCR) Conclusions on the International Protection of Refugees
    1985   "Refugee Women and International Protection." 39 (XXXVI). Geneva: UNHCR.
    1989   "Refugee Women." 60 (XL). Geneva: UNHCR.

1990   "Refugee Women and International Protection." 64 (XLI). Geneva: UNHCR.

Wali, Sima

1990   "Refugee Women and Development." Paper prepared for the Expert Group Meeting on Refugee and Displaced Women and Children, Vienna, 2–6 July. Washington, D.C.: Refugee Women in Development (RefWID).

Williams, Holly A.

1990   "Families in Refugee Camps." *Human Organization* 49(2):100–109.

THREE

Torture, Refuge, and Trust

Stuart Turner

To understand the bleak personal world that some refugees are forced to inhabit, it is necessary to consider not only the context from which they have escaped, a context that often includes widespread conflict, state violence, and even torture, but also the way in which many have to live in their exile. The continuing experience of persecution in a country of asylum may come as a shock. Fundamental shifts in attitude and expectation are likely to be encountered—especially when these traumatic experiences are associated with a limited sense of mastery.

Trust is an aspect of relating, not just interpersonal relating but also intrapersonal and between persons and other external objects such as may be seen in religious and political commitments. The experiences of the refugee may have a direct, intimate, and occasionally devastating impact on each of these trust relationships.

This chapter sets out, first, to describe some of the experiences of refugees in the country of persecution; second, to list some of the ways in which the experience of persecution continues; third, to identify some of the personal psychological reactions to oppression; and finally, to illustrate the impact and limitations (ethical and methodological) of therapeutic interventions on these reactions. Together, these insights illuminate the trust relationship.

STATE-ORGANIZED VIOLENCE, INCLUDING TORTURE

Torture is the use of "severe pain or suffering" intentionally inflicted for such purposes as gaining information and confessions, punishing, intimidating, coercing, or for any reason based on discrimination. Moreover, this attack is always carried out by or with the approval of a public official (United Nations 1984). It forms part of the systematic process of state control of dissident beliefs and the oppression of groups and communities. However, it is not merely the survivor of torture who suffers and in fear may be driven into exile. The systematic and repressive nature of the violence affects all people who share an ethnicity, religion, or political ideology with the immediate victim. Indeed, it is the intention of the state that this should be the case.

Seen in this way, torture can be identified as part of a broader spectrum of activities, perhaps best described under the phrase "organized state violence." This has been illustrated by Ignacio Martín-Baró (1988), vice-rector of the University of Central America and one of the Jesuits tragically murdered in El Salvador in 1989 because of his human rights work. He described two aspects of the same violent process operating in his country, "dirty" and "psychological" warfare. Between 1980 and 1983, one out of every two hundred Salvadorans was a direct victim of the dirty war. Many were killed by the so-called death squads, which operated with state support and impunity. From 1984 onward, there was an attempt to shift to a more sophisticated (and politically more acceptable) psychological warfare. This required that brutal actions were carried out on a few individuals in such a way that the wider population was literally terrorized. For this to be successful, the state had to make sure that the population was well informed about the violence taking place and was maintained in a state of fear by a sequence of unpredictable actions involving acts of intimidation alternating with conditional protection.

Systematic harassment, detention, interrogation, and searches do not fall within a narrow definition of torture, but these clearly share similar repressive intentions. Harsh beatings randomly inflicted in police stations and the sudden rounding up of civilians by soldiers, threatening all the inhabitants of a village, are not regarded as forms of torture. Yet the effects may be identical to the application of electric shocks to skin and genitals, the painful mutilation of a victim's body, and the half-drowning of "submarino" torture, which are all included in lists of physical tortures. The threshold between torture and other repressive violence therefore appears to be arbitrary and to some degree meaningless.

In his autobiographical writing, Jacobo Timerman gives personal insight into the way different types of violence, widely differing in apparent severity, share a common purpose and produce devastating results. He wrote from his own experience of torture and torture centers.

> Nothing can compare to those family groups that were tortured often together, sometimes separately, but in view of one another or in different cells, while one was aware of the other being tortured. The entire affective world, constructed over the years with utmost difficulty, collapses with a kick in the father's genitals, a smack on the mother's face, an obscene insult to the sister or the sexual violation of a daughter. Suddenly an entire culture based on familial love, devotion, the capacity for mutual sacrifice collapses. Nothing is possible in such a universe, and that is precisely what the torturers know. (Quoted in Kolff and Doan 1985:53)

So it is the meaning of the violence, rather than its form, that appears to be of greater importance. Often, it is enough for both parties to know what *might* happen for the victim to experience fear and for that to become the critical, the only, reality. Fear of this degree may lead to profound long-term psychological changes regardless of the degree of objective life risk or even of the actual experience of physical violence.

The meaning of the attack justifies further scrutiny. In Timerman's illustration, the torturer is attacking the heart of a family, the "love, devotion, the capacity for mutual sacrifice." In doing this, the aim is to destroy a trust relationship between people. More than this, it is an attempt to prevent such relationships from developing again. How can a person afford to enter into the commitment of trust, when that emotional bond renders him or her so vulnerable to the cruel strength of state violence?

Another way of examining the same issue is to consider not the meaning of torture as perceived by a victim but the purpose of torture from the perspective of the torturer. Torture in the modern world bears only a superficial relationship to torture of ancient times (Rasmussen 1990). Then, although very frequently abused, it was ostensibly part of a quasi-judicial process, the aim of which was to elicit a confession and determine guilt. Principles of "justice" have developed, and torture as an openly acknowledged judicial technique has thankfully passed out of general service. Rather, it has entered into the shadowland of Orwellian doubletalk. It is overtly denied by governments, yet to be effective people must know it (covertly) takes place. It may have the overt purpose of gathering confessions, yet operating as it does outside the rule of law, these are not required for sentence to be passed or (covertly) executed. Like the Queen in Alice's Wonderland, who "had only one way of settling all difficulties"—the command "off with his head" (Carroll 1983)—the state can indulge in extra-judicial execution with impunity. Information as evidence is not required. So why torture?

The gathering of information is one of the most common justifications for torture, but once again the critical distinction between overt and covert motivations must be drawn. The person or group under scrutiny is usually (overtly) labeled "terrorist" (although the records of Amnesty International (e.g., Amnesty International 1990) testify to the widespread use of torture against people committed to nonviolent action or who are oppressed solely because of who they are, the color of their skin, or their religious affiliation). Even the "information" that provides the tenuous justification can often be obtained through informers and all the other secret techniques available to states; in any case, suspects can be killed by "death squads" without any sham of justice or judicial process. So the overt rationale does not stand up to scrutiny.

The covert value of extorted information is its ability to shatter relationships, in fact, to destroy trust. Information extracted under torture becomes a weapon of repression. Even when the individual has been able to resist the pressure to inform, he or she must still battle to convince friends and supporters, who may struggle to trust the released survivor because of their assumptions about his or her behavior under torture. Similarly, since anyone released will likely deny passing information, it is all the harder to be believed even when one has resisted. In much the same way, Cambodian women who were known to have been detained sometimes faced stigmatization by their communities because it was assumed that they had been sexually violated (Muecke, this volume). A denial had no meaning; it was not believed. The mere knowledge of detention was sufficient to break trust within family and community.

Repression depends on the violent destruction of communal opposition. No individual alone can seriously attack a state; opposition groups can be overcome with the military superiority of the armed forces in civil war. However, if open civil war is impractical or cannot be acknowledged for other political reasons (as was the case in El Salvador from 1984, according to Martín-Baró's thesis), then the other weapon available to the state is the systematic disruption of communities, achieved by directly attacking these trust relationships. The man arrested because his comrade gave information about him or the sister murdered because a brother was forced to reveal a secret—these are the clues to one of the genuine purposes of organized state violence. Information, extracted under torture, becomes the currency of further violence and the symbol of the dislocation of trust.

THE REFUGEE EXPERIENCE IN THE UNITED KINGDOM

Under the United Nations' convention relating to the status of refugees (United Nations 1951), refugees are people who have a "well-founded fear of persecution for reasons of race, religion, nationality, membership of a particular social group or political opinion." Many will have experienced torture, but all to some degree will have been made aware of the broader aspects of organized state violence.

It has been estimated that there are over 16 million refugees in the world as well as about 23 million internally displaced people (*World Refugee Survey* 1992), including the disproportionately small number of about 700,000 in Europe (Andreassen 1989). Many of the refugees now in the United Kingdom arrived from other parts of Europe in the upheaval of the 1930s and 1940s; many others chose to come to the United Kingdom because of earlier colonial relationships. In the last decade, the nationalities and ethnic groups of asylum seekers have continued to be varied; official statistics list twenty-one main countries of origin, with many smaller countries also identified by geographic region (table 3.1).

TABLE 3.1.   Applications Received
for Refugee Status or Asylum,
by Nationality, 1979–1989

Afghanistan	640
Angola	315
Czechoslovakia	355
Ethiopia	2,190

TABLE 3.1. *(continued)*

Ghana	2,540
Hungary	320
India	1,345
Iran	15,485
Iraq	2,775
Lebanon	605
Libya	565
Pakistan	1,930
Poland	1,235
Seychelles	575
Somalia	4,065
South Africa	535
Sri Lanka	7,910
Sudan	345
Turkey	5,870
Uganda	3,475
Zaire	715
Other African	865
Other American	605
Other Middle Eastern	350
Other Asian	285
Other European	285
Others, including stateless	565
Total	54,935

SOURCE: Refugee Support Centre Information Package, quoting official statistics; available from RSC, King George's House, London SW9 9ES, U.K.

Although the British media tend to portray refugees and asylum seekers arriving in "floods, influxes, waves, torrents, streams" (Döveling and Hoffman 1989), this is a stereotypical, false representation. In any comparison (e.g., with the number of refugees in the world as a whole, the number of asylum seekers arriving in other European countries, even the total population of the United Kingdom) the number of asylum seekers to the United Kingdom is tiny (Nettleton and Simcock 1987) and the proportion gaining refugee status smaller still. Yet the nationalistic response is to seek controls, perhaps deliberately to confuse refugees with other migrants, to attempt to restrict the ways people can arrive. Two recent U.K. policy changes may illustrate this point.

In 1987, the United Kingdom enacted a law, the Immigration (Carriers' Liability) Act, which put a responsibility on air and sea carriers to ensure that anyone traveling on their service carried valid papers. Failure to meet this rule leads to a financial penalty against the carrier. Of course, it is in the nature of the asylum seeker's condition that exit from a country of persecution is often clandestine.

Sometimes this is arranged by bribing local officials to gain safe passage with valid papers, but for many it involves the use of forged or illegally obtained passports and other documents. A law ostensibly directed at the control of other immigrants, therefore, has an impact on a much more vulnerable group of people who may be in very real fear for their lives. Moreover, knowledge of this regulation is likely to deter others from attempting to travel to the United Kingdom. However this act is to be understood, it must, if it is effective at all, export to other borders and to other agencies the responsibility for excluding a proportion of potential asylum seekers.

In 1989, the United Kingdom received increased numbers of Kurdish people from Turkey This was portrayed in some quarters as a process of economic migration rather than as an escape from persecution, despite reputable evidence of widespread human rights abuses, including torture (e.g., Amnesty International 1988, 1990). Histories of organized violence, including torture, were also compatible with the results of medical examinations of the first few to arrive (Turner et al. 1989), findings subsequently supported by many health professionals in Turkey (Yuksel 1989). The official British response was to institute new visa controls as provided for by international law (Aleinikoff, this volume). U.K. immigration officials were sent to Turkey to screen people; only those granted visas were permitted to travel to the United Kingdom. Once again the decision-making process passed outside national borders and presumably has deterred a proportion of asylum seekers as well as people migrating for other reasons. It has been suggested that visa requirements are likely to be an "insurmountable obstacle for asylum seekers who are already uneasy about letting their plans for escape be known to anyone in authority" (Andreassen 1989) and that these restrictive rules may "increase the level of misery and danger" to the asylum seeker (Rudge 1989).

The reception of asylum seekers is also a matter of considerable importance. For a person who has faced persecution, violence, and even torture at the hands of officials in his or her own country, it is inevitably the case that an official request to reveal hitherto deeply guarded secrets will be met with some hesitation. Yet it is often on the basis of such an interview that decisions will be made about the individual's future status. This problem is compounded if the circumstances of reception involve unpleasant or overcrowded detention centers, prolonged detention, separation of the family unit, and very long delays in achieving a decision about status. Following an inquest into the death of a Ugandan asylum seeker to the United Kingdom, it was concluded that his suicide was "aggravated by official indifference and lack of care" (ibid.), a sad indictment of the statutory authorities.

A campaign (Charter 87) in the United Kingdom has made modest proposals for reform, including (1) a right for a full and fair hearing of the asylum case within a reasonable time, (2) a right to independent legal representation and medical examination, (3) a right of appeal (with a stay of deportation) in the case of a negative decision, (4) detention only under exceptional circumstances and then under judicial review, and (5) a right to certain social and economic necessities. These steps toward a positive asylum policy have so far been rejected, and although some asylum seekers do obtain some of these benefits, there has been a consistent refusal to apply these principles to all cases.

During the 1980s, there was a shift in decision-making practice. Fewer asylum seekers now obtain full refugee status; correspondingly more receive exceptional leave to remain in the United Kingdom. At first sight this may appear to be a minor difference. At least there is no return (*refoulement*) to a country of oppression. Yet the implications of this decision may still be very serious for the individual and his or her family. Exceptional leave, unlike refugee status, carries no permanent safety (being subject to annual review) and carries no automatic rights for the dependents of the asylum seeker who may have been left behind in the original country. Family separation is common and, although outside the control of the asylum seeker, often constitutes a perfectly understandable source of prolonged fear and guilt.

Given that the asylum seeker has often already sustained a severe attack, through no fault of his or her own, and has been left at least psychologically wounded, a caring and just response might involve official procedures that were not just neutral but positively designed to facilitate recovery. It would require an understanding of the overwhelming pressures that make some people risk everything in flight. This process would inevitably need to include work on the reestablishment of trust relationships, between individuals and between the individual and the state. In the context of a perceived just world, continued victimization and marginalization stand to have important consequences for people already sensitized by prior experience.

INDIVIDUAL PSYCHOLOGICAL REACTIONS

In a recent review of the literature (see Turner and Gorst-Unsworth 1990, 1993 for more detailed accounts and reference lists), the notion of a single "torture syndrome" has been challenged; instead it has been proposed that four common themes can be identified in the psychological sequelae of torture. These are (1) incomplete emotional processing (akin to posttraumatic stress disorder, or PTSD), (2) depressive reactions, (3) somatic symptoms, and (4) the existential dilemma.

The common elements of this approach include a rejection of the specific post-torture syndrome and a return to theories of normal psychological functioning. It highlights the abnormality of the experience rather than the individual and points to a series of dimensional (quantitative) reactions rather than a categorical (qualitative) disorder.

Etiological processes have been suggested for each of these reactions. In particular, it was proposed that the trauma of the torture itself would show the clearest relationship with PTSD; the consequential losses (including for asylum seekers loss of family, community, culture, and language) would be more closely associated with major depression.

Implicit in this approach is the recognition both that individuals react differently to state violence, as they do to many other psychological stressors, and that the persecutory experiences may continue. Torture is an activity with particularly complex psychological and physical sequelae. The survivor has not merely been an accidental victim of natural disaster but has received the focused attention of an adversary often determined to cause the maximal psychological change. This perversion of an intimate relationship (Ritterman 1987; Schlapobersky and Bamber 1988) for sociopolitical reasons may involve a deliberate intention to disrupt the normal healing process to maximize the psychological scars.

Given that one of the main covert purposes of torture is the destruction of trust as a basis for interpersonal and intercommunity relationships, an individual psychology is an insufficient explanation of these events. However, the claim that socially caused damage can only be socially repaired (Martín-Baró 1988) is far too extreme. Refugees are individuals as much as they are members of a group. Certainly, the community from which they have escaped can be construed as a social victim, but the actual experience of violence or torture is in its essence both personal and intimate. Both psychological and sociopolitical understandings and approaches must complement each other in achieving a resolution of this pain.

For refugees in particular, the possibility of social reconstruction within a changing country (e.g., Chile or Czechoslovakia) may have been abandoned with the decision to seek exile. As has already been demonstrated, the refugee may have had to face multiple traumas in his or her search for sanctuary. These add to the experience of alienation and may significantly limit the opportunity for successful resettlement and return to the country of origin even if the political climate there changes. A refugee may have had to accept not only enforced exile but also separation from family and dependents, prolonged periods of uncertainty and fear, further detention, and official interrogation. Moreover, the processes of isolation and cultural bereavement are enhanced by the fears that the refugee community may well contain people acting as informants to the country of origin.

Reference will be made here to two studies carried out in London. The first of these is a retrospective investigation of 100 consecutive psychiatric referrals (Ramsay, Gorst-Unsworth, and Turner 1993) seen in a London center. There were 78 men and 22 women, with an age range of 18 to 66 years and a mean age of 31 years. The sample was mixed; 58 were from the Middle East, 29 from Africa, 8 from Sri Lanka, and 5 from various other countries. Sixty-eight had experienced one or more forms of physical torture, and all subjects had been exposed to organized violence, including psychological threats and abuse. Sexual torture was used against 17 men and 6 women; it included injury or shocks to genital areas as well as more direct sexual assaults, including rape and anal insertion of batons. The second study is a pilot investigation of attitude change in survivors of torture (Gorst-Unsworth, Van Velsen, and Turner 1993). The numbers are smaller (n = 31), but the sample is very similar in terms of demography.

Incomplete Emotional Processing

For many, the trauma of organized repressive violence causes a characteristic reaction best understood in terms of a (hypothesized) normal function, emotional processing, that has been overwhelmed by the scale of the damage. Similar reactions follow disasters and other extreme traumatic events.

It is suggested that each of us carries a set of predictions about our own social and physical environment (internal models of the world or cognitive schemata). It is this facility that allows us to plan in advance ways of dealing with difficulties. Each daily event is compared against this set of predictions, and when discrepancies are identified, the internal psychological model can be adjusted accordingly (or, alternatively, that aspect of reality can be ignored). This internal adjustment has been termed cognitive processing. Some discrepancies also have emotional consequences. Passing or failing an examination, gaining or losing a job, for example, all require in addition to a factual cognitive change important emotional reactions.

Emotional processing, therefore, is a parallel process by which the emotional reactions are worked through (Horowitz 1976; Rachman 1980). It requires an awareness of the emotional reactions with a gradual decline or habituation over time. Large reactions are dealt with in smaller "chunks." In normal bereavement, for example, levels of distress may vary considerably, sometimes triggered by external cues or by an internal mechanism, at other times displaced by successful activity. These manageable amounts of distress can usually be tolerated when they occur, and as they subside, one takes another step toward emotional resolution.

In a reaction to extreme trauma, memories, nightmares, or even vivid flashback experiences produce such marked psychological reactions, with overwhelming emotional distress, that the only viable response is to attempt to shut them out, by internal "numbing" or avoidance of external triggers. The emotional disturbance cannot be tolerated and therefore cannot be processed. Intrusive and avoidance states alternate, but in neither is there the opportunity for change. Emotional processing leading to relief requires more than a brief reexposure to manageable rather than overwhelming amounts of fear and distress.

The notion of a dimensional reaction of this type has a similarity to the categorical reaction, posttraumatic stress disorder, which has now been recognized in the current American Psychiatric Association's *Diagnostic and Statistical Manual of Mental Disorders* (1987). From the retrospective study case notes examination, 31 percent met the research criteria for PTSD and 54 percent had received clinical diagnoses of PTSD. However, the data did not support the suggestion of a discontinuity between the two conditions of "well" and "disordered." Instead, the evidence indicates a wide range of degrees of difficulty.

Moreover, it was also found that different patterns of traumatic stress reaction could be identified. Straightforward violence appeared to be more closely associated with subsequent intrusive behaviors (unpleasant thoughts, dreams, or flashbacks); the more intimate attack of sexual torture appeared to lead to a strongly defensive avoidance state (Ramsay, Gorst-Unsworth, and Turner 1993). PTSD, not formally validated with groups of torture survivors, is therefore likely to be an oversimplification in theory and application.

In spite of recent developments in disseminating information about traumatic stress reactions (e.g., media involvement in postdisaster distress reactions), for many people, the survival process has been associated with uncomprehending and unforgiving reactions from friends, families, and even professionals, leading to secondary and continuing victimization.

Depressive Reactions to Loss

Associated with the experience of organized state violence, there are many consequential loss events, events recognized as leading to a major depressive reaction (Brown and Harris 1978). These may include bereavement, personal injury (loss of function), loss of home, and loss of employment. Leaving the country of oppression may only serve to increase the problem, with separation from family and community, from culture, and from language. The reception of asylum seekers is obviously of critical importance. Attempts to reduce the impact of these further traumas following arrival in the country of asylum are seldom made.

From a retrospective case notes examination of asylum seekers in the U.K., 42 percent met research criteria for a major depressive disorder and 55 percent had received clinical diagnoses of depression. Again, the evidence suggests a dimensional response with a range of severities. The depressive reaction was much less strongly associated with history of trauma, a finding compatible with the prediction that a wide range of loss events may be important in its pathogenesis (Ramsay, Gorst-Unsworth, and Turner 1993).

In a recent American series of 52 Southeast Asian refugees (Mollica, Wyshak, and Lavelle 1987), major depression was the most common diagnosis in the whole sample, being diagnosed in 37 of the 52 subjects. Moreover, the relationship with loss was demonstrated. Those Cambodian widows who had experienced at least two of the three traumas of rape, loss of spouse, or loss of children had the highest levels of depressive symptoms. They perceived themselves as socially isolated and living in a hostile social world.

Somatic Symptoms

It is hardly surprising that following physical torture, applied to the individual as a means of achieving psychological change, there should be complex meanings assigned to physical symptoms (Turner and Gorst-Unsworth 1990, 1993). Nowhere is it more important to move away from a Cartesian mind-body dualism and accept an interactional psychosomatic model (Turner and Hough 1993). The trust relationship between patient and physician is often put at risk by an unwillingness on the part of the doctor to accept the personal reality of physical symptoms in the absence of demonstrable injury or identifiable organic pathology.

The Existential Dilemma

Torture is a "catastrophic existential event" (Bendfeldt-Zachrisson 1985). Those who survive (and they are probably the minority) have to come to terms with a world in which such acts of barbaric cruelty are not just nebulous possibilities but stark personal realities. Even survival may bring its own guilt, whether by virtue of the enforced confessions, the information painfully extracted, the actions needed to survive, or the more magical notion that one death might have led to another being saved. Life in such a condition is the material of powerful testimony and autobiography.

> Writing and publishing "If This Is a Man" (1960) and "The Truce" (1965) marked a decisive turn in my life not only as a writer. For several years afterward, I had the feeling that I had performed a task, indeed the only task clearly defined for me. At Auschwitz, and on the long road returning home, I had seen and experienced things that imperiously demanded to be told. And I had told them, I had testified. (Levi 1987)

One of the common themes of these testimonies is the shift from a more comfortable position of greater or lesser denial into a more radical reaction—the "decisive turn" of Primo Levi. Survivors must to some extent come to reconcile the "new self" with the "new reality" of the external world. This may lead to active opposition to a system as well as to repression under the burden of violence and threat. There is the potential for personal growth, but commonly, the reactions seem to be more mixed and problematic.

Just as interpersonal relationships are changed, so the relationship between a person and larger entities such as the qualities of love and goodness, religious faith, or even a political ideology may be damaged by torture or other organized state violence. Similarly, the man or woman who was "betrayed" by a close friend or relative may never again have quite the same confidence in anyone. Such a person may also find that his or her personal world philosophy is irreparably dented by the experience.

Yet often of equal significance, the trust of an asylum seeker in his or her chosen safe country may be sadly misplaced. One man asked why it was that he had been detained in his own country for a matter of days but was held in the United Kingdom in prisonlike circumstances for three months. Implicit in the concept of trust is the notion of hope. Those who hope for little may have their trust in others less damaged by such experiences than those with higher expectations.

In an attempt to unravel this issue, data on some of these attitudes and feelings have been collected as part of a pilot interview survey (Gorst-Unsworth, Van Velsen, and Turner 1993). Survivors of torture and other forms of organized violence (n = 31) frequently reported feeling that the experience had changed them, that they felt different and misunderstood by others who had not shared their experiences. More seriously, many reported that they felt misunderstood even by those friends, doctors, or lawyers who were trying to help. This sense of alienation, of being apart from others, is probably common to many victim groups and may be an important reason for the development of self-help groups, for example, rape counseling or survivor groups following natural disasters. The experience commonly changed the individuals' religious or political beliefs, and many reported a lasting effect on their priorities in life. Another factor likely to be important in producing alienation from health professionals is their role in torture. In this sample, 46 percent (18 out of 39) reported some involvement of doctors and other health professionals in torture. This result is similar to findings in other surveys.

Guilt was reported by the majority and was associated chiefly with separation from other family members. Nearly half were separated from all family members, including dependents. For many, this separation would continue for long periods, the fear and uncertainties produced thereby being a major cause of continuing distress. Worse than this, the mere fact that the asylum seeker had escaped would be more likely to draw the attention of the authorities to his or her family and friends left behind.

A DIFFERENT WAY FORWARD

There has been wide variation in the attitudes professionals have taken vis-à-vis the precarious situation of the asylum seeker and the refugee who have been the victims of repressive violence. On the one hand, rehabilitation centers have been set up to offer specific medical treatment for individual refugees in safe countries (Somnier and Genefke 1986); on the other, it is argued that the only valid response is social and political (Martín-Baró 1988). Removing the evidence of the distress of torture has even been seen as (indirectly) colluding with the frequent tendency to avoid the reality of its existence in the world. There are few other situations that provoke such a wide range of reactions within the professional community. This failure to achieve less polarized ways of working stands to have a negative impact on survivors (Manz, this volume).

Moreover, the work is beset with its own problems. Mollica (1988) has reported the feelings of hopelessness that overtook his Indochinese Psychiatry Clinic. The "trauma stories" of the clinic's clients had a powerful influence not only on the clients themselves but also on the institution. Yet he also asserts that listening to these trauma stories is at the heart of therapy. It is tempting to avoid this painful process, but as a step to the rebuilding of trust in others, it is vital. It may be the first step into an unknown world, and it is the ability to take such steps that characterizes the trust relationship. That someone else can listen to such a story without apparently being overwhelmed or immediately rejecting may be a powerful way for the individual to start to reclaim his or her place in history, to reassert his or her existence within space and time (Schlapobersky and Bamber 1988).

Testimony, initially used as a technique of political opposition to the human rights abuses in Chile (Cienfuegos and Monelli 1983), now provides, in many modified and usually simplified forms, a common basis for psychotherapy for survivors of torture and other forms of organized violence (Turner 1992). It illustrates that it is possible to take a sophisticated view of therapy that acknowledges some of these tensions. By making previous life history as well as future political commitment, personal relationships, work, and social connections understandable, it allows the individual to begin to reclaim a personal space and a sense of self-worth.

The technique in its original form included one or two initial interviews with a therapist in which basic background information and a general account of state violence were elicited. In subsequent sessions, a tape recording, including a detailed description of the traumatic events, would be made. The therapist would help the client to clarify and expand this description by asking simple questions. The typed transcript of the growing testimony statement would be reviewed in subsequent therapy sessions. A written document (15–120 pages), edited jointly by client and therapist, would be the final result.

Producing a testimony not only helps to relieve symptoms; it also helps survivors to integrate the trauma story into their personal histories by allowing them to understand its significance in the context of political and social events. It has been said that the purpose of torture is to transform political distress into private personal pain; the aim of therapy is to reverse this by reframing the experience (Jensen and Agger 1988). The torturer may try to instill a sense of personal responsibility and therefore guilt in his victim for actions forcibly carried out under torture. The failure to protect others being tortured, the apparently chance witnessing of children or women being tortured or killed, the final inability to withstand further pain or mutilation and the release of secrets; these are powerful barriers to any return to normal social life, especially in trust relationships. Exploring these actions in the preparation of a testimony statement helps the survivor to set these events within a larger context; the inevitability of personal action in such circumstances becomes a reason for anger at the perpetrators of violence rather than a cause for self-condemnation.

So one of the primary aims of therapy is to help the traumatized survivor rewrite his or her own story, to reframe or reinterpret key episodes within a context of compulsion and abuse. This approach also encourages a sense of personal dignity, by placing the survivor within a treatment setting in which he or she is an active participant. By explicitly acknowledging that torture affects ordinary people, who have many personal strengths and resources, it becomes obvious that therapy should depend on self-help principles as much as possible.

Some refugee organizations in first world countries offer psychological help only to those who have already achieved asylum, believing that without the security this legal status carries there is no possibility of meaningful work. This is to deny help to large numbers of people whose needs may be even greater. It is a spurious argument, equivalent to denying medical aid to people solely because they are over a certain age and hence statistically nearer to death. Although psychological work with people who have not yet received asylum is often more difficult, it should be attempted and appropriate support should be offered. Indeed, it has been argued that it is an important part of the ideological commitment to be able to demonstrate that help is available from the preasylum state onward (Jensen and Agger 1988).

Similarly, therapeutic work directed to individual refugees ignores the fact that these are people within larger communities. In the absence of a basic understanding that state violence affects communities of people and that there is a need for complementary formulations at sociopolitical as well as medical and psychological levels, any attempt at therapy is likely to have a very restricted value. By ignoring the broader social issues, it is less likely that restitution of the ability to trust will occur.

CONCLUSION

For those refugees and asylum seekers who have been victims of organized state violence that included torture, it is likely that there will have been a deliberate attack on trust. This provides one of the most important covert justifications of state violence. By inflicting damage on trust relationships, the state can attempt to prevent the emergence of a united opposition.

Unfortunately, the experiences of asylum seekers in exile may add to these feelings of marginalization and oppression. To recover from the traumatic stress of torture requires a positive and enabling approach. The more traumatized the individual, the more work is necessary to aid recovery. This effort is usually not primarily psychological but has more to do with the basic necessities of existence: family preservation, food, accommodation, and support. Yet this ideal is not even closely realized; rather, the reverse commonly seems to operate. Whether in a large refugee camp in a neighboring country or in a more remote first world country, the individual is likely to experience further traumatization. In the groups presented here, separation from family may continue over long periods and may be an important source of guilt. Under the UN convention on refugees, status may take several years to be resolved. There may be substantial periods of detention. This all conspires to produce a failure to resolve earlier stress and lays the person open to suffer the more under each new adversity.

Experiences of organized violence appear commonly to have profound and probably long-term effects on attitudes and priorities. Political and religious outlooks may change. Experiences of this type often force the survivor to confront very basic human assumptions. It is no longer possible to assume that the world is a comfortable place or to reconcile the new understandings with previous beliefs. A process of radicalization may follow, leaving the individual either more oppressed or more determined to fight for change. In both cases, trust will have been one of the first casualties.

Finally, there are therapeutic approaches, which include psychological and sociopolitical understandings. One of the best known of these, testimony, has been used to illustrate this point. By talking in detail about the trauma story, there is the opportunity for emotional processing; by setting the events within a sociopolitical context, there is the possibility of reinterpreting these experiences, of rewriting the trauma story itself.

REFERENCES

Amnesty International
  1988   *Turkey Briefing.* London: Amnesty International Publications.
  1990   *Amnesty International 1990 Report.* London: Amnesty International Publications.
American Psychiatric Association
  1987   *Diagnostic and Statistical Manual of Mental Disorders.* 3d ed. rev. Washington, D.C.: American Psychiatric Association.
Andreassen, Dag
  1989   "Refugees and Asylum Seekers coming to Europe Today." In *Refugees: The Trauma of Exile,* ed. Diana Miserez, 57–61. Dordrecht: Martinus Nijhoff.
Bendfeldt-Zachrisson, F.
  1985   "State (Political) Torture: Some General, Psychological, and Particular Aspects." *International Journal of Health Services* 15:339–349.
Brown, G.W. and T. Harris
  1978   *Social Origins of Depression.* London: Tavistock.
Carroll, Lewis
  1983   *Alice in Wonderland.* London: Andrew Dakers.
Cienfuegos, Ana Julia, and Cristina Monelli
  1983   "The Testimony of Political Repression as a Therapeutic Instrument." *American Journal of Orthopsychiatry* 53:43–51.
Döveling, Bernhard, and Karl H. Hoffman
  1989   "Proposals to Project Accurate, Positive Images: The View of the German Red Cross." In *Refugees: The Trauma of Exile,* ed. Diana Miserez, 307–310. Dordrecht: Martinus Nijhoff.
Gorst-Unsworth, Caroline, Cleo Van Velsen, and Stuart W. Turner
  1993   "Prospective Pilot Study of Survivors of Torture and Organised Violence: Examining the Existential Dilemma." *Journal of Nervous and Mental Disease* 181: 263–264.
Horowitz, Mardi Jon
  1976   *Stress Response Syndromes.* New York: Jason Aronson.
Jensen, S.B., and I. Agger
  1988   "The Testimony Method: The Use of Testimony as a Psychotherapeutic Tool in the Treatment of Traumatised Refugees in Denmark." Paper presented to the First European Conference on Traumatic Stress Studies, Lincoln, England.
Kolff, Cornelius A., and Roscius N. Doan
  1985   "Victims of Torture: Two Testimonies." In *The Breaking of Minds and Bodies,* ed. Eric Stover and Elena O. Nightingale, 45–57. New York: W. H. Freeman.
Levi, Primo
  1987   *If This Is a Man* and *The Truce.* London: Penguin.

Martín-Baró, Ignacio
   1988   "From Dirty War to Psychological War: The Case of El Salvador." In
                  Flight, Exile, and Return: Mental Health and the Refugee, ed. Adrianne Aron,
                  2–22. San Francisco: Committee for Health Rights in Central America.
Mollica, Richard F.
   1988   "The Trauma Story: The Psychiatric Care of Refugee Survivors of Vio-
                  lence and Torture." In *Post-Traumatic Therapy and Victims of Violence*, ed.
                  Frank M. Ochberg, 295–314. New York: Brunner/Mazel.
Mollica, Richard F., Grace Wyshak, and James Lavelle
   1987   "The Psychosocial Impact of War Trauma and Torture on Southeast
                  Asian Refugees." *American Journal of Psychiatry* 144(12):1567–1572.
Nettleton, C. and A. Simcock
   1987   *Asylum Seekers in the United Kingdom: Essential Statistics*. London: British
                  Refugee Council Research and Development Unit.
Rachman, S.
   1980   "Emotional Processing." *Behavior Research and Therapy* 18:51–60.
Ramsay, Rosalind, Caroline Gorst-Unsworth, and Stuart W. Turner
   1993   "Psychological Morbidity in Survivors of Organized State Violence in-
                  cluding Torture: A Retrospective Series." *British Journal of Psychiatry*
                  160:55–59.
Rasmussen, O. V.
   1990   "Medical Aspects of Torture." *Danish Medical Bulletin* 37 (Suppl. 1): 1–88.
Ritterman, M.
   1987   "Torture: The Counter Therapy of the State." *Networker* (January/Febru-
                  ary): 43–47.
Rudge, Philip
   1989   "Reflections on the Status of Refugees and Asylum Seekers in Europe."
                  In *Refugees: The Trauma of Exile*, ed. Diana Miserez, 62–70. Dordrecht: Mar-
                  tinus Nijhoff.
Schlapobersky, John and Helen Bamber
   1988   "Rehabilitation and Therapy with the Victims of Torture and Organized
                  Violence." Paper presented at the annual meeting of the American Asso-
                  ciation for the Advancement of Science, Boston, Mass.
Somnier, F. E., and Inger K. Genefke
   1986   "Psychotherapy for Victims of Torture." *British Journal of Psychiatry*
                  149:323–329.
Turner, S. W.
   1992   "Therapeutic Approaches with Survivors of Torture." In *Intercultural Ther-
                  apy: Themes, Interpretations and Practice*, ed. Jafar Kareem and Roland Little-
                  wood, 163–174. Oxford: Blackwell.
Turner, S. W., and Caroline Gorst-Unsworth
   1990   "Psychological Sequelae of Torture: A Descriptive Model." *British Journal of
                  Psychiatry* 157:475–480.
   1993   "Psychological Sequelae of Torture." In *International Handbook of Traumatic
                  Stress Syndromes*, ed. J. Wilson and B. Raphael, 703–715. New York: Plenum
                  Press.

Turner, S. W., and Alex Hough
    1993   "Hyperventilation as a Reaction to Torture." In *International Handbook of
                Traumatic Stress Syndromes,* ed. J. Wilson and B. Raphael, 725–733. New
                York: Plenum Press.
Turner, S. W., Tom Landau, Jill Hinshelwood, and Helen Bamber
    1989   "Torture of Turkish Kurds." *Lancet* 1:1319.
United Nations
    1951   "Convention Relating to the Status of Refugees." New York: United
                Nations Office of Public Information.
    1984   "Convention against Torture and Other Cruel, Inhuman or Degrading
                Treatment or Punishment." New York: United Nations Office of Public
                Information.
U. S. Committee for Refugees
    1992   *World Refugee Survey.* Washington, D.C.: U. S. Committee for Refugees.
Yuksel, Sahika
    1989   "Torture in Turkey." *Lancet* 2:866.

FOUR

(Mis)Trusting Narratives: Refugee Stories of Post-1922 Greece and Post-1974 Cyprus

Mary N. Layoun

"*Mistrust*"
Although there is much that is praised in Homer, this we do not praise . . . in Aeschylus, when Thetis says of Apollo singing at her wedding

> *he prophesied children blessed with good fortune, with immeasurably long life, free from illness. He said my fate would be blessed by the gods and sang a paean of praise to me. And I, my hope was that the words from the divine mouth of Phoebus [Apollo] were trustworthy, he who was the master of prophetic art: But he himself who sang . . . he was the very one who murdered my son.*

PLATO, *The Republic, B*

> *When Thetis was married to Peleus*
> *Apollo rose at the sumptuous wedding*
> *banquet and blessed the newlyweds*
> *for the offspring that would result from their union.*
> *He said: never will sickness touch him*
> *and he'll have a long life. When he said these things*
> *Thetis was very happy, because the words*
> *of Apollo who knew prophesy*
> *seemed to her a guarantee for her child.*
> *And when Achilles was growing up, and*
> *his beauty was the pride of Thessaly,*
> *Thetis remembered the words of the god.*
> *But one day the old men came with news*
> *and told of the murder of Achilles at Troy.*
> *And Thetis tore her purple clothes,*
> *and threw*
> *[her] bracelets and rings to the ground.*
> *And in her lamentation she remembered the past*
> *and asked what wise Apollo was doing [now],*
> *where was the poet wandering who at banquets*
> *speaks so brilliantly, where was the prophet wandering*
> *when they killed her son in the prime of his youth?*
> *And the old men answered that Apollo*

himself descended to Troy,
and with the Trojans killed Achilles.

—C. P. CAVAFIS[1]

The bitter irony of Thetis's question on learning of the death of her son is only intensified by the blunt answer of the old men. The god who had promised a long and healthy life for her son, the god in whose "guarantee" she had placed such trust, proves himself "faithless." Apollo betrays Thetis's trust, and she, in turn, forsakes him. Trust *and* mistrust are here mutually generated, and the "mistrust" or "faithlessness" of the title refers to Apollo no less than to Thetis. This poetic citation of divine/human faithlessness or mistrust—and the clear suggestion in the poem's headnote of the threat of that mistrust for the state—is not an incongruous one for the theme of trust and the refugee experience that was the original context for the efforts gathered here.[2] For the retrospective insistence on trust *betrayed* is at least as striking as that of trust itself in refugee testimonials, oral histories, and literary and nonliterary narratives.[3] But more specifically for my purposes here, this insistence on mistrust clearly marks written and oral refugee accounts of the 1922 Asia Minor "catastrophe" and of the 1974 Turkish invasion and occupation of Cyprus. For the refugees in the former instance (largely Greek but also Armenian, Russian, and occasionally Jewish) and in the latter (Greek Cypriots and Turkish Cypriots), "trust" is resolutely a thing of the past, overwhelmingly belied by the refugee present. It is a sense of *mis*trust or trust betrayed—and the frequent suggestions that such mistrust was already present in the prerefugee past—that calls attention to itself. It is this *mis*trust in the fictional and nonfictional refugee accounts of the 1922 Greek catastrophe and of the 1974 Turkish invasion of Cyprus—and the critical implications of that mistrust for refugee and nonrefugee communities alike—that is the focus of what follows.

Examples of such refugee mistrust are here drawn from literary and cultural documents rather than more strictly sociological or ethnographic accounts of "the refugee experience." But the former are no less suggestive or important elements of this experience. Rather, cultural texts and phenomena (as in popular song, wall posters, or cartoons) and literary texts consider and respond to, if not necessarily answer, questions in ways often virtually impossible in designated political and social forums.[4] But also, the disciplinary divide between appropriate "objects of analysis" is scarcely as vast (or as clear-cut) as might at first appear. More recently, sociology and anthropology have begun to figure literary and popular culture into their analytical accounts. In a similar fashion, the objects of "literary" and "cultural" analysis have expanded to include nonliterary historical and social documents and social movements. There is, then, scant cause for the alarm of the disciplinary police. For arguably common to the various disciplinary efforts to address "the refugee experience" is a recognition of the immediate and pressing need to redress the suffering of refugee populations. But it is also the effort to understand the context that created the refugee situation in the first place. And that context is most often one of radical upheaval and change. There is, then, an at least implicit recognition that the refugee experience has crucial implications for refugees and nonrefugees alike.

Bertolt Brecht has suggested that refugees themselves "are the keenest dialecticians. They are refugees as a result of changes, and their sole object of study is change." The "change" that precipitates the refugee's status and the attempt to understand both that status and its correlative change are, in the final analysis, scarcely only pertinent to the refugee. Certainly one of the objectives of our multidisciplinary effort here is also a comprehension of change, of trust and mistrust, as a crucial part of the refugee experience, but with implications for a critical understanding of refugee *and* nonrefugee situations. The "object of study" in what follows is the rhetoric of stories of the refugee experience and the implications of that rhetoric and those stories for the critical understanding of that as well as the nonrefugee implication in that experience.

The poem "Which Half," written in 1975 by the Turkish Cypriot poetess Nessié Yassin, evokes and problematizes the notion of trust and a past betrayed as it questions the "change" that incurred the betrayal.

> They say you should love the homeland
> that's what my father always told me too
> But my homeland is divided in two
> Which half should I love?[5]

The poem's present of loss and dismemberment—"my homeland is divided in two"—is juxtaposed to the authority of the past—"my father always told me . . ." In that past, allegiance was presumably clearly designated. Society and father established the patriarchal boundaries of what "should" be—"love"—and of its specified object—"the homeland." But what in the past appeared to be a source of stability and power—the directive of society and father, the boundaries of the "homeland"—is in the present a source of anguish, conflict, and instability. The present from which the *memory* of authority and certainty, of familial and national coherence, is evoked is also the present of that memory violated. The lyric present is itself predicated on the story past of betrayal. "Trust"—or, more properly, the *memory* of trust—in the authoritative word of the collective ("they") and of the father, in the homeland toward which they counsel love, is, in the present, trust betrayed. And implicitly, the transgression that marks the narrative present marks the only apparently unproblematic trust of the past as well. In fact, it is from the present of transgression and betrayal that the past is approached or remembered at all. There are suggestive implications in this tension between (past) trust and (present) mistrust for understanding, rethinking, and, arguably, even reorganizing refugee and nonrefugee communities alike.

Some of the implications for understanding and rethinking refugee "change" that are tacit in Yassin's poem are rather more explicit in Dido Soteriou's novel of the 1922 Asia Minor catastrophe, *Matomena xomata*.[6] This narrative, too, is informed by the memory of violated trust. A mainland Greek serving in the Greek military in Asia Minor angrily comments to the novel's first-person narrator on an argument among his fellow soldiers about who is to blame for the failure of their mission (the Greek invasion of Asia Minor): "Did you hear them? Worthless, cheap chatter! They don't look for the root of the problem, the fools. It's the same old story: Venizelos, King Constantine.[7] These guys, at least, have an excuse; they don't know what's happening to them. But those in power? The leaders? None of them wants to see that what we're doing is suicidal" (217).[8]

But unlike Yassin's poem, this passage does not invoke the lyric memory of a past trust and coherence betrayed. The story past that Soteriou's first-person narrator, Manolis Axiotis, recalls is *already* one of betrayal;[9] if the narrator was unable to discern that betrayal then, his interlocutor, quoted above, certainly claims to have so discerned the betrayal of trust. And he locates it directly in the deception and willful blindness of political leaders who nurture ignorant trust among the troops in the field and among the civilians at home. The arguing soldiers are "fools" for failing to locate "the root of the problem" and, instead, entrusting their fate to Venizelos or Constantine. The narrative present makes clear what was perhaps less apparent in the story past; the choice between Venizelos and King Constantine was really no choice at all. It is "those in power" and their cohorts—the political leaders who designed and directed the "suicidal" Greek invasion and occupation of Asia Minor—who are indicted in this passage. If the patriarchal directive in Yassin's poem is implicitly proffered in good faith, without intentional duplicity on the part of the father or the community, the military and political directives repeatedly indicted in Soteriou's novel are adamantly otherwise characterized.

But perhaps what is most interesting here is not the (arguably unsurprising) story of "trust" betrayed or violated; it is a simultaneous suggestion of having known better, of a kind of narrative skepticism or *mis*trust to which the narrator lays claim even in the prerefugee past. And this often emphatic assertion of narrative skepticism is made precisely in the narrative *present* of retelling the story *past*. Retelling the story of refugee dislocation and uprooting, then, makes possible (but not inevitable) a narrative configuration in which what the narrator recounts is not only the trajectory of a violently uprooted past leading inexorably to the misery of the narrative present as refugees. That trajectory is certainly omnipresent in literary and historical accounts of the refugee experience. But implicitly and sometimes explicitly, the narrative organization of meaning in the past—the dominant stories of family, home, village, ethnos, religious community—is told as questionable, as not self-evident. Something of this critical narrative stance is apparent in the passage from Soteriou cited above as the first-person narrator recounts in the present his growing mistrust of the "official stories" that circulate in his (memory of a) prerefugee past.

Here Brecht's characterization of the refugee as a "dialectian" attempting to understand change is worth reiteration. For the mistrust and skepticism of "official stories" to which the story lays claim is precisely a way of rethinking and understanding change. The dominant narratives of the past are actually or fictionally told as already suspect, as already invoking mistrust. It is this insistence on past and present *mis*trust or skepticism of the dominant narratives in circulation—religious, regional, familial, ethnic, national, international—on which I would like to focus for a moment.

Whether or not this assertion is true in fact—whether the narrator "really" mistrusted what she or he claims to have mistrusted—is less significant than that the assertion of skeptical trust is made at all. And it is most often made at the same time as the assertion of "trust" betrayed. This narrative construct, then, might seem to be double-edged, even contradictory. If the dominant narratives were suspicious even in the past, why "trust" them at all? And then, why claim that such "trust," which was arguably limited anyway, was betrayed or violated? These might appear to be logical objections—ones that refugee agencies and organizations, as they represent and request alleviation of the urgent needs of refugees, must do their best to address (or, perhaps, to avert).[10] But the apparent logic of those objections collapses some crucial distinctions on which I would insist. The choices and values implied by this logic—of mobility and unobstructed circulation among various narratives and among meanings within those narratives; of some neutral position of unimpinged-upon reflection, outside of or beyond dominant narratives; of limitless possibility or, reversing but not altering the logic, of utter determinism—are surely themselves marked by the presumption of the secure distance of these questions and their speakers from the violent uprooting and loss of certainty that characterizes much of the refugee experience as it is retold. But this putatively safe remove or distance from disruption is precisely one of the things challenged by refugee stories. As Cavafis' poem "Mistrust" suggests, the sumptuous wedding table and nuptial celebration of Thetis and Peleus are, contrary to appearances, *not* distant or at a safe remove from the ravages of the Trojan War and its betrayals at all. The poetic retelling of "mistrust" is a counsel of sorts to those who would not reexamine their present "faith." For the imminent betrayal of uncritical trust is, figuratively at least, as close as the poem sung in your ear or facing your eyes on the page.

Thus to postulate past mistrust of dominant narratives in a present in which those narratives have been brutally exposed as inadequate is scarcely surprising or inexplicable. The retrospective skeptical qualification of past "trust" is, instead, a way of ameliorating the grimness of the narrative present. To tell the story of becoming refugees is to attempt to reconcile the teller of the story with the seemingly unresolvable conflicts that cast her or him in the role of refugee narrator in the first place.

This process of attempted reconciliation is ironically figured in another novel of Asia Minor refugees by Soteriou, *The Dead Are Waiting*,[11] in which the first-person narrator, Aliki, is a young girl from Smyrna. The first half of the novel is the account of her life in Smyrna; the second half opens with the story of her becoming a refugee, though, ironically, she leaves Smyrna with her wealthy aunt for a vacation in Greece just a few days before Smyrna's fiery demise.

> As soon as we landed in Piraeus, full of smiles and plans for tourist excursions [in Greece], we found ourselves in front of a strange sight: a large crowd was gathered, [standing] here and there, [looking] gloomy and dazed. Young and old women, their heads covered with scarves, shouted and gestured nervously. But it was impossible to distinguish exactly what they were saying and why the police were pushing them back. Later some sailors jumped into their midst, battered [looking and] glaring fiercely. They began to shout [at the police].
> —Why are you hitting the women, eh? What are you hitting them for? Who did they hurt? Are you afraid that they'll disturb the peace? The peace, eh? They're asking about their children; they don't know what's become of them in the massacre [in Asia Minor].
> As we were trying to listen and understand what was happening, a sailor pointed to us and said:
> —There, the first refugees have [already] come from Smyrna.
> My Aunt Ermione turned and looked at us, as if expecting a denial.
> —Are they talking about us? Just listen to the way rumors are started. (131)

For these women, at least, their story of becoming refugees is one they hear first from others. Before they themselves are aware of the refugee story in which they are cast, they are so narrated by others. As they search for a room in Piraeus, they are repeatedly turned away because they are "refugees." It is at some unidentifiable point in that process of being identified by others as refugees that they in fact *become* refugees. When they finally find "a dark, dismal room with six beds," Aliki admits, "When we became real refugees, we didn't understand. Within a few days, the whole world had turned upside down" (133).

Yet it is in the first half of *The Dead Are Waiting*—recounting life in Smyrna *before* the 1922 catastrophe—that the putative certainty and coherence of things begins to turn upside down. In fact, this situation is marked in the very first lines of the novel, where the narrator is remembered as a young girl.

> A small girl sets out on the uneven cobblestone path of Aidini, a provincial city in Asia Minor. Her dark face and black eyes are framed by blond curls elegantly covered by a light, pink hat—a cheerful sign of a rosy, carefree life. Those childish curls,

that were as soft as silk and shone like gold in the sunlight, gave to the pallid girlish little face a strange joy, a promise, a hope. . . .

But they weren't real. They had bought them for her and sewn them to the child's hat to cover, to camouflage [*exoraisoune/opov*], an ugliness, a stubborn case of scabies that had forced her parents to shave her head. . . .

Because of this, one of the first lessons that that little girl learned was how even the ugliest things in life can be whitewashed [*opov*] as long as you didn't hesitate to hide reality with a beautiful, gold-plated lie. (9)

The potentially treacherous contradictions of apparently "cheerful signs" of "rosy, carefree" narratives—of family, of religious community, of nation—are urgently evoked by the young-girl-now-grown.

Although the narrator acknowledges that to begin her story by recalling "a pink hat with a few fake blond curls" will seem strange to many, she insists that "this insignificant detail preoccupies me, it almost challenges me." And if the apparent insignificance of fake blond curls marks the story's setting out, the threat of imminent and premature closure is also signaled from the opening page by the sound of "volleys of gunfire from Nazi firing squads in Athens." And so the narrator is "in a hurry, in a hurry to say those things that consume me before what might be my turn [in front of the firing squad] comes." The story that begins with the "lie" of a little girl's fake curls is, in the narrative present, threatened with occlusion by the Nazi occupation of Greece during World War II. This fictional pretext of urgency in the narrative present is equally a rhetorical strategy that implies the story of the little pink hat and fake curls retold with a difference: its symbols, signs, and road markers read critically rather than naively. Faced with the possibility of death before a firing squad, the narrator hastens to tell her story and, from the beginning, as she "sets out," to disavow her readers/listeners of naive trust in what might *appear* to be the case. Her implied audience is forced to recognize, as she herself was as a young girl, "cheerful symbol[s] of a rosy, carefree life" as something other than what they appear. There is the implicit assertion here of having known better, of the apparent scheme of things as untrustworthy, not what they seem. And yet, of course, the young girl of the opening pages continues down the road and through the novel. Her story of becoming a refugee is told as unavoidable, as beyond her control. But the narrator-as-young-girl already knows that the predominant narratives that appear to order her prerefugee life are dubious, precariously held together, not altogether trustworthy. In the retrospective moment of the narrative present—and with the looming threat of death, the absolute end of re-membering and narrating for the narrator—the retelling of her story is simultaneously the indictment of uncritically trusting faith or belief. What would seem to be at stake here, then, is not just trust or mistrust but a sense of critical community and memory that tells not simply the past but also the present.

With Soteriou's *The Dead Are Waiting* as a provisional pretext, we can return to the question of whether dominant narratives of family, nation, and state or religious community could be perceived as dubious even in the past. The logic of the objections referred to earlier—which would question skeptical faith or trust in dubious narratives at all—implicitly postulates the notion of some definitive space outside of those dominant narratives from which their participants and narrators could construct other, less dubious narratives. But based on literary and testimonial accounts of the refugee experience, that space is often imperceptible, if not, for all practical purposes, nonexistent. To question, to mistrust, or even to refuse existing narrative configurations is not thereby to accede to the possibility of some leveraged Archimedean point outside of them. Participation in dominant narratives is not necessarily unequivocal belief in them; it is not necessarily the *non-* recognition of their contradiction by lived experience. What seems far more often the case is that narrators of and characters in dominant narratives attempt to redefine their positions both individually and collectively, to shift their place(s) within the narrative, to suggest an alternative telos and/or a different informing rationale for the narrative, and sometimes at least, to propose another story and another way of telling that story. The alternatives are thus not simply between utter determinism, on the one hand, and unlimited possibility, on the other; between total belief in narrative(s) and absolute mistrust of them, between a prerefugee moment of trust and a refugee experience of mis- or distrust. If the story of trust betrayed is a touchstone of the refugee experience, so is the story of the resolute unavailability of any handy exit from the exigencies *and* contingencies of a specific historical moment. The extent to which the massive forces that cause their becoming refugees neither originated with nor were controlled by them is apparent in virtually all refugee stories. Nonetheless, one of the overwhelming concerns of telling the refugee experience—literally or autobiographically—is to understand, to come to terms with, those forces. The simultaneous assertion of trust skeptically held and violently betrayed is a predominant component of the coming to terms with the refugee experience in the testimonials and cultural texts of both post-1922 refugees from Asia Minor and post-1974 refugees of the Turkish invasion and occupation of Cyprus. But, no less significantly, it is also a way of attempting to tell-with-a-difference, to reconfigure, the future.

For, finally, if the focus thus far has been on notions of trust in the story (past) and narration (present) of the refugee experience, there is also a crucial figuring of the future in this rhetorical economy. It is here that I would reinsert the notion of critical community as one potentially underlying refugee narratives—for the tellers *and* for the audiences of those stories. The assertion (in the narrative present) of trust betrayed is the assertion, at least implicitly, of a claim for what *should have been* (in the past of the story), for the necessity of a critical community "then." But equally, it is a claim for what *should be* (a future). It is a moral or ethical claim; it is an assertion of potentially different value or meaning or narrative order. It prefigures the future and what should, or perhaps would be, if the story (and its telling) were different, if the critical community could establish and maintain itself. This is both the threat and the promise of (stories of) the refugee experience. And it is one recognized by the "host" countries or communities in which the refugees seek (often temporary) asylum and the original countries or communities from which they flee.

The resettlement documents and directives of governmental and international relief agencies suggest this clearly enough in their often explicit recognition of the potential threat (or promise) of "destabilization" posed by the refugees—the potential for a radical reorganization of their own communities *and* of their "host" countries or communities. For example, the international committee that directed and oversaw the resettlement of the Asia Minor refugees in Greece (1923–1927) explicitly notes the potential threat of the refugees as a radicalizing force on the "indigenous" Greek population. The refugees were, therefore, to be settled as far from the cities and other "indigenous Greek" communities as possible. This is a particularly interesting situation because the refugees of 1922 in Greece were, according to the nationalist rhetoric of the day, not remarkably different from the residents of their "host" country. In fact, they considered themselves for the most part more "Greek" and "Christian" than the "indigenous" mainland Greeks.

Elsewhere I have suggested the ways in which various narratives of nationalism in crisis—of which the refugee experience is one extreme instance—make radically different propositions about the past of the story, the present of narration (and of becoming a refugee), and the future of what should or could be.[12] But often this future, too, is pointed at ironically or skeptically. This is not to impugn the moral or political force of that postulated future. It is, rather, only to suggest that there are far more complex narrators, narrative characters, and stories in operation than might at first appear to be the case. For certainly, our abilities to read/hear/retell stories have been no less influenced by historical and cultural circumstances that situate our own seeing and hearing in relation to the narration and story. And so it is also to suggest that we listen to or read and respond to or retell refugee stories with an eye and ear to their immediate distress and urgent needs. But there might well be something more to address in refugee stories than their sorrows and loss. There can also be an incisive critical edge to refugee stories, a persuasive argument for calculated (mis)trust in dominant narratives, a skeptical recounting of failed critical communities, an urgent appeal for new critical communities. And those elements of the refugee experience implicate, metaphorically at least, nonrefugee communities as well. This would seem to be the implicit suggestion of Soteriou's novels or Yassin's poem.

The *memory* of "trust"—as in Thetis's trust, or at least hope, that Apollo's promises would prove true—is a crucial narrative factor in the assertion of that trust and of its betrayal. It is not only the promises made (and believed, even skeptically) but their repeated re-membering, their reevocation, that crucially figures "trust." And that memory of promises/trust past is necessarily juxtaposed to the violation and rupture of the narrative present. It is, I suggest, just that juxtaposition, at least potentially, that contributes to—or forces—a more intensely critical perspective on stories and narratives. On pasts, presents, and futures. This is the process of "the refugee study of change" to which Brecht refers.

There is a suggestive instance of this fierce interaction of trust and mistrust—of memory and story past, narrative present and potential future—with which I will conclude. Toward the end of Michael Cacoyannis's documentary on the Turkish invasion of Cyprus and its immediate aftermath, *Attila 1974: A Testimony on Film* (1974), the camera pans a Cypriot mountain range in midautumn. It appears to be late afternoon. A group of women sit on a veranda sewing, embroidering, and reading. Some of them talk in turn, each one adding to the comments of the others, scarcely looking up from their work or reading. They speak less to one another than to an unseen audience.

> *1st Woman:* The Turks came down from the hills and we just ran.
> *2d Woman:* We move from village to village to escape them; the fear and terror of it only God can understand.
> *1st Woman:* They brought us up here to this house.
> *3d Woman:* The Turks took my only son prisoner.
> *2d Woman:* May God punish those who started this disaster, who brought on the Turks and this ruin. We left with only the clothes we were wearing.
> *3d Woman:* If it wasn't for those Fascists[13] the Turks would never have set foot on the island. Do you hear me?
> *2d Woman:* When Makarios was here no one bothered us. Not the Turks, not anyone. Because Makarios was an educated man. And he knew how to govern our island the way it should be governed.
> *3d Woman:* Our island was very prosperous. Everyone had their own car. My son's cars were taken by the Turks and shipped to Turkey. He was ruined.
> *2d Woman:* We're waiting for a solution from the United Nations, a fair solution to "the Cyprus problem" [*to kypriako*], that will rid us of the barbarians who came and invaded our island. If the UN can't solve "the Cyprus problem" then why do we go on?

The scene fades as the second woman finishes speaking and looks up from her work, directly into the camera, which frames her face front. The three women have told their respective stories of the preinvasion past, the invasion itself, and the situation of their narrative present as refugees. And in closing, or in the closing framed for them by the camera and the film director and editor, the direction of the stories and narration moves from past and present to a promise or at least a hope for the future. It is clear that the hopes entrusted to other (national) promises in the past— in Makarios and the Cypriot government, in the economic "prosperity" of preinvasion (and precoup) Cyprus—have been rather brutally called into question. But equally clear, visually as well as abstractly, is the potential power of a critical community in disruption to which these women attest. Of course, it is the task of governments, official agencies, and party leaders to keep that potential in rein, under control. This aspect of the "refugee experience" as both threat and promise is not an obscure one. In this instance, what would these refugee women do if the United Nations does not or cannot intervene satisfactorily in their disrupted lives? The barely suggested potential of critical community here is truncated—but not effaced—by the sequential structure of the film itself. For this exchange among refugee women is followed by an interview with a UN special representative who speaks of (unsuccessful) UN efforts to resolve "the Cyprus problem." But the almost ironic implication of the scene's closing lines is not only a function of the documentary's cut to an interview with a UN representative. It is also a function of the second woman's virtually expressionless citation of that source from which Cypriots, refugees and nonrefugees alike, were told by the Cypriot government and the mainland Greek government they could expect resolution—the United Nations.

There is a poignant irony in all this. The "trust" of these women—especially the second speaker but by implication all of them—in the "promise" of UN resolution to the Cypriot "problem" is framed by the likely impossibility of that trust. And it is framed by the representations of "trust" violated in the more local and immediate sources of resolution. The familial, village, religious, social networks of Cypriot society and even the Cypriot state have "failed" to provide the mediation they were presumed to afford.

What, then, is the closing appeal of these women, the second woman in particular? Is it really "trust" in the UN that this filmic sequence demonstrates? Or here too is the assertion of trust inflected by the story of trust violated?

In the struggles between official rhetoric and popular sentiment and between popular action and official machinations and maneuvering, cultural interpretations of refugee experiences, of the reconstitution of national (if not state) identities, play a crucial role. And in these contexts, the fierce negotiations and re-formations of gender roles, of "the family," of sexuality, critically inflect and often indelibly shape those national definitions, those social imaginaries.

It should come as no surprise that these negotiations are the site of violent contestation for representation, meaning, and identity/organization. In this struggle, though, the lines that "societies and cultures draw" to designate "those who can be trusted from those who cannot" are, of course, of distinct significance.[14] It is the negotiation of those lines in specific historical conjunctures, their violation and reassertion or re-formation, that is visible in narrative action in the examples cited above.

For certainly the forcible recasting of a group of people as refugees is grounded in violence and in a violent rupture of life as it was conceived *and* as it was lived. Previous everyday negotiations across borders—whether national, religious, ethnic, class, racial, or gender—are radically challenged, forcibly terminated, and of painful necessity reshaped. But I argue, at least based on cultural representations of the refugee experience and on oral narratives/histories both of refugee life and of sociocultural life before the refugee uprooting, that it is not only in times of peace (so-called) or in pre- and postcrisis moments—in other words, not only in times when "trust" is (re)established—that these renegotiations take place. It is also, and most suggestively, during and subsequent to the ruptures to which the very designation "refugee experience" points.

The refugee experience of the community or nation in crisis as it is represented in cultural and oral narratives potentially challenges established boundaries of community or nation. For it is precisely those inviolable boundaries that the refugee knows only too well to be violable. Thus the telling of refugee stories is sometimes also a radical reconceptualization of the very definitions and ground rules of community or nation and of the roles of those who claim to speak for and from them. Refugee stories reconstitute—with a difference that is often ignored in official political discourse—boundaries and official and unofficial rules for crossing over them in ways that are only arguably unimaginable or impossible. It is change for which they seek to account, and the respectable boundaries of the normal and everyday are no longer respectable or respected. Their stories of critical mistrust are crucial to our understanding of their—and our own—predicament. Not only for that reason, we would do well to attend to them.

NOTES

1. Cavafis's ambiguously ironic title suggests the notions of "mistrust" and "trust" that are taken up in this chapter. The original Greek of the title is *apistia*, without faith/trust/belief. But from the citation of Homer and the poem that follows that citation, "mistrust" or "faithlessness" is not just an attribute of Thetis but also—perhaps most essentially—of the god Apollo, who is faithless and untrustworthy in his relations with Thetis.

2. See Daniel and Knudsen 1990.

3. It should be stated from the outset that what follows is less an account of lived refugee experiences as such than of the cultural inscription—the retelling—of those experiences as story and narration.

4. Subsequently, the Cavafis poem was set to music and became a popular, if unofficial, Cypriot national anthem. For, as of 1990, Cyprus had no national anthem. Ironically, and scarcely fortuitously, the Cypriot government uses the Greek national anthem on those occasions—the signing on and off of the state radio and television stations, national holidays, public governmental functions—when a national anthem would be played.

5. On this point, see, e.g., the discussion of the fiction of the Palestinian writer Ghassan Kanafani, in Layoun 1990.

6. *Blood-Drenched Earth* (Athens: Kedros, 1962).

7. Venizelos and Constantine represent the two dominant and opposed figures/positions in Greek politics of the time. The former was a "liberal" who aligned himself with the major European imperialist powers of the day—France and especially Britain. At their behest and, in the final analysis, on their behalf—but using the rhetoric of "recapturing the glory of greater Greece," *e megali idea* or "the Great Idea"—Venizelos sent Greek troops into Asia Minor in May 1919. Constantine represented the monarchist forces—"conservative," allied with Germany, purportedly opposed to the expansionist politics of Venizelos. The monarchists were voted into power in 1920, defeating Venizelos, on a platform of ending the war and bringing the Greek troops home immediately. They did neither.

8. Literally, the phrase reads "that what we're engaged in is the dance of Zalongo," a reference to a valorized historical incident during the Greek War of Independence against the Ottoman Empire in the first decades of the nineteenth century when Epiriot women and children from the besieged village of Zalongo danced off the edge of a cliff rather than be captured by Ottoman forces. The gender reversal in this passage is noteworthy: the exhausted and virtually defeated Greek soldiers in Asia Minor are posited as parallel to the besieged women and children of Zalongo.

9. This formal distinction between *narrative time(s)*—the when (and how) of telling the story—and *story time(s)*—the when (and how or what) of the events being narrated—is crucial here, though not necessarily for the same reasons that structuralist narratology has insisted on. For a classic discussion of the formal aspects of narrative, see Chatman 1978, esp. 62–84, for a discussion of narrative and story times.

10. The representation by private agencies, governments, church groups, individuals, and refugee organizations of refugee conditions and needs to official relief-granting agencies is another suggestive way to consider the issue of the multiple nuances of trust and the refugee experience.

11. *Oi nekroi perimenoun* (Athens: Kedros, 1959).

12. In the context of more recent Palestinian culture and history, see Layoun 1992; of recent Cypriot culture and history, Layoun 1994; or of Occupation Japan, Layoun nd.

13. That is, the far Right Cypriot coup—orchestrated by the military dictatorship then in power in Greece, Turkey, the U.S.'s Henry Kissinger, and the Cypriot right-wing extremists "Eoka B"—that preceded by 8 days and provided a convenient pretext for the Turkish invasion of the island.

14. Daniel and Knudsen 1990:7–8.

REFERENCES

Cacoyannis, Michael, dir.
  1974   *Attila 1974: A Testimony on Film.*
Cavafis, Constantine
  1963   *"Apistia" in Poiemata, 1896–1918* (Poems). Athens: Ikaros.
Chatman, Seymour
  1978   *Story and Discourse: Narrative Structure in Fiction and Film.* Ithaca: Cornell University Press.
Daniel, E. Valentine, and John Chr. Knudsen
  1990   "Trust and the Refugee Experience: A Proposal." UNU/WIDER. Manuscript.
Layoun, Mary N.
  1990   *Travels of a Genre: The Modern Novel and Ideology.* Princeton: Princeton University Press.
  1992   "Telling Spaces: Palestinian Women and the Engendering of National Narratives." In *Nationalisms and Sexualities,* ed. Andrew Parker, Mary Russo, Doris Sommer, and Patricia Yeager, 407–423. London: Routledge.
  1994   "The Body of Woman and 'Transnational' Reproduction: Or, Rape by Any Other Name?" In *Scattered Hegemonies,* ed. Inderpal Grewel and Caren Kaplan, 63–89. Minneapolis: University of Minnesota Press.

n.d.   "Occupying the National Family: Narratives of National Reformation and 'Production Control.' " Manuscript.

Soteriou, Dido

  1959   *Oi nekroi perimenoun* (The Dead Are Waiting). Athens: Kedros.

  1962   *Matomena xomata* (Blood-Drenched Earth). Athens: Kedros.

FIVE

On Ropes of Memory:
Narrating the Palestinian Refugees

Muhammad Siddiq

I

The term "refugee" (*lāji'*) is associated in modern Arab sensibility with the establishment of Israel in 1948 and the resultant decimation of Palestinian culture and
society. Technically, not all Palestinians became refugees during that cataclysmic
event; most Palestinians, in fact, went on living within historical Palestine, the
national homeland. Yet the fate of the refugee became paradigmatic of Palestinian
experience in general. After 1948, the Palestinians became "a refugee nation."[1]
Paradoxically, perhaps, the refugee experience has since served as a major catalyst
for the consolidation and development of Palestinian political consciousness and
national identity. These, of course, are constitutive components of the modern
nation-state that, thus far, has eluded the Palestinian people.

Palestinian literature provides a compelling imaginative account of the travails
that accompanied this sudden and violent transformation into a refugee nation.
The primary interests of this literature lie in the emotional and psychological
effects of this collective trauma on individual refugees and in the general political
and moral implications of the refugee experience as a whole. In this chapter I
explore a few of the salient issues that the literary representations of refugee experiences raise in their wake. Because the space of Palestinian narrative is always a
highly contested one and because the terms "literary," "representation," "refugee,"
and "Palestinian" are unfathomably broad and problematic, the intention to keep
the discussion reasonably focused will often have to be negotiated against an endless number of discursive demands and practices. Some of these demands will
inevitably have to be engaged, but only to the extent that they help delineate more
sharply my interests here.

By and large, the profiles of the refugee one encounters in Palestinian literature are documentary, often autobiographical in nature. Little poetic license is

generally allowed for the imaginative transmutation of historical and experiential phenomena into literary and aesthetic artifacts. A significant cognitive consequence flows directly from this inherently discursive quality of Palestinian literature: the "literary" representation of the refugee provides a reliable index to the actual experience of the nearly one million refugees who fled or were driven out of their homes by the Israeli armed forces in 1948.[2] In many fundamental respects, the refugee holds the key for comprehending the Palestinian condition, and Palestinian literature offers valuable insights into the complex image of the refugee.

This may be another way of saying that the representation of refugee experience in literary narratives faithfully reinscribes through the metaphor of individual lives the collective historical experience of the Palestinian people. In this sense, Palestinian narratives can indeed be viewed as "national allegories."[3] Either way, the theoretical premise informing the generalization is fairly transparent: It postulates the existence of intrinsic connections between realms of discourse that are sometimes considered polar opposites, for example, literary/discursive, private/public, individual/communal, imaginative/documentary, aesthetic/political. The shattering, centrifugal force of the diaspora on Palestinian society, culture, and psyche impels Palestinian writers to subordinate all such distinctions in Palestinian narratives to one overriding concern: how to reassemble from bits and pieces, across disciplinary and generic lines, a continuous, recognizably Palestinian discourse with which to beguile the insidious effects of diaspora and deterritorialization on Palestinian national identity.[4] The collective political unconscious that motivates this communal urge is never far from the surface of any Palestinian literary text.

The literary narratives of Palestinian refugees comprise significantly more than what is available in print. Because Palestinian culture is largely oral, Palestinian refugees often express their experiences and sentiments through folklore and other traditional literary forms and genres. Foremost among these is popular oral poetry, which is composed extemporaneously in the Palestinian dialect during weddings and other public celebrations. The forms of this strophic poetry (*zajal;* better known in rural Palestine as *ḥadādī,* and the poet, as *ḥādī* or *ḥadda*), though diverse and versatile, are fully standardized so that both poet and audience are familiar with their constitutive formal features. The virtuosity of the individual popular poet, much like that of his classical Arab predecessor, resides in his ability to fill the familiar literary patterns with new and original content. Palestinian refugees carried these literary forms into their refugee camps, and wherever they congregated in their diaspora they often drew spiritual and psychological solace from partaking in what is so intimately familiar and reassuringly repeatable. To suggest how central memory became for the preservation of Palestinian identity in the diaspora, it may suffice to point out that Palestinian refugees assiduously named schools, hospitals, clinics, and even sports clubs in the refugee camps after the cities, towns, villages, and neighborhoods of the lost homeland.

Partly as a result of the adverse conditions of Palestinian dispersion, however, little of this rich oral culture has been recorded, documented, and studied, and only an infinitesimal portion has been translated into foreign languages.[5] This problem is further compounded by the evident privileging of written over oral texts, which, in modern times, has been a mainstay of Western hegemonic logocentrism. The insidious authority of this bias is so pervasive that extra caution may be necessary to guard against unwitting complicity with it. Richard Poirier's blurb for Edward Said's book, *After the Last Sky: Palestinian Lives,* is a case in point. Poirier writes, "It is Said's great accomplishment that thanks to this book, Palestinians will never be lost to history."[6]

Now, irrespective of the merits of the book itself, this extravagant statement is virtually inconceivable about any other people, not even extinct ones. For to predicate the fate of an entire people—a highly resilient, resourceful, and heroic one at that—on their representation in a book written in English, the language of England and the United States—the two countries most responsible, with Israel, for the creation and continuation of the Palestinian diaspora—is to recognize as paramount the supremacy of colonial culture. By asserting, implicitly, that only what is *written* in the language of the colonialists is guaranteed survival, this statement mortgages not only the past and the present but also the future to the colonialist moment. And while it is true that the narratives of the actual refugees project a categorically different trajectory, the urge to play up to the hegemonic discourse of colonialism is becoming increasingly more pronounced in Palestinian literary and political discourses, with certain but as yet unknown implications for the prospects of Palestinian national identity.

II

Considered on their own, the written literary narratives of Palestinian refugees constitute one sustained epic quest for return to home(land), self(hood), and nation(hood). The multifaceted quest unfolds in several stages and involves a progressively heightened awareness of the dialectical tension between the following pairs of concepts: border-margin, homeland-state, and refugee-revolutionary. For the purposes of this discussion, it is possible to collapse the various stages into two major ones, the first spanning the period from 1948 to the mid-1960s, the second from the mid-1960s to the present. Attention to the dynamic interaction between these pairs of concepts will orient the following discussion.

III

The examination of Palestinian literature written during the first phase reveals that the notion of "border" entered Palestinian consciousness retrospectively: only after they had crossed it in flight or under compulsion does the border-as-physical-barrier come into being for the refugees. Before that defining act, Palestinian refugee characters reveal little awareness of political borders. This fact accurately reflects the "natural" state in which most Palestinians, indeed most Arabs, lived before the arbitrary partition of the Arab world into separate and "independent" states at the hands of the colonialist powers, notably Britain and France, during the first half of this century. Tender recollections of one's home, neighborhood, and village far surpass in number and degree of vividness abstract reflections on homeland, country, and state in the narrative of Palestinian refugees. It will not be incorrect to conclude on the basis of this observation that before 1948 Palestinian patriotism was more local and regional than national in scope and outlook.[7]

Once awareness of borders is registered in consciousness, however, it lodges itself permanently there. What is more, this awareness is invariably accompanied by an acute feeling of estrangement and marginalization. Palestinian poets were the first to grasp this dialectical relationship and to inscribe it in numerous poems during the 1950s and early 1960s. The structure of emotions and sentiments one finds in these poems is fairly straightforward: the refugee both rejects and is rejected by the new environment into which he has been forcibly cast. Fresh memories of erstwhile home and ancestral lands, often still within sight of the refugee, conspire with the abject conditions of life in the refugee camps to keep the refugee's gaze reflexively fixed on the border. Words such as *gharib* (stranger), *musharrad* (fugitive), *lāji'* (refugee), and *nāzih* (wanderer) enter Palestinian poetic diction during this period and provide new linguistic means to grapple with the new experience. Instructively, *'ā'id* (returnee) and *'awdah* (return) are the only two words to have enjoyed greater currency in this poetry—surely a measure of the refugee's optimistic outlook concerning the expected duration of their *ghurba* (exile). The following fragment of a poem by Fadwā Ṭūqān expresses the range of emotions involved in this typical situation.

> How can I see my land, my rights usurped,
> And remain here, a wanderer, with my shame?
> Shall I live here and die in a foreign land?
> No! I will return to my beloved land,
> I will return, and there will I close the book of my life,
> Let the noble soil tenderly cover my remains.[8]

This fragment displays a number of typical literary and discursive characteristics. Stylistically, the rhetoric is direct and polemical, its tone stridently declamatory. Thematically, the designation of "here" as "a foreign land" is instructive on two accounts. First, the identification of the adverb of place only in terms of lack, its being "not there" in the occupied land, renders the latter a metonymy for the entire homeland. Second, being anywhere outside of Palestine amounts to being in "a foreign land." This point is particularly important because it simultaneously records the alienation of the Palestinian refugees in the Arab countries and foreshadows future developments in Palestinian political thinking toward Palestinian specificity and particularism.

In yet another poem, Fadwā Ṭūqān imbues the concept of return with powerful dramatic and emotional content.

Where to? He did not know. But his yearning
Was persistent, compelling.
From his own land,
A distressed voice was calling him,
Ringing in the depths of his heart,
Drawing him across the "boundaries" of exile.
. . . .

Like an infant he pressed cheek and mouth to the soil,
Shedding there the pain he had borne for years.
Revived by its tender breath,
He heard the whispered reproof,
"You have come back?"—"I have, here is my hand,
I will remain here until I die, Prepare my grave."[9]

As the translator of these fragments notes, the enclosing of the word "boundaries"
in quotation marks (brackets) in the original indicates refusal to accept the legitimacy of such boundaries.[10] This "refusal" seems to originate in the refugee's psychological inability to accept as legitimate borders that arbitrarily separate him
from what grounds his personal identity: his home, land, and place of birth. The
only will the refugee characters are able to marshal during this phase is passive: it
consists primarily of this refusal to accept their new condition. The moral rightness
of their claim for repatriation, enshrined in and annually reaffirmed by the United
Nations resolutions since 1948, lends added force to this intensely felt conviction.
Hence also the sense of certainty concerning the inevitability of return that ani-
mates the above fragments. Moreover, the recurrent symbolism of death at the
end of both fragments imparts to the theme of return an emphatic note of finality.
To die in the homeland is to pledge oneself never to leave it again. The ardent
desire for a closure, also evident at the end of both fragments, expresses in a literary trope a deeply felt existential and psychological reality.

It is important to note also that the poet herself is from the city of Nablus,
which, at the time of the writing these poems in 1959, had not yet come under
Israeli occupation. In other words, even though the poet was not technically a
refugee at the time and was living in her native town, she, like all Palestinian writers and poets, readily recognized the fate of the refugee as the compelling
metaphor for Palestinian experience in general.

IV

This holds equally true for Palestinian writers and poets who stayed put in Palestine in 1948 and consequently became citizens of the state of Israel. Imīl Ḥabībī,
one of Israel's most prominent Arab citizens who served for many years as a Knes-

set member representing the Israeli Communist party, frequently evokes this potent metaphor in his work. The story "Love in My Heart" exemplifies this tendency. A Palestinian political prisoner from the newly occupied West Bank is flabbergasted when her cellmate, a Palestinian woman from Haifa, Israel, expresses a liking for a popular song that vents the yearnings of the refugees to return to their homes. The following account of the exchange between the two Palestinian women is revealing:

> I asked her: "What moves you in this song about return when you had never left your homeland?" She answered: "My homeland? I feel like a refugee in a foreign land. You at least dream of return and the dream sustains you. Whither shall I return?"[11]

Admittedly, Habībī writes this tongue in cheek, because the refugee from the West Bank is a spoiled brat who wears thin her political consciousness. The sentiment of the woman from Haifa, however, is quite genuine, and the choice of a prison cell to dramatize the estrangement of the Arab citizens from the institutions of the Jewish state is singularly apt. For one thing, incarceration for Palestinian nationalist activity is a fairly common experience among Israeli-Arab writers and intellectuals. For another, prison stands in a relationship of metonymy, not metaphor, to the state of siege under which the Arabs of Israel lived from 1948 to 1964. During these sixteen years the Arabs lived under a military government that severely restricted their physical movements, largely confining them to their towns and villages.[12] Moreover, for a significant number of Palestinian citizens of Israel, the term "refugee" is a literal, not a metaphoric, designation. These are Palestinians who never left the territory that became part of the state of Israel but happened to be outside their villages during the war of 1948. When the fighting subsided, they were prevented from returning to their homes and villages, many of which had in the meantime been demolished by the Israeli army precisely to foil such an eventuality (Morris 1987). In Israeli legal and administrative jargon, these "internal refugees" are designated by the oxymoron "present absentees."

Such, for example, was the fate of al-Birweh, the birthplace of Mahmūd Darwīsh, the best-known living Palestinian poet. The destruction of their village caused the poet's family to relocate to another village, where Darwīsh grew up under the stigma of "refugee." The indelible memory of these traumatic childhood experiences informs many of Darwīsh's haunted lyrics about a homeland that readily blends with the image of the beloved, on the one hand, and a prison cell, on the other. In a poem entitled "On Man," Darwīsh summarizes the predicament of the Palestinian in starkly discursive terms.

> They gagged his mouth,
> Bound his hand to the rock of the dead
> And said: Murderer!
> They took his food, clothes, and banners,
> Cast him into the condemned cell

And said: Thief!
They drove him away from every port,
Took his young sweetheart,
Then said: Refugee![13]

Much like Ṭūqān's poems, Darwīsh's also ends on a positive note. It asserts, on the implicit basis of historical and natural precedent, that the wrong inflicted on the Palestinians will inevitably be rectified.

V

A different and far less sanguine view of the predicament of the refugees obtains in the Palestinian prose narratives of the same period. The works of Ghassān Kanafānī and Samīra 'Azzām amply illustrate this bleak outlook.

Kanafānī himself became a refugee at the age of twelve in 1948 when his family fled Acre to South Lebanon and thence to Syria, where they settled in a refugee camp on the outskirts of Damascus. A poignant account of this border crossing into exile is contained in one of Kanafānī's earliest and most autobiographical short stories, "The Land of Sad Oranges."[14] The story is narrated retrospectively by an eyewitness to the events to a younger brother, that is, a second-generation refugee, who was too young to remember the exodus from Palestine. The subject of the narrative, however, is the rending disillusionment of the father who crossed the border into Lebanon believing that his sojourn there will be no longer than the time it takes the regular Arab armies to liberate Palestine from the Zionists and reinstate him and all his fellow refugees in their homes and lands. As the appointed day of liberation—15 May 1948—comes and goes, unleashing in its wake an endless torrent of communiqués about fantastic Arab victories, the father realizes the onset of permanent exile and lapses into a state of terminal despondency. The last memory the narrator has of him is transparently symbolic: the suicidal father is lying distraught on the floor; next to him is a shriveled orange he had carried with him from Palestine and a loaded gun.

Total breakdown in the traditional value system, especially the central concepts of trust and honor, also motivates the harrowing action of Kanafānī's first novella, *Men in the Sun*.[15] Three hapless refugees attempt to cross the border from Iraq to Kuwait in search of work. Too poor to afford the exorbitant price demanded by professional, notoriously duplicitous smugglers of Basra, they unwittingly succumb to the persuasive sweet talk of a fellow Palestinian who undertakes to smuggle them, for a lower rate, across the border in the empty water tank of his truck. The three die by asphyxiation at a desolate checkpoint in the middle of nowhere in the desert. On the outskirts of Kuwait City, the driver strips the refugees of their meager personal belongings and dumps them on a garbage heap.

There are other border crossings in this novel, and they all involve a breach of trust. One of the three refugees, As'ad, is double crossed by a fellow Palestinian who undertakes to smuggle him out of Jordan, where he is wanted for "political offenses." The only condition this driver, Abū al-'Abd, insists on is that near a border checkpoint between Jordan and Iraq, As'ad would get off, circle around the installation in the desert, to meet with the driver on the other side of the checkpoint. The driver pledges "on [his] honor" to wait for As'ad at the designated meeting place. To assuage As'ad's nagging doubts, Abū al-'Abd appeals to his patriotic sense by "reminding" him that he and As'ad's late father had "fought side by side in Palestine." Having collected the handsome fee in advance, Abu al-'Abd leaves As'ad stranded in the desert, eventually to be picked up and ferried across the border by a Western couple who, unlike the hapless Palestinian refugees, have no difficulty crossing the borders of Arab states. (The strong suggestion that the Western couple are engaged in espionage adds poignant irony to this whole episode.)

Kanafānī's diagnosis of the refugee condition is remarkable for its ruthless frankness and perspicacity. The refugee appears here in his naked vulnerability: a passive victim of malicious circumstances he neither controls nor comprehends. To be a refugee is to be deprived not only of home and country but also of individuality and all attributes of personal identity. For this reason the refugee is perhaps more akin to the patient and the prisoner than he is to the exile, the immigrant, or even the migrant worker—categories with which the refugee obviously shares many common characteristics.[16] If a paradox might be allowed: total anonymity and invisibility are constitutive conditions of refugee "identity." The death of the three refugees inside the empty water tank—unseen, unheard—and the dumping of their anonymous corpses on a garbage heap are powerful symbolic reminders of the supremacy of these conditions.

Estrangement and alienation are by far the dominant emotions in the experience of the Palestinian characters of Kanafānī's novella. The oldest, Abū Qays, feels a total "stranger" in Basra. In his case, physical dislocation from his native land causes psychological disorientation and loss of all sense of direction. Lying at the wet bank of the estuary of Shaṭṭ al-'Arab, he is overwhelmed by a kinesthetic sensation akin to what he used to experience in his fields in Palestine after every rain. The intense sensation transports him, momentarily, on ropes of memory, to the home and twelve olive trees he had left behind. The sight of a lonely seagull circling aimlessly above finally awakens him from the reverie, only to plunge him into the nightmare that eventually transpires in the plot.

Kanafānī wrote *Men in the Sun* in 1961 while in hiding from the Lebanese authorities, who were after him ostensibly because his travel documents were not in order but actually because he had attacked in print a powerful conservative Arab government, presumably Saudi Arabia. The action of the novella, however, is set in 1958, which marks a high-water mark in the history of pan-Arabism. (Both the Iraqi revolution that overthrew the pro-Western Hashimite monarchy and the short-lived union between Egypt and Syria took place during that year.) The liberation of Palestine, as is well known, was always a major pillar of pan-Arab ideology. The cutting irony of *Men in the Sun* resides in the gaping distance between the rhetorical valorization of the Palestinian cause and the actual dehumanization of the Palestinians at the hands of the Arab regimes.

VI

Samīra 'Azzām, another Palestinian refugee writer (by coincidence also from Acre), treats refugee experience less symbolically and more discursively. In a story entitled "Because He Loves Them,"[17] she traces manifestations of behavioral deviance among Palestinian refugees to their abnormal condition. A Palestinian employee of the UN Relief and Work Agency is dismayed at the downfall of an intimate friend who was caught stealing from the camp's rationing center. The realization that the friend, like other Palestinian "deviants" the employee knows, is a victim of the abject conditions of life in the refugee camp prompts him to seek a drastic remedy. To wean his fellow refugees from the handouts that threaten to turn them all into ration addicts or deviants, and to remind them of the principal cause of their tragic condition, the employee sets the rationing center on fire. The conclusion of the story thus redefines the meaning of the title: "Because He Loves Them."

An equally poignant analysis of the malaise of refugee life is proffered in another short story by Kanafānī, "Farther than the Borders."[18] This story dramatizes in graphic terms the plight of the Palestinian refugees at the hands of an unspecified (i.e., typical) Arab regime. A Palestinian prisoner escapes from prison and then returns voluntarily to confront his custodian (an Arab official) with a long list of abuses to which the Palestinian refugees are routinely subjected. What is particularly instructive about these abuses is that they are all committed for reasons of state. Internally, to deter public unrest, the regime routinely "punishes" the Palestinian refugee camps, and the indigenous population gets the message loud and clear. Externally, the regime displays the plight of the refugees to foreign visitors to raise funds for itself at their expense.

What makes this abuse possible, the fugitive asserts, is that the Palestinians have no state to protect them. States, even individual citizens of states, can abuse the refugees with impunity because the Palestinians live in "A World Not [Their] Own," the title of another short story by Kanafānī. At the conclusion of his harangue, the fugitive of "Farther than the Borders" puts the Arab official on notice: The Palestinian refugees have all but exhausted their tolerance for the duplicity of the Arab regimes and the official should not be surprised if the camps erupt in anger before too long.

"Farther than the Borders" succinctly recapitulates the major characteristics of earlier refugee narratives and foreshadows future trends. Its protagonist is at once a refugee, a fugitive, a prisoner, and a potential revolutionary. True to the general condition of the refugees, he remains nameless and, thus, anonymous. The list of grievances he presents to the "official," however, afflicts the refugees, qua refugees, and not only him. This distinction is crucial and marks a significant development in the consciousness of the refugees because it reorders causes and effects, general rules and specific manifestations, in a manner more consonant with reality. In many earlier refugee narratives a strong sense of personal guilt and shame motivates the characters' action. In turn, the perception of their plight in personal terms prompts individual refugees to seek individual remedies. The fatal consequences of this dangerous illusion were presented in the harrowing end of the three characters of *Men in the Sun*. (Since the fourth Palestinian in that novella, the driver of the trolley, is a castrate, the conclusion of the plot is far more bleak than is readily apparent. The four Palestinians represent four different age groups and are thus representative of the Palestinian people as a whole. At the end of the novel, nobody is left to perpetuate the Palestinian species.)

VII

By the early 1960s, the estrangement of the refugees from the structures of power instated to "represent" them and to redress the injustice inflicted on them by Israel had become both complete and self-evident. The list includes, but is not limited to, the traditional Palestinian leadership, the UN, the Arab states, and practically the entire world, which stood by and watched the Palestinians rot in the squalid refugee camps year in and year out. Worse still, the refugees observed with dismay and stunned disbelief how the world bought into Israel's propaganda and applauded her valiant effort on behalf of Jewish "refugees." As the hope for a speedy repatriation dimmed, the refugees clung more desperately to the moral rightness of their cause. Israel's relentless and largely successful effort to monopolize the role of victim in world public opinion necessitated casting the refugees in the role of aggressor. This, in turn, compounded further the refugees' estrangement from the international order and aggravated their sense of marginalization.

If during the first phase of our chronological schema Palestinian literature invested much in diagnosing the Palestinian condition, during the second it mustered as much energy for prescribing a cure for that condition. While the final objective remained the same, namely, return of the refugees to their homes and return of the Palestinian homeland to the Palestinian people, the means of achieving it changed. The reorientation in literary focus coincided with and abetted political changes that were gathering momentum in the refugee camps. The end result was a paradigm shift in Palestinian political thinking leading eventually to the emergence of the Palestinian guerrilla organizations and the launching of armed struggle against Israel in the mid-1960s. This was by far the most important development in Palestinian life since 1948.

As far as the anatomy of the refugee is concerned, the shift prescribed reliance on the refugees themselves rather than on external sources to effect the desired change in the Palestinian condition. The refugee as passive victim of sundry external pressures of earlier narratives gives way now to the politicized refugee as active agent of change in his environment. Paramount in this metamorphosis is the role of consciousness and human agency. These, in turn, reinscribe, at one remove or another, the writer's underlying ideology. Jabrā Ibrāhīm Jabrā and Ghassān Kanafānī represent two polar opposites on this issue; all other refugee narratives fall somewhere in between.

The refugee characters of Jabrā's many novels come invariably from the Palestinian bourgeoisie. Much like the writer himself, they all experience dislocation and hardship as a result of the calamity of 1948, but they all deftly contain the negative fallout and proceed to build successful careers in different professions in the various Arab capitals. (Jabrā was stranded in Baghdad, where he had been teaching, during the 1948 war and, like all Palestinian refugees, could not return to his home in Jerusalem.) Externally these characters appear well adjusted to their new surroundings, but internally they are in incessant turmoil. What bedevils their inner world are intimate childhood memories violently interrupted in Palestine in 1948. Being, without exception, artistically inclined, these characters often seek comfort in sublimation: they all try to transmute their traumatic experiences into artistic creations. Paradoxically, the more accomplished the artifacts they produce, the more vivid grow the traumas that nurture the artistic vision. Eventually, all Jabrā's characters realize that the only way off this perilous spiral is to confront the original cause of the trauma, the Israeli occupier, directly by joining the guerrilla organizations. The presence of these organizations in the background lends verisimilar plausibility to this recurrent denouement.

Thus the largely psychological, often recognizably Oedipal quest of Jabrā's "refugees" piggybacks on the national cause to garner wider significance. (The recurrent ending also effects poetic closure.) The individual subject of this narrative is constituted a fortiori. The narrative is needed only to realign the innate attributes of personality for optimal realization and expression of individuality. Jabrā's fictional exiles are heroic individuals whose experiential realm happens to be the Palestinian tragedy. As fully individualized subjects, they have much in common with Palestinian intellectuals writing autobiographically on Palestinian exile from the safe distance and comfort of their private homes in Arab and European capitals.

By contrast, Kanafānī's refugee characters invariably come from the lower classes and camp dwellers. They cultivate political consciousness of necessity, not choice. A combination of intolerable material conditions and despair of the established order of things always precedes and prompts the initiation of these characters into political activism. *Umm Sa'd* (Sa'd's Mother, 1968)[19] amply illustrates this causal sequence. Sa'd's mother, the older refugee woman of the novel bearing her name, approves of her son joining the guerrillas after a sleepless night caused by extensive leaks in their makeshift barrack during a heavy storm. Similarly, the change from passive victims to armed combatants necessarily involves clashing with the existing structures of power. Before they can reach the border with Israel, the refugees-turned-guerrillas have to cross a far more dangerous border: the tight siege that the Arab regimes maintain, as a matter of course, around the refugee camps. When Sa'd and a number of his comrades try to break out, the Jordanian authorities apprehend them and throw them in prison. To check the spread of this phenomenon in the camps, the authorities mobilize their collaborators, the appointed traditional Palestinian "dignitaries," and instruct them to keep the restless refugees in line. In *Umm Sa'd*, the effort fails because the refugee-guerrillas are armed with a class perspective that enables them to view the traditional Palestinian leadership and the Arab regimes as part of the enemy camp. In Kanafānī's post-1967 work, the refugees' desire for repatriation adopts a political vernacular in which the discourses of national and class liberation converge. This, in turn, invites a reexamination of the fundamental concept of return.

Kanafānī addresses this issue systematically in a subsequent novel, *'Ā'id ilā Haifa* (Returning to Haifa, 1969).[20] The plot features a Palestinian couple who flee their city during the fighting in 1948. Amid the panic and chaos, the distraught mother forgets her infant, and when she tries to return to the house to collect him, she is blocked by "a torrent of people moving in the opposite direction." The couple eventually settle in the West Bank, which was annexed by Jordan in 1950 and, until 1967, was officially part of the Hashimite kingdom. When, in the wake of Israel's occupation of the West Bank in 1967, the borders between the occupied territories and Israel are reopened, the Palestinian couple, after much hesitation, decide to return to Haifa to check on the fate of their son and house.

To their surprise, they discover that the house survived intact, with only minor changes in the interior decoration, and, what is immeasurably more important, the son also survived. The shock of recognition occurs when they discover, first, that the Jewish occupant of their house is a refugee survivor of the Nazi concentration camps and, second, that Khaldūn, the Arab infant they left behind, is now Dov, an officer in the Israeli army who considers himself a Jew in every respect. The details of the halting dialogue that ensues between the parties are less important than the imperceptible change the visit causes in the Arab couple. This is the first time in Palestinian literature that the question of return to the houses the refugees left behind in 1948 is raised, discussed openly, and thoroughly demystified. What this novel and indeed all of Kanafānī's post-1967 novels suggest is that the concept of return can no longer be confined to the specific material property the refugees left behind. Nor, in fact, can the refugees "return" in any literal sense because, by the time they become politically and psychologically capable of forcing their way back, they will no longer be the same refugees who left. At the time of his assassination by the Israeli secret service in 1972, Kanafānī was well on his way to developing a transcendental definition of return that imbues it thoroughly with progressive ideological content. The trajectory of this line of reasoning postulates at the end of the struggle for national liberation a transformed Palestinian refugee returning to a significantly different old/new Palestine.

In retrospect, Kanafānī's forecast concerning the prospects of the refugees appears to have been overly optimistic. Instead of a triumphal return, on a higher plane of consciousness, to a radically transformed, secular, and progressive Palestine, the refugee camps themselves have since become regular targets for military and paramilitary attacks. Enabled by the concerted slant in the Israeli-Western narrative equating Palestinians with terrorists, Israel, the Arab regimes, and armed factions of every stripe routinely attack refugee camps with impunity. A graphic reminder of this grim reality surfaced recently in Kuwait when, during the campaign of terror against the Palestinian community following the Gulf War, Kuwaiti vigilantes wrote the following graffiti on the walls of Palestinian camps: "Amman 1970, Beirut 1982, Kuwait 1991." (The first date refers to the massacre of Palestinian refugees by the Jordanian army during what came to be known as "black September" in 1970; the second refers to the massacre of refugees in the camps of Sabrā and Shatīlā by the Maronite phalangists under the protection of the Israeli army in 1982.) As a result of that campaign, the Palestinian community in Kuwait was reduced within a few months from four hundred thousand to less than fifty thousand. The harrowing narrative of the survivors of this new exodus, many of whom are refugees for the third and fourth time, is still being assembled and will, undoubtedly, inspire its own literary representations in due course. Nor, judging by the drift of events, does it promise to be the last chapter in the Palestinian refugees' tale of woes.

NOTES

1. Zolberg, Suhrke, and Aguayo 1989:227.

2. For a thorough and comprehensive discussion of the Palestinian refugee problem, see Morris 1987; for the role of the UN, see Buehrig 1974.

The Israeli writer S. Yizhar describes scenes of expulsion of Palestinian civilians by the Israeli armed forces during the 1948 war in a well-known short story entitled "Khirbet Khizā" (Khiz, 'a Village), in Yizhar [1949] 1977. An English translation of excerpts from this lengthy story appeared in *Jewish Quarterly* 4 (Spring 1957).

3. See Jameson, 1986:65–88; for a rigorous critique of Jameson's view, see Ahmad 1987:3–25.

4. This existential/political urge may also explain the tendency of Palestinian writers to shun literary specialization and to experiment with all genres, modes, and forms of expression. To take just two examples, the late Ghassān Kanafānī wrote short stories, novels, plays, works of literary criticism, historical treatises, and editorials and political commentaries for several daily newspapers while being a full-time political activist, the spokesman for a major Palestinian guerrilla organization, and the editor of its weekly. Similarly, Maḥmūd Darwīsh is at once a leading Arab poet, an accomplished writer of literary prose, a political commentator, the editor of a prestigious literary periodical, and an active member of the Palestinian Writers' Union and the Palestine National Council. It fell to Darwīsh to draft the declaration of the establishment of the Palestinian state in November 1988.

5. For a translated sample of that rich oral heritage, see Muhawwi and Kanaana 1989; for a highly suggestive incorporation of Palestinian folktales in novels, see Barakat 1974 and Shammas 1988.

6. Said 1986; cited blurb appears on the back cover.

7. See Siddiq 1984:38 ff.

8. Translated by A. L. Tībāwī (1963:517).

9. Ibid.

10. Ibid., n. 42.

11. Habībī 1970:116, 117; my translation.

12. For a review of this historical background, see Jiryis 1976 and Lustick 1980.

13. Darwīsh "On Man," trans. Johnson-Davies (1980:3).

14. Kanafānī 1978:57–62.

15. Ibid., 9–56.

16. For an informative discussion of the various categories involved in intellectual and cultural border crossing, see JanMohamed 1993. For a more general discussion of this issue, see Hicks 1991.

17. ʿAzzām 1963.

18. Kanafānī, "Abʾad min al-Hudūd" (1973).

19. Kanafānī 1973:1:24–336.

20. Ibid., 341–414.

REFERENCES

Ahmad, Aijaz
  1987   "Jameson's Rhetoric of Otherness and the National Allegory." *Social Texts* 17 (Fall): 3–25.
ʿAzzām, Samīra
  1978   *Al-Sa a wal-Insan: Quisas* (The Clock and the Man: Stories). Acre: Marktabat al Aswar.
Barakat, Halim
  1974   *Days of Dust.* Washington, D.C.: Three Continents Press.
Buehrig, Halim
  1974   *The UN and the Palestinian Refugees: A Study in Nonterritorial Administration.* Bloomington: Indiana University Press.
Darwīsh, Mahmud
  1980   "On Man." In *The Music of Human Flesh,* trans. Denys Johnson-Davies, 3. Washington, D.C.: Three Continents Press.
Habībī, Imil
  1970   "Al-Hubb Fi Qalbi" (Love in My Heart). In *Sudasiyyat al-Ayyam al-Sitta* (Sextet of the Six Days), trans. Muhammad Siddiq, 116–117. Haifa: Matbaʾatal-Ittihad.
Hicks, D. Emily
  1991   *Border Writing.* Minneapolis: University of Minnesota Press.
Jameson, Fredric
  1986   "Third World Literature in the Era of Multinational Capitalism." *Social Texts* 15 (Fall): 65–88.
JanMohamed, A. R.
  1993   "Worldliness-Without-World, Homelessness-as-Home: Toward a Definition of the Specular Border Intellectual." In *Edward W. Said: A Critical Reader,* ed. Michael Sprinker, 96–120. Oxford: Basil Blackwell.

Jiryis, Sabri
    1976   *The Arabs in Israel.* Trans. Inea Bushnaq. New York: Monthly Review Press.
Kanafānī, Ghassan
    1973   *Al-Athar al-Kamila* (Complete Works). Vol. 2. Beirut: Dar al-Tali a lil-Tiba
                a wal-Naahr.
    1978   "The Land of Sad Oranges." In *Men in the Sun and Other Palestinian Stories,*
                trans. Hillary Kilpatrick, 57–62. Washington, D.C.: Three Continents
                Press.
Lustick, Ian
    1980   *Arabs in the Jewish State: Israel's Control of a National Minority.* Austin: Univer-
                sity of Texas Press.
Morris, Benny
    1987   *The Birth of the Palestinian Refugee Problem, 1947–1949.* Cambridge: Cambridge
                University Press.
Muhawwi, Ibrahim, and Sharif Kanaana
    1989   *Speak, Bird, Speak Again: Palestinian Arab Folktales.* Berkeley, Los Angeles, and
                London: University of California Press.
Said, Edward W.
    1986   *After the Last Sky: Palestinian Lives.* New York: Pantheon.
Shammas, Anton
    1988   *Arabesques.* New York: Harper and Row.
Siddiq, Muhammad
    1984   *Man Is a Cause: Political Consciousness and the Fiction of Ghassan Kanafani.* Seat-
                tle: University of Washington Press.
Tibawī, A. L.
    1963   "Visions of the Return: The Palestine Arab Refugees in Arabic Poetry and
                Art." *Middle East Journal* (Autumn): 517.
Yizhar, S.
    [1949] 1977 "Khirbet Khiz." *7 Sippurim.* Tel-Aviv: Hakibbutz Hameuchad.
Zolberg, Aristide R., Astri Suhrke, and Sergio Aguayo, eds.
    1989   *Escape from Violence: Conflict and the Refugee Crisis in the Developing World.*
                Oxford: Oxford University Press.

SIX

Refugees as Foreigners:
The Problem of Becoming German
and Finding Home

Jeffrey M. Peck

I

Since the fall of 1991, foreigners, primarily refugees and asylum seekers, have been attacked in Germany. Stephen Kinzer (1992), reporting in the *New York Times*, wrote that "there were 600 [such attacks] in the first three months of 1992." The German newsmagazine *Der Spiegel* has devoted numerous covers to the topic. One article, "Asylum: The Politicians Are Failing" (6 April 1992), dealt with the impotence of the government in addressing this problem. The photographs in this article depicted the literal storming of the gates by asylum seekers anxious to get into Germany; other issues have addressed the "ethnic Germans," for example, "Millions of Russian-Germans Are Coming" (21 October 1991). Others dramatically announced "Violence against Foreigners, HATE" (30 September 1991). Since reunification on 3 October 1990 and especially after the collapse of East Germany (GDR) (starting with the fall of the wall on 9 November 1989), foreigners in general and refugees in particular have been in a precarious situation. They have been the target not only of neo-Nazi and proto-Fascist skinheads but also of the hostility of other German citizens, who are frustrated by the overflow of people and the concurrent drain on the economy.

The "asylum question" has become the most decisive and divisive political issue in Germany, as evidenced by state elections (5 April 1992), where far Right parties made sharp gains. In the southern province of Baden-Württemburg, the right-wing Republican party scored 11 percent of the vote, and in northernmost Schleswig-Holstein, the German People's Union won more than 6 percent. Kinzer's *New York Times* piece further reported that "rightist parties warned that the country was being overrun by asylum-seekers from Eastern Europe and the third world." More alarming, especially in the context of my analysis, are comments by the leader of the People's Union, Gerhard Frey. Exploiting the often used image of being overrun, submerged, or washed away by foreigners (which even the respected *Spiegel* depicts), Frey states, "Old parties showed themselves unable to deal with the flood of so-called asylum seekers." Even more distressing is the language that represents the traditional and dangerously polarizing discourse around ethnicity and race, for instance, in Frey's words, "We are not unfriendly to foreigners. . . . We are friendly to Germans" (Kinzer 1992).

The events of 1992 prove that there is a clearly articulated dichotomy between Germans and foreigners based on race. On the one hand, the various non-Germans are increasingly divided by race or more often by color, both among themselves and in relation to the Germans; on the other hand, it appears that the disastrous economic situation is mitigating the aggression directed only against foreigners of color by displacing frustration on any immigrant who is perceived as draining the German economy.

On 22 September 1991, in a small Saxon town called Hoyerswerda in the territory of eastern Germany, foreigners, that is, guest workers and asylum seekers, were attacked by neo-Nazis and skinheads. While the attacks were condemned all over Germany for their violence and blatant xenophobia and racism, another issue loomed more dramatically. A *Spiegel* reporter sums it up.

> Hoyerswerda marked a turning point, less because a few dozen young xenophobes have given the go-ahead to fanaticism with steel balls and Molotov cocktails thrown at dormitories for asylum seekers and guest workers. Much worse: Thousands of adult citizens, in spite of decade-long stereotypical East German education about "People's Solidarity" accepted these criminal attacks silently, when they were not jubilantly welcoming it.[1]

According to the chief official for foreigner affairs in Hamburg, the response of the citizens who applauded the actions was "about the worst thing that has happened on German soil" since "the Night of Broken Glass," on 9 November 1938, when Nazis systematically attacked Jews, their businesses, and synagogues.[2] The population of this East German town had been "freed," so to speak, on the same date, 9 November, fifty-one years later when the Berlin Wall came down. This dramatic change was inspired by their countrymen, who had been refugees on their way out of East Germany through Hungary and Czechoslovakia, a year before. Now all former GDR citizens were themselves a different sort of refugee in their new homeland. They were literally "renewed" Germans, who, in the euphoria of the regime's collapse that had led so swiftly to unification, did not foresee the catastrophic economic results that would make them into "second-class Germans" and make some wish that a wall could again be built, this time to keep refugees out. Drastic measures—cutbacks in jobs, higher rents, and fewer social benefits—made these Germans feel that they were losing out to "foreigners," who were taking away their jobs, their apartments, and even in some cases, they thought, their women. They felt and still feel threatened on all sides. In short, while they may have gained a German Heimat, they have lost a home.

As of this writing, the German government and its politicians are overwhelmed and paralyzed, unwilling to make a decision on asylum policy. What is clear, however, is that the refugees keep coming: in March 1992, 35,059 asylum seekers, 4,000 more than in February and more than in any month previously. If this were to be estimated for the year, it would be 400,000 versus 256,000 in 1991.[3] The political battles among the major parties continue about changing asylum laws, restricting immigration with quotas, and economic supports for Eastern Europe and third world countries to encourage their citizens to stay home. However, the question remains, especially for the concerns raised in this volume: not only what will Germany do, but what do these events mean for refugees and other foreigners who are seeking a home, trying to belong?

The terrible situation for foreigners and refugees has largely to do with the Germans' treatment of foreigners and their own racism. Turned into a "foreigner problem," these attitudes make the victims the perpetrators of their own fate. While the refugee can be distinguished from the "immigrant" or even the more general "foreigner" based on motivations for leaving a homeland, the way that the Germans regard these people is not distinguished by the outsider's desire or need to stay in Germany. Although some make the unacceptable suggestion of expelling the guest workers or other particular groups of foreigners, most foreigners who are nonwhite, especially the guest workers, refugees, and asylum seekers, do not plan to return to their homes, at least in the near future. The majority of these people are simply going to stay. This means that the German government and the German people are confronted with millions of non-Germans who are living among them; Germany is in fact "a country of immigration" *(Einwanderungsland)* made up of black, brown, and yellow peoples. Those that are white, especially the Poles and other Eastern Europeans who are not ethnic Germans and Soviet Jews, may have an easier time, since they are not marked as "other" by their color.

Race and racism clearly figure into the refugee debate much more than most would like to admit. Germany is not alone in Western Europe in this regard, yet defenders of Germany's foreigner and refugee policies continuously draw on these comparisons to explain (or excuse) the problem. One has to reiterate that to understand the specific examples of racism in Germany is not to say that it is better or worse than its European neighbors. The attention to Germany's own special history makes us better able to examine the manifestations of racism today which at least in part evolve from particular historical conditions. German history resonates, particularly in the case of Hoyerswerda, which recalls Nazi pogroms against a people who also were not considered German. To distinguish the specificity of the German situation, a number of aspects have to be addressed: its citizens' relationship to the foreign (normative and prescriptive social attitudes), Germans' own difficulty in thinking of themselves in positive national terms (rejecting any forms of national identification or pride), Germans' lack of experience with foreigners (a limited colonial tradition), and the inheritance of Germany's systematic elimination of "foreign" peoples (the extermination of Jews, Slavs, Gypsies, Jehovah's Witnesses, and gays). However, the reasons distinguishing the German situation from the French, English, or Swedish situations should not be used as excuses on either side of the political spectrum, either uniformly contra- or proforeigners. Indeed, it would be grossly unfair to cast the Germans today as all antiforeigner. Antiracist and proforeigner debates and demonstrations directly after the events in Hoyerswerda showed solidarity with the victims. In fact, many Germans proudly declared, "I am a foreigner."

Yet this kind of identification with foreigners is also extremely problematic and illustrates the way that the Germans try to come to terms with racism, xenophobia, and the question of their own identity. While linking the Nazi past to present-day xenophobia and racism is necessary, such a focus on the terrible events of the past often overly historicizes the relationship. It therefore often fails to draw enough attention to how these traumatic events and the racist attitudes shaping them continue to influence current policy and politics of identity, albeit manifested differently. Notions of national identity on the Left and the Right—of being German or not wanting to be German—continue to influence foreigner and refugee policy, especially vis-à-vis race. Even though Germany's liberal asylum policy was based on the inequities and horrors of its past, it has proven to be inadequate to cope not just with the influx of refugees but also with the necessity of developing definitions of foreigner, refugee, asylum seeker, guest workers, and immigrant and adequate laws to accommodate this complex reality. On the one hand, all of these non-Germans are collectively called "foreigners" and are (mis)treated accordingly; on the other hand, the legal categorizations are so highly differentiated as to distinguish different varieties of "Germans" (*Aussiedler* [ethnic German immigrant from eastern territories] or *Übersiedler* [immigrants from the former GDR]) from asylum seeker (one who has applied for political asylum), from guest worker, and from refugee (one fleeing his country). Even East Germans, initially welcomed as German brothers and sisters, are no longer greeted so enthusiastically. As Nora Räthzel (1991:46–47) points out,

> In the course of extended immigration, East Germans seem to have lost their Germanness and become the Other. Now they are not seen as embodying the typical characteristics of the true industrious German, but as possessing a number of negative attributes. . . . All of these negative characteristics, however, have to do not with their being "German by blood," but with their being socialized by the Communist system. East Germans are considered as socially and culturally different, not different by nature [by blood]. The result is that the concept of Germanness becomes yet further diffused. The biological and social construct of "the German" are no longer identical.

Consequently, even aside from the influx of foreigners, the new Germany will not be able to maintain a nationalized notion of home based on cultural, social, and biological homogeneity and represented in a West German state that is ostensibly reaffirmed by the inclusion of the former GDR. Such a state cannot, in fact, exist if Germany officially becomes a country of immigration, since it is not all Christian or all white—in other words, all German. Räthzel comments,

> While the Federal Republic claims not to be a country of immigration, no less than fifteen per cent of its workforce are migrants. Consequently, concern focuses mainly on "integrating" migrants to keep in place the homogeneity of the Kulturnation [cultural nation], while racism itself is untackled: indeed, racism does not exist, only Ausländerfeindlichkeit [xenophobia]. It is within this logic, of the German nation as having a homogeneous population of German citizens, that battles are fought between those wanting to preserve such homogeneity, and those on the Left who challenge this notion by rejecting any notion of national identity at all, because they see it as so closely bound up with form of the state. (Ibid., 45)

Thus the "foreigner problem" is in large part a racial problem. Germany hesitates to officially acknowledge that it is a land of immigration because once the "problem" is "removed" by legal and subsequent social recognition that might develop under more auspicious conditions of immigration, the racism underlying the problem will be all the more evident. It will not have necessarily disappeared with "integration" into German life, and it will show that the focus on foreigners and xenophobia has diverted attention from racism.

Both the Left and the Right are blinded by their inability to construct a new and more heterogeneous identity, one that acknowledges the benefits of immigration and the racial prejudices that have to be overcome. By announcing themselves as "foreigners," these Germans make the mistake of identifying themselves with the victims and therefore avoid dealing with the racism and the violence coming from the Germans themselves.[4] The interviewer in the article I cite points out that "in spite of the many attacks and in spite of Hoyerswerda, racism is rarely straightforwardly addressed." Instead, "the president of the Federal Republic speaks of 'the crisis of human understanding,' social psychologists of 'the natural fear of the foreign' and 'normal reactions to stress.'" The psychologist responds by emphasizing that for Germans the notion of racism is itself taboo and therefore ignored, just as are the problems of dealing with the Nazi past. Again, racial and ethnic division is constructed by the inability to name racism for what it is and to continue to reify the notions of German and *Ausländer*.

For refugees and foreigners, this means being patronized, spoken for, and consistently seen as victims; foreigners are interesting to view in an exoticized or folkloric milieu in Germany or on vacation, in ethnic restaurants, or at "cultural festivals." But even with the best intentions, they are still separated and set apart, objectified and depersonalized, as black, brown, or yellow people whose bodies mark them as different and make them in the worst case literal objects of violence. In short, they are constantly reminded in everyday life that they are not Germans and that they do not belong. The experience of all foreigners proves that since the decision does not rest with the foreigner but with the Germans, the refugee may do what she or he can to assimilate but can do nothing to become German.[5] The fact that, for the Germans, being German is so opaque, reified, and objectified leaves little space for refugees and foreigners to enter, no matter how well they master the behavior, speech, and habitus of "the German."

The discourses, both public (legal) and private, push and pull on the foreigner/refugee, who is torn between the variety of categorizations that all mark her or him from outside. The economic and personal misery of most refugees, who for the sake of asylum must prove that they are politically persecuted and not just financially destitute, makes any effort to take discursive or material power back into their own hands all but impossible. The future of refugees in Germany is being decided now; the attacks will continue unless the Germans change their fundamental notions of German identity and home, the discourse used to articulate that reality, and their relationship to race.

II

COME TOGETHER AND LEARN TO LIVE AS FRIENDS
—ADVERTISEMENT IN GERMANY FOR PETER STUYVESANT CIGARETTES

UNITED COLORS OF BENETTON
—ADVERTISEMENT IN GERMANY AND ABROAD FOR CLOTHING

ALLE BERLINER SIND AUSLÄNDER (All Berliners Are Foreigners)
—ADVERTISEMENT SPONSORED BY THE WEST BERLIN CITY GOVERNMENT'S OFFICE FOR FOREIGNERS

These advertisements draw attention to public discourses in Germany about being foreign. The specific messages conveyed in them ostensibly represent the multiracial, multiethnic, and multicultural paradise that one would infer from the happy, smiling faces depicted. The natives, at least the "colored peoples" in these ads, are anything but discontent. In fact, the images of white, black, and Asian faces smiling broadly at each other and at the spectator give the impression of racial harmony and ethnic equality.

In the first two ads, the beautiful people and beautiful children seem to tell us how wonderful the world would be if only we could "live as friends."[6] Perhaps for yuppies of the international set with commodified faces and smiles to match and for their offspring who seem to have wandered into a like-minded Benetton ad, dealing with racism and xenophobia, or at least "com[ing] together," is as easy as smoking the right cigarette or wearing the right clothes. As long as adults and children normalize their habits and their habitus, multiculturalism is palatable. Although the characters in these ads and on these billboards have all the ethnic and racial markers that should make them exotic, their difference seems to be flattened to a mere marketing ploy. Their "colors" somehow all turn "white" when clothed in the internationalism of the marketplace. Their "foreignness," upgraded by money and class, is unthreatening. And the fact that the ad for a German cigarette is in English, in the vocabulary of easy American "neighborliness," and is coupled with strikingly American images is not surprising, since marketing and image packaging are an American specialty.

In a country like Germany, with 200,000 non-German refugees *(Asylanten)* (1990), 750,000 German refugees (Übersiedler and Aussiedler) (1989), and more than 4.5 million foreigners (Ausländer)[7] and serious problems of racism and xenophobia to match, these ads work at a level unintended by even the most clever advertisers. For an interpreter of cultural reproductions and representations sensitive to the German context in which these images appear, these ads provoke the public, both German and foreign, to ask why their Ausländer cannot be like these "proper" foreigners depicted: well behaved, clean, internationalized (read: neutralized), smiling, and congenial. While supposedly celebrating difference, the ad actually negates it by universalizing and minimalizing the context and by reducing individual ethnic or national groups to generalized ethnic markers. By limiting background or topography, the location remains nonspecific and non-German; more important, by focusing on color (black, yellow, white) and facial physiognomy (noses, mouths, lips, cheekbones, eyes) that could denote a variety of national or ethnic groups, the ads leave the viewer uncertain exactly what particular foreigners these are. The images can, in fact, be divided into the following four categories:

1. "Mediterranean"—Turkish, Greek, Italian, Portuguese?
2. "Aryan"—German, Dutch, Scandinavian, American?
3. "Asian"—Japanese, Chinese, Korean?
4. "black"—African-American, black African? (What about Afro-German?)[8]

The ad works to dichotomize the binary opposition central to German public and private discourse—German/foreigner to "noble" foreigner/"rejected" foreigner.[9] The former, at least as far as the ad implies, are as acceptable as the Germans. These noble foreigners distinguish themselves from the unwanted foreigners who live in Germany and must put up with racism and xenophobia daily. And yet these ads reinforce the assimilationist tendencies of "cultural integrationists," some conservative proponents of "multiculturalism," and the prevailing government opinion that foreigners, at least those who want to gain German citizenship, must "become German."

But what does it mean, in fact, to "become German"? To speak the language, to behave in a certain way, to have a passport? Although a distinction between refugees, immigrants, and exiles is useful, for the German situation and this analysis, the differentiation between refugees (German and non-German) and foreigners is more pertinent for what it both exposes and conceals. Outside official German political discourse the two categories collapse. Simply not being German, being an Ausländer (from outside the country) elides the political distinctions that are invisible to the average German. How can identification, acceptance, and security, the basis of trust, be established when foreigners/refugees do not feel, or are not allowed to feel, that they belong?

The particularly German notion of Heimat,[10] defined as home or homeland, precludes the kind or degree of integration necessary to belong, to feel "at home," of ultimately establishing trust between an indigenous population whose notion of Heimat is tied to a past and a place that foreigners can never reach, no matter how long they live in Germany. In the terms used by David Lowenthal for the title of his book, *The Past Is a Foreign Country,* Germany is historically and topographically inaccessible to all those seeking refuge, except those Germans from the former GDR and the ethnic Germans from Eastern Europe whose unique situation actually contributes to the dilemmas of the "non-German" immigrants.

This discussion brings us to the third advertisement, this time not for cigarettes or clothes but literally for improved understanding between the different ethnic and racial groups living in Berlin. Sponsored by the city's office for foreigners, the sign was the visual representation of the office's program, Miteinander leben in Berlin (Living together in Berlin).[11] The sign is filled with twenty-five individual black-and-white portraits of faces, many ostensibly "foreign" and others that may well be "German." The differentiation is clearly not intended to be bold. Each picture is a type; these are not only ethnic and racial minorities but also old people and young, those who are good-looking and average, high society and punk. This is a collection of "everyday Berliners" more natural and less manicured, although stylized as are the other ads. With such a variety of characters and charming personalities, the poster erases the forcefulness of ethnic markers and the identity of who is German and who is not. It is a noteworthy liberal attempt to sensitize Berliners to the foreigners living among them, but in my opinion, it fails when set alongside—as it often is in the Berlin subways—the high-gloss, color, and full-body images of more conventionally appealing "beautiful people."

III

The attention paid to cultural significations is meant to illustrate some of the contradictions in German society toward its foreigners that begin at the semantic level and spill over into cultural, national, and racial connotations. Let us first look at the words themselves, the central terms in the political debate, such as "Ausländer" (foreigner), "Asylbewerber" (asylum seeker), and "Flüchtling" (refugee), and the investment in the categories that define the problem and set the semantic and ethnic boundaries for a political and economic battle. The most problematic, at least for this analysis, is Ausländer. Literally meaning "from outside the country," the term traditionally was interchangeable with the word *Fremder,* meaning "the stranger." Originally the primary difference was that the former was someone who came to Germany from any country and the latter denoted an ontological condition or a psychological state of anyone who was alien or strange in a new place. In practice, this distinction meant that someone who moved from Frankfurt to Berlin would be *fremd* (the adjectival form) but not *ausländisch*—or the state of feeling different, unusual, and exotic and not fitting in—no matter where he or she was. The changes that have taken place around the term "Ausländer" are more important here, since according to Germany's Basic Law (1949), there are very important exceptions for people from particular countries. With these categories begin some of the special problems for defining a refugee, defining a German politically, ethnically, and culturally, and making Germany "home."

Since the official West German viewpoint, as stated in the Basic Law, still formally considered reunification a goal, even when it was ostensibly given up as a realistic option by conservatives and liberals alike, the East Germans were citizens *in spe* of the FRG as were the group called "ethnic Germans" or *Volksdeutschen* (the word *Volk* here is not to be ignored). This group was composed of those Germans and their descendants who were displaced during World War II and who were living in Poland, Rumania, and the Lower Volga area of the former Soviet Union. The status of Aussiedler is based on their being part of the German nation (Staatsangehörige) or German Volk (Volkszugehörige) after 31 December 1937, as stated in the FRG's Basic Law (Art. 116). The fact that they were born to German parents guarantees them rights that Turks, for instance, who have lived in Germany for twenty years do not enjoy; nor do the Turks' children, who were born there, speak the language, and know the culture.[12]

Neither of the two groups are officially considered "Ausländer" but are still *Flüchtlinge* with special connotations: those from the GDR, *Übersiedler* (literally, those settling from over there,)[13] and from the eastern territories, *Aussiedler* (literally, those settling from outside). The German government and the conservative organizations representing these displaced Germans make it very clear in their literature that these people are not "Ausländer" and enjoy a special status. The specificity of the terms "Übersiedler" and "Aussiedler" differentiate them from other foreigners whether they are, on the one hand, Americans and Western European or, on the other hand, Soviet Jews. The Ausländer of the first group, white Americans, French, English, Dutch, and Scandinavians, called by Dieter Thränhardt "noble foreigners," are not coincidentally all primarily white and often blond or light complected (the "Aryan" category). These people are not considered Ausländer anymore, since the term is reserved for the "Mediterranean" types, primarily Turks, Roma and Sinti Gypsies, and those who like the former originally came to Germany in the 1950s and 1960s as part of Germany's postwar "economic miracle." They were called at the time "Gastarbeiter" (guest workers), a euphemism, since they were welcomed by their employers, rather than their German hosts. To this group one must add the Persians, North Africans, black Africans, Pakistanis, and Tamils who arrived as refugees. The former GDR also had its share of guest workers from Vietnam, Cuba, Angola, and Mozambique.

In Thränhardt's view, these foreigners can be divided into two groups, the "strange" and the "rejected," with the Turks being the most disdained. I would offer yet another organizational scheme based on skin color that parallels Thrän-hardt's categories and further differentiates the five major groups of foreigners and refugees.

1. "Germans"—GDR citizens in the West and now all citizens of the former GDR. They resemble the West Germans racially and physically. They were welcomed in the years after the Wall was built (1961), up until and including the collapse of the GDR, but are now disdained and even hated because of the financial drain they have caused. This resentment spawns increasing awareness of distinctions in habitus, the way they dress and the way they talk.

2. "Almost Germans"—Ethnic Germans from Poland, Rumania, and the Soviet Union. They resemble the Germans physically, that is, they are Caucasians, light skinned, and blond or light haired. They are generally welcomed, but economic stress has strained their integration.

3. "Noble foreigners"—Thränhardt's category.

4. Eastern European "Ausländer"—Primarily Poles, who are not ethnic Germans. They are white but disliked because their economic situation drives them to behave in Germany in unacceptable ways, for example, setting up cheap "Polish markets" and aggressively buying up foodstuffs and electronic equipment to take back to Poland. On 8 April 1991 Poles no longer needed a visa to enter Germany and thousands of Poles crossed the border.

5. "Ausländer"—Turks and other Mediterraneans, Südländer (people from the South), Roma and Sinti, Indians, Pakistanis, and Tamils. These are people with dark skin and hair who are considered greasy and dirty, not "white."

6. Asian "Ausländer"—Vietnamese in the former GDR. Since reunification these people have borne the brunt of resentment. Thousands have returned home. Many would like to stay but find it impossible to get work.

This hierarchical categorization emphasizes the complexity of being an Auslän-der in Germany, differentiations that slide from official political discourse sup-porting diversity to racial slurs like "Türken raus!" (Turks get out!) written on walls in Kreuzberg, the Turkish section of Berlin. Being German is associated with being white and being clean, in contrast to the darker peoples whose color often connotes uncleanliness and, by extension, disorder and even chaos. While one might say that the Ausländer from Eastern Europe are preferred to the foreigners from the South because many of them are financially better off, their preference also has to do with their being whiter. To be an Ausländer is not just to be "fremd" but also to be unwanted, because you are different, strange, and, importantly, do not have a German name, speak German properly, behave like the Germans, look like a German man or woman, or are not Christian. (Jews and Muslims fall into this category, and each presents a special situation.)[14] There is a high priority to follow norms that go beyond a reasonable political expectation for good citizenship and conformity to standards of living. If one adds race to this constellation, then the foreigners are faced with an impossible task.

The clichés of German or Prussian notions of orderliness, cleanliness, and obedience still weigh heavily on the foreign population when trying to adhere to German behavior. The comments about foreigners, although often based on economic frustrations, are projected onto how they are subjectively experienced in everyday life by the Germans. "Es riecht hier wie eine türkische Küche" (It smells here like a Turkish kitchen—meaning a lot of garlic has been used, not traditional for German cooking) or "Es ist wie eine Judenschule" (It's like a Jewish school—meaning people are raising their voices or moving around [i.e., Germans are more orderly and controlled]). Does the transcendence of behavioral patterns that could help one triumph over such stigmatizing clichés make one German, make one belong?

But belonging means being at home, and such criteria bring us back to my original intention to unpack this metaphor on which the debate turns. "Heimat" is a term that first of all is difficult to translate simply into other languages. It has a unique meaning that is connected to a German landscape, a German history, and a feeling of being German. Used by the Nazis to glorify a specific national, ethnic, and racial quality of their people and country, the term is not only linked to home, a city, and a region but also to a sentiment attached to a place, often rural and even bucolic. In short, it has historical, topographical, and ontological status; Heimat is "abgesehen von allem anderen, immer ein vertrauter Raum" (above everything else, always a trusted space).[15]

It is ironic that the notion of Heimat and German are so territorially bound *(bodenständig)*, when German law grants nationality according to the "law of blood" *(ius sanguinis)* to those who have German parents rather than to those who are born on German soil *(ius solis)*. However, the term "space" is insufficient to describe territory in German, since it neglects the depth of emotionalism and materiality of *Boden*. The connection of "Blut und Boden" was not lost on the Nazis, who exploited a previously untainted German tradition. The eighteenth-century notion of Kultur in Germany (rather than French civilization) which was identified with inner moral development was part of a socialization process, its forms, and its norms that were passed on and identified through the family (blood) and a place (Boden) rather than through a nation-state (Kultur statt [instead of] Nation). Since German citizenship is based on blood rather than place, being born "German" links you not only to your father, mother, and grandparents but in an extended sense to all other Germans before you. What, then, of the foreigners, especially the refugees? Is it possible to gain discursively what one can practically never reach biologically?

For the German, Heimat, at least theoretically, becomes the site where past and present are connected. More recently, this notion was extended territorially to a united East and West in a new political entity that incorporates all Germans. For foreigners, this Heimat, especially in its newly constructed form, becomes an ever more uninhabitable space whose lack they bemoan in their literature. The Greek woman writer Dadi Saderi writes, "Home, homelike, homeland / I feel uneasy when I hear the words / is homelessness my home then?" Taking into account the weight of the term "Heimat," it is not surprising that the writing on "home" by foreigners seems always to be coupled with explicit or implicit reference to homelessness. Experiencing Heimat, especially in recent times, results from being absent, exiled, or rejected from the country of one's origin. One writes about it when in exile or after return, as exemplified by the fixation on the topic in the genre of so-called Gastarbeiterliteratur (foreign literature and refugee literature). The Turkish writer Aras Ören, in the final book of his trilogy about life in Kreuzberg, *Die Fremde ist auch ein Haus* (A Foreign Country Is a Home Too), "offers the aesthetic anticipation of a functioning multicultural society."[16] Yet one must admit he carefully avoids using the term "Heimat" for home. However hopeful he may be at the end, even after recounting hostility toward foreigners, Turks in Germany must still resign themselves oxymoronically to a "permanently temporary" status.[17]

Tentativeness and uncertainty pervade foreign and refugee experience in Germany. But at this point one must try to specify how the German experience is unique in comparison to other European countries.[18] The German word *Ausländer* and the discourse surrounding it classifies, organizes, and ultimately neutralizes people from over twenty countries into an undistinguishable and anonymous mass whose reification reduces them to a manageable and unthreatening lot. Paradoxically, German authorities administratively overdefine and distinguish foreigner groups—Ausländer, Aussiedler, Übersiedler, among others—while simultaneously reducing them, in Azade Seyhan's terms, to "a monocultural paradigm." On the one hand, they are distinctly differentiated in order to grant specific groups (who are not Ausländer) certain privileges and, on the other hand, to erase distinctions for any group that is not German, thus further isolating and excluding these foreigners.

From the unilateral perspective of the dominant culture, the discourse of the German is natural, obvious, universal. The strategies of this totalizing discourse are deemed adequate to the task of defining and objectifying the other. They often amount to no more than an effort to script a blueprint of theoretical categories designed to contain the ethnic subject. The polarities that mark these categories (white/nonwhite, German/foreigner) only serve to reaffirm the central position of the subject who distances, masters, and controls the other in appropriate representation.[19]

Germans construct the foreigner in word and image as something separate from themselves, in binary terms that put "the German" in a position of authority, one who can often capriciously invoke or destabilize trust through symbols of what it means to be German. The rules are constantly shifting, unpredictable, and systematically disabling. The dichotomy German and foreigner, overdetermined by the power of the former, oppresses the other and cuts off dialogue that might encourage each side to enter the symbolic worlds of the other, where cultural communicative interaction takes place. As long as the ethnic/foreigner/refugee is objectified and distanced, he or she is not a threat to the subject who holds him or her at a safe distance. Consequently, the dominating subject is protected from questioning her "natural" relationship to herself and her position as center and the other as periphery. If one believes that culture is a process and always emergent, then only through this "cultural dialogic" can new meanings about "being German" be produced.[20]

Even the well-meant efforts of liberals and leftists to ameliorate the situation—reflected in the funding of functionaries, offices, and informative material about Ausländer—seem to falter at this level where culture and discursive analysis coincide, since by continuing to use the term "Ausländer," overdetermined by conservative politicians, they perpetuate the reification of an opposition that needs to be deconstructed from within no matter how severely it has been questioned from without. Bureaucracies, even well-meaning ones, are often thwarted because, on the one hand, they are regimented and efficient and, on the other hand, interminably inadequate and capricious.

But Germany, of course, has not traditionally been regarded as a land of immigration. However, as the strongest economic power in Europe reinforced at least in numbers by the unification with the GDR, Germany's appeal has grown. Memories of the war that drove so many out of Germany fifty years ago might seem to preclude it as a choice of residence. However, any reservations Soviet Jews, Poles, or other Eastern Europeans may have are mitigated by the security in a nation that has proven its commitment in the last forty years to democratic principles or to faith in the continuing economic miracle.

In fact, it was precisely the economic miracle of the 1950s and 1960s that brought the first Gastarbeiter to Germany and laid the foundation for the subsequent history with which I am concerned here. With only limited colonial territories—Southwest Africa (now Namibia), Togo, and Cameroon, lost in 1918—Germany's confrontation with foreigners, especially those who looked so different from them, was a rather new phenomenon in the 1950s. In 1955 the official import of guest workers—recruitment migration—began when a formal contract was agreed on with Italy, and others soon followed: 1960, Spain and Greece; 1961, Turkey; 1963, Morocco; 1964, Portugal; 1965, Tunisia; and 1969, Yugoslavia. In fact, in 1964, a Portuguese guest worker was feted as the one millionth worker. Ten years later in 1973, the import of foreign workers was stopped.

The relationship of the two groups—refugees and guest workers—cannot be overlooked; the connection between economics, xenophobia, and racism is clear, according to Alfons Söllner.

We now know, not the least from German history, that a politics built around projection and xenophobia can succeed only if it manages to suggest a rational core. In the case of asylum policy, the fact is that the refugee structure changed abruptly just at the moment when West Germany was overtaken by an economic crisis and structural unemployment. Generally speaking, asylum policy is not to be separated strictly from economic policy. The mediating link between the two spheres is the policy towards foreigners, for which the stop on worker recruitment in 1973 is an important event.[21]

At this point the German population saw itself in the media as "überflutet" (flooded over) by a "Zustrom" (stream) of refugees, and the response for many was to build a verbal as well as a legal bulwark against this metaphorical flood. "Überfremdungsängste" (fears of overforeignization) dominate the rhetoric of the right-wing movements and are not negligible in legitimate conservative politics. Ausländerfeindlichkeit has become a main tenet of the right-wing Republican party's political and ideological program.[22] How is this to be explained when once the Germans welcomed these foreigners, both workers and refugees in the 1950s, and what changes took place in the twenty years between the two phases?

At this point one can only draw on historical events in Germany, such as World War II, and the particular definitions of terms like "Heimat" that set Germany apart in what is often called the "century of refugees." It was not coincidence that Adolf Hitler unleashed a war that would result in millions of displaced persons wandering across Europe in the war's aftermath, including forced laborers from the East in Germany, inmates of concentration camps, and expatriated Germans in Communist countries. More than the war itself, the ideology of Volk was tied to specifically German notions of a racial and ethnic community expressed in terms like "Lebensraum" (living space needed for Germans) and "Heim ins Reich" (the call for all Germans to return home to the Reich) that were exploited by the Nazis. This residue remains, especially when it is stimulated by new territorial claims. For example, during the demonstrations in the GDR against the Honecker regime, chants of "Wir sind das Volk" (We are the people) shifted to "Wir sind ein Volk" (We are a/one people). It not only led the way to reunification of the two Germanies but also inspired many observers to raise serious questions about the force of nationalism and its right-wing manifestations in a future unified Germany. The fact that incidences of xenophobia have risen and tensions are more strained between Germans and foreigners in the West and especially in the East since reunification reinforces fears of renewed nationalistic and ethnic fervor, not unlike what is taking place in Eastern Europe and the former Soviet Union. The government official responsible for foreigners recently announced after an attack on a home for refugees in one of the eastern provinces that "Fremdenhass" (xenophobia) arose from the unwarranted fears of citizens losing their jobs to the foreigners and "[die] Überbetonung des Nationalen" (the overemphasis on nationalism).[23]

The most "scandal[ous]" example pointed to by one critic is "that the condition of belonging to the Volk goes back to the bureaucratic remnants of National Socialism."[24] This situation is played out perversely when "das richtige Blut" (the correct blood) can only be proven by using lists compiled by the Nazis to separate those who were "rassisch Deutsch" (racially German) from those who would be sent to concentration camps. A membership document in the SS can still be used today to prove one's Germanness, that is, that one is an authentic "ethnic German." Roland Tichy pointedly concludes, "And German citizenship is built on what one knows to be such a purely racist SS definition!"[25]

IV

"Heimat" is not a place of rest; rather a transit camp for the utopia of social harmony.
—KARSTEN WITTE[26]

It is noteworthy that a critic commenting on the German term "Heimat" should use the metaphor of the "transit camp." As the middle ground or intermediary point between one country and another, rather than as the traditional notion of a safe and secure haven, Witte's definition of Heimat fits the situation of refugees in the Federal Republic. The German word *Flüchtling*, which was originally applied to those who were fleeing communism, more than the English *refugee* emphasizes the movement of leaving one's home to find another. The German Heimat becomes the literal (as well as the metaphoric) space where the inaccessibility or exclusion from social and often economic "harmony" is more the rule than the exception. Further differentiating the German terms, one critic adds that Flüchtling reflects the moral and social dimensions appropriate to its origins: "The term Asylant, since 1980 in the Duden [German dictionary]," is seen by critics as "reducing an individual to the purposes of his being in Germany. It fossilizes a social status." Further, "the concept of Asylant ignores the situation [*Lebenszusammenhang*] out of which someone has fled." The associated terms built out of this status such as "Asylschwemme" (asylum flood), "-Lawine" (asylum avalanche), "-Zeitbombe" (asylum time bomb), "-Springflut" (asylum spring flood)" or "Asylschnorrer" (asylum parasite), "-Erschleicher" (asylum black marketeer), respectively, refer to the asylum seeker either in terms of a massive wave of humanity that can be dangerous, suffocating, and even deadly or in terms of those who do nothing, are lazy, useless, expensive to the state, and generally undesirable.[27]

The descriptions of the refugee/asylum seeker are based on the very same values and standards of commodification that rendered the ethnic images so appealing in the advertisements. The depicted "social harmony" is utopian, and this world is represented in the ahistorical and neutralized images of the beautiful people. While they are frozen in permanently impressed smiles, the "real" refugees are more literally stuck in a "permanently temporary" state, not belonging to their homeland and not fitting into Germany. The real transit camps that they live in are way-stations between the past and the future, between the world they left and the world they want to enter. They are temporally and topographically imprisoned in between, in a border area whose walls are racial and economic rather than concrete.

The difficult and often dangerous political or economic conditions under which refugees left Iran, Sri Lanka, or Ethiopia make their status even more tenuous than the Ausländer, whose situation, as I have shown, is difficult enough. Although the latter chose to come to the Federal Republic, the circumstances, especially in the early years of their arrival, were encouraged by the respective governments and the Federal Republic. While the guest worker remains unwelcome and may find a return to his homeland economically and often existentially difficult, the refugee/asylum seeker, based on his official status as someone who is "politically persecuted," risks punishment or death.

The differences in terminology, Aussiedler (ethnic German), Übersiedler (refugee from the former GDR), DDR-Flüchtling (refugee from the former GDR), EG Bürger (citizen of a common market country), Gastarbeiter (guest worker), heimatlose Ausländer (homeless foreigner), Kontigentenflüchtling (status established for Vietnamese boat people based on a law of 22 July 1980), Asylberechtigte (person eligible for asylum), Asylbewerber (refugee applying for asylum), Ostblock Flüchtling (East bloc refugee), defacto Flüchtling (persons who do not fall under the legal categories of refugee but are permitted to stay), and Illegale,[28] in the descending order of status, emphasize the necessity to find ever narrower and more complicated legal definitions to cover a human reality that is expanding and that does not always fit such objectifying and limiting categories. As is often the case with minority groups, their categorization reflects political battles over power, territory, and financial allocations for other people's authority over them. Just as for the Germans who in the 1950s and 1960s "called for a work force, and got people," today it is often forgotten that foreigners and refugees are individuals, and while being classified, organized, and managed, they must also be fed, clothed, respected, and treated with the dignity that they may well have lost in their escape.

There are alternatives to this objectification and flattening out of people and their individual experiences into indistinguishable faceless masses. Poetry, novels, and film, as Michael M. J. Fischer points out in his chapter in this volume, often give a "different spin" to the critical narratives that record refugees' experiences. Such imaginative and evocative texts present the potentiality of "secondariness": to take advantage of literature's indirectness and mediation to provide opportunities to test out solutions and reactions, in some cases even through fictional coverups to protect refugees from political or physical retribution. Precisely because literature is indirect and analogous and offers models of experience or action not possible in real life, it complements more documentary or "realistic" representations to which we have often become inured. Literature can "defamiliarize" the circulating narratives that have become all too commonplace.

The recently published *In die Flucht geschlagen: Geschichten aus dem bundesdeutschen Asyl* (Forced to Flee: Histories/Stories from West German Asylum) is the only attempt in Germany that I know to chronicle in literary form the experiences of refugees from eleven countries who made it to the Federal Republic. These documentations emphasize, as was stated in the conference proposal, "the peculiar cultural inflection that this universal [trust] takes in different cultural and historical contexts."[29] As part of the "foreigner problem," these writers express in poetry and prose their common estrangement and alienation, although they come from a variety of countries. Just two examples suffice.

> Said, Iran
> *"Brief eines Emigranten"* (Letter of an emigrant)
> *Ich krieche mühsam hierher,*
> *setzte mich geräuschvoll hin,*
> *strecke meine Gefühle von mir, nehme viel Platz ein-*
> *und werde nicht benötigt.*
> (With difficulty I crawl here / sit down with a great deal of noise / spread out my feelings in front of me / take up a lot of space / and am not needed.) (91)

> V. I. S. Jeyapalan, Sri Lanka
> *Ein Raum in Frankfurt* (A space/room in Frankfurt)
> *Ein verirrter Bastard*
> *hundemüde, mit dem Gesicht nach unten im Bett,*
> *hat die Strassen durchkämmt, um zu überleben.*
> *Seine Tage kriechen hin.*
> (A lost bastard / dog-tired, with his face turned down in the bed / has combed the streets, in order to survive. / His days creep on.) (133)

Words such as *Teilung* (division), *Freiheit* (freedom), *Tod* (death), *Ort* (place), *suchen* (search), and of course *Flücht* (flight) dot the remaining pages of these refugees' testimonies to the breakdown and loss of trust. However, the subtext of all of the pieces, whether temporally or topographically, is the loss of home and the difficulty of recovering what was lost; this is the utopian vision that Witte refers to. Unfortunately, as was already clear from the German Romantics who themselves made Heimat a powerfully mythical motif, this paradisically harmonious world cannot be recaptured on this side of heaven or dream, no matter how economically well off Germany is today.

V

Solutions may emerge in Germany, as many suggest, by changing the principle of citizenship from blood to territory. This would mean that anyone born in Germany automatically would be German, as in the United States. While this would not immediately change the German attitude toward what constitutes "being German," it would lead to a dramatic increase in Germans who are "foreign" and a different color. The increased numbers of these "nonwhite/foreign Germans" would make them more visible than they are now, relegated to being markers for difference that often only reinforce the dominance of whiteness. Representation does indeed seem to constitute a greater part of racial and ethnic relations than one might think.

This transformation could change the false impression that "becoming German," at least legally, means giving up your national or ethnic identity, that is, of "integrating" in the official terminology. While the sudden transformation of approximately 700,000 children born of "foreigners"[30] in the Federal Republic into citizens would not itself solve the problem, it would contribute to the impression—when linked to dual citizenship—that one can have more than one identity simultaneously, for example, part German, part Turkish.[31] If we have learned anything from poststructuralist thinking and feminism, it is that identity is heterogeneous and constructed across time and space, situational and in constant flux. "The assumption of, or desire for, another safe place like 'home' is challenged by the realization that 'unity'—interpersonal as well as political—is itself necessarily fragmentary, itself that which is struggled for, chosen, and hence unstable by definition; it is not based on 'sameness,' and there is no perfect fit."[32] Such theorists, especially women, have also found the term "home" to capture this displacement. In the words of one critic, Afro-German women experience the dilemma even more profoundly. "[Their] most commonly shared experience . . . is the isolation that results from socialization in a predominantly all-white environment with virtually no affirmation of a 'double identity.' An identity of 'feeling neither Black nor White' (Oguntoye, Opitz, and Schulz 1986:155) is often accompanied by a consciousness of having the (only) 'outsider' position. . . . Due to their imposed status as 'outsiders' in German society, many of these Afro-German women express anger and loss at being denied a 'feeling of community' ('Heimatgefühl')."[33]

While most foreigners/refugees do not need theory to tell them what they already experience, as the lives of these Afro-German women show, it might be salubrious for "the Germans" to confront their own heterogeneity, racially as well as politically. They could see it at least as a site from which they make decisions, write laws, and expound discourses on how to treat foreigners in legal and racial terms. It must be made easier for foreigners in general to get citizenship and for refugees to be granted asylum, for the former to get double citizenship at least until the age of eighteen and for the latter to be able to work while waiting for a decision about asylum. With an additional million "Germans," at least in successive generations, it would be possible to transform the German population into a legal and ethnic mixture. Black or brown faces are not yet seen in positions of authority, for example, as public officials elected by foreigners, as policemen, or as announcers in the media. When Turks or Tamils are visible in "real" identifiable situations in everyday German life and not only as "types" on billboards that conceal racism and xenophobia, then perhaps there can be a change in German attitudes toward foreigners. Germany needs immigration laws in addition to asylum laws.

While the term "Ausländer" may continue to designate someone who is foreign, it need not represent a choice between two alternatives: on the one hand, difference that leads to an exclusionary or totalizing nationalism, regionalism, or ethnicity, or, on the other hand, an internationalism that literally whitewashes away specificity and individuality. If "home" could be accepted as an ambivalent and dynamic notion, then those seeking home, Germans as well as foreigners, might find there to be more space provided for by an increasingly porous term that was expanding to accommodate a more heterogeneous German population. It remains to be seen, however, if a shift can be made from such a discursive strategy to the materiality of this position. It also remains to be seen if a united Germany burdened by economic hardship that causes tensions between East and West, German and foreigner, can overcome divisiveness and division and make a home, if not a Heimat, for its many peoples.

NOTES

I would like to thank Rekha Kamath, Ewald Böhlke, and Ulla Haselstein for offering constructive suggestions that have been incorporated into this chapter.

1. " 'Lieber sterben als nach Sachsen' " (We'd Rather Die than Go to Saxony), *Der Spiegel*, no. 40 (30 September 1991): 30.

2. Ibid.

3. " 'Sie kommen, ob wir wollen oder nicht' " (They come whether we want them or not), *Der Spiegel*, no. 15 (6 April 1992):26.

4. Stated by the psychologist Birgit Rommelsbacher in an interview entitled "Rassismus Ost und West schaukeln sich hoch" (Racism, East and West, Increases Dramatically), *Die Tageszeitung*, 11 February 1992, 11.

5. This point is often used against foreigners, since they are accused of not wanting to assimilate or integrate with the Germans. The Turkish ghetto of Kreuzberg exemplifies for many Germans the Turks' self-chosen segregation. It is worth noting that a number of articles about foreigners and particularly Turks use a picture of the nameplates in a Kreuzberg building, all with Turkish names, as if this is to prove that they either want to live together or have any choice (since it is difficult or impossible for them to get apartments elsewhere) and that their Turkish names represent foreignness, rather than Germanness.

6. For more detail on the difficulty of "becoming German," also see Klimt 1989, where she discusses her work with Portuguese migrants in Germany.

The Peter Stuyvesant cigarette company continued its "multicultural" theme in a new advertising campaign featuring billboards and a contest. The billboards show a foreign face with the appropriate foreign background and the slogans, "Komm, verstehe Ireland" [Come, understand Ireland], "Komm, erlebe die Weite" [Come, experience the amplitude], or "Komm, meditier mit mir" [Come, meditate with me]. The competition gives one the chance to spend two weeks with an Eskimo family, an Egyptian ship pilot, a flying farmer in Australia, an Irish priest, or a Japanese monk.

The Benetton campaign is discussed in detail in chapter 2, "Europa in den United Colors of Benetton: Ein Kulturmarktbericht," in Claus Leggewie, *MULTI KULTI: Spielregeln für die Vielvölkerrepublik* (Berlin: Rotbuch, 1990):26–36.

7. The statistics have been compiled from a number of excellent studies that are useful as sources, e.g., Tichy 1990; Meinhardt 1990; Hönekopp 1991.

Recent statistics establish the number of citizens with "non-German citizenship" at 4.6

million. Two-thirds of these have lived in Germany for more than ten years. Over 70% of their children under sixteen have been born in the Federal Republic of Germany (FRG).

8. See Oguntoye, Opitz, and Schulz 1986; Obermeier 1989:172–180. Obermeier's essay appears in a special issue of the *New German Critique,* "Minorities in German Culture," referred to hereafter as *NGC.*

9. The sociologist Dieter Thränhardt develops these categories in his article, "Patterns of Organization of Ethnic Minorities," *NGC* (Winter 1989):13.

10. A number of studies have been done on this term and its meanings, e.g., Seliger 1987; Greverus 1979; Dericum and Wambolt 1987; Bienek 1985.

11. This office counsels foreigners and puts out a great deal of material on citizenship, marriage, asylum laws, prejudice, and the various groups of foreigners living in Berlin. It also puts out its own monthly magazine, *Top: Berlin International-Ein Informationsforum,* which has information on meetings, films, changes in laws, and book publications.

12. In the period before German unification, organizations representing die Vertriebenen (those who were pushed out), who are made up largely of Aussiedler, lobbied very hard to keep Chancellor Helmut Kohl from "giving up" the Polish land and boundaries that were formally "German." Until it became clear that the position was internationally untenable, Kohl skirted the issue because he thought he and his party, the Christian Democrats, needed the support of these groups to win elections. Before coming to Germany, many of these Aussiedler spoke of West Germany as "meine Heimat" to which they "zurückkehren wollen" (wanted to return) ("Aussiedler," 8–9. The brochures of one of these organizations is called, in fact, "Ihre Heimat sind wir" [We are your homeland]).

13. For the former East Germans, the Übersiedler, the situation is unique. Up until 1961 approximately 3.3 million GDR citizens fled to the West. When this access was closed off by the building of the Wall, those who wanted to leave could either legally file a petition, at great cost to one's personal life, or illegally escape over the Wall, under the ground, or hidden in the trunk of a car. For those privileged enough to travel to the West, a decision to stay there would mean hardship for their families remaining in the East. These "refugees" (they were called "Flüchtling") who arrived in the West were greeted as heroes (especially if they escaped dramatically) and like the Aussiedler immediately received special benefits, e.g., counseling, housing, jobs, money, language courses, and voting rights. In August and September 1989, the first massive exodus from the GDR since the early sixties began when Hungary opened its borders with Austria and thousands of GDR citizens left their *homeland* for West Germany.

Even at departure, GDR citizens, whether they wanted to stay or not, had been brought up to identify with the GDR, to see themselves as citizens of the GDR, and to see it as their home. I would venture to say that GDR citizens at that time, whether old (knowing prewar Germany) or young (only knowing the GDR), would identify themselves as Germans when they would not identify themselves as GDR citizens but never as citizens of the FRG. By going to West Germany, East Germans attached themselves to a suprapolitical notion of Germanness and West Germans could celebrate their own German identity when they looked in the faces of their fellow (East) Germans, who had been barred from participating completely in this identification. This was illustrated most dramatically on November 9, 1989, when the Wall came down and thousands of East Berliners rushed into West Berlin. Aside from celebrating freedom to travel to the West, the revelry and euphoria of that evening and the following days, before German unity was even a realistic option, represented the reunification of German and German in the city whose division had continually represented the separation of a people who had once been together as a nation. It was in fact this prefix *re-* (*wieder* in German) that later symbolized in the *Wieder-vereinigung* (reunification) the problematic territorial, historical, and national link to a previously unified German nation.

With reunification, Germany could be whole again; all Germans could be safely housed (*beheimatet*) in one nation-state. This equation of one people, one country strengthened those who would exclude people who did not fit under this racial or ethnic umbrella. While German racial ideology of the Nazi years appears to be minimized (*verharmlost*) by forgetting this period in history, it ironically surfaces in right-wing ideology and remains undetected in conservative and even liberal discourses, such as the advertisements with which I began this chapter. The reification of Ausländer was reinforced when Germany's population swelled by 16 million GDR citizens, the majority of whom voted for reunification. Some cynically call it *Anschluss,* referring to Hitler's 1938 welcomed "takeover" of Austria with Germany.

14. Because of Germany's Nazi past, the German Jews who live in Germany today (only around 15% of the small Jewish population) are still regarded by many as not quite German, even as foreign, although they are virtually indistinguishable from the rest of the German population. For Muslims, the situation is much more serious, since much of the resentment against Ausländer is connected to the fact that many of them are Muslim and do not fit into the Christian traditions associated with being German. For a very insightful discussion of the notion of home(land) and Islam, see Morley and Robbins 1990:1–23.

15. Harry Pross, in Dericum and Wambolt 1987:14.

16. Heidrun Suhr, *"Ausländerliteratur:* Minority Literature in the Federal Republic of Germany," *NGC* (Winter 1989): 87. This example and the one above from Dadi Saderi are also cited from this article, p. 71. The article also provides a very useful bibliography for the subject.

17. This category, used by an anthropologist to describe the status of Portuguese migrant workers in Germany, can also be applied to Turks and other foreigners of the "strange" and "rejected" classification. See Andrea C. Klimt, "Returning 'Home': Portuguese Migrant Notions of Temporariness, Permanence, and Commitment," *NGC* (Winter 1989): 47–70.

18. Although I am not able to go into comparative analysis in the limited space here, this chapter has shown that comparisons to other European countries are necessary for assessing the situation and status of Germany's refugees and foreigners. Especially when one bristles at the use of categories like "racist" to characterize particular aspects of German policy toward foreigners, it is easy to find similar examples of racism in France, for example. Although racism is rampant in France, the French grant refugees and foreigners very different privileges of citizenship that have to do with French colonial history and a different notion of the nation-state. It should also be mentioned here that the percentage of foreigners in the Federal Republic (1990) was 7%, which placed it in the middle between eight other European countries (Luxembourg, 26.5%; Switzerland, 15% (with seasonal workers 25%); Belgium, 8.6%; France, 8%; Sweden, 4.6%; England, 4.5%; Austria, 3.9%; and Holland, 3.8%). These statistics are from Tichy 1990: 25 in a section appropriately entitled "Wie schwer es ist, Deutscher zu werden" (How difficult it is to become a German). Ger-

many and Switzerland are two of the countries where it is most difficult and most complicated to get citizenship. I also recommend the chapter in Meinhardt, "Migration and Rassismus," 80–99.

19. Azade Seyhan, "Introduction," *NGC* (Winter 1989): 3–4.

20. See a more detailed discussion of trust and the semiotics of culture in the conference proposal by Daniel and Knudsen, "Trust and the Refugee Experience," 2d draft (29 September 1989), 11–12. This discussion, of course, only summarizes theories of cultural semiotics and interpretive ethnography popular today in cultural studies.

21. Söllner, *NGC* (Winter 1989): 149.

22. In recent election material of the Republican party, the headline read, "Berlin muss Deutsch bleiben!" (Berlin must stay German!) The text is accompanied by an inflammatory photo of a Turkish man with arms raised defiantly signifying protest or victory. Helmeted policeman ready for "battle" are also in the scene.

23. "Ausländerbeauftragte mahnt die Politiker," *Berliner Morgenpost*, 10 March 1991, 4.

24. Tichy 1990:153.

25. Tichy 1990:32.

26. Witte, cited by Miriam Hansen, "Dossier on *'Heimat'*" in *NGC*, no. 36 (Fall 1985): 7. Witte refers here, as do other critics in this special issue of *NGC*, to the $15\frac{1}{2}$-hour film by the German filmmaker Edgar Reitz. It was released in 1984 as an eleven-part TV series in Germany and was shown the next year in the United States. The film is controversial in part for the same reasons that the term itself is so problematic for becoming German. It raises questions about the use and abuse of history and its representations that both affirm and deny everyday experiences and memories of Germans.

Witte's further definition of *Heimat* in the context of this chapter supports the position I am taking: " *'Heimat'* always implies a totalizing grasp, whether directed towards a territory or towards the integration of those who speak a common language. At the same time, *'Heimat'* is conceivable as the locus of a diversity which has succumbed to unification [this was written before 3 October 1989], a non-territorial space which no longer asserts a presence but remains a trace of the past. *Heimat* would signify an elsewhere, a memory of origin for those who went away" (ibid.).

27. Anja Tuckerman 1989:21.

28. I use Tichy's (1990:38–39) categories here. The additional term *Scheinasylant* (false asylum seeker) is also often used.

29. Daniel and Knudsen 1989:7.

30. Tichy 1990:156.

31. The most recent information I have found at the time of completing this article (April 1991) established that there are 4.6 million people in Germany with "non-German citizenship." "Two-thirds of these have lived there for over 10 years. Over 70% of their children under 16 were born in the Federal Republic." The article continues, "In fact, we are dealing with immigrants [*Einwanderer*]. Former 'guest workers' and their families have already become inhabitants [*Inländer*]—without German citizenship nor the prospect for naturalization." The article, published in the liberal *Frankfurter Rundschau* (4 April 1991, 4), was also citing the progressive organization League for Human Rights and their call for facilitating the naturalization process, which as it is now *"spaltet Ausländer und Deutsche"* (splits foreigners and Germans). This formulation supports my argument to break down the

dichotomy between these two groups and these two terms. They also note that the new *Ausländergesetze* (laws for foreigners) may make it somewhat easier for young *Inländer* to get citizenship, but it does not deal adequately with the issue of dual citizenship. Finally, it states that in comparison with neighboring countries the FRG has the lowest rate of naturalization.

32. Biddy Martin and Chandra Talpade Mohanty (1986:208) develop their argument about identity politics through Minnie Bruce Pratt's "Identity: Skin Blood Heart," the autobiographical narrative of a "white, middle-class, Christian-raised southern . . . lesbian."

The problem of being a Turkish woman in Germany has received special attention, with articles in major magazines like *Der Spiegel* and books of interviews such as Franger 1984.

33. Obermeier 1989:175.

REFERENCES

Bienek, Horst, ed.
1985   *Heimat: Neue Erkundungen eines alten Themas.* Munich: Hanser.
Daniel, E. Valentine, and John Chr. Knudsen
1989   "Trust and the Refugee Experience: A Proposal for a Workshop at the United Nations University, World Institute for Development Economics Research." Manuscript.
Dericum, Christa, and Philipp Wambolt, eds.
1987   *Heimat und Heimatlosigkeit.* Berlin: Karin Kramer Verlag.
Franger, Gaby, ed.
1984   *Wir haben es anders vorgestellt: Türkische Frauen in der Bundesrepublik* (We Imagined It to Be Different: Turkish Women in the Federal Republic). Frankfurt: Fischer.
Greverus, Maria
1979   *Auf der Suche nach Heimat.* Munich: Beck.
Kinzer, Stephen
1992   "Far Right Gains Sharply in German State Elections." *New York Times,* 6 April, A1, A6.
Klimt, Andrea
1989   "Returning 'Home': Portuguese Migrant Notions of Temporariness, Permanence, and Commitment." *New German Critique* (Winter): 47–70.
Hönekopp, Elmar
1991   Report. Conference of Ministers on the Movement of Persons Coming from Central and Eastern European Countries. Vienna: 24–25 January.
Leggewie, Claus
1990   "Europa in den United Colors of Benetton: Ein Kulturmarktbericht." In *MULTIKULTI: Spiegelregeln für die Vielvölkerrepublik,* 26–36. Berlin: Rotbuch.
Lowenthal, David
1985   *The Past Is a Foreign Country.* Cambridge: Cambridge University Press.
Martin, Biddy, and Chandra Talpade Mohanty
1986   "Feminist Politics: What's Home Got to Do With It?" *Feminist Studies / Critical Studies,* ed. Teresa de Lauretis, 191–212. Bloomington: Indiana University Press.

Meinhardt, Rolf, ed.
    1990   *Türken raus? Oder Verteidigt den sozialen Frieden.* Reinbek bei Hamburg: Piper.
Morley, David, and Kevin Robbins
    1990   "No Place Like Heimat: Images of Home(land) in European Culture." *New Formations* 12 (Winter): 1–23.
Obermeier, Karen
    1989   "Afro-German Women: Recording Their Own History." *New German Critique* (Winter): 10–27.
Oguntoye, Katharina, May Opitz, and Dagmar Schulz, eds.
    1986   *Farbe Bekennen: Afro-deutsche Frauen auf den Spuren ihrer Geschichte.* Berlin: Orlando Frauenverlag.
Pross, Harry
    1987   "Heimat auf den Begriff gebracht." *Heimat und Heimatlosigkeit,* eds. Christa Dericum and Philipp Wambolt, 11–22. Berlin: Karin Kramer Verlag.
Räthzel, Nora
    1991   "Germany: One Race, One Nation?" *Race and Class* 32 (3): 46–47.
Seliger, H. W., ed.
    1987   *The Concept of Heimat in Contemporary German Literature.* Munich: Iudicium.
Seyhan, Azade
    1989   "Introduction." *New German Critique* (Winter): 3–10.
Söllner, Alfons
    1989   "The Politics of Asylum." *New German Critique* (Winter): 127–155.
Suhr, Heidrun
    1989   "*Ausländerliteratur:* Minority Literature in the Federal Republic of Germany." *New German Critique* (Winter): 71–104.
Tichy, Roland
    1990   *Ausländer rein! Warum es kein 'Ausländerproblem' gibt.* Munich: Piper.
Thränhardt, Dieter
    1989   "Patterns of Organization of Ethnic Minorities." *New German Critique* (Winter): 10–27.
Tuckerman, Anja
    1989   "Vorwort." In *Die Flucht geschlagen: Geschichten as dem bundesdeutschen Asyl,* 11–22. Frankfurt: Luchterhand.

SEVEN

Starting Over:
How, What, and for Whom Does One
Write about Refugees? The Poetics and
Politics of Refugee Film as Ethnographic
Access in a Media-saturated World

Michael M. J. Fischer

LANGUAGES, PSYCHOLOGIES, AND MEDIA
OF COMMUNICATION

In examining the refugee experience, either second hand or by directly interviewing survivors, the social scientist is immediately struck by how familiar it all sounds.
—STEPHEN L. KELLER (1975)

In the nearly twenty years since Stephen Keller penned those words in his pioneering study of the refugees of the partitioning of India and Pakistan, we have continued to be inundated with accounts and news broadcasts of refugees. Refugees, indeed, have become a major sociological category of the twentieth century, one to which events of unprecedented scale have marked certain generic terms with prototypical horror and iconic imagery: "the massacre" (Armenians), "the Holocaust" (Jews), "displaced persons" (Europeans), all of which occurred in the first half of the century. To these have now been added innumerable others identified usually by national tags: Palestinians, Cambodians, Vietnamese, Cubans, Ethiopians, Biafrans, Tamils, and so forth.

Indeed, practically no society in the world—with the possible exception of North America, Australia, Scandinavia, and Switzerland—can be said to have escaped fundamental disruption and reorganization caused by warfare and global restratification during the course of this century. Although the category "refugee" remains an important legal one, both for humanitarian relief work and for immigration policies, as a sociological category it threatens to become archaic amid the various kinds of migrant flows as the world reshuffles populations. Three kinds of refugees are often separated in the older literature: refugees from warfare or civil war, refugees from natural disasters such as floods or earthquakes, and economic migrants (who are always mentioned, if only to be then excluded, as if to mark the instability of the category itself). Refugees are usually those who must flee their nations of origin, but surely internal refugees, those forced into temporary camps because of communal riots (e.g., in India, or famine refugees triaged by political manipulation in Ethiopia), suffer similar problems. And so many categories blur. Even in terms of psychology, Keller (1975:266) notes the heterogeneity of the category in terms of causes, albeit finding uniformities in psychology across the types: "What the [Punjabi] refugees underwent, what they thought about and felt, and how they acted in situations of extreme stress directly parallels the accounts we have from inmates of concentration camps, the survivors of Hiroshima and Nagasaki, and those people who have lived through large scale disasters such as explosions, floods, and tornadoes."

But things do change, though it is not always clear what is a real difference that makes a difference. The other day, I began reading through a packet of letters between my father, a refugee from Vienna, and my uncle, who spent time in an English internment camp. I suppose I was hoping for some description of what the internment camp was like. What I got instead was the poignancy of letter writing: the lament for relatives one was sure were no longer alive, the loss of sense of belonging, the difficulties of finding money for the basic necessities, the happiness of having new children, and the pain of one's nephews and nieces being where one could not watch them grow. In sum, the sense of a fragmented world held together fragilely by intermittent bits of paper that it took great effort to find the time to write. How different I thought, for my Iranian friends, who can pick up a telephone. And then as a social scientist: What difference, in fact, does this technological change make? Does it make any? How important is the content of the cultural forms that are used to express the experiences that refugees go through? Of what influence are the previous iconographies of refugees on the ways in which the world responds?

What is needed is a starting over, much as refugees themselves need to start over, by perhaps taking into account the ways in which refugees represent themselves and are represented. This chapter is a preliminary effort to listen to refugees in a slightly oblique way, but one that (a) pays attention to the ways in which the media intervene in the creation of public cultures and politics; (b) views the world as a nonhomogenizing global network in which massive demographic movements are occurring which affect both national politics and international cultural flows in interactive ways; and (c) problematizes the sentimental essentializing categories of romanticism that certain kinds of refugees become entrapped by and attempt to use to gain sympathy with little effect, especially those romantic tropes of essential and exclusive connection between soil and identity, the tropes of authenticity or autochthony. Such terms inevitably fall apart as soon as they are subjected to a historicizing gaze, and their mobilization invariably are indexes of either receding agrarian pasts or nationalistic ideologies whose deployment in a fast-pluralizing world is archaic and violence inducing.

Let me begin with three methodological examples from film to illustrate the importance of "listening." The first has to do with the ways in which the visual media are often not used analytically and especially the ways in which dominant news broadcasts obfuscate; the second has to do with the ways in which juxtaposition can be used in film as a powerful form of cultural critique; the third has to do with the ways in which these media can be used by refugees to intervene in the international public culture that affects their future. I am especially interested in the cultural information that film can deliver about the ways in which people view themselves. Among the things most poorly developed in the literature are the frames of narration—the cultural resources—that refugees bring with them. At issue is figuring out ways to make use of such resources but also to create a public environment that can help facilitate refugees' starting over. For those refugee populations caught in camps with no place to go, perhaps the best help is shedding light on the political forces that keep them locked there. For refugees in Europe facing racist hostilities, or in America engaging in escalating "identity politics," the task is perhaps first to deconstruct the essentializing of romantic tropes that still power nationalist chauvinisms and fears and next to expose the economic bottlenecks that turn communities into desperate competitors (imagined or real). If this battle can be fought in Europe and America to demonstrate that multiple communities can share the same space and that individuals can assert multiple identities, then perhaps similar grounds for moral argument can be established elsewhere, where today the old calls of nationalist exclusivity are rising again. With the collapse of the cold war bipolar hostilities, there is a slim chance that regional restructurings might provide hopeful futures for communities that now seem to threaten each other.

The semiotics of trust play ambivalent roles in these narratives. On the practical level, trust is often a category attributed to American gullibility, or to the sensibilities of comfortable, rich Europeans, or to limited groups of clinicians and therapists who over time build up rapport. On the cosmic level, soteriologies both theistic and karmic have been deeply shaken. Jean-François Lyotard, drawing on Emanuel Levinas and others, has suggested that we need to construct a language of immemorials (as opposed to inert memorials to past traumas that freeze into clichés and arrested thought), an ethnography of differands (acknowledging perspectives that do not translate into one another), of blocking together visual figurations and verbal discourses that do not allow arrests (Readings 1991). This is a call to a world that can no longer find refuge in fantasies of homogeneity. Stephen Tyler (1986), in a different vein, suggests that ethnography itself needs to become therapeutic rather than encyclopedic.

I will draw on several "ethnically" defined examples, focusing on film and secondarily but complementarily on novels, as sources for the "cultural hermeneutics" in guiding (a) activity in new lives and (b) articulation of refugees' desire for respect and trust from their host communities. The chapter is an attempt to discover if film and literary critique can be turned to more than mere descriptive or analytic ends: as access to languages of refugees with different cultural riches. The two modes of communication, film and written fiction, may work differentially; they may complement rather than repeat or reinforce each other.

Three Preliminary Methodological Examples

First, compare Ted Koppel's (31 May 1992) "Nightline" account of the Los Angeles riots with Mike Davis's account in the *Nation* (5 April 1992). Davis analyzes these riots much as anthropologists have analyzed many previous ones: the targets of destruction are not random. Some two thousand shops were burned in Los Angeles; most were Korean. The first to be attacked (though, ironically, it survived) was the store in which a black girl, Latasha Hawkins, had been shot months earlier by a Korean storekeeper in a dispute over a $1.79 purchase. "For our sister Latasha," black youths on the street would tell Davis during the riots. Moreover, Davis points out, both in the 1965 Watts riots and now in the South Central riots, no Los Angeles Police Department trooper was killed and very few sustained injuries (in contrast to the slogans on the walls urging the killing of cops). In these and other ways, the riot showed itself to be systematically patterned. But for Koppel, there was no pattern, just anarchy. His program, for instance, had no map to show which shops burned.

The point, of course, is an obvious one and holds as well for the television coverage of the Gulf War against Iraq: the film-television-video medium can be used to sanitize and depoliticize events (e.g., there could have been footage of the carnage of Iraqi soldiers through the night-vision cameras of the American helicopter gunships). Hence the importance of getting filmic material produced and scripted by refugees themselves, or by members of their communities. (This is what in cultural studies is being called "positionality": who is speaking, what perspective is being taken, and how is the editing of the narratives and visuals being done?)

Second, among the strongest cultural criticism techniques that film can make are "juxtapositions" of contrasting points of view. Good examples are the opening classroom scene in *Boyz 'N the Hood*, shot from the point of view of black children listening to a white teacher telling them about their ancestors, the Pilgrims in Massachusetts, and the scenes in *Europa, Europa*, in which we watch, through his eyes, a Jewish lad forced to recite the catechisms of first the Communists and then the Nazis, both denying his identity.

Third, film can deliver more than powerful cultural criticism. It can reshape perception and set the terms of debate. The Kayapo Indians of the Amazon basin have been given video cameras and have used them to record interactions with Brazilian officials, thus making the international community witness and placing the Brazilian state on the defensive in ways that could not be achieved without the camera.

Questions: Can film and video be used to counter the sanitized Ted Koppel–style news broadcasting and to intervene on behalf of refugees in ways that redefine the politics of their home countries, their countries of transit, and their host countries? Can film be used as a way to help refugees externalize and narrate their experiences, as a therapeutic for themselves and as a political tool to empower themselves in a new world?

There are then, to recapitulate, several general issues. First, we no longer live in a world of stable traditional societies ephemerally disrupted by singular, localized traumas. Rather, our world is one in which massive social trauma requires the reconstruction of civil societies at large in new pluralist ways. Second, the repetitiveness of refugee accounts and the secondariness of accounts in a world of prior circulating images about refugees mean that we need to pay attention to the cultural tools that refugees possess which allow them to break out of trauma. We need to pay attention to the cultural forms used by social actors, not treating them as uniform victims but recognizing their philosophies and narratives of survival and reenergization, their modes of mourning and working through trauma, the dynamics of how second and third generations deal with traumas, their forms of diaspora networks and communications, and the changing social forms of violence they have endured. Finally, we need to pay attention to the semiotics of trust, not as a static psychological category that gets ruptured and repaired but as a field of dynamic strategizing and cultural formations. Film can help both as a cultural access and as a tool of intervention and therapy, if attention is paid to the positionality of the filmmakers as well as the cultural forms drawn on to construct the film.

CULTURAL LANGUAGES OF REFUGEE FILM

Iranians: Distrust and Persian Finesse

MF: Tell me about trust.

MA: Trust? *Etemad* [the Arabic term used in Persian and Turkish], as in *amud,* the central pillar that holds up a tent, and *etminan,* "to be sure about"? No, there's no trust here among Iranians in exile. It is not only the different political factions, or the legacy of the shah's secret police, and now Khomeini's secret police and informers. Even in business we trust Americans more than Iranians. Let me tell you the list of scams that Iranians play on each other. . . . And of course there is a kind of cutthroat competition in the carpet business here that would not be possible in the Tehran bazaar where guilds knew everyone's business and regulated practices. There is of course also a litigiousness that Iranians, like other immigrants, have learned to play in the States, including manipulation of bankruptcy laws, where you declare bankruptcy and then buy your property back at the foreclosure sale at half-price.

There are two lessons from this brief exchange. First, refugees and immigrants need to negotiate not only in a strange culture but even among themselves in a "loose social structure" wherein information about others is much harder to come by than in Iran, where one always knew someone who knew the other party and could both supply information and exercise a kind of moral check. This applies to negotiating marriages and funerals and other core identity ritual events as well as to more profane activities (Fischer and Abedi 1990: chap. 5). Second, the tonalities of this exchange, which would need to be heard, set up a classic picaresque or tragicomic set of premises, which can be richly exploited in film and needs to be set off against the deep tragic laments and language of exile out of which Iranians build much of their most profound poetry and fiction. The two forms—comedy and tragedy—perform quite different functions: the comedy is a teaching device for negotiating the pitfalls and misunderstandings of the real world and is present and future oriented; tragedy is a more meditative device for expressing the pain of separation, nostalgia, and grief and is more past oriented. This duality fits as well with the split between the inner *(batin),* private, real, melancholic sense of gravitas as opposed to the exuberant public *(zahir)* masques necessary in a corrupt, superficially pleasurable world of appearances, where cleverness *(zerangi)* is required.

A study done in California shortly after the Islamic revolution of 1978 using Iranian psychiatrists and a few of their cases as a probe suggested that depression and grief at separation from home were expressed in cultural forms of sadness that were parallel to, or drew on, the religious mourning frames of Shi'ism even if people were not particularly religious. The Karbala story of mourning for the martyrdom of Imam Husain provides modes for expressing grief that can be of use when people are stunned by loss and have no words of their own (e.g., the case of the bereaved husband of a murder victim in Fischer and Abedi 1990:272). More recent studies of the semiotics of the television programs produced by the exile community in Los Angeles describe a split imago. On the one hand, program logos and opening/closing clips are drawn from ancient pre-Islamic motifs, from Pahlavi era motifs, or from Albert Lamorisee's celebratory film, *The Lover's Wind* (ca. 1975). These and other techniques, says Hamid Naficy, fetishize Iran as "a ruined land in the throes of death." There was the constant "depiction of the body in crisis: bodies maimed by torture and bodies wounded and destroyed in the war with Iraq" in news clips; in interviews with Mujaheddin and others who could show scars; in accounts of assassinations, hangings, stonings, raping of women, shortages, and disruption of utilities; and in hyperbolic descriptions of Iran as "a total ruin and a vast cemetery." Naficy notes that it is the destruction that is foregrounded and a tragic sense of helplessness that is promoted. "Even when action and resistance is shown, it is injected with tragedy. . . . We see demonstrations in Los Angeles . . . accompanied by an extradiegetic song on the soundtrack . . . whose refrain is, 'lonely homeland, indigent homeland.' Sometimes such visual or verbal invocations of home as a ruin [are] inappropriate. . . . If Islamic Iran is designated as a signified for 'ruin,' then any picture of ruins will do" (Naficy 1988: 8).

On the other hand, if the tragic mode dominates the programming, the interstitial commercials are celebrations of consumer capitalism, masking "the inner pain and displacing it with pleasure of consumption," including "reconstruction

and renewal of the self . . . from cosmetic plastic surgery to transformation of one's
legal status" (ibid., 9). Naficy notes a growing orgy of this sort of displacement by
1987 when some programs were three-fourths commercials. And two other techniques of split imago reinforced these psychological processes: singers on music
videos were split into superimposed figures and pastiche magazine formats constantly juxtaposed "self-other, home-exile, here-there, and present-past" (ibid., 10).
Repetition and sensory overload, Naficy hypothesizes, turn these features into a
"form of closing the self off from the threatening outside . . . tantamount to
whistling in the dark when alone or carrying a boom box" (ibid., 12).

Iranians are only a decade-old refugee group, and already their cultural forms
may have gone through a cycle of grief work from mourning to a split imago nostalgia to a current optimism with the albeit still tentative stabilization of power in
Tehran. At least the more successful feel that they can be participants in a global
market between Iran and the United States. Many are beginning to buy land in
Iran, commenting, "Inja khuneh khaleh nist" (One's aunt's house is not here).
There is, of course, a younger generation now, for whom Iran is primarily their
parents, memories, and a smattering of Persian.

Comedy, at least in Iranian film (Fischer 1984), can be a powerful vehicle for
displaying misunderstandings of cultural forms and thereby the forms themselves.
Two refugee films and two videos are initial examples. *Agha-ye Avareh* (Mr. Exile) is
a comic video about immigration to California, composed of a series of skits that
follow an Iranian Charlie Chaplin-like Everyman in suit coat, loosened tie, and
canvas shoes carrying a green flight bag as he tries to find a house to rent, get a
job, and so forth. Events in Iran intervene not only in his nightmares of Khomeini,
revolutionary demonstrations, and sounds of the Iran-Iraq warfare but also in his
rejection by Pakistani, Indian, and Mexican employers and even by redneck winos,
because he is an Iranian. Trust? There is none, neither from the other immigrant
groups nor from various Iranians who appear to help but actually take advantage
of him. Ghassem Ebrahamian's film, *The Suitors,* is a polished weaving of such situation comedy skits into a deadpan black humor story about a working-class *hajji*
who returns from Iran to New York with a young bride. Four young male friends
throw a party for him; they slaughter a sheep in their apartment bathtub, and its
blood drips into the apartment below causing the superintendent to fear an Iranian terrorist cell. A police SWAT team clears the building, storms the apartment,
and kills Hajji, leaving Hajji's widow in the clutches of his four young friends. One
of these, together with Hajji's business partner, essentially kidnaps the young
woman in an effort to marry her and thereby claim the insurance. She escapes
with the aid of another of the young men and attempts to fly to Europe in a suitcase but, on the runway with the other baggage, thinks better of flying in the hold,
unzips the suitcase from inside, and climbs out, only to face New York again without baggage, without friends, without passport or papers.

The appeal of the film is in the emotional tonalities and familiarity of the set
pieces: the U.S. immigration official who insists on seeing the face (all the way to

the ear) of Hajji's wife (humiliation); the reminiscence scenes about the gourmet delights of breakfasting on sheep's head soup (nostalgia); the comic slaughtering of the sheep in the bathtub complete with arguments about which way to face the animal toward Mecca and incompetence with the knife (wry self-deprecation); the police scenes with the hapless Iranians trying to maintain their innocence, dignity, and rights in the face of the New York police; Hajji's funeral *(porseh)*, with the competition of the young men to attach the widow to themselves (gender warfare, familial discourse, and greed for the inheritance), and her attempts to escape.

The scenes are neatly stitched together with a kind of symbolic logic, done in neither slapstick comedy nor full melodrama. There are playful Freudian clichés (the street lads who try to pick her up taunt her with a huge snake; in the final airport scene, the camera focuses for a second on a cat carrier, a pussy in a cage). And there are deft uses of American counterpoint background details: the initial airport scene focuses ever so briefly on passing Hasidim, surely as weird-looking as Hajji in his three-day growth, wool cap, and collarless worker's shirt, laden with suitcases and samovar, followed by a young chadored woman; there is a scene of Miryam, the widow, lounging in the apartment in her slip, reading fashion magazines, while the radio spews out adult dating ads (in a language she does not understand); the scene of the blood dripping into the apartment of Lou, the building supervisor, brilliantly has Lou listening to a Christian fundamentalist preacher, fully as wackily paranoid as Lou's and the New York policemen's fantasies about Iranians as terrorists; and the television show watched by the gas station attendant is an apt counterpoint to the deadly dating game being played at the same time with the widow by Hajji's partner and the young man he has selected to marry her.

Parviz Sayyad's film, *The Mission,* portrays the human, ethical, and ideological negotiations of royalists and revolutionaries in New York, where again the attraction of the film is in the emotional tone of the set-piece scenes and the moral human interactions of the lead characters within the story of an idealistic young man sent by the Khomeini regime to assassinate a former SAVAK (secret police) colonel. Reza Alamehzadeh's *The Guests of Hotel Astoria* is a portrait of Iranians stranded in Istanbul waiting for visas, the complicated stratagems and strategies they are forced to employ, and the complex learning experiences of who (not) to trust.

Gholem Hossein Sa'edi's video, *Othello in Wonderland,* is a satire of how producing a Shakespeare play under the Islamic Republic would lead not merely to censorship by the mullahs but also to their playing all the roles themselves and in the end turning the action into a passion play of martyrdom. It gets funnier and funnier as the action proceeds, although its message is quite dark. From his exile, Sa'edi has written as well a trilogy of powerfully enigmatic allegories on the revolution and a series of essays on the dark theatricalization of the state in Iran and the conditions of being a refugee in exile. In these, he articulates perhaps as powerfully as anyone a range of Persian terms, differentiating between those refugees who are exiles *(avareh)* and those who are migrants *(muhajir).*

The latter are those who can assimilate in their host culture; but avareh feel themselves paralyzed in a limbo or purgatory *(barzakh)*, unable to move forward into a new life, unable to return to their roots. The feeling is not a freezing of time but a slow dying from gradual gangrene. Thus avareh live in a world of memory, idle talk, jokes, folkloristic references, and parables. Sa'edi gives the word a tragic depth (its Urdu/Hindi cognate, *awaara*, vagabond, is the title of the international blockbuster Bombay film hit of the 1950s starring Raj Kapoor), for he was just such an avareh dying of despair. But others have found inspiration and renewal in the liminal spaces where cultures meet and cross-fertilize.

There is one final set of films that should be mentioned with regard to the other Iranian refugees—the domestic refugees from the Iran-Iraq war who devastated the cities of Khuzistan in southern Iran. These films, made in Iran, present the traumas and coping strategies of the poor and displaced of Iran in quite powerful ways, drawing on modernist camera techniques and emplotment devices and ideas from such sources as Alberto Moravia and Alfred Hitchcock. Good examples of such films are *The Peddler* and *The Blessed Marriage* by Mohsen Makhmalbaf. Or Bahman Beza'i's *Bashu, Garibeh-ye Kuchak* (Bashu, the Little Stranger), about an orphan boy fleeing burning Khuzistan and being taken in by people in the north with whom he has no common language. "Gharibeh" (stranger), like "avareh," is a deeply resonant term in Persian, one with many religious connotations.

None of these films and videos is widely distributed. Still, those who see them are likely to feel closer to the dilemmas and imagination and cultural resources of Iranians as people, rather than exoticized Others, statistics, or bureaucratic categories. There are, in fact, two audiences for these films: Iranians themselves, for whom they serve as entertainment, perhaps as externalizations that can be used for a kind of self-reflection and critique (as novels are said to provide) and as a therapeutic in helping to articulate and share problems; and non-Iranians, for whom they can be informative (visually, behaviorally, providing access to the humor and other intimate cultural cues) but also therapeutic in breaking through stereotypes and providing material with which to open conversations with Iranians. If, as Stephen Tyler has suggested, ethnography in the late twentieth century should be a therapeutic, then such cultural vehicles may serve this end.

Vietnamese: Feminist, Romantic Tropes of Distrust

We live in constant suspicion. . . . [T]here is no mutual trust.
                    —LY, AGE 37, VIETNAM, 1982

I am like a piece of silk, floating in the midst of the market, knowing not into whose hands it will fall, sitting on a reed, leaning against an apricot branch, between the peach tree to the east and the willow tree to the West, whom shall I befriend for a lifetime?
For the Vietnamese exile, it speaks for the exodus or silent popular movement of resistance that continues to raise problems of conscience for the international community.
                    —SURNAME VIÊT GIVEN NAME NAM

What is one to make of Trinh T. Minh-ha's film, *Surname Việt Given Name Nam*? Celebrated in some circles as a feminist statement, a film about Vietnamese by a Vietnamese refugee and a critique of its own modes of production, it is dismissed in others as pretentious, sentimental, lacking in communicative skills and in precisely the critical skills that it proclaims to possess. While it is flawed, if one takes the time to disassemble (analyze) it into its cultural units and strategies, it offers interesting access both to key components of Vietnamese cultural forms and to a rhetoric of distrust.

There are at least four narratives: a historical narrative composed of documentary images, photographs, old footage, poetry, folk songs and dances, and so on, about colonialism and the anticolonial struggles; a feminist narrative about the lives of Vietnamese women in Vietnam, France, and the United States, based in part on Mai Thu Van's interviews in her book *Vietnam, peuple, des voix;* key to both of these, a mythic narrative drawn from *The Tale of Kieu,* the national epic of Vietnam, written by Nguyen Du (1765–1820); and a metanarrative about the making of films such as this one.

The film opens with the historical narrative: a color sequence of women dancing in coolie hats that we will later learn is a folklorized California event; the title spattered with drops of rain, while on the sound track is heard what may be thunder or a bomb explosion; black-and-white stills of women in coolie hats, the historical reference of the contemporary coolie dance, but then as the camera pulls back from their heads, these women hold rifles and schoolgirls hold demonstration banners. This back and forth between past and present will inform the film, using (a) photos of both family members and collective events and (b) romantic figurations of nature or love, which are then historicized and given embattled meanings. A color photo of a young woman in a scarf is followed by a black-and-white photo of a child, a figure on a boat, a woman spinning silk, a photo of a young woman, then the camera is panned down across foliage to a horrified crying woman and across to the screaming faces of other women and children. Meanwhile on the sound track a female voice sings a lullaby with ominous overtones: "I am like a piece of silk, floating in the market, knowing not in whose hands it will fall. The country lies under a heavy storm; my child lies under a heavy storm; I wish to use my fragile body to protect my child, but the earth is shaking, shaking, and my baby's cradle is shaking."

The historical narrative is overlaid with the metanarrative: there is white print against a black screen while a woman's voice tells us about the difficulties of her life in Vietnam, eventually coming to what is printed on the screen. We will then be shown her face: she is the woman in the scarf. The print says: " 'In principle a foreigner is already a spy. Even a socialist. . . . Or even you. We live in constant suspicion. . . . There is no mutual trust.'—Ly, 37 years old, employee, Vietnam, 1982." Here the non-Vietnamese viewer can still take the statement as one about the oppressive Communist regime, but later this kind of statement will be directed toward the interview process in general, toward the making of films, toward the viewer's curiosity.

The metanarrative and historical narrative work on each other also in terms of what constitutes change. Another woman says, "There is always a tendency to identify historical breaks and to say this begins here, this ends there, while the scene keeps on recurring as unchangeable as change itself." Meanwhile, however, the sound track has the sound of a train speeding up, and the visuals of a demonstration appear, a demonstration of girls marching, a young woman speaking into a microphone, and a male audience applauding. The woman's voice continues, "Life seems suddenly fragile and vulnerable. The past disappears from the ruins." And now the feminist narrative comes on line.

> Nobody knows whether Ho Xuan Huong really existed or whether she was a mere name: she wrote poems in the nineteenth century, but they were notorious for the scandals they caused and they continue today to define the principles of right speech and a good manner of womanhood. Though some men went as far as affirming that poems signed in her name might not be hers. They might, of course, be written by a man. Who, one might ask, who was this feminine man whose womanness was violently attacked and trashed by male poets of the time and who wrote feminist poetry on free love or single mothers or labia minor and labia majora divided against polygamy and double standards of morality, who ridiculed male authority and religiosity, and who challenged the norms of Confucian patriarchy?

The demonstration is problematized by a woman saying, "When he claps, she has entertained, when she claps, he has made a significant contribution." A woman doctor tells the story of her life's struggles, while a Chinese-style song tells of the hard work of the female, while an old poem is recited in accented English translation ("We are absurd petals in a puff of wind, in an indifferent world . . .").

And now finally we are given the mythic core: "In Vietnam, almost everybody poor or rich uses verses from the Doan truvng tan thanh fluently in their daily expressions, also known as the *Tale of Kieu.*" The tale is borrowed from a Chinese novel, but the effect in Vietnamese verse did for the Vietnamese vernacular what Dante did for Italian (liberation from Chinese and Latin, respectively). For the literate, the poem is filled with allusions to Chinese classical lore, but it is also much beloved by ordinary folk. The heroine sells herself as a concubine to Scholar Ma (who turns out to be a pimp and she is swept into a series of ill adventures) to get money to free her husband jailed on a vague charge by a corrupt bureaucracy. There is also a vivid peasant rebel modeled on Nguyen Hue, who led the Tay-son revolt and who routed 200,000 Chinese troops in the Tet offensive of 1789. Prostitution and the loyalty that causes some to sell themselves to preserve their families are also traditional allegories of political allegiance (Nguyen Du may have seen himself as a political Kieu). In the later nineteenth century, the poem about a divided soul took on new meaning as the southern provinces fell under French rule. In the 1920s and 1930s, the French hired a Vietnamese scholar to analyze the *Tale of Kieu* and use it to rally people to the French; the nationalist opponents pilloried this scholar as Scholar Ma. The poem then took on renewed allegorical force during the American war. And now among refugees and exiles abroad, it remains a text that is known by heart, often used as a text for divination and a constant source of comfort.

Although the film initially only stresses the *Tale of Kieu* as a feminist account— "loved for its unorthodox approach to sexuality . . . she not only freely chooses her lover, she also eagerly loves three men. Her life offers a revisionist interpretation of the Confucian principles of chastity that govern the conduct of women"— by the end it is made clear that the *Tale of Kieu* operates as the key trope for all of the other narratives of the film and for the Vietnamese sense of identity, whether living under an oppressive regime at home (the interviews stress this oppressiveness) or with divided loyalties abroad. How many other nations have a woman as the key nationalist hero? But the trope of divided loyalty, of selling oneself to preserve one's loved ones, is not unlike the romantic tropes of Polish nationalism (traitorous patriotism, embodied in the figure of Konrad Wallenrod, engaging in hopeless uprisings).

Other heroic women of Vietnam are invoked: the two sisters who led the Vietnamese in their earliest uprisings against the Chinese are now seen parading annually on elephants in the Los Angeles annual celebrations. ("It is fantasized that to conquer the female armies, the only successful strategy the Chinese soldiers finally came up with was to strip themselves to the skin and expose their thing shamelessly to the sight of their female opponents. The women fighters retreated in disgust and the sisters committed suicide.") Then there is Trieu Thi Trinh, a young peasant woman who led thirty battles against the Chinese: she was nine feet tall, with breasts three feet long that went flying over her shoulders as she rode her elephant; she too committed suicide rather than return to serfdom when her army was finally defeated. And accounts are given of the crafts and businesses that women ran.

The film then turns to America, interrogating the now American-Vietnamese filmmaker's techniques as well as the lives of American Vietnamese students in California. Distrust is foregrounded here too; a Vietnamese-accented voice says, "Interview—an antiquated device of documentary: truth is selected, renewed, displaced, and speech is always tactical." And again: "The pose is always present, . . . the original text is already always an impossible translation that renders translation impossible."

Here one is reminded again of the repetitions of history: "Mother, who had experience of fleeing war on foot, was convinced not only that we had to reduce our belongings to the minimal but also that the clothes we wore should be dark so as not to draw any attention to ourselves as women." And also of the ways in which history and trauma inscribe themselves on the body and psyche: the scramble for food and beds in the refugee camps and the overflowing toilets ("I was so obsessed by this that even today when I go to national parks, it is a real ordeal for me to use these restroom facilities.") Mai Thu Van, whose interviews in Vietnam provided the basis for the script of the women in Vietnam in the first half of the film, writes to Trinh T. Minh-ha, "A million Vietnamese dispersed around the globe: it will take more than one generation for the wounds to heal."

And finally, the distrust about the interviewing, scripting, and acting in the film comes full circle as the American-Vietnamese women, who each acted two parts (a woman in Vietnam and herself in America), tell how they felt about being in the film and the filmmaker talks about the ways in which film has been used by America to rewrite and falsify history.

> War is a succession of special effects. The war became film before it was shot. Cinema has remained a machine of special effects. If the war is the continuation of politics by other means, then media images are the continuation of war by other means. . . . It is said that if the Americans lost the other, they have certainly won this one.

Photo stills are reviewed from the Vietnam war, while Vietnamese women speak, translated in subtitles, calling for human compassion, asserting that there are images that are emotionally moving. *The Tale of Kieu* is once again invoked: we are reminded that different governments appropriated its image of woman differently, that it was used to denounce feudalism, colonialism, and American imperialism; today, "for the Vietnamese exile, it speaks for the exodus or silent popular movement of resistance that continues to raise problems of conscience for the international community."

What is the reception of this film among Vietnamese refugees? The women-actresses in the film say they have broken the code of silence of women's traditional coping with trauma because they want the story told. They want to celebrate the strength of Vietnamese women and memorialize their suffering.

Is there something that film like this can do, that the private clinical stories of individuals does not do? For the refugees themselves? For the non-Vietnamese who try to help the refugees? For the public culture of the societies that receive these refugees?

What is left out of this film? In France, at least, the three quite distinct waves of refugees and their profound differences in experience and in politics are left out. For instance, might an open discussion of political factions be therapeutic for refugees in making them see their own experiences in a comparative light and in a light that suggests the social patterns of which they are a part?

Lebanon and Palestinians: Toward Feminist Critiques of Male Fetishism

> Male Voice: You shall see nothing but the splinters of time.
> Female Voice: I will see misery . . .
> Male Voice: You will see nothing unless you live here.
>   —*CANTICLE OF STONES*, WRITTEN AND DIRECTED BY MICHEL KHELEIfi

> *"I Will Not Be Sad in This World"*
>   —ARMENIAN MUSIC ALBUM USED IN *THE ADJUSTER*, WRITTEN AND DIRECTED
>   BY ATOM EGOYAN

If *The Tale of Kieu* is a key to the Vietnamese codes of Trinh T. Minh-ha's film, and if a split imago complementarity between the batin and zahir, between purity and cleverness *(zerangi)*, between comic film and tragic poems and stories, compose Iranian discourses of survival, so too there is an interesting dialectic to be hazarded between, on the one hand, the films of the Belgian resident and Palestinian filmmaker Michel Kheleifi and the stories of such Palestinian or Lebanese male writers as Ghassem Kanafaani, Elias Khouri, Tawfiq Awaad, and Halim Barakat and, on the other hand, the feminist counterdiscourses of the Decembrist poets of Beirut analyzed by Miriam Cooke (1988) and the feminist writers against warfare (Hanan al-Shaykh, Etel Adnan, and Andree Chedid) analyzed by Evelyn Accad (1990).

Michel Kheleifi's films are avowedly engagé, political, even polemical. They are efforts to "continue war by other means." Of his three feature films to date, *Canticle of Stones*, a tribute to the *intifada*, is arguably the most interesting, particularly for the features that make both Arabic-speaking and English-speaking audiences dislike it—namely, its stilted poetic language and modeling of itself on Marguerite Duras and Alain Renais's *Hiroshima, Mon Amour*. The stilted language, say some Arab audiences, only shows that someone living in a French-speaking environment has lost touch. On the contrary, reply Kheleifi's defenders, it is an attempt to find a poetic style that will elevate and grace the topic of news broadcasts with more lasting aesthetic power. The use of the well-known Palestinian band Sabrin, of a well-known elderly Palestinian spinster, *bint* A. F. Darwiche, who has refused to move from her childhood home, and of documentary footage might, however, have more power. It is worth trying to explore the reasons documentary footage often has tremendous power when inserted into a narrative film, beyond the usual explanation that it is somehow more "real." Documentary film, after all, is also constructed and partial: other camera angles, other bits of the event, can change the meaning of a documentary profoundly. Perhaps the two most important bits in *Canticle of Stones* are, first, a father in the Gaza Strip bitterly attacking the Israelis for the death of his son, when in a casual line he admits that the reason the Israelis opened fire was because hundreds of Palestinian youths had run out to attack them, and second, the heroine's lover promising to accompany her to Gaza but failing to show up, leaving instead a note with directions to friends there. In the first bit, the senseless tragedy and the intensity of the fear on both sides become palpable, a conundrum in which there is fault on all sides but in which there is causality of human dimensions, not just faceless, inexplicable evil. Here there can be problem solving, negotiation, movement. Demonization of the other, by contrast, allows for no problem solving or negotiation. In the second, presumably to accompany the heroine would put the lover, and perhaps her, in senseless danger. Certain things cannot be understood until experienced ("unless you live here"); learning or guiding another in such circumstances requires a different kind of trust.

Accad argues that however sensitive male-authored novels (and filmscripts) are, however much they point out the ugliness of war, nonetheless they are caught up also in a fascination with war, death, heroism, and proving masculinity. Miriam Cooke argues that the women poets of the Beirut civil war have often found a voice and style that undercuts the ideological male discourses, revaluing the actions of snipers and warriors not for their macho actions but for their more mundane acts and using the latter as a vehicle to critique their warlike activities. In a similar fashion, Accad analyzes three novels written by women as dramatizing the self-destructive cycles of socialization, sexuality, and violence, in which the female central characters come to terrible ends. In Hanan al-Shaykh's *The Story of Zahra*, Zahra is raised in southern Lebanon and visits an uncle in Africa; she finds herself oppressed in both places, beaten by a religiously fanatic father, made the object of advances by male relatives and friends of the family, but above all having conflicted feelings about a mother who uses her as a cover to have affairs and who abandons her each time a man comes along. In the second part of the novel, she is traumatized by the civil war in Beirut and her brother's mindless participation in the fighting, not for a cause, but for the feeling of power that killing gives him. She tries to divert a sniper from killing, using her sexuality, but finds herself first yielding to the sexuality and then failing utterly to achieve any control either over her lover's actions or her own body. She becomes pregnant, he wants her to get an abortion, she cries, he relents, he then shoots her. This grim cycle is hard to break, and in Etel Adnan's *Sitt Marie-Rose*, the woman hero tries to stand up against the young men of Beirut, only to be "tried" and executed by them for blocking their will. In Andree Chedid's *La maison sans racines*, when two young women from enemy camps attempt to lead a peace march, one of them is wounded by a sniper; a grandmother who takes the wounded woman's place then sees her granddaughter cut down by a sniper and herself dies of grief.

These texts are part of a growing, sharp feminist exploding of the shibboleths of the Middle East, exposing male ideologies but also accounts by Westerners who excuse events in the Middle East as being "the way of Middle Eastern culture" (see also the recent books by Malti-Douglas [1992] and Mernissi [1991]). There is a dense modeling here not only of problems deeply seated in psychological conflicts of socialization, sexuality, and violence, as well as in political and economic conflicts, but also of solutions, of ways individuals can reach out to one another to begin to build a different kind of world. They are, perhaps, also accounts that can help people who have been through these traumas to externalize and work through them. As al-Shaykh says of her experiences meeting women in the Gulf who lived in harems, about which she wrote in her second novel, *Wardat al-Sahra*, it was by seeing these other lives that she was able to see her own in perspective, to see its limitations and to find ways to escape them.

If these texts and films by exiles from the Middle East focus on the dynamics of the social trauma in their homelands causing waves of exiles and displacements, another kind of exile film raises the issues of displacement and the disjunctions of passion that continue in more "normal" worlds in which exiles and other kinds of displacements of modernity intermingle. Atom Egoyan's film *The Adjuster* may be read on many levels, but one level is signaled by the sound track (the eerie wail of the ney-flute Middle Eastern music that seems to invoke Jalalu'ddin Rumi's Masnavi, "Listen to the reed, how it tells a tale, complaining of separations . . .") and by the photographs of Beirut that the non–English-speaking elder sister burns. On the surface, the film is about an insurance adjuster, Noah, who puts his fire clients in the same motel (a Noah's ark perhaps: there is the single woman, the older couple, the gay couple, the two sisters, all of whose emotions he caters to or plays on in his elaborate scam/effort to help [his surname is Render]). Noah lives in the model house of an unfinished, bankrupt development with a refugee from Beirut named Hera (goddess of marriage?), her little boy, and her elder sister, who are among his first clients. The film begins with the image of a hand backlit in the reddish glow of flames and ends with Noah looking at his hand as his and Hera's house goes up in flames and then a flashback to the fire when as an adjuster he entered Hera's life by saying, "I'm your adjuster" (metaphoric flames of Beirut and the ambiguous salvation of moving in with an American adjuster?). A hand dangles from the rearview mirror of Noah's car as he calls Hera in the middle of the night from his car phone to ask if she is having a nightmare and to express his own anxieties. At this level of symbolic play, the film is a meditation on mirrors, nightmares, photographs, and films, that is, on recapturing the past (photographs of Beirut, photographs of houses before they burned used by insurance adjusters to establish lifestyles and the value of lost goods), projections of passions (porn films that Hera classifies in her work as a censor [the goddess Hera punished the women who were seduced by Zeus; Noah, too, sleeps with all his clients]; films that Bubba and his wife stage to break their ennui, reflections of self (the mirrors in which Bubba and Noah look). Is that hand the hand of fate, or is it rather that by our own hands our passions lead us to schemes of self-destruction? Passion in this film is highly self-conscious, at a jaded once remove, whether it is the treatment of sex, voyeurism, grief, shock, or shame. One of Noah's clients refuses his efforts to have her inventory her losses so as to make a claim on her past lifestyle: she wants things to change, not return to the way they were. So too with the lives of many refugees: although the power of nostalgia is great (Bubba enacts this desire in one of its more negative modes), the return to status quo ante is neither possible nor in most cases desirable; moreover, it is not only refugees whose lives have been displaced by the processes of the modern world. The intermingling of many kinds of modern world displacements as the grounds of contemporary life is a constant register of *The Adjuster*.

Indians: Midnight's Children, When Will They Arrive?

It has become commonplace in India now to describe one instance of strife after another as "perhaps the worst since 1947." . . . At the worst stage of the violence [in Bhagalpur] in October-November 1989, some 40,000 people were forced to leave their homes and live in makeshift relief

*camps. . . . [A]n estimated 10,000 were still in "relief camps" towards the end of January
1990. . . . [D]estruction or removal of records is of course not unprecedented: the British practiced
it on a large scale in India after 1937. . . . Hindus . . . met us with studied silence, if not hostility. . . . [Muslim victims] begin to talk. . . . [T]here is a need for a public narrative of their
suffering. However, this narrative too assumes a set form. It appears in a ritualized account.
. . . [I]nformants . . . tend to become part of a collective subject that . . . appeals to her/him for
Relief, Justice, Mercy. . . . [O]ur nationalist historiography, journalism, and filmmaking have
tended to generate something like a collective amnesia. In cinema, of course, the great Bengali
director Ritwik Ghatak produced a series of unparalleled filmic statements about the pain, despair,
and hopes of those dispossessed and displaced by Partition. . . . But Ghatak remains an exception.
. . . Among Hindi/Urdu films . . . M. S. Sathyu's Garam have . . . sensitively portrayed the
collective insanity. . . . The more recent television serial "Tamas," based on Bhishma Sahni's
novel of the same name . . . marks a return to a less subtle nationalist statement in which agents-
provocateurs and mysterious evil folk pull the strings.*
—GYANENDRA PANDEY (1992)

Violence and, to a lesser extent, communalism are important themes in Indian
cinema, but as Pandey points out, cinema is normally used to deny the politics
and corruption that drive communal violence. One wonders, if film were used
otherwise, could it be an aid to stabilizing and advancing peaceful democracy?
There is a wonderful scene in one of Ghatak's films in which an actor is saluted
by an old woman for presenting the pain she had endured, for externalizing it, for
making it available as a witnessing but also as a scene for thought, as an immemo-
rial.

Partition, its causes and dislocations, have been the subject of much novelistic
writing, from Kushwant Singh's powerful novella *Train to Pakistan,* which shows
how a village determined to avoid the ethnic strife around it was unable to do so,
to Bapsy Sidwa's more recent *Ice Candy Man,* based in part on recollections of a
man in Houston, Texas, forty years after the event, still carrying his scars. If *Train
to Pakistan* and *Ice Candy Man* parallel some of the feminist writings of Lebanon
cited above, and if the Pakistani exile Jamil Dehlavi's film *Born of Fire* parallels the
flute and fire-passion motifs of Atom Egoyan's *The Adjuster* (albeit romanticizing a
nostalgia for Turkey and sufi mysticism), it is the irritations and brilliant satires of
Salman Rushdie (especially *Midnight's Children* but also *Shame* and *The Satanic Verses*)
that engage the dilemmas of exiles and displaced persons both in the Subconti-
nent and in England, modeling the hybridity that constitutes the migrant and exile
experience, exploiting this hybridity to re-vision history in ways alternative to conventional wisdom, to draw attention to and legitimate the decolonization of the
English language through the introduction of linguistic resources from other cultures, to expose the dependencies and psychological conundrums that migrants,
exiles, and refugees are trapped in, and to redeem a cosmopolitan sensibility that
eschews the nationalist chauvinisms that constitute so much of migrant and exile
problems both in countries of origin and in host countries (see Fischer and Abedi
1990: chap. 7). Rushdie is part of a major stream of new writing about these expe-

riences in both the Anglo-American and Franco–North African worlds (Hargreaves 1991).

Holocaust: Mourning and Generational Transfer

A brief word is in order about the work of the many films on the Holocaust. Eric Santner (1990) has analyzed a series of efforts by male German filmmakers to make films about the Holocaust that try to work through the German trauma, that try to facilitate the process of grief work, of mourning in the sense of nonencryptment. Santner thinks that each attempt ultimately fails. This is not the place to analyze the problem in any detail, or to evaluate whether or not he is correct, but simply to raise the issue that one use for film is not only for the refugees but also for those left behind. An argument can be made that a film like *Shoah* is quite innovative in the technique of having the presence of the filmmaker work as a kind of transference figure within the film: Claude Lanzmann acts as a provocateur getting people to articulate thoughts and arguments that they might not otherwise articulate. The results are often disconcerting and lead to further thought and argument: immemorials.

The Holocaust literature is important for a second reason: there is now a growing rich literature on children and grandchildren of Holocaust refugees, that is, on the effects of social trauma in the second and third generations. Studies are now becoming available not only of the children of the refugees but also of the children of the perpetrators (Bar-On 1989). As Frantz Fanon (1961) pointed out in his work on the struggles for Algerian independence, the psychological damage of torture rebounds also on the torturer.

Refugees in Europe and America: Toward Multicultural Polities

It soon became apparent that we were not the first "therapists" but that the refugees had already discovered this process. Otherwise there would be no way to explain how refugees too young to have clear memories of the events of 1947 were able to tell stories of those days in great detail.
—STEPHEN KELLER 1975

A cinematic discourse about the fate of non-European refugees and immigrants in Europe is being generated only slowly: Rainer Werner Fassbinder's *Angst Essen Seele Auf* (1973) was an important first step; but not until a decade later, with such films as Hanif Kureishi's *My Beautiful Laundrette* (1986) and *Sammy and Rosie Get Laid* (1988), do we begin to get films made by members of immigrant communities about themselves. In Berlin, a pair of very low budget films has been made by Mathias Drawe and Ragit Tuneay about a friendship between a Turk and a German (*Die Kunst ein Mann zu Sein*, 1989; *Der Koenig von Kreuzberg*, 1979). "The King of Kreuzberg" (a neighborhood full of immigrant Turks) is built on the conceit that the Turk periodically is seized by a nervous unease *(nervose Unruhen)*, a compulsion to fly (do something great). He tries to balance on one foot, hands outstretched, back bent, hands up like flaps. This compulsion gets him into trouble if it comes while shopping, riding the subway, or making love. The urge is connected to his identity of being of the lineage of Suleiman the Great (Turks have their high civilization heritage, but it goes unrecognized in Germany where they are just struggling immigrants). The series of comic skits finds him on a park bench, imposing on his friend, attempting a scam on an electronic bank teller machine, and so on. One of the nice things about the film is that while it alludes to problems of the homeless, of those who have no money, the lead character is well dressed. It is a story about the spirit, not about the stereotypes of being down and out. The humor is not unlike the similarly skit-constructed U.S.-Iranian immigrant film, *Agha-ye Avareh.*

In America, too, a cinematic discourse is slowly being built with such films as *El Norte* (Central American refugees fleeing through Mexico and illegally across the U.S. border), *Mississippi Triangle* (Chinese in Mississippi), *Mississippi Masala* (Asians displaced from Uganda to America), as well as those Iranian, Vietnamese-American, and Armenian-Canadian films mentioned above. A recent video, "History and Memory," made by a daughter of Japanese-Americans interned during World War II, explores the ways in which children maintain memories of events that occurred before their time, paying particular attention to the circuits of the stock of images that come now from a great variety of sources ranging from propaganda films and newsreels to Hollywood re-creations, advertisements, family snapshots, physical mementos, and verbal descriptions. What is important, not only for the fate of refugees and immigrants but also for the construction of a multicultural polity, is that increasingly there is an archive of films made by refugees and immigrants about themselves (rather than stereotypic formulations by Hollywood about others, whose theme is usually assimilation rather than use of alternative cultural resources) that draw on (and contribute to the larger polity) cultural resources of the lands they come from.

Novelistic and short story accounts are much richer: there is now an impressive and rapidly growing corpus of first-rate writers exploring the experiences and narrative vehicles and coping devices of refugees and new immigrants from within the rich cultural resources they bring with them. While it is important to distinguish between kinds of migrants and refugees—those made destitute by war, those with little education, those with few language skills, those psychologically traumatized, and so on (the reaction of working-class Muslims in Britain to Rushdie is sufficient warning that elite members of the community cannot be taken as spokespersons for the community at large)—it is equally important to seek out the cultural terms of reference, parables, mythic figurations, poetry, and philosophies that these groups bring with them, some of which can be conveyed by elite writers quite effectively. Bharati Mukherjee's novel *Jasmine,* for instance, introduces the figures of Kali and ideas like *sati* into the American landscape which transform the latter, in addition to making observations about Vietnamese refugee networks and Hmong interactions with church welfare groups.

One of the strongest refugee novels is Hualing Nieh's *Mulberry and Peach,* which opens with a hilarious scene between an immigration agent and Peach, who denies she is Mulberry.

> The immigration agent is standing in her doorway. He is dressed in a dark suit with a black and grey striped tie. He wears sunglasses, although it's an overcast day. The dark lenses disguise the only distinguishing part of his face: eyebrows, eyes, the bridge of his nose. Only the anonymous parts are visible: bald head, sharp chin, high forehead, beak nose, a pencil-thin moustache.
>
> Peach laughs. "Mr. Dark, you have a real good imagination. What you see isn't real. What I see is real. You know what I see when I look at you? A tiger with nine human heads."
>
> Peach laughs. "Mr. Dark, don't try to be so smart! You think I'm going to tell you that I was born in Nanking on 26 October 1929 so you can prove I'm Mulberry? Well, you're wrong, Mr. Dark. I was born in a valley when heaven split from the earth. Where the flowers fell people sprang up. That's how I was born. You people were born from your mothers' wombs."

When heaven split from the earth is not a bad description of the cataclysmic events of the Chinese revolution, when families were torn apart and individuals fled across vast lands trying to keep body and soul alive; not a bad description for the cataclysmic events that have shaken almost every society in the twentieth century, the United States being one of the few exceptions, an odd place, Mukherjee notes in *Jasmine*, where people think the language they speak is who they are (as opposed to those used to changing identities, names, and language as circumstances demand).

CONCLUSION

Then one day some friends forced him to take some time off and accompany them to the cinema. The theme of the picture forced him to look at that which he had been avoiding through constant work.

—STEPHEN KELLER (1975)

They are different from us—self-assertive—the children of pogroms and Pobedonostsev— the bearers of bright hopes.

—A. B. YEHOSHUA ([1989] 1992)

This chapter has raised two questions: First, can film and other cultural media be used to present refugees' own perspectives and humanity in ways that can redesign the public cultures of the emerging pluralizing global world, and if so, do film and written fiction function differently in pursuing these goals? Second, how can we write about refugees while acknowledging the secondariness of our accounts, yet directing attention to their problems on the psychological as well as social and political levels?

In answer to the first query, the argument here is speculative and simple. The film medium could provide a mechanism for public discourse to move in a therapeutic direction. (It can, of course, be used in other, regressive and repressive, directions as well: to create mystery and fear of difference, to create a sense of noir or random anarchy.) The suggestion here is that funding might be provided, as England has begun to do through Channel Four, for productions that present the refugees from their own points of view, not just as cases of disempowered victims, but as lively individuals, with their own cultural resources, who can make their own way if given a chance and who can enrich the host society. A critical discourse needs to be created to guide reception and encourage production of these films. For all its flaws, *Mississippi Masala* (flawed especially in its ending) was a great success in attracting crossover audiences of blacks, whites, and Asian Indians into the same theaters. The scene of the arbitrary search on the bus when the Asian protagonists are forced to leave Kenya is one of those reconstructed bits of ethnographic "realism" that work powerfully like the documentary insertions discussed above in regard to Kheleifi's films. Perhaps an even more powerful example is the series of new black films that foreshadowed the Los Angeles riots: *Do the Right Thing, Boyz 'N the Hood, New Jack City, Juice.*

The second query arises out of a certain repetitiveness and distance that seems to bedevil the literature on refugees. One of the defining features of ethnography and anthropology in the late twentieth century is the secondariness of our discoveries. No longer can we indulge in fantasies of discovering untouched societies or social problems. Journalists, social workers, travelers, and bureaucrats have all preceded us not only in investigating, seeing, querying, and listening but also in writing. Nor are there any societies left—perhaps with the exception of North America, Scandinavia, and Switzerland—that have not been fundamentally disrupted, deranged, and reorganized by the wars and disasters of this century. Increasingly, and, we hope, much to our readers' benefit, anthropology must take the circuits of preexisting narratives into account: for critique but also for comparative conceptual leverage and for a sense of historicity in our endeavors to avoid mere repetition of past mistakes.

Questions of representation, here, are fundamental: What are the forms of the diasporas that refugees become part of? What are the forms of violence that are enacted and recounted in the creation of refugees, and do these change over time? What are the forms of mourning that refugees use to work through their experiences and to enable them to rebuild a new life? What are the continuing dynamics for the second and third generations?

More generally, this chapter has tried to respond to the literature on refugees by pointing out some basic elements that seem to be missing: (a) a concern with cultural forms in which experience and philosophies of survival are encoded and made available for the psychological working through of trauma; (b) a reminder that many refugees turn out to be dynamic members of new societies (Keller's study of Partition makes this a central theme) and that to reduce the literature to "victimization" studies is to be unduly pessimistic; (c) a concern with media of communication that can help to transform the politics but also the psychology of refugees; and (d) a concern with the dynamics of refugees for the following generations, dynamics that can generate both passivity/dysfunction but also a sense of purpose and activity.

REFERENCES

Accad, Evelyn
 1990   *Sexuality and War: Literary Masks of the Middle East.* New York: New York University Press.
Adnan, Etel
 [1977] 1982 *Sitt Marie-Rose.* Sausalito, Calif.: Post-Apollo Press.
Alamzadeh, Reza
 1990   *The Guests of Hotel Astoria.* Film.
Bar-On, Dan
 1989   *Legacy of Silence: Encounters with Children of the Third Reich.* Cambridge: Harvard University Press.
Beza'i, Bahram
 1985   *Bashu, The Little Stranger* (Bashu, Gharibeh-ye Kuchak). Film.
Chedid, Andree
 [1985] 1989 *House without Roots.* London: Serpent's Tail.
Choy, Elaine
 1983   *Mississippi Triangle.* Film.
Cooke, Miriam
 1988   *War's Other Voices: Women Writers on the Lebanese Civil War, 1975–82.* Cambridge: Cambridge University Press.
Dehlavi, Jamil
 1986   *Born of Fire.* Film.
Drawe, Mathias, and Ragit Tuneay
 1979   *Der Koonig von Kreuzberg* (The King of Kreuzberg). Film.
 1989   *Die Kunst ein Mann zu Sein* (The Art of Being a Man). Film
Duras, Marguerite, and Alain Renais
 1959   *Hiroshima, Mon Amour.* Film.
Ebrahamian, Ghassem
 1987   *The Suitors.* Film.
Egoyan, Atom
 1992   *The Adjuster.* Film.
Fanon, Frantz
 1961   *Les damnes de la terre.* Paris: Maspero. Reprinted as *The Wretched of the Earth.* London: Penguin, 1982.
Fassbinder, Rainer Werner
 1973   *Angst Essen Seele Auf.* Film.
Fischer, Michael M. J.
 1984   "Towards a Third World Poetics: Seeing Through Short Stories and Film in the Iranian Culture Area." *Knowledge and Society* 5: 171–241.

Fischer, Michael M. J., and Mehdi Abedi
   1990   *Debating Muslims: Cultural Dialogues in Postmodernity and Tradition.* Madison: University of Wisconsin Press.
Ghatak, Ritwik.
   1961   *Komal Gandhar* (E flat). Film.
Good, Byron J., Mary-Jo Del Vecchio Good, and Robert Moradi
   1985   "The Interpretation of Iranian Depressive Illness and Dysphoric Affect." In *Culture and Depression,* ed. Arthur Kleinman and Byron Good, 369–428. Berkeley, Los Angeles, and London: University of California Press.
Hargreaves, Alec
   1991   *Voices from the North African Immigrant Community in France.* New York: Berg.
Holland, Agnieszka
   1991   *Europa, Europa.* Film.
Kapoor, Raj
   1951   *Awaara* (The Vagabond). Film.
Keller, Stephen L.
   1975   *Uprooting and Social Change: The Role of Refugees in Development.* Delhi: Manohar Book Service.
Khajaturian, Rafi
   1984   *Aga-ye Avareh* (Mr. Stranger). Film.
Kheleifi, Michel
   1990   *Canticle of Stones.* Film.
Kureishi, Hanif
   1986   *My Beautiful Laundrette.* London: Faber and Faber. Film.
   1988   *Sammy and Rosie Get Laid.* London: Faber and Faber. Film.
   1990   *The Buddha of Suburbia.* London: Viking.
Lamorisee, Albert
   ca. 1975.   *The Lover's Wind.* Film.
Lanzmann, Claude
   1985   *Shoah, An Oral History of the Holocaust: The Complete Text of the Film by Claude Lanzmann.* New York: Pantheon.
   1991   "The Obscenity of Understanding: An Evening with Claude Lanzmann." *American Imago* 46(6): 475–495.
Lee, Spike
   1989   *Do the Right Thing.* Film.
Lyotard, Jean-François
   1989   *The Lyotard Reader.* Cambridge: Basil Blackwell.
Makhmalbaf, Mohsen
   1986   *The Peddler* (Dastforush). Film.
   1988   *Marriage of the Blessed* (Arusi-Ye Khuban). Film.
Malti-Douglas, Fedwa
   1991   *Woman's Body, Woman's Word: Gender and Discourse in Arabo-Islamic Writing.* Princeton: Princeton University Press.
Mernissi, Fatima
   1991   *The Veil and the Male Elite: A Feminist Interpretation of Women's Rights in Islam.* New York: Addison-Wesley.

Minh-ha, Trinh T.
    1989   *Surname Viêt Given Name Nam.* Film.
Mukherjee, Bharati
    1988   *The Middleman and Other Stories.* New York: Grove Press.
    1989   *Jasmine.* New York: Grove Weidenfeld.
Naficy, Hamid
    1988   "Culture in Exile: Fetishized Iranian T.V. in the U.S." MS.
    1993   *The Making of an Exile Culture: Iranian Television in Los Angeles.* Minneapolis: University of Minnesota Press.
Nair, Mira
    1992   *Mississippi Masala.* Film.
Nava, Gregory
    1991   *El Norte.* Film.
Nguyen Du
    1983   *The Tale of Kieu.* New Haven: Yale University Press.
Nieh, Hualing
    [1976] 1981   *Mulberry and Peach.* London: Woman's Press.
Pandey, Gyanendra
    1992   "In Defense of the Fragment: Writing about Hindu-Muslim Riots in India Today." *Representations* (Winter): 27–55.
Peebles, Mario van
    1991   *New Jack City.* Film.
Readings, Bill
    1991   *Introducing Lyotard: Art and Politics.* New York: Routledge.
Rushdie, Salman
    1980   *Midnight's Children.* New York: Alfred A. Knopf.
    1983   *Shame.* New York: Alfred A. Knopf.
    1988   *The Satanic Verses.* London: Viking.
Sa'edi, Gholam Hosain
    1984   *Othello in Wonderland.* Film.
Sahni, Bhisham
    1960   *Tamas.* London: Penguin.
    1990   *We Have Arrived in Amritsar, and Other Stories.* Delhi: Orient Longman.
Santner, Eric
    1990   *Stranded Objects: Mourning, Memory and Film in Postwar Germany.* Ithaca: Cornell University Press.
Sayyad, Parviz
    1989   *The Mission.* Film.
al-Shaykh, Hanan
    [1980] 1986   *The Story of Zahra.* New York: Readers International.
Sidwa, Bapsy
    1990   *Ice Candy Man.* London: Jonathan Cape.
Singh, Kushwant
    1956   *Train to Pakistan.* New York: Grove Press.
Singleton, John
    1991   *Boyz 'N the Hood.* Film.

Tajiri, Rea
    1991   *History and Memory*. Film.
Tyler, Stephen
    1986   *The Unspeakable*. Madison: University of Wisconsin Press.
Yehoshua, A. B.
    [1989] 1992   *Mr. Mani*. New York: Doubleday.

EIGHT

Fostering Trust in a Climate of Fear

Beatriz Manz

This chapter is an analysis of the events that compel people to seek refuge beyond their communities and the constraints to the building of trust after their anticipated return. I argue that gaining trust among repatriates from highly polarized societies is only possible if the causes that lead them to become refugees are explicitly addressed and acknowledged and, as a by-product, if the fundamental schisms that separate the refugee population from their persecutors are redressed. The focus here is an examination of the depth of fear in the everyday experience of Mayan Indians of Guatemala so as to assess the possibilities for a successful reintegration.[1]

SCOPE OF FEAR

Several scholars have addressed the issue of fear and terror in recent writings on conditions in the third world. Some have referred to this phenomenon as a culture; when "torture is endemic" in the society, it perpetrates a "culture of terror" (Taussig 1984:467–497, 1987). A critical component of the culture of terror is silence and a negation of the truth. Often the logic of terror is difficult to decipher as an erratic concealment of deeds, mystery, and uncertainty alternate with overt and purposeful displays of terror. Rumors and fantasy abound. The boundaries of social behavior are not clear, the parameters blurred, the scope of misbehavior very broad. Punishment is arbitrary, irregular, and often fatal. The rule of law is nonexistent.

When these conditions exist in a society based on centuries of discrimination, inequality, and abuse, there does not have to be a moment of radical disjunction, although this does occur. Rather, there is a deepening of the lack of trust and estrangement. Persons become refugees when in assessing their relationship to the state it becomes clear that they are living in a situation where torture, death, and kidnapping have become pervasive, beyond levels routinely endured. Exiles and refugees experience the moment of flight in various dimensions. Some may have enjoyed prior participation and a sense of security; others, such as minorities or disenfranchised majorities, may have never felt integrated into the larger society as a result of racism and social repression.

A unique case for assessing the notion of trust among a dispossessed ethnic population is that of Guatemalan Mayan refugees. The term "refugee" here is used to include persons that fled their communities irrespective of whether they crossed state boundaries or remained within the internationally recognized political borders. The external refugees are in Mexico or the United States. The refugees that have remained within the country are known as the communities of population in resistance (CPR). They have successfully eluded the Guatemalan military for ten years by hiding in the lowland tropical rain forest or in highland forests. Others are dispersed in Guatemala City or other areas such as the plantation zone where anonymity is easier to maintain.

For non-Mayan urban middle-class persons (known in Guatemala as *ladinos*), a radical disjunction is likely to occur which propels them to become refugees as they experience a sense of isolation and overwhelming fear. In contrast, Mayans have lived for five hundred years within a society dominated by others with ever-present isolation, fear, and oppression. Official denial of repressive actions against Indian communities is the norm. A radical disjunction, therefore, is more likely to occur to a ladino than to an Indian. The roots of fear and suspicion among Indians are too deep for establishing trust; even developing minimal levels of confidence in the ability to achieve basic security—a more realistic goal—is a daunting task. Thus consideration of what it would take to build this confidence within the Guatemalan refugee population must begin with an understanding of the breadth, depth, and length of the culture of terror that has characterized Latin American societies for the last five centuries as well as the particular characteristics of the Guatemalan refugees—the most durable refugee population in Central America.

HISTORY, FUNCTION, AND PERSONAL TESTIMONY

When the Spanish Inquisition was imported to the New World, it quickly evolved into a system of terror that helped maintain control over the indigenous population. The violence that became an institutional feature of colonial rule and life resulted in the deaths of millions of Indians.[2]

Historical reportage and literary fiction are useful forms to contextualize the feeling of fear.[3] The first words sent by Spanish conquistadors from the "new world" were of simple and friendly people. There were only a few voices that reported on the mistreatment at the hands of these conquerors. One eyewitness who wrote about the brutality the original inhabitants were subjected to was the Spanish priest Bartolome de las Casas. He wrote in horror, for example, of seven thousand children dying in three months, of mothers drowning their babies in sheer desperation and yet others inducing to abort. Indians were forced to work ceaselessly with minimal rest. The Spanish supervisors, whom he called "cruel brutes," "treated the Indians with such rigor and inhumanity that they seemed the very ministers of Hell, driving them day and night with beatings, kicks, lashes, and blows and calling them no sweeter name than dogs." What was called " 'moderate labor' turned into labor fit only for iron men: mountains are stripped from top to bottom and bottom to top a thousand times, they dig, split rocks, move stones and carry dirt on their backs" (Goodpasture 1989:10). Others had to wash gold in rivers staying in the water all day with their backs bent constantly, breaking them. The Indians were kept in captivity, constantly and fiercely abused. "Even beasts enjoy more freedom when they are allowed to graze in the fields." This treatment, de las Casas observed, was "designed to destroy all Indians." Antonio Montesinos, a Dominican friar, was also horrified at the cruel decimation and pernicious abuse of the Indians. He asked the Spanish, "By what right or justice do you hold these Indians in such cruel and horrible slavery? By what right do you wage such detestable wars on these people who lived mildly and peaceful in their own lands. . . . [W]hy do you oppress and fatigue, . . . so you may extract and acquire gold every day? . . . Are they not men?" (ibid., 12).

Terror was part and parcel of this genesis, "the mediator par excellence of colonial hegemony: the space of death where the Indian, African and White gave birth to a New World" (Taussig 1987:5). De las Casas's and Antonio Montesinos's pictures of the "new world" also remind us of how little has changed. The physical and verbal abuse persist. Ladinos generally hold the Indians in contempt, subjecting them to ridicule. As one anthropologist noted, "Fear has always been an intrinsic part of the psychodynamics of the ladino-Indian relationship," often with bloody effects. The ladino ruling class "feared the Indians as a potentially rebellious people who had to be periodically reminded of their conquered status; and the periodic reminders have, quite naturally, reinforced a fear already long present in the minds of the Indians" (Adams 1988:284).

In the past four decades the military and agrobusiness elites have escalated the customary abuse with widespread torture, assassinations, kidnapping, and outright massacres of entire villages. The increase in violence had to be justified. In 1954, the Guatemalan "authorities" found the justification: they were able to organize and receive U.S. support around the common denominator of anticommunism (Aguilera Peralta et al. 1981:prologue). The target, quite clearly, was not communism but democracy. And inversely: to fight for democracy was (and still is) to be a Communist; to challenge the terror is to challenge the state. All attempts at unmasking the official lies, masquerading as truth, are labeled subversive activities. And, in Guatemala, subversives are by definition people without rights. Even a cursory look at Guatemala would reveal that being a subversive—to subvert the existing state of affairs—should be viewed as a moral virtue rather than a depravity. That inability or unwillingness to adapt to the given antisocial environment should be assessed as healthy, since such adaptation would not be conducive to the evolution of social harmony. Moreover, this horrific devastation, particularly in the early 1980s, grew to hideous dimensions with little public attention throughout the world.

A vehement state of secrecy, vulnerability, and humiliation is the pillar of an authoritarian state. Ariel Dorfman (1985:A17), writing about Chile, illuminates the notion of secrecy and unreality. People "are isolated from each other, their means of communicating suppressed, their connections cut off, their senses blocked by fear." Occasional manhunts reactivate the government's control of fear. Government officials are not in the slightest embarrassed by the absurdity of their actions, by their efforts to deny reality. They sarcastically relish it. "By eliminating news, the Government hopes to eliminate reality," Dorfman observes. When asked about "the disappeared," even if thousands of prisoners are taken to a national stadium, a government will respond cynically, "What prisoners?" "What stadium?" But cynical tactics can still have an effect, as Dorfman reveals, as individuals "refuse to act and tend to become passive: when people do not know what is happening near them, they are given the pretext for not caring. What is endangered is the existence of community—the nation's moral foundation. I have found many people who . . . float apart in fragments, reduced to private worries, merely trying to survive."

In the past two decades Catholic bishops in Latin America, both at Medellín and at Puebla, have defined "institutional violence" as the dominant feature of society. The Guatemalan refugee crisis must be situated, quite appropriately, within a discussion of terror. Their plight is neither limited to an individual experience of suffering nor rooted in culturally defined moral and political deficiencies; rather, it reflects centuries-old oppression as well as contemporary-style "low"-intensity warfare. The refugees see their plight neither as an isolated event in their social history nor solely in a personal sense. Since colonial times the Indian community provided security, stability, comfort, and familiarity—the social elements needed for fostering trust. One of the critical new elements in the terror campaign was the violation of this last sanctuary for Indians: the community. The society went beyond economic and ethnic division, becoming violently torn apart and destroying the most intimate bonds of family and community. The most isolated of villages was penetrated, intruded, and disrupted. In the 1980s a modern Guatemalan army was aided by sophisticated strategies of control, thus going much beyond the previous periodic reinforcement.

One of the leading social psychologists in Latin America, Ignacio Martín-Baró (one of the Jesuits assassinated by the military in El Salvador in 1989), explains two interacting structures operating in social psychology: "the structure of the individual (the human personality) and the social structure (each historical society)" (Pacheco and Jiménez 1990:ix). That is, we need to look at individuals' perceptions of their social reality as well as their position within it. Guatemalan refugees tend to see the current persecution from a collective perspective within a social and historical context.

The relationship between the massive flight of Indians from the highlands and rain forest of Guatemala and the military's policies of extermination and relocation is well documented.[4] Within this context, more personal histories of the last several decades of terror highlight the drama of an everyday struggle for survival. Rigoberta Menchú's testimony about her brother's murder by the Guatemalan army is a firsthand account of the fright that millions of Indians have experienced. "The captain gave a panoramic description of all the power they had, the capacity they had," she recounts. "We, the people, didn't have the capacity to confront them. This was really being said to strike terror into the people and stop anyone from speaking." One's closest relatives are forced to witness the horror, unable to intervene. "My mother wept," she continues. "She almost risked her own life by going to embrace my brother. My other brothers and my father held her back so she wouldn't endanger herself." The result is great fear mixed with bitter anger. "My father was incredible; I watched him and he didn't shed a tear, but he was full of rage. And that was rage we all felt. But all the rest of us began to weep, like everyone else" (Burgos-Debray 1984:178).

Felipe Ixcot Jalben, a refugee from the province of Quezaltenango who fled to the United States, where he now lives in a church sanctuary, tied the exploitation of the Mayan people by the Spaniards to the terror he experienced at the hands of the Guatemalan army. "What then did the conquest bring for us, the indigenous people?" he questions. "It brought us the terror of the destruction of a culture, of a people, and of a social organization. It was also the first step in the imposition of a system of exploitation and humiliation that persists to our day and under which we still live and suffer" (1985:141).

He emphasizes historical relationships between dominant elites and Indians, stressing the ways in which ideologies are used as an excuse for butchering Indians. He defines the struggle for human rights as an autochthonous movement. "The history and struggle of our people is not a struggle provoked by Cuba or Russia or any other outside power," he states. "What we are doing is following the example of our ancestors." He feels strongly that "our struggle is based on the values of our ancestors, the Mayans," and asserts that "we are not giving ourselves, selling ourselves, lending ourselves to the interests of the Russians or the Cubans or any other people, but that we are inspired by our own ancestors to defend our land and customs, our lives and culture" (ibid., 142).

Just as witnesses and those targeted by oppression can capture the essence of their reality, novelists such as Miguel Angel Asturias, the Guatemalan Nobel Laureate in literature, wrote brilliantly about the climate of fear created by the tyrannical rule in his appropriately titled novel, *El señor presidente*.

> The fourth voice murmured faintly: "There's no hope of freedom for us, my friends; we must put up with this as long as God wills. The men of this town who desired their country's good are far away now: some of them begging outside houses in a foreign land, others rotting in a common grave. A day will come when no one dares walk the streets of this town. Already the trees don't bear fruit like they used to. Maize is less nourishing than it was. Sleep is less restful; water is less refreshing. The

air is becoming impossible to breathe. Plagues follow epidemics, epidemics follow plagues, and soon an earthquake will put an end to us all. My eyes tell me that our race is doomed! When it thunders, it is a voice from heaven crying: 'You are evil and corrupt, you are accomplices in wickedness!' Hundreds of men have had their brains blown out against our prison walls by murderous bullets. Our marble palaces are wet with innocent blood. Where can one turn one's eyes in search of freedom?" (1963:201)

An important dimension of Latin American oppression is the depth of terror that descends from the desire of ruling elites for total control aimed more than anything at neutralizing resistance, especially among the Indians. Terror exists, not in isolated acts of violence, but in the body politic as a whole.

Fear is a constant reality. The military and economic elites would like to think of themselves as omnipotent. The population at times feels overcome by the sensation that tyrants could know what everyone is doing and could direct any action with impunity. Asturias captures that feeling.

Everything seemed easy until the dogs began barking at him in the monstrous wood which separated the President from his enemies, a wood made up of trees with ears which responded to the slightest sound by whirling as if blown by a hurricane. Not the tiniest noise for miles around could escape the avidity of those millions of membranes. The dogs went on barking. A network of invisible threads, more invisible than telegraph wires, connected every leaf with the President, enabling him to keep watch on the most secret thoughts of the townspeople. (Ibid., 39)

While the fear is more intense for the Indians, it is part of the culture of the poor. The Salvadoran novelist Manlio Argueta reveals the role of the Catholic church in perpetuating a discipline, sense of obedience, and fear of sinning and hell among the poor. "And we don't feel pain in our souls when we talk about our neighbor," he writes. "We used to. We couldn't even think bad thoughts because we believed we would be condemning ourselves. For everything there was damnation. For everything there was hell. For everything there was fire as punishment. Our tongue was always tied by our fear of sin" (1983:53).

Another significant element of class relations is that the poor are expected to know their assigned place in society and resign themselves to that, always showing submission.

We always wanted to be good. We believed that to be good was to bow one's head, not to protest, not to demand anything, not to get angry. . . . [W]e were always being offered a celestial paradise. The reward for being good. To respect one's neighbor was really to respect the landowner. And to respect the landowner was to conform to his whimsy. If there were no beans to eat after working on the plantation, it was because the landowner couldn't manage, the landowner was suffering losses. . . . We used to confuse goodness with resignation. (Ibid., 52)

Argueta's most telling line of the assigned position of the poor in Latin American societies, especially those with large indigenous populations, is perhaps the resignation associated with the traditional Catholic church allied with the rich, contrasted with a born again wisdom and liberation: "We used to confuse goodness with resignation." But still personal liberation cannot be fully realized while the social conditions remain in a state of oppression and distress. Real liberation and trust cannot be cultivated and sustained separate from the society that binds individuals.

THE IMPOSITION AND CULTIVATION OF FEAR

In Guatemala, the people are subjected to a violence barely concealed below the surface of society. Suspicion is cultivated in the rural areas by the existence of misnamed *patrullas de autodefensa civil,* self-defense civil patrols, military commissioners, and other selected or coerced informers. This foreign military imposes a network of informers, pits neighbor against neighbor. A network of spies extends throughout the countryside. In the early phases of the militarization of the countryside, patrollers were even taken to the city to seek out and denounce refugees from their home communities (Manz 1988a:38–41).

Jon Sobrino refers to the situation in El Salvador that claimed the lives of his friends and fellow priests at the University of Central America as "a world of death" (*Sojourners* 1990:17). He poses the question, "Why haven't these people of El Salvador and Guatemala committed collective suicide? After so many centuries of being oppressed and repressed—new governments, new superpowers—why haven't they said, 'History makes no sense?' " And his answer reflects an extraordinary aspect of the lives of many Central Americans. "Because they have hope. Hope for what? Just to live" (ibid., 18).

Yet the hope is mixed with the constant terror that the massacres may begin again, or that a family member may disappear or be murdered at any time. This fear is sometimes so debilitating that it makes daily life nearly unbearable for the survivors (Manz 1988a:92). Organizations such as the Mutual Support Group (GAM), Ethnic Communities—We Are All Equal (CERJ), and the National Committee of Widows of Guatemala (CONAVIGUA) are attacked for exposing human rights violations and calling for the dissolution of the civil patrols that are used in rural areas to attack them.

The terror aims at paralyzing and rendering the majority impotent so that resistance to oppression and democratic participation becomes impossible to conceive of, much less implement; life becomes a struggle to maintain the routine of survival. In the culture of terror the goal is to turn not only against neighbor and family but, more significantly, inward, directing one's fear against oneself: the enemy is oneself because the individual's motives and actions are subjected to constant scrutiny. Individuals must always prove their loyalty and lack of subversive intent.

The eternal question of the government is, when will you reveal your crime? Everyone is perceived as guilty. The object is to prove and constantly re-prove one's innocence. But, as we will see, the collective and communal nature of Mayan culture and the identification of an individual's predicament with that of others like oneself makes many of the goals of terror somewhat more bearable.

Terror becomes the key ingredient in maintaining the power of the state when the legitimacy of the state is fundamentally in question. Without fear, power is undermined. And social terror—whether massive or incremental—is the basis for individual fear. When the state relies on terror as the basis of rule, it is acting against the needs of the people, and thus, by a widely accepted definition of the state, it is illegitimate (Montealegre 1982:187–210). Yet, illegitimate as it may be, the state, backed by a superpower, has seemingly endless staying power. The following reflections from the diary of a Guatemalan judge are illuminating.

> In Guatemala there are two systems of law: the formal system you are taught at Law School and the real system. In the real system there are areas in which everyone knows the law is totally irrelevant—such as the disappeared, the habeas corpus, and crimes committed by military officers.
>
> The fact that the formal system exists allows the real system to continue. It veils the real system. It protects the real system. It is its accomplice.
>
> A person who comes from a democratic culture will not understand Guatemala. He will read that the constitution protects freedom of speech. But there has never been freedom of speech in Guatemala: you speak out and they kill you. . . .
>
> He will read that the constitution protects private property. But tomorrow someone from the upper class or the military could come and force you to sell your small finca for any price he wants. What naivete to imagine that a piece of paper has more power than an officer with a machine gun!
>
> He will read that the constitution protects life, but, in fact, the constitution protects regimes that kill and never admit it. They hint at their crimes, but only to deepen the fear of the people.
>
> The law is the facade that makes it possible for the upper class and the military to pretend that they live in the twentieth century while they uphold, in fact, the brutality and the injustice of a savage past. (Gleijeses 1988:15–16)

The government simultaneously denies any involvement in the terror while maintaining the terror. Martín-Baró pinpoints the government's role in terror and institutionalized lies. In its attempt to create an official story, the government filters reality. "Above all, the object is to create an official version of the facts, an 'official story,' which ignores crucial aspects of reality, distorts others, and even falsifies or invents still others" (1989:10). And on the relation of violence and social contract, he writes, "Structural violence cannot be reduced to an inadequate distribution of available resources which impede the satisfaction of the basic necessities of the majority. Structural violence includes an ordering of that oppressive inequality, through the use of legislation which hides behind the mechanisms of the social distribution of wealth and establishes a coercive force obligating the people to respect them. The system therefore closes the cycle of violence, justifying and protecting those structures that privilege the few at the cost of the many. . . . [V]iolence is already present in the social order."[5]

Some suggest that a culture of terror has in fact become "a necrophiliac culture" because it is ruled by those who possess "the passion to tear apart living structures" (Giddens 1985:300). In listening to the testimonies of survivors regarding the manner and symbols employed to torture, rape, kill, and burn people alive, one certainly realizes the perpetrators acquire the ability to distance themselves from the suffering. I was particularly taken by one account, because it was one of the first testimonies I heard in 1982 as refugees fleeing Guatemala entered the Lacandón rain forest in Mexico, or because it seemed stunningly slow and brutal, or because of the moving explanation given by the witness. The military action began in a familiar way: soldiers arrived at a village and dragged a man from his home, hitting and shoving him with guns. Using abusive, insulting language they demanded information or confession. The answers did not satisfy the soldiers. After overwhelming physical and verbal abuse while the villagers, including his wife and small children, watched, the soldiers decided to apply more serious torture. According to the eyewitness, they inserted a pointed instrument, like a long needle, into one eye. The man shrieked and screamed, blood covered his face. They took out one eye, then the other, but still the man did not know what he had to say. The soldiers made fun of him, they taunted him that he must be tough, that he obviously did not want to cooperate. He insisted he knew nothing about the guerrillas. Finally, they took the man down the river to drown him, pushing and shoving him. He could no longer see. There they submerged him underwater and then let go, but the man would not drown. The witness who related this episode of torture thought that probably, though the victim could not see, he knew his children were watching, and he was sad and tried not to die. He was a proud man who wanted to spare his family suffering and sadness. Several times they kept him underwater, until finally, he could not be strong anymore, he could not resist, and he gave up and died. There was nothing more he could do.

I was as much taken by the images of the incident as by the interpretation of the gentle and soft-spoken witness. I sympathized with the feeling of vulnerability, of fate, of not knowing what the authorities want, as well as the strong message that the witness conveyed of a father who loves his children, is desperately trying to convey that love, and seeks to escape death as part of that love. The witness said nothing about those that committed the deed. He was totally focused on detailing the incident from the victim's point of view. But knowing that the army had modern state-of-the-art weapons yet chose to use rudimentary means to commit this heinous crime heightened my awareness of their urgent need to create terror among survivors. It is not enough to kill; they must terrorize those they will allow to live. I did not see the incident, but since then on my trips to Guatemala I have felt more frightened. Its one thing to be shot and die instantly, quite another to be kidnapped or killed like that good, honorable man.

CONSTRAINTS TO OVERCOMING FEAR

What are the effects on children, particularly when they have been forced to witness terror? One study reflects on the destructive experiences of war for refugee children. According to the report, the events that lead to the exodus are not "isolated traumatic events; they become traumatic processes that continue to destroy the psyche way after they have occurred. . . . This is the origin of nocturnal terror, fantasies of persecution and a generalized sense of fear" long after and even far distant from danger (Thomas 1985:30). Though difficult to assimilate, because the atrocities "defy human comprehension," nothing is gained by covering up, denying, burying, or making children forget. Remembering and understanding are essential for mental health—to avoid being trapped in pathology.

Jacobo Timerman (1987:31–32) has captured better than anyone the meaning of terror and the difficulties of "eradicating fear and ending anxiety about more horror in the future." This problem prompted Latin American psychologists to organize a conference in Buenos Aires entitled "The Culture of Fear in Totalitarian Regimes" at which the psychological characteristics generated by fear were outlined.

> Sensation of vulnerability: In the face of life-threatening situations there is a sense of personal weakness. The individual feels "identified" and "persecuted" and loses all possibility of privacy and intimacy in his personal life. He becomes susceptible to arbitrary behavior beyond his control.
>
> State of alert: The senses are exacerbated and the individual cannot rest in the face of imminent danger and the life-threatening situation this poses. This can be expressed in various symptomatic ways.
>
> Individual impotence: The individual recognizes that his own resources and strength are inadequate to deal with adversity. The individual in this situation feels he has no control over his own life and that decisions about his future are not in his hands. This impotence, and the allied feelings of vulnerability and helplessness, give rise to a sense of abandonment in the face of violence.
>
> Alteration of the sense of reality: As one of the objectives of inducing fear is to deprive an individual of his ability to act, the ordinary sense of reality is deliberately disrupted and rendered useless. It comes to seem practically impossible to verify what is objective fact against subjective experience, and the boundary between what is real and possible on the one hand and what is fantasy and imagination on the other tends to dissolve. Reality becomes confusing and threatening, with no clear borders, and so loses its guiding role in subjective processes. (Ibid., 32)

Martín-Baró (1989:14) refers to the work of Joaquín Samayoa in understanding that the "cognitive and behavioral changes caused by war bring with them a process of dehumanization." This process of dehumanization hinders four important human abilities: to think lucidly, to communicate truthfully, sensitivity to the suffering of others, and hope.

Martín-Baró departs from a position of adaptation, passivity, and alienation. He claims that the evidence shows "the essentially active role groups and individuals play as subjects no matter how alienated they may be." Referring to El Salvador, he goes on to state, "There is no doubt that for many Salvadorans, the war is something imposed on them; but for a significant number, the war is something they themselves help to cause and develop. Looking at their participation in those processes from a merely adaptive perspective would lead to misunderstanding" (ibid., 15–16). War, Martín-Baró suggests, defines all that is social. "By its very dynamic, a war tends to become the most all-encompassing phenomenon of a country's situation, the dominant process to which all other social, economic, political, and cultural processes must be subordinated, and which, directly or indirectly, affects all the members of a society" (ibid., 7–8). We tend to emphasize only the physical aspects of war and not others, such as the psychological aspects.

Latin American psychologists point out the limits of psychotherapy and underscore the social nature of the problem. "But in speaking of psycho-social trauma, one should emphasize two other aspects that are frequently forgotten: (a) the injury that affects people has been produced socially—i.e., its roots are not found in the individual, but in society; and (b) its very nature is nourished and maintained in the relationship between the individual and society, through various mediations by institutions, groups, and even individuals" (ibid., 14). Timerman (1987:29) also highlights the need for "collective treatment" of mass trauma. Others refer to the possibility of a "collective overcoming" of trauma (by refugee children) when conditions are suitable (Ronstrom 1989:147).

SOCIAL CONTEXT AND THE ROLE OF INTELLECTUALS

Psychotherapy needs to be complemented at the macrosocial level, "establishing a new framework for coexistence, a new 'social contract' that would allow collective interaction without turning disagreement into mutual negation." There is a need for greater social sincerity so as to "learn about realities before defining them, to accept facts before interpreting them" (Martín-Baró 1989:19). Martín-Baró's research centered on El Salvador, a society less polarized than Guatemala. To move in the direction he is positing, or to achieve a new social contract in a country like Guatemala, would be substantially more difficult.

Given the historical legacy of Guatemalan society and the recent experience of terror, what are the possibilities for engendering minimal confidence in personal security, if not trust? Most observers agree that what has changed in Guatemala in the last several decades are the waves or the "varying levels and intensity" of terror, not its existence (Aguilera Peralta 1980:111). When Guatemalan refugees return they are not under the illusion that they are returning to a democratic, peaceful society that has renounced violence as a means of rule; they return to a society that has temporarily abated its tactics, but not its strategy, of terror. The terror does not exist merely as an internalized psychological state but primarily as the state's objective to destroy all mediating structures in society that stand between the state and the individual—including, when necessary, the family (Franco 1986: 5–17). Even memory itself becomes a target.[6]

Social scientists in Latin America are cognizant of the implications of terror for the role of intellectuals in society. In Western academic research there is a tendency to emphasize a separation of subject and object, academics and fellow members of society. Yet there are many who have little difficulty sorting out our roles as citizens/witnesses/researchers. Some of us believe there are no ethics in silence, that we bear a responsibility, that the subject we choose is not value-free, and that informants are not specimens for observation, analysis, and documentation, to be classified, theorized, and filed. A balance is possible and essential. As Paulo Freire (1988:30) phrased it, "Separated from practice, theory is a pure inoperative verbalistic act; torn from theory, practice is blind activism. Because of this, there is no authentic praxis outside of the dialectical unit action-reflection, practice-theory." I concur with the position that

> being partial, which always assumes the taking of a stance, does not have to eliminate objectivity. It is absurd, as well as an aberration, to ask impartiality of those who study the problem of drug addiction, child abuse, or torture. What should be asked and required, is that those phenomena be analyzed with all the rigor and with a total openness to the data given by reality. This means that objectivity is not the same thing as impartiality. But the axiological options, which lead to rejection of certain things and to desire others, must constitute a horizon which sheds light on our subject of study, not as something superfluously added, but as something intrinsic to the scientific, academic or professional activities themselves. (Pacheco and Jiménez 1990:67)

PROSPECTS

Guatemalan refugees have experienced the terror unleashed on their communities and the difficulties of exile since 1982. In my years of research, I have not found a refugee who feels the government, the military, or the ladinos (especially professionals or the landowning elite) can be trusted, because of the intrinsic oppression and discrimination in their daily lives. Trust can only be conceived in the framework of fundamental structural changes in the society. The mutual mistrust that exists is a deeply rooted component of the social relations that are remnants of colonial society. A step in the direction of regaining confidence (not trust) could come about through organization and collective resistance to a system of domination that has destroyed families and communities. The ability of Guatemalan refugees to identify with one another and to cultivate bonds of solidarity and unity is a major cultural asset. Their tenacity and strength can best be explained by their strong sense of community and a tradition of collective action and solidarity. They became refugees, by and large, in a communal exodus, and that itself impels them to respond collectively. If anything, the common refugee experience by necessity strengthens the bonds and accelerates trusting relations that under normal circumstances might be cause for customary hesitation and precaution. In addition to their own solidarity, a decisive expression of solidarity from others (within Guatemala and elsewhere) to counter the silence, isolation, and indifference becomes a critical step in recovering confidence among the refugees. Along with solidarity it would seem essential as well to acknowledge the wrongdoing and pass judgment, what Central Americans are calling "the right to the truth—el derecho a la verdad." As a Guatemalan lawyer states, "Truth has tremendous power. People want to know, where are the disappeared? Were they tortured and by whom? Even if there is no prosecution." Acknowledging what happened would be socially therapeutic. Guatemalans might be willing to settle for a general recognition of the crimes. "The fact that you ignore the [identity of the] culprit does not mean you ignore the crime" (LaRue 1991). The right to truth is essential if the goal is healing, to move the knowledge of the isolated event from the private domain to the official sphere. To recognize, to acknowledge, to render a public admission of wrongdoing, and thus begin to leave the pain behind.

Traditional Western psychological methods might be inadequate for interpreting the wholesale destruction and heightened disregard for human rights; tragically, the separation of psychological theory from political activity only serves to perpetuate the slow disintegration of communal existence that occurs within—and is the goal of—the culture of terror. In Latin America, there is an effort to heal this great divide between the personal and the political.

Guatemalan refugees are today planning their "voluntary, organized and collective" return.[7] I find myself posing the same questions that haunted the Chilean novelist Ariel Dorfman: "How can those who torture and those who were tortured co-exist in the same land? How to heal a country that has been traumatized by repression if the fear to speak out is still omnipresent? And how do you reach the truth if lying has become a habit?" (Dorfman 1991:59). But, though more difficult than in Chile, a slow healing process must begin and with it, one hopes, the restructuring of society that such a process could bring forth.[8]

I reserved the last words, because they are hopeful words, for a Guatemalan woman who has suffered from the terror described above but amazingly is attempting to forge unity and set her view to a brighter future. Menchú, in addressing the opening session of the the Second Continental Meeting "500 Years of Resistance" held in Guatemala in October 1991 spoke of her dreams for the future, of the importance of unity between Indians and poor ladinos. The pain, suffering, and blood shed by her ancestors and brothers and sisters today, said Menchú, is something one can draw lessons from. In her call for unity she assured those listening, fellow Indians and also "my ladino and mestizo compatriots" that "we are open, we have a great conscience, we are not intransigent . . . and if at one point we struggled hard, and we have called things by their name, and if our forefathers lost their lives in the big social confrontation in this continent, it was because we had no other recourse." This is a time for harmony. "We must live together in a pluri-cultural society, and respect one another, to find room for everyone, and resolve together the problems that bind us. This is a challenge brothers and sisters. . . . We are talking of unity, compañeros." Menchú spoke of new concepts of education, development, politics, and participation of the disenfranchised in their future and destiny. This will require "reflection and analysis and action in the interests of the great majority . . . [as well as the need to] work without frustrations to solve the difficulties we will encounter along the way." She referred to the construction of a diverse and open culture, with room for everyone, as well as mutual respect.

The week-long continental meeting, held in the highland city of Quetzalte-nango, concluded with a call for unity among Indians, African-Americans, and the popular sector. As a special guest to that historic event, I felt in Quetzalte-nango that the emergence of democracy in a country such as Guatemala could lay the basis for the arduous path toward reconciliation, social justice, and trust.

NOTES

I am indebted to several students from the University of California, Berkeley, especially Tim Nonn, Amy Ross, and Alex La Croix, for their invaluable assistance in writing this chapter. I would also like to thank the participants at the UN-WIDER workshop at Bergen, Norway, for their thoughtful response.

1. In 1982 there was a mass exodus of Guatemalan Indian peasants. Ten years later these refugees are still in UNHCR camps or live as "invisible" refugees in Mexico. It has been estimated that out of a total population of eight million, one million Guatemalans (mostly Mayans from several ethnolinguistic groups that make up the estimated four million Indians in that country) were displaced in the 1980s. More than one quarter of a million fled the country, mainly to Mexico but also to the United States. Their case is not widely known, and yet Guatemala is considered one of the worst violators of human rights in Latin America. In 1992, as their refugee status ends, the refugees' main concern is human rights. At the local level there are issues regarding adaptation to new social conditions, resolution of personal conflicts, emotional scars, fears, divisions, and tensions the displacement experi-ence created between those that left and those that remained, and serious disputes that are likely to occur with new land-starved settlers who were given possession of the refugees' land.

2. For background on the colonial period, see Helms 1982; Smith 1990; Thomas 1991; Wolf 1990.

3. The Peruvian novelist Mario Vargas Llosa relishes telling that "the novel was for-bidden in the Spanish colonies by the Inquisition" because it was considered "dangerous for the spiritual faith of the Indians as for the moral and political behavior of society, and, of course, they were absolutely right." He goes on to express gratitude to the Inquisitors, "for having discovered before any critic did the inevitable subversive nature of fiction." Vargas Llosa offers the explanation or excuse for my utilizing fiction in a work on social psycho-logical reality. Latin American novelists can capture the meaning of daily life in a way that social scientists often seem to miss. The "revenge of the novel" is quickly recognized, as is the often blurred line between fiction and reality. Referring to writers such as Gabriel Gar-cía Márquez, he states, "History and literature, truth and falsehood, reality and fiction min-gle in these texts in a way that is often inextricable. The thin demarcation line that separates one from the other frequently fades away so that both worlds are entwined in a complete-ness which the more ambiguous it is the more seductive it becomes because the likely and the unlikely in it seem to be part of the same substance" (Vargas Llosa 1991:24–25).

4. For background on displacement, see Manz 1988a, 1988b. For a general background on Guatemalan society in the decades of the 1970s and 1980s, see also Black 1988; Carmack 1988; Figueroa Ibarra 1991.

5. *The Jesuit Assassinations: The Writings of Ellacuría, Martín-Baró and Segundo Montes, with a Chronology of the Investigation* (Kansas City: Sheed and Ward, 1990:10–11).

6. For a description of the new tactics, symbols, and defiance used by the mothers of the disappeared in Argentina to counter the denial by the military authorities, see Navarro 1988:241–256.

7. The refugees, through elected representatives, have drafted and sent to the Guatemalan government six conditions for their return. The right to (1) return voluntarily, in a collective and organized way; (2) take possession of their lands; (3) organization and freedom of association; (4) life and integrity, both personal and of the community; (5) presence of international and national delegations; and (6) freedom of movement both within the country and internationally. It is noteworthy that the Guatemalan refugees in Mexico refer to the process not by using the term "repatriation" but by consciously referring to it as "return" *(el retorno)*.

8. Patricio Aylwin, the first president of Chile after 17 years of military dictatorship, took a step in the direction of healing by allowing an acknowledgment and making official past misdeeds, which could be followed in a country such as Guatemala. A commission was appointed—the Rettig Commission—to investigate the human rights abuses committed during General Pinochet's dictatorship.

9. Remarks made by Rigoberta Menchú during the opening session at the II Encuentro Continental held in Guatemala City on October 7, 1991. For a full account, resolutions, and summary, see the official document, II Encuentro Continental, "Canta, levántate America, voz de tantas raices," in *Campaña, 500 Años de Resistencia Indígena y Popular,* Quetzaltenango, del 7 al 12 de octubre de 1991 (Guatemala: Secretaría Operativa, Noviembre 1991). The year 1992 marks two crucial anniversaries: what the original inhabitants of the continent call "500 years of resistance" and the Indian culture, a "culture of resistance," as well as ten years as refugees.

REFERENCES

Adams, Richard N.
>   1988   "Conclusions: What Can We Know about the Harvest of Violence?" In
>   *Harvest of Violence: The Maya Indians and the Guatemalan Crisis,* ed. Robert M.
>   Carmack, 274–291. Norman: University of Oklahoma Press.

Argueta, Manlio
>   1983   *One Day of Life.* Trans. Bill Brow. New York: Random House. Originally
>   published as *Un día en la vida,* San José, Costa Rica, 1982.

Aguilera Peralta, Gabriel
>   1980   "Terror and Violence as Weapons of Counter-Insurgency in Guatemala."
>   *Latin American Perspectives* 7 (2–3):91–113.

Aguilera Peralta, Gabriel, et al.
>   1981   *Dialéctica del terror en Guatemala.* San José, Costa Rica: Editorial Universitaria Centroamericana.

Asturias, Miguel Angel
>   1963   *El señor presidente.* New York: Atheneum.

Black, George
    1988   *Garrison Guatemala*. New York: Monthly Review Press.
Burgos-Debray, Elisabeth, ed.
    1984   *I, Rigoberta Menchú: An Indian Woman in Guatemala*. London: Verso.
Carmack, Robert H.
    1988   *Harvest of Violence*. Norman: University of Oklahoma Press.
Dorfman, Ariel
    1985   "A Rural Chilean Legend Come True." *New York Times*, February 18, A17.
    1991   *Death and the Maiden*. London: Nick Hern Books.
Figueroa Ibarra, Carlos
    1991   *El recurso de miedo: Ensayo sobre el estado y el terror en Guatemala*. San José, Costa
                Rica: Editorial Universitaria Centroamericana.
Franco, Jean
    1986   "Death Camp Confessions and Resistance to Violence in Latin America."
                *Socialism and Democracy: The Bulletin of the Research Group on Socialism and Democ-
                racy* 2 (Spring/Summer):5–17.
Freire, Paulo
    1988   *La importancia de leer y el proceso de liberación*. Mexico: Editorial Siglo Vein-
                tiuno.
Giddens, Anthony
    1985   *The Nation-State and Violence*. Berkeley, Los Angeles, and London: University
                of California Press.
Gleijeses, Piero
    1988   *Politics of Culture in Guatemala*. Ann Arbor: Center for Political Studies, Insti-
                tute for Social Research, University of Michigan.
Goodpasture, H. McKennie, ed.
    1989   *Cross and Sword: An Eyewitness History of Christianity in Latin America*. Mary-
                knoll, N.Y.: Orbis.
Helms, Mary W.
    1982   *Middle America: A Cultural History of Heartland and Frontiers*. Washington, D.C.:
                University Press of America, 1982.
Ixcot Jalben, Felipe
    1985   "The Traditions and Culture of the Mayan Quiché People." In *Sanctuary: A
                Resource Guide for Understanding and Participating in the Central American Refugee's
                Struggle*, ed. Gary MacEoin, 139–147. San Francisco: Harper and Row.
LaRue, Frank
    1991   Lecture delivered at University of California, Berkeley. 21 November.
Manz, Beatriz
    1988*a*   *Refugees of a Hidden War: The Aftermath of Counterinsurgency in Guatemala*.
                Albany: State University of New York Press.
    1988*b*   *Repatriation and Reintegration: An Arduous Process in Guatemala*. Washington,
                D.C.: Georgetown University, Hemispheric Migration Project/Center for
                Immigration Policy and Refugee Assistance.
Martín-Baró, Ignacio
    1989   "Political Violence and War as Causes of Psychosocial Trauma in El Sal-
                vador." *International Journal of Mental Health* 18 (1):3–20.

Monteaglegre, Hernán
    1982   "The Security of the State and Human Rights." In *Human Rights in the Americas: The Struggle for Consensus*, ed. Alfred Hennelly and John Langan, 187–210. Washington, D.C.: Georgetown University Press.

Navarro, Marysa
    1988   "The Personal Is Political: Las Madres de Plaza de Mayo." In *Power and Popular Protest in Latin America*, ed. Susan Eckstein, 241–258. Berkeley, Los Angeles, and London: University of California Press.

Pacheco, Gerardo, and Bernardo Jiménez, comps.
    1990   *Ignacio Martín-Baró (1942–1989): Psicología de la liberación para América Latina*. Guadalajara: Instituto Tecnológico y de Estudios Superiores de Occidente, Departmento de Extensión Universitaria, Universidad de Guadalajara.

Ronstrom, Anitha
    1989   "Children in Central America." *Child Welfare* 68 (2):145–153.

Smith, Carol A., ed.
    1990   *Guatemalan Indians and the State, 1540–1988*. Austin: University of Texas Press.

Sojourners
    1990   "The Greatest Love: El Salvador's Sacrament of Salvation, an Interview with Jon Sobrino." April: 16–21.

Taussig, Michael
    1984   "Culture of Terror—Space of Death: Roger Casement's Putumayo Report and the Explanation of Torture." *Comparative Studies in Society and History* 26:467–497.
    1987   *Shamanism, Colonialism, and the Wild Man: A Study in Terror and Healing*. Chicago: University of Chicago Press.

Thomas, David Hurst, ed.
    1991   *Columbian Consequences: The Spanish Borderlands in Pan-American Perspective*. Vol. 3. Washington, D.C.: Smithsonian Institution Press.

Thomas, Noëlle, comp.
    1985   *Report from Workshop to Exchange Experiences of Psychosocial and Psychotherapeutic Work with Displaced Populations in Central America, Mexico City, 18–22 February 1985*. Stockholm: Rädda Barnen (Swedish Save the Children).

Timerman, Jacobo
    1987   *Chile: Death in the South*. New York: Alfred A. Knopf.

Vargas Llosa, Mario
    1991   *A Writer's Reality*. Syracuse: Syracuse University Press.

Wolf, Eric
    1959   *Sons of the Shaking Earth*. Chicago: University of Chicago Press.

NINE

Transforming Trust: Dispossession and Empowerment among Palestinian Refugees

Julie M. Peteet

Until the Afghan refugee crisis, Palestinians had the dubious distinction of being the world's largest refugee community. Estimates of 2,428,100 means that nearly half the Palestinian population of 5.2 million are refugees.[1] Nearly 100,000 refugees came to Lebanon in the wake of the establishment of the state of Israel in Palestine.[2] They were predominantly residents of villages and towns in northern Palestine. Provisionally settled into the refugee camps and the towns and cities of Lebanon, by the mid-1980s this number had swelled to between 300,000 and 400,000 as the second and third generations expanded. Meanwhile, a succession of Israeli governments has refused to consider their return or to offer monetary compensation for the loss of property and livelihoods. The majority of those entering Lebanon were quickly transformed from landowning or sharecropping peasants to traumatized, stateless exiles dependent on the assistance of international agencies.

Refugees speak of bewilderment and trauma during those first years and an intense longing to return to their homes and lands. For many, the first years of exile were like a period of mourning. The loss of the land and the rupture of identities and social relations grounded in it was akin to the loss of a loved one. Unable to defend their communities, landless and penniless and now recipients of relief and charity, they felt an intense loss of trust in themselves. Honor was also implicated in the loss of trust in oneself and one's immediate community. With the leveling of statuses and identities in the refugee camps, there was the loss of the ability to summon recognition, an indication of one's honor and respect in the community.

Tension and, eventually, armed conflict were perhaps inevitable as Lebanon found itself host to a large refugee population. The refugees were socially unwelcome to the working class, who viewed with trepidation the competition of unskilled labor. In addition, the refugees found their right to work, travel, and engage in political activities circumscribed by the host government. The Maronites[3] were quick to sense a threat to their political hegemony from the largely Muslim refugees and feared their presence would upset the sectarian balance and political status quo by serving as a focal point for the growing discontent of Lebanese Muslims and their eventual mobilization against Maronite domination. To compound matters, in the late 1960s and early 1970s, Israel sustained a policy of military attacks on Lebanese civilian targets in an effort to compel the government to control armed Palestinian activity and turn the local populace against them (Khalidi 1986:20–21).

In the late 1960s, the Palestinian community in Lebanon underwent a sweeping transformation. In November 1969, after a year of sporadic clashes with the Lebanese army, the resistance's open, armed presence was accepted by the government in an agreement known as the Cairo Accords. It assumed authority in the refugee camps in an uneasy relationship with the United Nations Relief and Works Agency (UNRWA). The latter, long distrusted by the refugees, continued to operate (although in diluted form) while the resistance movement proceeded to provide internal security, a vast network of quasi-governmental social services, and employment opportunities for camp residents.

NURTURING TRUST: THE CULTURAL CONTEXT

This chapter explores the concept of trust within the configuration of Palestinian space/place, resistance, and identity in the Lebanese arena. Trust, while underlying a certain predictability and therefore cultural practice and communication, points to feelings of safety and well-being. It also refers to an absence of hostility. Such a reference brings to the surface some of the problems associated with the notion of trust as inhering in social life. Trust, while basic to social life, is a multilayered sentiment and relationship. For Palestinians, trust, in a broad sense, is not axiomatic. It is closely tied to notions of family, where trust is assumed. Trust is continuously established and reestablished in a process of negotiation in the course of social activity. Yet it is also a cultural assumption that guides a broad variety of relations. Thus, while trust is present at many levels, it must be sustained and nurtured rather than simply taken for granted. Within the family, trust is, to a large extent, built into the meaning of kinship relationships. Family is a bulwark of sorts against precisely the mistrust that colors extrafamilial social relations. It is in the domain of extrafamilial relations that trust must be nurtured.

Trust is a fragile and situational concept, easily broken but difficult to restore. Perhaps the most fruitful use of trust as an analytical tool is to recognize its situatedness and thus fluidity. Trust inheres in differential zones of interaction, such as family, nation, international community, religious community, and on the intrapersonal level. It should not be extracted from a specific historical or cultural context. In an Arab context, one is cautioned not to trust people beyond the circle of kin. The world is a place where one must constantly negotiate and nurture trust, and these processes and the resulting relations ensure a certain measure of safety and well-being.

In the contemporary concern with a deterritorialization of culture and identity, it is impossible to ignore the obvious: people do refuse and resist uprooting. Palestinians became refugees as the result of being forced into exile or seeking temporary refuge from conflict and subsequently facing a denial of return. In the age of the nation-state and its accoutrements such as passports, citizenship, and diplomatic representation, the stateless are exceedingly vulnerable and face the world with circumscribed options.

CONFLATIONS OF SPACE, PLACE, AND IDENTITY

Being a refugee stands as a framework for experiencing, interpreting, and acting on the world, giving location to self and community in an immediate sociopolitical order and in an international community. Refugee status, as a legal and social category, sharply nuances the boundaries of the permissible and the possible for Palestinians in Lebanon. It is the "perilous territory of not-belonging" that has produced great cultural creativity but also "mutilations" (Said 1984:50). These mutilations should caution against any flippant romanticization of the deterritorialization of culture and identity. For Palestinians in exile, it has been crucial to establish a historical and cultural inventory of a relation to Palestine, to verify in international political and scholarly discourses that they are rooted in Palestine, which they "know," to counter an internationally circulated image of them as unrooted, temporary sojourners who can be transferred from one region to another.

While conflations of space, place, culture, and identity can be transposed into metaphors expressive of a national exclusiveness integral to a politically rightist discourse, such conflations can assume centrality as well in instances of resistance to colonial projects. The distinction between space and place is one of scale and affinity. Place, or village, in the Palestinian consciousness is what ties a person to the space of Palestine. Palestinians identify and refer to one another in terms of village or region of origin. This is "place"—as distinct from "space"—where "its people were bound together by ontic forces." Even though this distinction between "place" and "space" is made by E. Valentine Daniel (1990) with respect to South Asia, it holds true broadly for the Palestinian case as well. "Ontic forces" are understood as being forces in which one finds oneself embedded and which constitute a way of *being-in-the-world.* In other words, one is linked to a place by a sense of identity with and belonging to that has roots in deep and enduring affect. Space, by contrast, is what Daniel refers to as "an epistemic unit"; it provides one with a way of *seeing the world.* A "way of being in the world" summons an intimacy that "a way of seeing the world" does not and cannot afford (ibid., 232–233). In a thoroughly "epistemicized world"—in Daniel's sense—one cannot go on with the business of living or just being for one cannot take one's eye off the many details of everyday life that spawn a culture of suspicion and mistrust.

The insistence on return evidences an active refusal to endorse contemporary colonial projects in Palestine.[4] Like the Afghan refugees discussed by M. Nazif

Shahrani (this volume), discussion of the notion of trust among Palestinians in Lebanon forces a focus on resistance. Resistance to exile itself and resistance to the legal designation "refugees" are central motifs of Palestinian exile culture. Resistance as an analytical concept is a point of entry to understanding these refugee communities. They insist on a specific connection between space, place, culture, and identity. Yet this connection between a time and place in the past and contemporary struggles to return to it should not gloss over the experience of exile itself, which of course also evinces a clear connection between place, space, and culture. Palestinians are desirous of a specific territorialization of place, space, culture, and power, one rooted in the past but oriented toward the future. Reterritorialization is only conceivable through resistance and empowerment. Palestinians seek return, rather than assimilation or resettlement elsewhere, to a site where the restoration of trust as a cultural basis for everyday life and security is territorialized. For such an enterprise, a national entity is crucial. Palestinian nationalism underlays a contemporary conflation of space and place, of epistemic and ontic units, where bonds with places of origin are only possible in space defined as Palestinian. The achievement of a generalized sense of trust is sought in the geopolitical reality of a Palestine where relations of power do not cast them as the "other." In this configuration, space as an epistemic unit is not to be overly juxtaposed to place as an ontic unit, for I would argue that place in the ontic sense, in this particular instance, is ensured by control over the definition and identity of space.[5] The living room walls of nearly every Palestinian home in Lebanon sport a bronze map of Palestine mounted on a black velvet–covered plaque. The map is of Mandatory Palestine, which includes the occupied West Bank and Gaza Strip as well as all of pre-Partition Palestine. These maps are produced by workshops sponsored by the Palestine Liberation Organization (PLO). Young Palestinians all over the Arab world also wear small gold maps of Palestine, hung charmlike on a thin gold chain around their necks. This definition and assertion of space, expressed through its incorporation into domestic and personal items of adornment, gives cultural meaning and visibility to the conflation of space and place, the epistemic and the ontic.

It is important to note that the refugees are located in Lebanon in Palestinian discussions of state and placement. While a state is conceivable in the occupied territories, it cannot accommodate all diaspora Palestinians. And while desirous of state and citizenship, certainly not all Palestinians would actually reside in a future state. Many of the refugees are not originally from the West Bank or Gaza Strip. The refugees in Lebanon, who come from the Galilee and coastal towns, are considered at most risk and are placed in primary position for relocation to a future state.

VIOLATING TRUST

Refugeeness is a process of becoming rather than a onetime set of events bounded in time and space. For many Palestinians in Lebanon, uprooting has occurred more than once. Decades of Israeli bombing in the South, the Lebanese civil war (1975–1991), and Israeli invasions (1978 and 1982) have caused dislocations on a large scale for both the Lebanese and the Palestinian communities.

With uprooting, trust has been violated on several levels and yet affirmed on the internal or communal level. In spite of linguistic, cultural, historical, and a largely common religious heritage and practice, Palestinians feel betrayed by other Arab governments and increasingly by the masses of the Arab world. After nearly three months of warfare and siege in 1982, the Palestinian resistance movement forces withdrew from Beirut in a mass-led demonstration of celebratory mourning. Women held up signs that read: "We are not Arabs." Their trust in the international community and its organs of justice has ranged from initial faith in the 1950s and early 1960s that the United Nations and the Arab states would restore Palestine to the realization that Arab states seek their own national interests and will not allow the Palestinian cause to interfere with those projects and that the UN is fairly limited in what it can accomplish on the international political scene.

Trust with those external to the community has been severely tested in Lebanon, where state and private militias have launched murderous attacks on the refugee camps and individual Palestinians over the past two decades. With time, a sense of trust has been circumscribed through violent events, increasingly limiting the space within which they can move. With trust in others diminished, the differences between them and other Arabs have tended to be magnified. In Lebanon, Palestinians were gradually hemmed in and the space within which they could move with safety shrank. During the civil war, areas to the north of Beirut, largely under control of the Christian militias, were dangerous terrain for a Palestinian. With Israeli invasions and occupation of the south in 1978 and 1982 and the establishment of proxy militias, Palestinians found their safety in large parts of the south in serious jeopardy. With the war of 1982 mobility was all but confined to the home (whether in the refugee camps or in urban areas) as armed men from an assortment of the rightist militias accompanying the invading Israeli army entered the major coastal cities of Lebanon and Beirut and rounded up thousands of men. A people who routinely design day-care centers and kindergartens with underground shelters as an integral architectural component are clearly not inclined to trust.

The homologous shrinking of space and the limits of safety pushed trust inward to the community and the family. The identification of an inner direction to trust must be cast in a historical frame. The 1950s and early 1960s is the period when one may speak of ruptured identities and disorganization in the refugee camps. The emergence of an inner-directed trust is closely bound up with the rise of the resistance movement in the late 1960s. These two periods are distinguished in Palestinian discourse: the former is referred to as the "days of passivity," of a reliance on charity and of waiting for external forces to restore a pre-1948 Palestine; the latter period is celebrated as the "days of euphoria." Ruptured identities were mended during the time when the resistance became an epicenter of trust empowering the community and giving it control of local affairs and security. J. Abu-Lughod (1988) describes all Palestinians as exiles, not only those in camps in neighboring Arab countries or even those in the currently occupied West Bank and Gaza Strip but also those who live in their homes within the 1948 boundaries of Israel as a minority within a Jewish state. To fully comprehend why trust can only be realized and flourish in the context of Palestine, it is necessary to understand the state of statelessness in a world of borders and passports and therefore the determination of a people to retain their national identity in the face of unrelenting crises and conflict and in their insistence on justice—a guiding motif of Palestinian resistance culture and political strategies.

Uprooting: The Deterritorialization of Trust

Palestinians in Lebanon refer to 1948, the year of the disaster *(al-nakbah)*, as the temporal marker signifying the beginning of the contemporary and ongoing state of statelessness, of life in exile *(al-ghurbah)*.[6] For Palestinians, there is an isomorphism between space and place. How does one deal with this while recognizing the validity of Akhil Gupta and James Ferguson's (1992:7, 20) claim that an "assumed isomorphism of space, place, and culture" is problematic? The idea that "multiple grids" should replace physical site and territory for the mapping of cultural difference pushes discussion toward sentiment and relation. A focus that highlights the progressive politics of the isomorphism may be a fruitful line of inquiry and lend ethnographic immediacy both to how ideas of place become pronounced and to how these ideas can be guiding ideological motifs of anticolonial movements.

Palestine has been reterritorialized to ground a new place, culture, and identity while the refugees are denied a similar grounding of place and culture in the desired space of their homeland. Since 1948, Palestine's topography has been transformed to remove signs of its original inhabitants. In the Zionist project, the Palestinians were denied or placed in zones where their physical existence would be distant from a now transformed space. Similar to the Greek refugees of Asia Minor during the consolidation of the Turkish state, there was no cultural or political place for the Palestinians in the new state (Hirschon 1989).[7] They were expected to resettle elsewhere. In these ethnic-national-sectarian clearings of the land, both groups were expected to settle elsewhere, in a place where they could easily blend with their fellow ethnic–sectarian group members and where time would eventually dilute memories of former homes and histories. In spite of the passage of time and of dwelling in culturally and linguistically familiar communities, seventy years for the Greeks of Asia Minor and nearly forty-five years for the Palestinians, in neither instance has memory receded and identity been regrounded in new locales. The refugee camp and community *is* hierarchically interconnected with the space/place of both origin and exile. The refugees now dwell in another space/place where they occupy a distinct, though fluctuating, position in a local hierarchy of power. New locales, and the experiences generated in them, have been incorporated into identities formed in exile but always originating and grounded in the homeland.

What kind of meaning does occupying a borderland with extreme swings in power have for the development of trust? If trust is a critical component of culture, what are the implications of a radical disjuncture between space/place and culture? We need to turn our attention to how trust is formed, re-formed, and deformed in the absence of rootedness and in the presence of continuous conflict, upheaval, and spatial movement.

The Refugee Camps and the Social Geography of Trust

UNRWA established and operated fifteen refugee camps in Lebanon. They provided the poorest refugees with tents, monthly rations of basic food supplies, primary and eventually secondary education, medical services, and refugee residency in Lebanon. Arrayed around the Lebanese urban centers of Beirut, Tripoli, Saida, Sur, and B'albak, the spatial distribution of the camps, from the far north to the southern border area, was clearly intended to obstruct the emergence of a geographically contiguous, cohesive Palestinian sociopolitical entity. While many clans, families, and villages were fragmented in space, they did attempt to reside together. As the refugees strived to settle, as much as possible, along family and village lines, the social mapping of the camps had a resemblance of sorts to pre-1948 Palestine, a familiar and safe social landscape. An attempt was made to cast space as place using former regional and social maps. Internally, the camps are loosely but distinctly organized (mapped) into areas defined by former village boundaries. As recently as the early 1980s, one could find one's way in the camps by asking for village areas. If one wished to locate the home of a person who is from Safed, one could ask, "Where do the people of Safed live?" In short, the camps were structurally arranged to mirror rural Palestine in a desire to re-form a physical and social geography of trust.

While this initial mapping endowed the community with a sense of the familiar and facilitated adjustment, it was soon to be overlaid with a mapping and naming of another sort. Transformations in Palestinian identity and politics are apparent in the contemporary mapping of the camps. Resistance offices and facilities have augmented villages as spatial referents. It is not uncommon to be given directions to someone's house that locate it as "next to the resistance office" or "across the alley from the resistance kindergarten" (Peteet 1991:24–25). Thus definitions and perceptions of space were transformed as the resistance provided an epicenter from which trust radiated. Shifting briefly to the West Bank, camp streets are being reclaimed by their inhabitants, refugees who came in 1948. Formerly unnamed streets are now marked by neatly hand-painted street signs named after martyrs of the *intifada*, such as Martyr Ahmed Street. This claim to space through inscription with potent symbols of the resistance ethos and movement registers a recovery of trust. It signifies a taking back of space by endowing it with names of critical mean-

ing in contemporary culture. As such it entails the admission and playful incorporation of new conditions. Such inscriptions encode a message to the occupying
authorities, informing them that in spite of twenty-four-hour surveillance of the
camp by high-tech telescopes, the ringing of the camp with guard towers, and regular army patrols through its streets, the camp is Palestinian territory and its streets
embody the spirit of those who died for Palestine. These street signs are elements
in a construction of memory that is dynamic and historically located. They serve
notice that the power to define and control space is henceforth challenged and is in
the process of being reconstrued.

What is the relationship between transformations in spatial cognition and discourse and the concept of trust? Given their existence as an exile community in
Lebanon and their spatial fragmentation, there was no single contiguous geographic area that could be referred to as "Palestinian." Yet there were areas that
were spatial junctures where Palestinians came together. These were the camps
and resistance-controlled urban areas such as Beirut's al-Fakhani neighborhood
adjacent to the camps and home to numerous PLO offices. Until 1982, the population of these areas was largely Palestinian and under their control and protection.
With the 1982 departure of the Palestinian armed forces and much of the institutional infrastructure, the area was remapped and repopulated by the Lebanese.

The Palestinian relation to space and place is one of multiple, intersecting, and
overlapping positions. While spaces/places are empowered and disempowered
sites, their power content shifts temporally and spatially and can do so with amaz-
ing rapidity. The meaning of space could shift with little warning from a zone of
trust and safety to a zone of danger, suggesting caution and warranting dissimulation. Because of the fragility of power, trust cannot be territorialized in any long-
term sense.

More than other Palestinian communities in exile, the one in Lebanon is the
most precarious and, until the Gulf war, the most endangered. In Lebanon, they
daily crossed borders whose meaning fluctuated over very short periods with
regional and local political events, from the protected state of the 1970s to the vulnerability of the 1980s when a Palestinian military presence in Lebanon was
severely diminished. The camps were a borderland of sorts, a remnant and a reterritorialization of Palestinian culture. Yet they were also defined by borders. Those
areas on the margins of the camps, which gave way to urban Lebanese neighborhoods, constitute another borderland. Danger lurks here in the form of Lebanese
militias and armed civilians who, since 1982, have beaten, kidnapped, detained,
and killed Palestinians. Living in such a "perilous territory of not-belonging" is
more than a state of mind, a sense of alienation and difference; it also signifies
danger and exposure, a stripping away of the protection that can come from
belonging to an internationally recognized state. In these borderlands, where identity is threatened and threatening, where trust and safety are in doubt, dissimulation colors behavior and culture. Unlike their parents who came at a later age,
Palestinians raised in Lebanon can switch dialects fairly easily when moving in

Lebanese circles. The "tomato joke" was one of the most common of the civil war and had resonance throughout Palestinian society. In Lebanese Arabic pronunciation a tomato is called "bandura," while Palestinians are clearly distinguished by their pronunciation "banadura." The joke, which has many variations, goes something like this: At a roadblock where rightist militiamen are trying to sort out Palestinians from Lebanese for kidnapping, they show each man a tomato and ask him what it is. When the Palestinian says "banadura" he is detained, while those who say "bandura" are free to proceed. This seemingly morbid joke was told with either profound sadness or great glee by Palestinians. It was recited to show that the Lebanese were targeting Palestinians for attack and unfortunately some fell into the trap by using a Palestinian dialect. Conversely, the Palestinians laughingly used the joke to affirm their cleverness at escaping Lebanese attacks. In an act of dissimulation, the Palestinian would pronounce tomato in a Lebanese dialect and thus be spared "disappearance." But in both instances, it underscored Palestinian differentiation from the Lebanese and the need to practice dissimulation to ensure safety, if not survival.

It is important not to turn to an essentializing Palestinian experience or identity in discussing those moments of movement through borderlands, for the dangers associated with them were not the same for all Palestinians. Their meanings were gendered and had a clear class dimension as well. Because cultural constraints circumscribe female mobility, women in the refugee camps moved in more spatially bounded arenas. For women, the world exterior to the camps was an alien and dangerous one. It was also a subject of curiosity to the women, who moved in it to a much lesser extent than did men. During the era of Palestinian military power in Lebanon, however, women moved with safety in Lebanese areas but usually with less frequency than men. Paradoxically, as danger approached and Palestinians as a community were endangered, women's mobility was enhanced. While trust in the world exterior to the camps was completely suspended, Palestinians placed some trust in Arab cultural practices that ensured the safety of women during times of conflict. While men remained close to home to avoid potentially deadly encounters with Lebanese militiamen, women moved out of the camps for provisions and to deal with the refugee bureaucracy.

Middle- and upper-class urban Palestinians possess the material means to escape or at least soften the worst aspects of being a refugee. If they are Christians, they have usually acquired Lebanese citizenship, which affords them some protection from militiamen seeking Palestinians. Their capital assets and skills have allowed them to move out of Lebanon. During shelling of the camps they are physically distant from danger. In short, they have more options that ensure safety.

The camps are not transit points from one locale to another. Palestinians live in a state of being permanently transient. Permanence in this instance is not to be confused or associated with assimilation. Exile itself has taken on the qualities of permanency while the dream, the organizing, the focal point for the future, is the transition to Palestine, to a situation where a certain level of trust is grounded in institutions of state. More significant, the experience of daily materialities is never distanced from the state of being a refugee. For a child growing up in a camp, there is an air of permanency because it is the only home and way of life known, until it is rocked by an assault by hostile forces that precipitates another uprooting. For the parent or the young adult displaced two or three times, refugeehood is reaffirmed. Any semblance of permanency is quickly and violently revealed to be illusionary. Impermanence is also a daily reality for the refugees from 1948 who are living in camps in the occupied territories. But given the specificities of exile within one part of Palestine, their impermanence differs in form from that of the refugees in Lebanon. In the occupied territories, the refugees, remnants of a 1948 Palestine still on Palestinian soil, fear they will be the first to be "transferred" to Jordan if the Israeli Right is able to execute its plan to transfer Palestinians out of Palestine. Thus nearly all Palestinians occupy an indeterminate zone of existence between transition and permanency, between a continuing process of becoming a refugee, of not-belonging yet rebuilding shattered lives and homes, attempting trust and permanency on a day-to-day basis yet always assuming the eventuality of a Palestinian entity where one is no longer marginal, insecure, or needs to practice dissimulation.

CONTESTING CATEGORIES OF IDENTITY

Among the first cultural projects associated with the rise of the resistance movement and the empowerment of the exile community was to interrogate and transform the discourse of refugeehood. Political and military empowerment enabled them to define themselves rather than quietly accept the labels of international agencies and the host population. Palestinians in refugee camps in Lebanon do not refer to themselves as refugees. They are "returners" *(al-a'idin)*. In vehemently rejecting the imposed term of reference and consciously choosing to refer to themselves as "returners," they were constructing a lexicon of both refusal and resistance. In spite of being identified by the local, regional, and international community as refugees, they refused to accept this designation. Rather than choosing terms of self-definition that stated where they were—seekers of refuge in—they defined themselves as people seeking to go back to where they came from. The distinction lies in the prepositions *to* or *in* and *from.* To be a "returner" implies that one is going back to a place one belongs to. The distinction is one of action. To refer to oneself as a "returner" evokes a political commitment that underwrites agency. Return is contingent on an active commitment to struggle *(nidal).*

The term "refugees" *(laja'een)* was rejected because it implied a passive acceptance of the status quo and suggested the possibility of resettlement elsewhere.[8] Rejection of this term in the mid-1960s indicated an adamant refusal to accept a deterritorialized existence and identity. This insistence was all the more pronounced given the 1967 war and UN Resolution 242, which "did not deal with the Palestinians as a people with a national cause, but rather as a random agglomeration of atomized individuals of no fixed identity" (Khalidi 1992:31).

In the Lebanese arena during the 1950s and 1960s, the label "refugee" carried with it certain negative connotations. To call someone a refugee was to hurl an insult. Lebanese insults often implied, if not explicitly stated, that Palestinians "left their lands," as if becoming a refugee was an act of volition. Palestinians bristled at the idea that others misunderstood what had happened to them in 1948. Mistrust and distance, indeed objectification, were evidenced in the jokes about Palestinians that circulated. Lebanese joked about going to the "zoo" (the refugee camps) to stare at the refugees, as if they belonged to another, extrahuman, category of being. Interestingly, the Palestinians incorporated into their own exile discourse the notion of the camps as "zoos." But they did so in a fashion that spoke from a position of moral superiority. When exasperated with the number of foreign visitors who came to the camps (who are "tourists," in a sense) to observe from a distance refugee life—to read their lives as signs—women vented their anger and despair to whoever listened: "You think this is a zoo and we are on display? We are human beings. We have feelings! We live this life every day! What can you know of our lives?" In rejecting objectification and criticizing distance, they implied that to categorize them in such a fashion was to display one's own rudeness and lack of humanity. As the resistance movement increasingly took power in the camps, foreign visitors were received in a different manner. Given that they could only enter the camps with the approval of the resistance and usually in solidarity delegations, the bitterness gave way to offers of hospitality. Telling stories of expulsion, uprooting, and life as a refugee was an attempt to lessen the distance between the Palestinian and the other, to create knowledge and thus empathy. It was in such an atmosphere that trust could be established with others. This could only come about through the empowerment of the community, an empowerment that allowed for control over the glances of others.

Along with "returners," other terms suggestive of agency assumed prominence as signifiers of a reconfigured self and community. Women and men now referred to themselves as *thuwwar* (revolutionaries), *fedayeen* (guerrillas), *munadaleen* (strugglers), and, of course, as exiles, terms indicative of a determination to overcome refugee status and actively design one's future. The emphasis in self-definition was less on where one was and more on how one would get back to a place of origin and belonging, to a place where trust could be restored and reconstituted in a particularly Palestinian fashion and according to Palestinian dictates.

In a world of material loss and deprivation, Palestinians were compelled, at some points, to accept the legal identity of refugees. Pierre Centlivres and Micheline Centlivres-Dumont's (1988) discussion of Afghan refugees in Pakistan reminds us of the problems associated with the concept of "refugee" when international legal categories are juxtaposed to widely divergent but historically specific cultural conceptions of identity and experience. To ensure material survival, Palestinians

and Afghans had to be eligible for rations and assistance.[9] To do so meant registration as refugees and possession of a UNRWA-issued ration card. The bitterness of assuming this identity is apparent in the distaste with which they speak of
accepting rations. The humiliating experience of standing in long, disorderly lines
to receive monthly rations of flour, sugar, soap, and so on, was often relegated to
young children. Adults who grew up in the camps speak with caustic humor of
being sent to stand in line in order for their parents to avoid the indignity of
accepting assistance from foreigners and foreign agencies. But legal refugee status
was a necessity. Access to sorely needed rations depended on it, as did medical
care, education, and access to scholarships for higher education. Possession of
refugee status was critical in another sense as well: future eligibility for return was
seen as possibly being contingent on possession of documentary evidence of a presence in pre-1948 Palestine.

Camp dwellers are considered by other Palestinians as having an identity less
diluted or tainted by exterior elements. Assuming an original, unpolluted identity,
borderlands and areas exterior to the camp were seen as embodying cultural elements threatening to this purity. Similar to the quintessential peasant (Swedenberg 1990), camp dwellers, descendants of peasants, were elevated to the position
of signifiers of central motifs in contemporary Palestinian culture. They both experienced on a daily level and represented for those on the exterior suffering and
resistance. This assumed purity of suffering, resistance, and identity stemming
from the inescapability of the camps. Outsiders have options that offer means of
escape and thus a diminution of suffering. Moreover, camp Palestinians are known
to carry a heavy burden of resistance, the bulk of the fedayeen being young men
from the camps. Air and artillery raids target the camps with a frequency unparalleled elsewhere. Exiled urban Palestinians, the middle and upper class, jokingly
threaten children acting spoiled or making unreasonable material demands, "I
ought to send you to the camps! There you'll learn what real suffering is. You'll
learn to be a real Palestinian!" Clearly suffering and resistance are conflated with
an assumed purity of identity that inheres in life in the camps

The implications and meaning of legal refugee status, simultaneously rejected
and sought, fluctuated with the fortunes and power of the resistance movement
and the general welfare of camp residents. During the oil boom years of the 1970s,
the standard of living in the camps rose considerably. Young men, either skilled
laborers or clerically and managerially trained, formed part of the movement of
labor to the oil-producing states. In the camps and elsewhere in the Arab world,
their remittances fueled an enhanced standard of living. The oil boom and its economic effects coincided with the empowerment of the resistance movement in
Lebanon and its development of an infrastructure of quasi-governmental services
for camp residents. For over a decade, reliance on rations and UNRWA services
declined in scope. Passports, while always a desired item, were now critical for the
international travel and education necessary to compete in an increasingly global
labor market. In this market, Palestinians were disadvantaged by their stateless-

ness and the attendant difficulties associated with obtaining visas and work permits. In the wake of the 1982 Israeli invasion of Lebanon, the era of communal self-reliance came to an abrupt halt. Subsequently the resistance movement's capacity to provide protection and services to the civilian population was severely diminished. With the safety net provided by the resistance movement pulled from beneath them, claims to refugee status were quickly resurrected. Not only did they entitle holders to rations, medical care, and education but they also provided the documentation necessary for legal residency in Lebanon. This occurred at a time when the Lebanese were anxious to rid their country of as many Palestinians as possible. Internationally defined and recognized refugee status was essential for preserving a Palestinian presence in Lebanon. For many, the post-1982 war situation evoked memories of the 1950s when, newly arrived in Lebanon, they had to rely on UNRWA for most of their basic needs.

Desire for and reliance on legal refugee status is a barometer of sorts, indexing power, dependency, and, more ominously, exposure to mistreatment from the host population. Palestinians found not only services and national pride in the PLO but most essentially protection from abuse by sectors of the host population. The open, armed presence of the resistance movement ensured the borders of a community where trust was possible, even if only in clearly demarcated spaces.

LOOKING BACK: TRUST AND THE POWER OF PLACE

When Palestinians discuss what it means to be a refugee, the elderly in particular will often dramatically juxtapose exile to rootedness and belonging, qualities that ground trust in space and place. Because the *jeel al-nekbah* (generation of disaster) are now elderly and knew Palestine, they are able to vividly juxtapose the past and the present. Narratives of life in Palestine evoke a nostalgic longing for a past that is irretrievable and confirm a contemporary reality that is painful and alienating. Now elderly peasant women reminisce about the "days of paradise" in their villages where food was plentiful and fresh from one's own fields. The fruits and vegetables of Lebanon just cannot compete with those of Palestine, they resolutely claim. There was order to the world then, and the rules were clear: "Girls didn't run around with bare arms and go out with boys and they accepted their parents' choice of a husband," a ninety-year-old woman told me. A "days of paradise" sort of nostalgia glosses over points of cleavage and differentiation in Palestinian society such as sectarianism, differences in wealth and power, political factionalism, and regionalism. Essentializing the past through a selectively reconstituted memory narrows the distance between people, providing a narrative basis for establishing a restored inward-looking trust. For the *jeel al-thawra* (generation of the revolution), born and reared outside Palestine, the present sense of mistrust of and alienation from the world around them is sustained by the sense of exile from a place made familiar only through the recollections of those who actually lived there. The tangibility of memory thus constructed and the political agency to which it gave rise were evident in the number of young people who supported the resistance movement. While it is a memory constructed elsewhere, it is hardly less meaningful than that based on firsthand knowledge and experience of the physical reality of Palestine. Experienced through everyday discrimination and deprivation, it is a material and emotional reality. The contemporary reality of everyday life in the refugee camps was framed in terms of a past that had come to an abrupt and violent end. Poverty and disaster were explained to children as a consequence of the loss of homes and land to the Zionists. "We can't give you these things because we lost everything to the Jews," parents told their young children when they asked why they were so poor and unable to purchase adequate food and clothing. An alternative to exile and the camps was ever on the horizon. Palestine was geographically close—just across the border. Young people sought to escape the abnormality of the camps and a refugee identity in which one was not the "other" and daily life was secure (Peteet 1991:26). The homeland was reconfigured as a place where trust suffused daily life and social relations. Disjunctures between the trust one could feel in a homeland and the trust that is absent in a place of refuge spawned a sense of the urgency of return.

Nostalgia is not confined to a past in Palestine. Exile itself is imbued with a nostalgia of its own. It has its own temporal markers that signify varying levels of trust and nostalgia. The term "ayyam Beirut" (days of Beirut) evokes a mournful longing for a period of protection, autonomy, and cultural creativity. For Palestinians who departed Lebanon in the wake of the 1982 war, it refers to an era when they enjoyed unprecedented autonomy and power. Palestinians who departed Kuwait in the wake of the Gulf War and now reside in Jordan lament the end of their presence in Kuwait and discuss life in Jordan against the backdrop of life there. It was an era of economic security and well-being, although without the security of being a citizen. Political organization was possible on a scale not easily achieved in other Arab countries, and large amounts of capital were raised for the PLO. Although their presence in Kuwait ended in disaster with Palestinian-Kuwaiti relations severely damaged, Palestinians speak of their lives in Kuwait as ones of material well-being, given the higher standard of living and the absence of high levels of unemployment when compared to Jordan.

LOOKING INWARD: ESTABLISHING TRUST IN EXILE

The narrative lines connecting the past, present, and future are critical junctures in restoring trust. In their introduction, E. Valentine Daniel and John Chr. Knudsen identify "the need and freedom to construct a normative picture of one's past" as central to restoring trust. Having discussed the nostalgia for the past and the more immediate past of exile itself, I would add that configurations of the present and the future are also central to the project of trust.

Palestinians feel a keen sense of betrayal and mistrust vis-à-vis other Arab countries and an international community that has either ignored them or assigned them to the "terrorist" camp. In turning trust inward to the Palestinian community alone, they distinguished themselves from their host Arabs. While Lebanese-Palestinian relations have been fraught with tension, conflict, and massacre, goodwill and political solidarity have also been evident. The lines dividing Palestinians and Lebanese, those to be trusted and those subject to less trust, respectively, are expressed in cultural and social terms and, more significant, in terms of moral qualities. Palestinians see themselves as being on a higher moral plane than the Lebanese, especially in the affairs of family, sex, and honor. Palestinians feel they conform to prescriptions of culturally appropriate behavior while the Lebanese are morally duplicitous.

The uprooting and displacement to refugee camps did not put in doubt trust among Palestinians. Indeed, it fostered trust where little had previously existed. The shared experience of exile among people who were previously strangers and the participation of nearly all camp families, in one way or another, in the resistance movement deepened sentiments of solidarity and trust, turning them inward.

The restoration of trust is closely related to the speed with which identities are reconfigured and shared with others. Once I asked Leila, a thirty-year-old activist, what it was like to be a Palestinian in Lebanon at a time when the resistance movement was just coming on the scene. She described it this way:

> I knew that I was not from this country. I didn't speak like they did. I saw it on their faces. I knew that UNRWA was paying rations for us. My family always spoke of Palestine and how much better off we were there. I felt like an outsider, but I knew I had an alternative—that is, a home in Palestine, a big house, and we owned a shop. But my situation was still better than that of others. We didn't live in the camps, and I wasn't working as a servant in a Lebanese home. For me the problem was not so much a material one but a psychological one, and it has affected me all my life.
>
> I attended a Lebanese school, and no Palestinians were there except my sisters and I. Until I was fifteen years old we were the only Palestinians there. I was always aware that I was a Palestinian—something different. The Lebanese made jokes about us, especially our accent. I began to feel more Palestinian than ever.
>
> One day five Palestinian girls from the camps joined our class. They had been in UNRWA schools, and since they were top students they were selected to go on to a private Lebanese high school. Soon after they joined the class, I addressed the teacher and he mimicked my accent. Suddenly one of the new girls stood up and began screaming and cursing at him. The Palestinian girls ordered a strike, and all the pupils followed until the teacher was forced to apologize to me. After that I sat with the Palestinian girls.

A sense of solidarity unbounded by class and the ability to confront a figure of power and respect were made possible only by the empowerment of the whole community. Sentiments of shared marginality and solidarity were achieved on the basis of a common status as refugees in a milieu where their empowerment cast them as active participants in making their own history rather than as victims who could be mistreated with impunity.

Trust is also sought and initially located through identifying and communicating one's identity as a Palestinian and then one's place of origin. When Palestinians meet for the first time, they quickly establish a connection that allows for the building of a relationship with some basic level of trust. After initial greetings and inquiries about what each person is doing in the present location (usually working or studying), the dialogue proceeds like this:

"Where are you from?"
"From Safed."
"Where are you from?"
"From Tarshiha."
"Where's your family living?"
"In Ayn al-Helwah."
"Mine is too!"

In this encounter, the two fellows are from nearby areas of Palestine and grew up in the same refugee camp in South Lebanon, yet similar dialogues occur between Palestinians with distant origins who meet in faraway places such as New York, Ohio, London, Moscow, the Gulf states, or wherever Palestinians encounter one another. Such dialogues usually include an inquiry as to the well-being and safety of the other's family, in reference to the latest crisis a Palestinian community may be undergoing. Over the course of the last fifteen years, the references were directed to events in Lebanon. Recently, solicitous inquiries were usually directed to those coming out of Kuwait or the occupied territories. A sentiment of shared experiences of discrimination, of the insecurity and vulnerability of the stateless, suffuses the dialogue, generating feelings of being bound together by refugee or exile status. Trust is more quickly established among those who have taken refuge in the same country or area. They have usually lived through experiences of exile specific to that place. As attacks on the Palestinian community in the diaspora multiply, however, trust is an assumed, minimum quality of all Palestinian social relations. Trust within the community does have limits. It can be taxed and pushed to limits by extreme crisis. In 1976, Tel al-Zaater camp, in largely Christian East Beirut, was besieged for nine months by rightist forces. When it fell, hundreds were massacred as they attempted to flee. The camp was later razed. Its inhabitants took refuge in West Beirut where they quickly overwhelmed local relief agencies. While kin ties were activated to shelter the refugees, eventually they were overtaxed, and in some cases relatives were compelled to move on. It was not uncommon for widows to prefer to live in proximity to others from Tel al-Zaater rather than their own kin because of their common experience and their awareness that in a situation of prolonged civil war their presence was burdensome to family members. In 1982, Shatila camp was the site of a massacre by Israeli-sponsored Lebanese rightist militias. In the aftermath of three months of siege, intensive aerial bombardments, and the removal of the Palestinian resistance movement's military and social institutions from Lebanon, families simply had few means to cope with members who were destitute. The crisis was extreme enough that relations once based on kinship and communitywide trust were now stretched to the breaking point and in many instances suspended.[10]

In a world where some refugees have lost homes and possessions two or three times, trust in the stability of material objects is hard to extend and sustain. For poorer refugees, attitudes toward desired material goods fluctuate between desire and rejection. Underlying this is an anticipation of loss. Edward Said (1984:52) writes self-reflectively, "Many exiles are novelists, chess players, political activists, or intellectuals. Each of these occupations requires a minimal investment in objects and places a great premium on mobility and skill."

CONCLUSION

Palestinians realize that their sense of loyalty and obligation to one another is now a cultural expectation of some currency. Yet they feel it should be more stringent. In such moments of self-criticism, Palestinians lambast themselves for not having the solidarity of Jews and Armenians, which they conceptualize in essentialist terms.

The inwardness that characterizes trust is based on shared experiences, history, and interests and shared location in a global and regional social order. Refugee status and the inwardness of trust served as the cultural and emotional basis of the emergence of the resistance movement in the camps. The resistance movement then lent tangibility to an inward-looking trust, serving as it did as the main source of protection and access to resources. For Palestinians, trust is ultimately tied to resistance and return, to a merging of space and place, the epistemic and the ontic.

NOTES

1. See U.S. Committee for Refugees 1991.

2. Sayigh 1979 remains the most solid social and historical account of the Palestinian community in Lebanon since 1948.

3. The Maronites are an eastern Catholic sect with a history of economic and political hegemony in Lebanon.

4. See Khalidi 1992 for a detailed discussion of the location of the concept of return in official Palestinian discourse.

5. See Daniel (1984, 1990) for a discussion of the distinction between place and space in a South Indian village.

6. See Malkki 1992 for a critical discussion of the concept of rooting, culture, and identity.

7. The Greeks of Asia Minor took refuge in Greece, a country with the same language and religion and many cultural affinities. Asia Minor refugees, however, have maintained a distinct identity over a seventy-year period, foregrounded in their bounded position in Ottoman society. They continue to distinguish themselves from the mainland Greeks, referring to themselves as "refugees" and "Asia Minor people." The point of difference is shared

history and experience in the Ottoman Empire and a conception of themselves as culturally more cosmopolitan and sophisticated. Refugee discourse imposed on refugee–mainland Greek differences a typology of cultural development such as rural-urban in which the Greeks were cast as "narrow-minded, ignorant, and uncouth" (Hirschon 1989:4–5, 10–11, 12).

8. Resettlement, what Khalidi (1992:39) dubs the "favorite solution" to the Palestine problem of American policy makers and others since the 1950s, has in fact never had any chance of implementation. Palestinian nationalism and unwillingness to consider the idea as well as the problems and difficulties of other Arab states absorbing as citizens large numbers of Palestinians have rendered this "solution" untenable.

9. Centlivres and Centlivres-Dumont (1988:148–149) observe that "circumstances have forced the Afghan refugees to conform to the image of a foreign-imposed identity" in order to establish access to the "very large stakes" associated with international relief and assistance. In their description of aid distribution, they contend that it is "welcome and generally well-organized, but goes against traditional forms of distribution which are collective and hierarchical in nature. In the camps when it is distributed these imbalances become evident."

10. See Sayigh and Peteet 1986 for a discussion of the implications of extreme crisis on ties of kinship after the 1982 Sabra-Shatila massacre and Peteet 1991 for a detailed discussion of the kinds of communities and relationships established by women survivors of Tel al-Zaater.

REFERENCES

Abu-Lughod, Janet
> 1988   "Palestinians: Exiles at Home and Abroad." *Current Sociology* (October): 61–69.

Centlivres, Pierre, and Micheline Centlivres-Dumont
> 1988   "The Afghan Refugee in Pakistan: An Ambiguous Identity." *Journal of Refugee Studies* 1 (2):141–152.

Daniel, E. Valentine
> 1984   *Fluid Signs: Being a Person the Tamil Way.* Berkeley, Los Angeles, and London: University of California Press.
> 1990   "Afterword: Sacred Places, Violent Spaces." In *Sri Lanka: History and the Roots of Conflict*, ed. Jonathan Spencer, 246–277. London: Routledge.

Gupta, Akhil, and James Ferguson
> 1992   "Beyond 'Culture': Space, Identity, and the Politics of Difference." *Cultural Anthropology* 7(1):6–23.

Hirschon, Renee
> 1989   *Heirs of the Greek Catastrophe: The Social Life of Asia Minor Refugees in Piraeus.* Oxford: Clarendon Press.

Khalidi, Rashid
> 1986   *Under Siege: PLO Decision-making During the 1982 War.* New York: Columbia University Press.
> 1992   "Observations on the Right of Return." *Journal of Palestine Studies* 21(2):29–40.

Malkki, Liisa
>   1992   "National Geographic: The Rooting of Peoples and the Territorialization
>   of National Identity among Scholars and Refugees." *Cultural Anthropology*
>   7(1):24–44.

Peteet, Julie
>   1991   *Gender in Crisis: Women and the Palestinian Resistance Movement.* New York:
>   Columbia University Press.

Said, Edward
>   1984   "The Mind of Winter: Reflections on Life in Exile." *Harper's,* September,
>   49–55.

Sayigh, Rosemary
>   1979   *Palestinians: From Peasants to Revolutionaries.* London: Zed Press.

Sayigh, Rosemary, and J. Peteet
>   1986   "Between Two Fires: Palestinian Women in Lebanon." In *Caught Up in
>   Conflict: Women's Responses to Political Strife,* eds. R. Ridd and H. Callaway,
>   106–137. London: Macmillan Education.

Swedenberg, Theodore
>   1990   "The Palestinian Peasant as National Signifier." *Cultural Anthropology*
>   63(1):18–30.

U.S. Committee for Refugees
>   1991   *World Refugee Survey.* Washington, D.C.: U.S. Committee for Refugees.

TEN

Afghanistan's Muhajirin
(Muslim "Refugee-Warriors"):
Politics of Mistrust and Distrust of Politics

M. Nazif Shahrani

To those who leave their homes in the cause of Allah, after suffering oppression,
We will assuredly give goodly home in this world; but truly the reward of the
Hereafter will be greater. If they only realized [this]! [They are] those who per-
severe in patience, and put their trust on their Lord.
—QUR'AN 16:41–42

He who flees with his religion from one territory to another, even if it is [only the
distance of] an inch, will be worthy of paradise and be the companion of his
father Ibrahim, Allah's bosom friend, and of His prophet Mohammad.
—HADITH, SAYING OF THE PROPHET MUHAMMAD

A refugee is a man who votes with his feet.
—LENIN

An important measure of the magnitude of the "refugee problem" in recent
decades has been the sheer number of refugees: an estimated 16,689,300 world
wide in 1990. The report prepared by the U.S. Committee for Refugees
(1991:32–34) also indicates that approximately 65 percent of these refugees (over 10
million) are from Muslim countries and are hosted by countries with a predominantly Muslim population. The refugees from Muslim Afghanistan, estimated at
well over five million in neighboring Pakistan (3.3 million) and Iran (2.3 million),
constitute the largest concentration of displaced people from a single nation in the
world today.[1] Precipitated by the fourteen years of political and military crises as a
result of the Soviet-sponsored Communist coup on 27 April 1978 and the Russian
invasion and decade-long occupation of Afghanistan (1979–1989), this very large-
scale exodus of Afghan refugees represents one of the less problematic cases of
refugee management experiences in recent memory, that is, it has been free of epidemics, hunger, and starvation, and there have been minimal conflicts and communal violence compared with refugee centers in other parts of the world (see
Boesen 1990:161). Alfred Janata (1990:67), a close observer of the situation in Pak-

istan, states "that nowhere in the world have refugees been received as well as Afghans in Pakistan."

What accounts for this relatively peaceful, orderly, and generally trouble-free management of the massive Afghan refugee communities during the past fourteen years in Pakistan and Iran? And how do notions of "trust" as constituted in the Muslim political cultures of Afghan refugees, Pakistani and Iranian peoples and governments, and their many international benefactors play a part in understanding the dynamics of the Afghan *muhajirin* experiences? These are some of the issues to be explored in this chapter.

AFGHAN MUHAJIRIN: A MUSLIM SELF-DEFINITION IN HISTORICAL CONTEXT

The choice of language and the use of a particular vocabulary, both in the discourse of the refugees as well as in the discourses about them, can serve to mystify as well as clarify the social processes and historical realities depicted (see Zolberg, Suhrke, and Aguayo 1989:274). The noun *refugee*—with its French origin in the late sixteenth century and its adoption in the English language a century later[2] and the more recently institutionalized legal meanings assigned to it by the 1951 United Nations Convention Relating to the Status of Refugees and the subsequent 1967 Protocol—is freely applied in reference to the Afghan muhajirin, especially by the United Nations High Commissioner on Refugees (UNHCR) and other international donor agencies and organizations and by the Western media. Indeed, "some 525,000 [Afghan] families in Pakistan, comprising some 3.3 million persons, which represent the entire registered refugee population residing in Pakistan," are recognized as statutory refugees by the UNHCR (United Nations 1990:35). Unlike the widely used term "mujahidin," Muslim fighters in the cause of Allah or "holy warriors" in reference to Afghan resistance fighters, the companion term "muhajirin," "those who leave their homes in the cause of Allah, after suffering oppression" (Qur'an 16:41, see epigraph above), the appellation of choice for the displaced Afghans, is for the most part ignored by the international relief organizations and the Western media.

Not surprisingly, therefore, according to Grant Farr (1990:137), the modern universal definition of refugees as people who crossed international frontier(s) because of a well-founded fear of persecution or violence in their homeland "is of least importance to the Afghans, and to the average Pakistani, but is the salient status to the international refugee aid organizations who control various resources for the refugees including rations, shelter and legal rights in Pakistan." The different notions of refugee status held by the displaced Afghans in Pakistan, the Pakistani people and officials, and the refugee relief organizations working in Pakistan, Farr suggests, are "the source of some of the problems between the Pakistan refugee relief effort and the Afghan refugees themselves" (ibid., 138). Indeed, it is argued that the different constructions of the self-definition of Afghan muhajirin and the current standardized normative definition of refugee applied by their benefactors are responsible, to a large measure, for the pervasive condition of what I call the "politics of mistrust" that appear to characterize relations among Afghan muhajirin communities and outside refugee relief establishments in Pakistan.

A complex set of "mixed motives determine the [international refugee] policy process," as Aristide R. Zolberg, Astri Suhrke, and Sergio Aguayo (1989:272) have suggested, where "humanitarian goals tend to be exaggerated" at the expense of political and religious considerations, because to the refugee relief organizations the humanitarian goals "have a legitimizing function." Such an approach to the definition of *refugee* for the purposes of policy implementation by those primarily concerned with the issues of the "adjustment and assimilation" of refugees in the Western host countries is understandable. However, it is not very useful for understanding the dynamics of refugee experiences in particular situations such as the Afghan muhajirin in Pakistan and Iran. For this purpose, while recognizing the importance of institutionalized legal definitions of *refugee*, we must also adopt an ethnomethodological stance that considers self-definition of the refugees themselves (ibid., 4). It is therefore to the examination of the self-definition of Afghanistan muhajirin and its implications for their relations with their Pakistani hosts and the refugee assistance establishment that we now turn.

Let us begin with an examination of the meaning and cultural and ideological significance of the term "muhajir" (pl. muhajirin)—the Afghan refugees' appellation of choice from other commonly used vernacular words available for self-definition. Two alternative terms for displaced people, widely used, by both Persian and Pashtu speakers in the country, are the Persian words *panahandah,* generally translated in English as "refugee, one seeking protection, one seeking political asylum"; and *awarah,* meaning "vagrant, homeless, tramp, refugee, evacuee, and vagabond" (Kashani and Kashani 1983:246,21). Both terms are used interchangeably primarily in reference to displaced peoples outside the Muslim world, whether caused by political violence or natural disasters. Both terms are also regularly applied in reference to the Palestinian refugees as in the popular expressions, *pana handagan-i Falastini* and *awaragan-i Falastini.*

Before the onset of the 1978 Communist coup in Kabul and the subsequent Russian intervention in Afghanistan, the use of the term "muhajirin" among the Afghans was limited to a large body of Muslim Central Asians (Turkistanis) who took refuge in Afghanistan following the establishment of the Bolshevik regime and the incorporation of Muslim lands in Turkistan within the domain of the former Soviet Union (early 1920s). For the Afghans in this context, the Arabic terms "hijrat" and "muhajir" did not simply mean a displaced person or a refugee but meant very specifically a "Muslim refugee."[3] Not surprisingly, the Afghans have deliberately chosen to describe their own flight from Communist oppression in Afghanistan as a muhajirat and themselves as muhajirin-i Afghanistan, not as panahandagan or awaragan-i Afghanistan.

Zafar Ishaq Ansari (1990:9) states that,

> in Arabic, the root "h-j-r" denotes "to dissociate oneself, to separate, to keep away, to part company, to renounce, to leave, to abandon, to give up, to emigrate." . . . Moreover, the root "h-j-r" also has the nuance of "dislike" as the motive for dissociating oneself from or leaving something or someone. . . . One of the derivatives of "h-j-r"—the third verbal form, muhajarah—specifically means "to emigrate," and a muhajir is "he who migrates."

Based on these literal meanings alone, a muhajir, or "Muslim refugee," is indeed a political actor—"a man who votes with his feet" in Lenin's words. However, "as an Islamic religious term," Ansari points out, "hijrah has come to denote migration from Domain of Disbelief [in Islam] to the Domain of Faith [in Islam], similar to the migration [of the Prophet Muhammad (pbh) and his companions] from Mecca to Medina [in A.D. 622]" (ibid.).

In this religious and historical sense, the concept of "hijrah" assumes a particularly potent symbolic and paradigmatic significance, especially for religiously minded Muslims in general and displaced Afghans in particular. In this Islamic religious construction, the "refugees' problems"—facing life-threatening violence (and death), persecution, oppression, war, and evil that engender the imminent threat of chaos, anomie, and meaninglessness—are confronted as a "problem of meaning" in the Weberian sense, as elaborated by Clifford Geertz (1973:87–125), and rendered susceptible to resolution. That is, as K. Newland (1981:6) has pointed out, as long as the forces generating refugees, such as "human greed, betrayal of popular will, lust for power, ethnic hatred, and so forth," persist, the refugee ordeal will remain as an ultimate problem of meaning common to the human condition; some may be experiencing it at a particular time, all are vulnerable to its likelihood.

Not surprisingly, attempts to address refugee experience as a problem of meaning have received considerable attention in the sacred narratives of major world religions, especially Judaism, Christianity, and Islam. A large portion of the sacred texts of all three religious traditions consists of the stories of the Exodus, the Exile, and dispersion and/or repatriation of persecuted religious communities led by various prophets and paradigmatic heroes.[4] The resolutions offered are by no means the same.

The Islamic treatment of religious exile and refugee life is firmly grounded in the biblical tradition. The Qur'an mentions hijrah by at least four major prophets—Noah, Abraham, Lot, and Moses—in the course of their prophetic missions.[5] Undoubtedly, as Ansari (1990:4) suggests, the mention of the example of these prophets in the Qur'an assures a degree of respectability to hijrah as a *sunnah* (practice) of the prophets in the eyes of faithful Muslims. However, what "has turned hijrah into a major Islamic virtue is the fact that during the lifetime of Muhammad (peace be upon him) Muslims resorted to hijrah twice, and in one of these the Prophet himself took part" (ibid.).

The first hijrah by Muslims from Mecca to the Christian Kingdom of Abyssinia began with the emigration of ten or eleven men and four women in A.D. 615, only five years after the prophethood of Muhammad had commenced. The motivation for this hijrah was primarily to ensure the safety of Muslims, especially those who lacked strong tribal support within Mecca, against persecution and mental and physical torture directed toward Muslims by the powerful Meccan opponents of the prophet. The fact that about one hundred Muslims made the journey (between A.D. 615 and 622) and found safe refuge in Abyssinia, so early in the history of Islam, was also a strong testament to the strength of their faith.

Unlike the hijrah to Abyssinia, which was voluntary and limited in scope, "the hijrah to Medina [in A.D. 622 by the Prophet Muhammad] was obligatory and involved almost the entire Muslim community. No Muslim was supposed to stay behind in Mecca. Exemption was allowed only to the 'weak'—women, children, and the sick—and those who could not afford to migrate" (Masud 1990:30). The strategic withdrawal of the Muslims was necessitated by the death of the Prophet Muhammad's uncle and guardian, Abu Talib, in A.D. 619 and the loss of considerable support among his own Meccan tribesmen. Indeed, the personal safety of the Prophet himself was endangered and the future of Islam seemed to be imperiled.

Also unlike the hijrah to Abyssinia, the hijrah to Medina was preceded by two pacts concluded (in A.D. 620 and 621) between Muslims of Mecca and powerful tribesmen from the town of Medina (Yathrib). As a result of the second pact, called *bay' at al-harb/hijra* (the pact of war or emigration), between the prophet and the people of Medina, "the people of Medina . . . swore allegiance to protect Muslims and to wage jihad against their enemies" (Ibn Hisham 1963:II, 303) (ibid., 31). After the completion of the emigration from Mecca, sometime during the middle of September in 622, all ties, including kinship, between Meccan Muslim emigrants

> were broken with both non-Muslims and Muslims who refused to migrate. Instead, a new bond of brotherhood (mu'akhat) between muhajirs (migrants) and ansars (inhabitants of Medina—generally supporters or local hosts) was established, which entitled them even to inherit from one another. . . . *Hijra thus meant to abandon one's property and relations in order to support the nascent community of Muslims in Medina.* Refusal to perform hijra meant to weaken the Muslim cause and to lend support (wala' or muwalat) to their enemies. (Masud 1990:31; emphasis added)

It is important to note that in this hijrah, as in the previous one to Abyssinia, the Muslim families were moving together, men, women, and children (ibid.). The most significant outcome of this historic event, the "hijrah par excellence for the Muslims" (Ansari 1990:5), was the formation of the initial nucleus of the Muslim political community, the *umma,* consisting of the muhajirin and their Medinan hosts, the *ansar.* This first community of Muslim "refugee-warriors"[6] then organized and carried out a prolonged armed struggle or jihad, from their place of refuge in Medina, against their Meccan oppressors.[7] Eight years and many battles later, in 630, their enemies in Mecca submitted, and the Muslim refugee-warriors triumphantly returned "home" to Mecca.

The Qur'an and hadith (texts relating to the sayings of the Prophet), the two principal textual sources of Islamic doctrine, make numerous references to the historic events of the hijrah and contain the injunctions that made it incumbent on Muslims to migrate when faced with serious adversity. For example, the Qur'an (8:72) says, "Those who believed, and emigrated and fought for the Faith [i.e., muhajirin], with their property and their person, in the Cause of Allah, as well as those who give (them) asylum and aid [i.e., ansar],—these are (all) friends and protectors, one of another (also see 2:218; 3:195; 4:100; 9:100, 117; 16:41–42; 28:8–9; 33:6; 59:8–9; 60:10).

Among the numerous sayings of the Prophet concerning hijrah as an obligation is the following. "I convey the following five commandments given me by God: attention (sam'), obedience (ta'a), migration (hijra), struggle (jihad), and organization [of community] (jma'a)" (Ibn Hanbal, quoted in Masud 1990:33).

From the examination of the Qur'anic and hadith texts on the original hijrah, a number of significant points of critical relevance to our discussion may be inferred. First, the obligation of hijrah as a physical movement was essential for the "self-definition of the nascent Muslim community." Not joining the migration resulted in exclusion from the society. Second, "hijra was closely associated with jihad" (ibid., 32). That is, displacement was not only for the sake of ensuring physical safety of the Muslims but it was also a concerted effort to build liberation of Muslim land with varying degrees of effectiveness and success (see Jansen 1979; Karpat 1990; Peters 1979, 1977).[8] Afghanistan's muhajirin in Pakistan and Iran, as refugee-warriors resisting the intervention of the former Soviet Union in support of their Afghan Communist allies in Kabul, represent one of the more recent examples of the two centuries of confrontations between Western and Muslim societies and polities.

BECOMING MUHAJIR: IDENTITIES AND MOTIVES

The particular motivating forces behind the decisions of individuals, families, and larger groups of Afghans are necessarily very complex and almost impossible to establish with any degree of certainty. From the very beginning of the Afghan exodus, however, the displaced Afghans have publicly couched their actions in the idiom of hijrah and jihad, as a grand Islamic religious ritual[9] in defense of Islam and their Muslim homeland. The majority of Afghans who have made the often perilous journey into Pakistan and Iran view their decision simultaneously as a political act of resistance against Communist usurpation of state power in Kabul and as a moral act of faith in the sanctity of Islamic principles and their commitment to defend them. Fortunately for the Afghan refugees, their self-conception was affirmed through the warm reception accorded them by their Muslim hosts, the people and governments of Pakistan and Iran, as expressed by a former Pakistani official:

> Refugees all over the world, whether they be Muslims or belong to any other faith, should be, and happily usually are, the responsibility not only of the country of asylum but that of the world community as a whole. . . . We in Pakistan, of course, have an added reason for providing shelter and succour to the [Afghan] muhajireen. It is a tradition left by the Ansar of Medina who welcomed the Prophet Muhammad and his followers when they migrated from Mecca due to the continued persecution by their own people. (Matinuddin 1990:217)

Shortly after the Soviet-inspired Marxist military coup of 27 April 1978 in Kabul, a strong popular Islamist armed opposition to the new regime began and grew steadily, invoking the Qur'anic obligations of jihad and hijrah to mobilize public support. Interpretations and commentary on the Qur'anic verses and hadith of the Prophet related to jihad and hijrah proliferated in the Afghan vernacular press on both sides—the Kabul regime as well as the Afghanistan muhajirin and mujahidin movements abroad (see Roy 1990; Shahrani and Canfield 1984). For the past fourteen years these twin notions have found a prominent place in the Islamist political discourse of Afghans as well as Muslim discourses elsewhere about them. The prolonged experiences of Islamist armed resistance (jihad) and migration for the cause of Islam (hijrah) have had considerable transformative effects on Afghan society and culture in general and the identity, organization, and conduct of Afghanistan's muhajirin in Pakistan and Iran in particular.

It is critical to understand that while the paradigmatic model of hijrah has been widely invoked, the actual decision to become a muhajir or not has been very personal, particularistic, and contingent on many other exigencies, both local and extralocal. Some of the most significant factors affecting Afghanistan muhajirin's decisions to migrate and the organization and management of their refugee experience appear to be the following: ethnolinguistic and sectarian affiliations and loyalties; proximity to potential place of refuge; subsistence base and occupational skills; local community organization and leadership; prior history of hijrat; and the history of perceived or actual relations of individuals, families, and larger collectives with the Afghan governments, past and present, as well as with the Afghan resistance parties and organizations both inside and outside the country. Also significant have been the tactics and targeting practices of the Kabul regime and the Russians in carrying out their war policies. It is in the light of these broader historical and sociological realities of Afghanistan that muhajirin behavior becomes comprehensible when viewed both as an Islamically informed and sociologically grounded social and political action.

COMPOSITION OF AFGHAN MUHAJIRIN IN PAKISTAN[10]

Available data indicates that over 97 percent of the refugees are from rural agricultural and pastoral nomadic backgrounds. Nearly one-half (48%) of Afghan muhajirin are infants and children who are nurtured by over one million Afghan women over the age of fifteen. Together women and children account for more than 75 percent of the refugees in Pakistan (Dupree 1990:121, 1991). Male refugees account for about 24 percent, and the majority of them are elderly, infirm, and disabled. Most able-bodied males, having secured the safety of their families in the refugee camps, return to Afghanistan and participate in the armed resistance. Ethnolinguistically, members of the traditionally dominant Pashtun groups inhabiting the eastern, southern, and southwestern provinces of the country along the Pakistani and Iranian borders constitute 85 percent of the muhajirin in Pakistan. The remainder are Tajiks (6%), Turkmens (1%), Uzbeks and Hazaras (each less than 1%), Nuristanis (2.9%), Baluch (3.6%), and other smaller groups (about 1%),[11] primarily inhabiting the central and northern provinces closer to the former Soviet borders, except for the Nuristanis and Baluch who live in eastern and southwestern regions, respectively (see English 1988:8–10; Sliwinski 1989:46). Over 75 percent of the Pashtun muhajirin have come from Afghan provinces bordering Pakistan and have in most cases maintained close contact with their home areas inside Afghanistan. Over 2.5 million Afghan refugees (out of the total of 3.3 million) are living in the North-West Frontier Province (NWFP), a predominantly Pakistani Pashtun tribal region bordering Afghanistan.

Although no comparable statistics are available on the ethnic composition of Afghan refugees in Iran, Pashtun tribes are said to predominate. "The inhabitants of Samangan, Kunduz, Baghlan, and probably Badakhshan [the northern provinces] suffered the highest war casualties, with more than 15 percent of the population killed or incapacitated," but not many of their inhabitants are among the refugees (Sliwinski 1989:47). The sheer length and the difficulty of routes from these regions to both the Pakistani and Iranian borders, coupled with government bombing and strafing of the suspected refugees en route, might have been responsible for large numbers of reported potential refugee victims and may have discouraged attempts by others to leave. However, with the prolongation of the war, "the refugees increasingly arrive[d] from distant regions" (ibid.). The testimony of an elderly Afghan muhajir, Muhammad Yusuf, illustrates the predicament of those contemplating exodus from the northern and central areas of Afghanistan.

> I was a tenant farmer in northern Afghanistan near the Soviet border. I didn't want to leave my homeland—it took eight years of war to make me and my family refugees. We left our village along with 18 other families, after being bombed everyday in retaliation for a Mujahidin attack. It took us six weeks to reach Pakistan. We were bombed twice on the way and ambushed as well. About 60 people in our convoys were killed—men, women and children. (Bryant 1988)[12]

It is worth noting that the great majority of Turkic (Uzbek and Turkmen) and Tajik muhajirin from northern Afghanistan are originally refugees from Turkistan (former Muslim Soviet Central Asia), people who have painful memories of their earlier flight from Russian Bolsheviks (Shalinski 1979).

LOCATION AND ORGANIZATION OF AFGHAN MUHAJIRIN IN PAKISTAN

The exodus to Pakistan occurred along some 1,500 miles of common borders and across an estimated 180 to 300 passes and entry points. On arrival in most places, the Afghan muhajirin encountered no Pakistani border officials or customs posts. Many Afghan Pashtun muhajirin sought refuge among their tribesmen on the Pakistani side of the border, often not very far from their home territories. Non-Pashtun refugees came later and had to move farther away from the frontiers. In many cases they settled nearer the larger cities and towns in NWFP, Baluchistan, and Panjab provinces. Urban-educated elite families, especially from the capital city of Kabul, planned and executed their escape over a period of time, often with the help of mujahidin operating near the city. The great majority of them chose to live in large cities, avoiding the refugee camps, and many (an estimated 100,000) left for a third country of asylum in Europe, America, or Australia. The flight of the rural villagers and nomadic groups ranged from utterly abrupt departures in desperation to well-planned family and community efforts such as the Kirghiz exodus from the Afghan Pamirs (see Shahrani 1981, 1984a).

STATE AND SOCIETY RELATIONS: POLITICS OF DISTRUST IN REFUGEE LIFE

The ethnic and geographic makeup of Afghanistan muhajirin in Pakistan, according to Marek Sliwinski, may be the result of "a conscious, ordered and planned Soviet [war] policy." He argues that

> from 1978 to 1981, the Soviets gave priority to isolating the resistance movements by creating a cordon sanitaire along the Pakistan border, and consequently this strip was depopulated [of Pashtuns] by aerial bombings. . . . [C]learing the northern and central zones around the capital was the next goal, and that was indeed the main task during 1982–84. Then came the control of trunk roads . . . linking the central area with the Soviet Union. These steps could not be achieved without expelling or exterminating the indigenous population. (Sliwinski 1989:50)

An added dimension to the policy of "migratory genocide" pursued by the Soviets and their Afghan Communist allies was their distrust of the rural population of Afghanistan, whom they viewed as backward, conservative, religious minded, and loyal to the reactionary anti-Communist Muslim clergy *('ulama)*. As such they were deemed expendable.[13] The feelings of mistrust on the part of Afghan rural villagers toward central governments in general and the new Marxist regimes in particular was mutual.

At least since the turn of the century, governments, with their attempts at centralization and secularization, have been suspicious of traditional rural-based tribal and religious leaders as potential forces of threat to the state, and when and where possible the governments have treated such leaders harshly. On their part, local traditional leaders in the rural areas have viewed the centralizing state apparatus principally as forces of political oppression, control, and economic extraction, legal and extralegal. Prior to the Soviet invasion, central governments in Afghanistan provided no significant social services to the rural population, and their legitimacy was based primarily on increasing monopoly over military and police forces, maintenance of order in the countryside, and, most important, the claims to defend Islam and Muslim Afghanistan against outside forces. By "inviting" the Soviet Red Army into Afghanistan and waging war against the rural population, the Marxist governments lost the modicum of trust and support that the previous government enjoyed. Therefore, rural opposition to the Communist regimes and their protectors, the Soviet Russians, became universal.

Traditionally, the relationship between modern state (government) apparatus and rural society in Afghanistan has been characterized for the most part by tension, suspicion, and mutual distrust. The state wished to transform rural society in its own image. Lacking resources to do so, the governments have been content with political control of tribal and rural regions. Under the prevailing and prolonged conditions of "politics of mistrust" between central Afghan states and rural society, the villagers and nomadic populations resorted to the creation of their own parallel power structures at the local level. That is, villages and local communities relied on trusted local community leaders to manage the affairs of their members, thereby insulating themselves from the state apparatus by avoiding contact with exploitative and corrupt government officials (for details, see Shahrani 1986*a*, 1986*b*). This tradition of reliance on the tightly organized local kin-based village and tribal communities led by the familiar, proven, respected, and trusted elders proved remarkably resilient and effective in serving the local community interests during the current crises, especially concerning the management of the muhajirin exodus and life in the refugee camps in Pakistan.

AFGHAN MUHAJIRIN AND PAKISTANI ANSAR: SHARED VALUES, OBJECTIVES, AND TRUST

At enormous cost to Pakistani society and economy, especially during the first few years after the conflict began in Afghanistan, Pakistan provided a "natural refuge" to their "brothers in faith, culture and kinship" (Hussain n.d.:6). It would be a mistake to assume there was no opposition to the flow of Afghan refugees into Pakistan. Indeed, there were many individuals and a few small political parties in Pakistan who vocally opposed the government policies toward the presence of Afghan muhajirin and mujahidin in Pakistani territory. Despite internal opposition, the policies of unwavering support for the Afghans, both muhajirin and mujahidin, by the government of Pakistan continued.

From the very beginning, the Pakistani authorities understood and appreciated the national, regional, and international political dimensions of the tragedy and fully shared the aspirations of the Afghan refugee-warriors. For the Pakistanis, caring for the Afghan muhajirin

> is not a job of merely feeding and sheltering . . . ; *the task is also to preserve the dignity and honour of a proud people. Pakistan is doing this just out of humanitarian and religious compulsion; it is a display of compassion combined with companionship*—a task which it cannot shuffle off. And while shouldering this heavy and increasing burden, Pakistan is sincerely working for a political solution of the Afghan crisis, a solution which will bring about the withdrawal of foreign forces restoring the sovereignty and non-aligned character of Afghanistan and create proper conditions for the return of Afghan refugees to their homes in safety and dignity. (Hussain n.d:6; emphasis added)

Therefore, both the Afghans and their Pakistani hosts (the ansar) viewed hijra to Pakistan as a necessary temporary measure and as a means of preserving the self-respect, dignity, and honor (personal, familial, communal, national, and Islamic) of the Afghan Muslim nation in the face of overwhelming Communist threats. Achieving this honorable objective for the Afghans has been contingent not only on finding safe haven for the muhajirin but also on the support of their armed struggle, jihad, until its fruition and the eventual return of all muhajirin "home" to Afghanistan.

The recognition of the importance of personal dignity and collective honor in the Afghan cultural tradition and willingness to assist in its preservation and defense by the Pakistani policy makers has earned them much goodwill from the Afghan muhajirin and laid an important foundation for establishing relations based on a degree of trust. The establishment and maintenance of any kind of relationship based on trust *(i'timad, itminan,* and *i'tibar)* in Afghan society requires, first and foremost, respect for the dignity, honor, and independence of the other. The positive image of the Afghan muhajirin held by the people and government of Pakistan, not merely as victims of a tragic conflict, but as determined Muslim political actors, has contributed immensely to the generally trouble-free management of the otherwise massive refugee problem in Pakistan.

Afghan muhajirin in Pakistan, compared with refugees in other countries, have enjoyed unprecedented rights and liberties. There are no (and never were) refugee transit camps with barbed wire and armed guards. Afghan refugees are granted freedom of movement, employment, and participation in trade and commerce throughout Pakistan. After entering Pakistan, Afghan refugees are allowed to proceed to Pakistani areas or particular refugee tented villages (RTV) where people from their own ethnolinguistic, tribal, or regional communities live. Once in the desired place, with help from the previously registered muhajirin in the camps and/or the mujahidin resistance party organizations, the identities of the new arrivals are verified and registered for relief assistance and the issuance of ration cards. Officially, provision of rations and other relief assistance has been contingent on residence in one of the more than 340 RTVs located primarily in NWFP (249 camps), with smaller numbers in Baluchistan (76 camps), Panjab (16 camps), and Karachi (1 camp). Those Afghans living in the cities amid Pakistani communities are deemed ineligible for such assistance (see Christensen and Scott 1988; Hussain n.d.:12).

Afghan "RTVs" ranging from 40,000 to well over 120,000 in population are not tented villages at all. Within a year or so after their establishment or following the arrival of the new muhajirin, tents were replaced by permanent Afghan-style adobe structures, hidden behind high mud walls. Architecturally and organizationally, Afghan RTVs look and work like traditional Afghan villages and urban *muhalahs,* or neighborhoods. That is, each RTV is made up of numerous kin-based communities *(qawm),* each organized around a mosque with its own trusted leadership, often closely linked to home-based branch(es) of one or more of the Pakistan-based mujahidin parties. In many instances actual villages or segments of them are relocated almost intact in an RTV. The RTVs have their own sprawling bazaars offering a fully array of consumer goods and products of the local craftsmen and artisans within the community. The most obvious difference between the Afghan RTVs and rural villages in Afghanistan is the enormous size and diversity of people living in exceedingly crowded conditions in the refugee camps, a situation that has caused much mental anguish among women muhajirin.[14]

Pakistani refugee administration officials have adopted a policy of minimal interference in the internal affairs of the Afghans in the RTVs. They have relied heavily on the traditional community leaders—that is, the *khans, rishafids, kalani qawn,* and the *maleks*—as the interlocutors only in communities where such leaders are important parts of the local organizational structure in the management of administrative relations with the muhajirin. In camps where no apparent political leadership was identifiable they have dealt directly with the heads of households or encouraged the formation of new Afghan leadership structures.

Pakistani administrators have also allowed the formation of the council of elders, committees, and even the selection of a *ra'is,* or president, for the very large RTVs by the Afghan refugee community leaders to help manage their own internal conflicts and concerns independent of the Pakistani administrative structures. Afghan resistance organizations and political parties are also permitted to maintain offices in the refugee camps and offer educational and health care services to the muhajirin. Indeed, in most cases, the party representatives, *namayandahs,* play important roles in the RTV councils and administration of community affairs.

By their presence in the muhajirin camps, the Afghan mujahidin parties and political organizations also play a critical role in monitoring corruption and pilfering in the RTVs. On the whole, the Pakistani approach of tolerating considerable autonomy by the Afghan community leaders in running their own affairs in the RTVs has worked well.[15] But the system has not been free of abuse and corruption by both Pakistanis and the new breed of emergent refugee community leaders known as the *rashan maleks,* or ration chiefs (see Centlivres and Centlivres-Dumont 1987). Under pressure from the UNHCR, the system left an estimated 300,000 to 400,000 muhajirin (primarily non-Pashtun groups from the northern provinces) unregistered for many years and therefore without access to refugee assistance benefits (see McPherson 1987).[16]

AFGHAN MUHAJIRIN AND INTERNATIONAL RELIEF ORGANIZATIONS: MISTRUST OF POLITICS

Assuming administrative control over the Afghan muhajirin by virtue of being the host country, the Pakistani government also became the intermediary between the refugees and all the international and bilateral relief assistance organizations and agencies. The donor agencies, especially the UNHCR and World Food Program (WFP), which collect and provide the bulk of the assistance, have assumed the role of directly monitoring the distribution of goods and services by the Pakistani refugee administration authorities in the RTVs. This task is accomplished through site visits and inspection tours of the RTVs by the relatively small number of UN field officers or visits to the camps by "high-powered delegations" from Geneva, Rome, and New York. This monitoring responsibility offers the UN agencies an opportunity to put pressure on Pakistan to provide accurate statistics, account for the assistance distributions, and conform with the political and strictly humanitarian objectives of refugee assistance for Afghan muhajirin.

In this capacity, UN officials have no real sustained contact with the Afghan refugees, and none is sought. UNHCR and other UN agencies providing assistance to the Afghan refugees have purposefully avoided the inclusion of Afghans in their staff for political reasons. The assumption is that Afghans are essentially *Homo politicus* and there is no room for people with strong political views in the task of providing humanitarian assistance. Therefore, having Pakistanis as intermediaries to insulate UN officials from political contamination by the Afghan "refugee-warriors" has been a blessing in disguise for both the UN and the Afghans. While appreciating the UN humanitarian help, the Afghans have been suspicious of the motives behind the UN aloofness toward the Afghan resistance and courting of the Kabul Communist regimes over the years of conflict. Such "politics of mistrust" characterizes the relationship among Afghan muhajirin and mujahidin in Pakistan and the UN officials, a phenomenon that may also be responsible in part for the failure of UN-negotiated peace efforts in Kabul.

In addition to the UN concerns about the close association of Afghan muhajirin with the armed resistance inside Afghanistan, UN officials, operating "according to an implicit liberal ethos which infers that refugees are individuals equal in rights which need to be defended against tribalism and feudalism, and protected against intermediaries such as malek and representatives of the [mujahidin] political parties" (Centlivres and Centlivres-Dumont 1987:4), have put pressure on the Pakistani refugee administrators to renounce reliance on traditional political leadership in the camps for the distribution of assistance. Compliance by the Pakistani officials in some instances has resulted in camp riots and, for some refugee households headed by women, inconvenience and additional cost in obtaining rations.

The pressures from both UN agencies and to some extent indirectly from Pakistani refugee administrators to ensure that Afghan muhajirin act like proper "refugees" (i.e., docile, grateful, cooperative, and apolitical) have not been insignificant. Pakistan officially has not acknowledged involvement of muhajirin in any overt political or military resistance inside Afghanistan, while permitting such activities in practice. The presence of well-armed and fractious resistance parties with considerable influence both in Pakistan and in the home districts of the refugees has played an important role in maintaining a degree of autonomy for social action at the local community level within the RTVs. Also important in this struggle for recognition and autonomy has been the presence of numerous nongovernmental organizations (NGOs) and voluntary agencies (VOLAGs), including some fifteen agencies from the Muslim world that have shown considerable sympathy for the political aspirations of the Afghans while healing their wounds in exile and at home inside the liberated areas during the past several years. Within this general context of multiple centers of power and resources (Afghan resistance, the Pakistani government, the UN, and NGOs), armed with persistent cultural traditions of political mistrust of outsiders and distrust of government politics at all levels, Afghanistan's "refugee-warrior" communities in Pakistan and Iran have shown remarkable resilience in pursuing the fulfillment of their Islamist religious and political objectives. Goals that are inspired and guided by the paradigmatic model of Islamic hijrah—fighting from the safety of refuge to remove the oppressive conditions at home—so that they may be able to repatriate.[17]

CONCLUSION

The exodus of millions of Afghan muhajirin to Muslim Pakistan and Iran because of a direct confrontation with colonialism and atheism has been viewed both by the refugees and by other Muslims around the world, especially those in Pakistan and Iran, as an act of profound religious and political significance. Their remarkably positive and trouble-free experiences in the refugee camps in Pakistan may not be fully comprehensible in terms of the standardized and universalized definitions and conceptions of "refugee" used in policy making. Instead consideration of their self-image and understanding of the sources of their cultural and religious inspirations as political and religious actors are crucial for any approach aiming to explain their conduct as displaced Muslims.

The most critical feature of the self-definition of Afghan muhajir is their reluctance, both conceptually and practically, to separate their decision to migrate from the desires to resist external and internal sources of oppression and to repatriate. The Islamic concept of "hijrah" as it is understood by the Afghans has played a crucial emotive and paradigmatic role in their actions. The fact that the historic hijrah of the Prophet, his companions, and his followers was fundamentally a task undertaken by Muslim families to help create, strengthen, and preserve the unity and integrity of the nascent Muslim community, the umma in Medina, is viewed with special significance by the Afghan muhajirin. That is, to the Afghans, the survival, integrity, and autonomy of their Muslim community is thought to be contingent on the well-being of their own Muslim families.

Therefore, for the great majority of Islamically minded Afghans, both historically and culturally, the defense of Islam, family honor, and the preservation of the integrity and dignity of qawn, or community, constitute the supreme virtues. From this perspective, the struggle for Islam is not simply the willingness to fight for the cause of some abstract set of high ideals; rather, it is understood first and foremost as an endeavor to protect their loved ones and their valuables, both tangible and intangible. Therefore, for most Afghan refugee-warrior communities in Pakistan, the increased opportunities for Islamic education and knowledge in the camps, especially among the young, and greater adherence to Muslim values also have had positive influences on the relatively healthy experiences of the Afghan muhajirin in Pakistan.

Thus, in political terms, hijrah meant maintaining the autonomy and the integrity of the umma, the extended religious "family" of a local community. This symbolic resource enabled the Afghan refugees to relocate with the political structure of a local community headed by a trusted leader intact. With the understanding of their Muslim Pakistani hosts, the Afghan refugees were able to maintain this internal political organization in the RTVs.

The Afghan refugees also brought with them a historical mistrust of central governments—a "distrust of politics." The survival of their local political autonomy in the RTVs enabled them to continue their pattern of insulating themselves from central governments— now the international relief organizations and, to a lesser extent, the Pakistani government—by relying on trusted local Afghan representatives. Ironically, the international refugee organizations' reciprocal mistrust of Afghan refugee politics and politicians further reinforced the autonomy of the RTVs, thereby indirectly strengthening the Afghan refugees' ability to help themselves.

What distinguishes the Afghan refugee-warriors' situation in Pakistan from refugees elsewhere is the recognition of and respect for the mutually reinforcing relationship between the humanitarian and political dimensions of their refugee life. The Afghan muhajirin's ability to maintain local community autonomy in the RTVs and the presence of armed mujahidin in the background "represent a transformation of refugees from being mere objects to being simultaneously actors and subjects in their own right" (Zolberg, Suhrke, and Aguayo 1989:278). This situation undoubtedly is "desirable for the refugees" as Zolberg et al. (ibid.) suggest, but it does not have to necessarily complicate "problems of the host countries" as the situation in Pakistan illustrates. No one doubts the fact that the "problems of the refugees" as well as "refugee problems" around the world "stem from distinctively political conditions" of mistrust, but wholesale distrust of refugee politics can result in overlooking or even undermining potent symbolic and cultural resources refugees may bring with them into exile. Are we and the concerned UN agencies willing to begin to address the political dimensions of the refugee problems as much as the humanitarian ones?

NOTES

1. These figures are based on 1990 estimates published by UNIDATA in the Third Consolidated Report issued by the Office of the United Nations Co-Ordinator for Humanitarian and Economic Assistance Programmes Relating to Afghanistan (UNOCA) in Geneva (United Nations 1990:35). In addition, the report adds that "as many as 1,000,000 Afghans are currently living in exile overseas." The figures for the internally displaced Afghans who have moved either to major urban centers within Afghanistan, including the capital, Kabul, or to the more remote rural mountainous regions are estimated at 1.5 to 2.5 million.

2. For an interesting history of the political context and religious association of the rise of the term "refugee" with the persecution of the Christian Huguenots in Spain and southern France, as well as the more recent refinements and modification of the definition of the concept, see Zolberg, Suhrke, and Aguayo 1989:5–33.

3. Turkistani Muslim refugees in Afghanistan also adopted muhajir as an important dimension of their identity (for details, see Shalinski 1979).

4. For an extensive history of Judeo-Christian religious refugees, see Norwood 1969; and for a recent treatment of the concept of "hijrah" in Islam and extensive bibliographic sources, see Ansari 1990; Masud 1990.

5. The word *hijrah* has been used in the Qur'an to mean "to reject" (23:69), "to shun" (74:5), "to depart" (19:46), and "to banish" (4:34). The shared meaning in all these usages may be deduced to be a distancing—physically and otherwise—usually from evil and disbelief (Masud 1990:32).

6. The expression "refugee-warrior" community, which appears in the title of this chapter, comes from Zolberg, Suhrke, and Aguayo 1989:275. They use this expression in reference to Afghan and Palestinian refugees in an attempt to distinguish them from other types of refugee communities. No reference to the Islamic notions of hijrah is made in their work.

7. It is significant to point out that as Masud (1990:32) asserts, in the Qur'an, "Most verses employing the derivative form [of hijrah] hajaru ('they migrated') are often paired with jahadu ('they waged war') and thus imply a close association of hijrah with jihad."

8. An important exception may have been the Palestinian opposition movements to Israeli occupation, especially during the earlier decades (1950s–1970s).

9. I have argued elsewhere (Shahrani 1984*b*) that hijrah is a form of Islamic ritual enactment. It embodies core symbols, has both didactic and transformative effects, and consists of all three distinctive phases of ritual actions—separation (exodus), liminality (exile), and reintegration (repatriation)—identified by Victor Turner (1969).

10. For a variety of obvious political reasons information about Afghanistan's refugees in Iran are scarce. Hence my focus on the situation in Pakistan.

11. Sliwinski (1989:46) provides the following figures for the prewar ethnic composition of Afghanistan's estimated population of 12 to 15.5 million: Pashtun (Pathans) 39%, Tajiks 26%, Hazaras 10%, Uzbeks 10%, Turkmens 3%, and others 12%.

12. For other narrative accounts of torture and suffering of the Afghan refugees at the hands of Kabul regimes and the Soviets, see Dadfar 1988*a*, 1988*b*; Helsinki Watch 1984; Helsinki Watch/Asia Watch 1985.

13. Edward Girardet (1983) has reported that Afghan Marxist government officials in Kabul reportedly said that "if only 1 million people were left in the country, they would be more than enough to start a new society" (quoted in Sliwinski 1989:51).

14. Despite generally hospitable policies of the government of Pakistan and the generous attitude of most Pakistanis, Afghan women muhajirin have suffered isolation and serious restrictions on their spatial mobility and participation in public life. This is due largely to a much greater emphasis on personal and communal honor among Afghan refugees and the insistence on stricter observance of the Islamic code of female modesty *(hijab)*. Particular problems experienced by Afghan women refugees are discussed at length elsewhere by others, including Nancy Hatch Dupree (1990, 1991), and because of space limitations cannot be attempted here.

15. The fractious and conflict-ridden Afghan resistance political parties and organizations (mujahidin) all vied for support, recruits, and loyalty from the ranks of the Afghan muhajirin. This was done to a large measure by their efforts to secure assistance and provide services to the refugee communities. Their violent squabbles were largely kept out of the refugee camps and only rarely affected life in the RTVs.

16. The UNHCR, in a dispute with the government of Pakistan over the possible "over-registration" of Afghanistan refugees, decided in 1986 to freeze the number of registered refugees at about 3.2 million. After that date no new refugees were added to the roll of the registered refugees until 1991, although Afghan muhajirin, especially from the central and northern provinces, continued to reach Pakistan in large numbers and were not offered benefits by the UNHCR. The unregistered refugees relied on assistance from relatives and compatriots from their region who were already established in Pakistan and were also extended help by various nongovernmental relief agencies operating in Pakistan.

17. In late April 1992, the Communist regime of President Najibullah in Kabul was forced out of power and the formation of an Islamic State of Afghanistan announced by a coalition of Afghani mujahidin parties. Sadly, after victory over their common enemy, interethnic and sectarian conflicts over access to power in the capital have resulted in continued bloodshed in Kabul. Fortunately the situation in the provinces and rural areas has remained peaceful, and according to a report in the *New York Times*, 31 August 1992, "Hundreds of thousands of the estimated 3.2 million who went to Pakistan have already returned to Afghanistan" (Ghazi 1992).

REFERENCES

Ansari, Zafar Ishaq
   1990   "Hijrah in the Islamic Tradition." In *The Cultural Basis of Afghan Nationalism*, ed. Ewan Anderson and Nancy Hatch Dupree, 3–20. London: Pinter.

Boesen, Inger
   1990   "Honour in Exile: Continuity and Change Among Afghan Refugees." In *The Cultural Basis of Afghan Nationalism*, ed. Ewan Anderson and Nancy Hatch Dupree, 160–174. London: Pinter.

Bryant, Margi, coord. ed.
   1988   *The Afghan Tragedy*. London: British Refugee Council.

Centlivres, Pierre, and Micheline Centlivres-Dumont
   1987   "Sociopolitical Adjustment Among Afghan Refugees." Presented at a

Symposium on the Crisis of Migration from Afghanistan: Domestic and Foreign Implications. Oxford University, 29 March–2 April, 1987.

Christensen, Hanna, and Wolf Scott
1988   *Survey of the Social and Economic Conditions of Afghan Refugees in Pakistan.* Geneva: United Nations Research Institute for Social Development (UNRISD), Report no. 88.1.

Dadfar, M. Azam
1988a   *The Impaired Mind.* Peshawar: Psychiatry Center for the Afghan Refugees.
1988b   *Psychological Consequences of War in Afghan Children.* Peshawar: Psychiatry Center for Afghan Refugees.

Dupree, Louis
1984   "The Marxist Regimes and the Soviet Presence in Afghanistan: An Age-Old Culture Responds to Late Twentieth-Century Aggression." In *Revolutions and Rebellions in Afghanistan: Anthropological Perspectives,* ed. M. Nazif Shahrani and Robert Canfield, 58–73. Berkeley: Institute of International Studies, University of California.

Dupree, Nancy Hatch
1990   "A Socio-Cultural Dimension: Afghan Women Refugees in Pakistan." In *The Cultural Basis of Afghan Nationalism,* ed. Ewan Anderson and Nancy Hatch Dupree, 121–133. London and New York: Pinter Publishers.
1991   "Observations on Afghan Women Refugees in Pakistan: 1990." In *World Refugee Survey: 1991.* Washington, D.C.: American Council for Nationalities Service, 28–30.

Eickelman, Dale, and James Piscatori
1990   *Muslim Travelers: Pilgrimage, Migration, and the Religious Imagination.* Berkeley, Los Angeles, and Oxford: University of California Press.

English, Richard
1988   "Preliminary Report on Conditions Affecting the Repatriation of Afghan Refugees." Geneva: For the Operational Unit for Repatriation to Afghanistan, UNHCR.

Farr, Grant M.
1990   "Afghan Refugees in Pakistan: Definition, Repatriation and Ethnicity." In *The Cultural Basis of Afghan Nationalism,* ed. Ewan Anderson and Nancy Hatch Dupree, 134–143. London: Pinter Publishers.

Geertz, Clifford
1973   *Interpretation of Cultures.* New York: Basic Books.

Ghazi, Katayon
1992   "Iran Asks Help in Sending Afghan Refugees Home." *New York Times,* 31 August, A3.

Girardet, Edward
1983   "In Afghanistan, Soviet Drive to Destroy a Nation." *U.S. News and World Report,* 12 December, 37–39.

Helsinki Watch
1984   *"Tears, Blood and Cries": Human Rights in Afghanistan Since the Invasion, 1979–1984.* New York: U.S. Helsinki Watch Committee.

Helsinki Watch/Asia Watch
    1985   *To Die in Afghanistan: Human Rights in Afghanistan.* New York and Washing-
               ton, D.C.: Helsinki Watch and Asia Watch Committees.

Hussain, Syed Shabbir
    n.d.   *The Long Wait: Afghan Refugees in Pakistan.* Islamabad: Kamran Publishing
               House. Pamphlet.

Janata, Alfred
    1990   "Afghanistan: The Ethnic Dimension." In *The Cultural Basis of Afghan
               Nationalism,* ed. Ewan Anderson and Nancy Hatch Dupree, 60–70. Lon-
               don: Pinter.

Jansen, Godfrey H.
    1979   *Militant Islam.* London: Pan Books.

Karpat, Kemal H.
    1990   "The Hira from Russia and the Balkans: The Process of Self-Definition in
               the Late Ottoman State." In *Muslim Travelers: Pilgrimage, Migration, and the
               Religious Imagination,* ed. Dale Eickelman and James Piscatori, 131–152.
               Berkeley, Los Angeles, and Oxford: University of California Press.

Kashani, Abbas Aryanpur, and Manoochehr Aryanpur Kashani
    1983   *The Concise Persian English Dictionary.* Tehran: Amir Kabir Publications.

Khan, Shan Zaman
    1990   "Afghan Refugees in Pakistan: The Possibility of Assimilation." In *The Cul-
               tural Basis of Afghan Nationalism,* ed. Ewan Anderson and Nancy Hatch
               Dupree, 144–153. London: Pinter.

Keller, Stephen L.
    1975   *Uprooting and Social Change: The Role of Refugees in Development.* Delhi: Manohar
               Book Service.

McPherson, Charlotte
    1987   "The Migration Patterns of Afghanistan Refugees with Particular Refer-
               ence to Those of Turkic and Tajik Origin." Paper submitted to the sym-
               posium: The Crisis of Migration of Afghanistan: Domestic and Foreign
               Implications. Oxford: Queen Elizabeth House.

Masud, Muhammad Khalid
    1990   "The Obligation to Migrate: The Doctrine of Hijrah in Islamic Law." In
               Muslim Travelers: Pilgrimage, Migration, and the Religious Imagination, ed. Dale
               Eickelman and James Piscatori, 29–49. Berkeley, Los Angeles, and Oxford.
               University of California Press.

Matinuddin, Kamal
    1990   "Afghan Refugees: The Geostrategic Context." In *The Cultural Basis of
               Afghan Nationalism,* ed. Ewan Anderson and Nancy Hatch Dupree, 217–230.
               London: Pinter.

Newland, K.
    1981   *Refugee: The New International Policy of Displacement.* New York: Worldwatch
               Institute.

Norwood, Frederick A.
    1969   *Strangers and Exiles: A History of Religious Refugees.* 2 vols. Nashville: Abingdon
               Press.

Peters, Rudolph
    1977   *Jihad in Medieval and Modern Islam.* Leyden: Brill.
    1979   *Islam and Colonialism: The Doctrine of Jihad in Modern History.* The Hague:
                 Mouton.
Pye, A. Kenneth, and William John Brian, Jr.
    1990   "Refugee and International Law." In *The Cultural Basis of Afghan Nationalism,*
                 ed. Ewan Anderson and Nancy Hatch Dupree, 21–37. London: Pinter.
Roy, Olivier
    1990   *Islam and Resistance in Afghanistan.* 2d ed. New York: Cambridge University
                 Press.
Shahrani, M. Nazif
    1981   "The Kirghiz Odysses." In *Odysses: The Human Adventure,* ed. Jane E. Aaron,
                 16–19. Boston: Public Broadcasting Associates.
    1984*a*   "The Kirghiz of Afghanistan Reach Turkey." *Cultural Survival Quarterly*
                 8(1):31–34.
    1984*b*   "Kirghiz Refugee Experiences and the Concept of Hijrah in Islam." Pre-
                 sented at a panel on Cultural Interpretations of Refugee Phenomena, 83d
                 Annual Meeting of the American Anthropological Association, Denver,
                 Colo., 14–18 Nov.
    1986*a*   "State Building and Social Fragmentation in Afghanistan: A Historical
                 Perspective." In *The State, Religion and Ethnic Politics: Afghanistan, Iran, and
                 Pakistan,* ed. Ali Banuazizi and Myron Weiner, 23–74. Syracuse: Syracuse
                 University Press.
    1986*b*   "The Kirghiz Khans: Styles and Substance of Traditional Local Leader-
                 ship in Central Asia." *Central Asian Survey* 5 (3/4):255–271.
Shahrani, M. Nazif, and Robert L. Canfield, eds.
    1984   *Revolutions and Rebellions in Afghanistan: Anthropological Perspectives.* Berkeley:
                 Institute of International Studies, University of California, Berkeley.
Shalinski, Audrey
    1979   "Central Asian Emigrés in Afghanistan: Social Dynamics of Identity Cre-
                 ation." Ph.D. dissertation, Department of Anthropology, Harvard University.
Sliwinski, Marek
    1989   "Afghanistan: The Decimation of a People." *Orbis* (Winter):39–56.
Turner, Victor
    1969   *Ritual Process.* Chicago: Aldine.
United Nations
    1988   *First Consolidated Report.* Geneva: UNOCA.
    1990   *Third Consolidated Report.* Geneva: UNOCA.
U.S. Committee for Refugees
    1985   *Afghan Refugees: Five Years Later.* Washington, D.C.: American Council for
                 Nationalities Service.
    1991   *World Refugee Survey: 1991 in Review.* Washington, D.C.: American Council
                 for Nationalities Service.
Zolberg, Aristide R., Astri Suhrke, and Sergio Aguayo
    1989   *Escape from Violence: Conflict and Refugee Crisis in the Developing World.* Oxford:
                 Oxford University Press.

ELEVEN

In Search of the Locus of Trust: The Social World of the Refugee Camp

Eftihia Voutira and Barbara E. Harrell-Bond

This chapter begins by questioning the proposition contained in the "founding document" by E. Valentine Daniel and John Chr. Knudsen (1991) on which the workshop on trust and the refugee experience was based and for which the chapters of this volume were written. In that document, Daniel and Knudsen submit that "trust is the least controversial concept by means of which we can reflect upon our own experiences with and knowledge of the refugee-problem . . . [and] the even bolder claim that trust is basic to being human." This is not to suggest that Erik Erikson (1963) and others are necessarily misguided in stating that specific psychological crises in children's development are linked to the issues of trust and mistrust. Nor do we suggest that J. Anthony Marsella, George DeVos, and Francis L. K. Hsu (1985:10, quoted in Daniel and Knudsen 1991:3) are wrong when they say that the self is "continuously defined in one's experience in interaction with others, and that it is this interactional process that contains the meaning of social experience" (ibid.). We do, however, want to challenge the validity of an unqualified acceptance of the concept of "trust" as a methodological tool in the analysis of human social relations, particularly as it relates to the study of refugees. In other words, can we assume that the inability of an individual to trust others is necessarily pathological or leads to pathological consequences?

The "glue" or cement, as Emile Durkheim put it, that holds human societies together is not trust per se but trust *in a system* of normative social relations, values, hierarchies, statuses, roles, obligations, sanctions, and so on. Certainly, "societies and cultures draw lines that divide those who can be trusted from those who cannot" (Daniel and Knudsen 1991:3). No doubt some social worlds are more capricious, particularly those that are in the process of rapid change. By implication, the social world(s) of refugees, perceived from the standpoint of radical uprootment, must be the most unpredictable and capricious of all.

Research on professionals in West Africa provides ample support for the claim that relationships that people admit to trust are very much the exception rather than the rule. In fact, Sierra Leoneans will always tell you that the *only* person a man can *really* trust is the one person who will not stand to gain by his death. This person is neither his wife nor his children; it is his mother. Men have only one mother (Harrell-Bond 1975:236)! The attitudes of the professional group toward relatives outside the immediate family were, to say the least, ambivalent, and non-familial social relations among other professionals were marked by "extreme competition and tension" (Harrell-Bond 1975, 1978). Food symbolism, patterns of food sharing, and attitudes toward the safety of accepting proffered food and drink were articulated in terms of the fear of being poisoned. While such fears of the potential malevolence of others might be interpreted as indicating a pathological level of distrust in others, for this group, in fact, this "belief" functioned as a means for rationalizing their disengagement from confining familial obligations and as a way to structure and manage social relations they perceived to be advantageous to their upward mobility.

Many, perhaps most, societies train children to be cautious, even suspicious of others, as a means for survival. Renee Hirschon has recorded how at least some sections of Greek society use "verbal play" (1992) or "verbal irresponsibility" (1989) to produce what she describes as the "doubting Thomas syndrome," which she claims to be "a feature which extends into all aspects of Greek life. . . . 'Don't believe it until you see it' is a principle which Greeks need to employ in all their social contacts" (1992:35).

In many parts of the world young children are allocated major responsibility for the care of other children. The growing evidence of sexual abuse of children by children in Western societies suggests that normative models may have a less direct correspondence to empirical reality than has been assumed, even in the very societies in which these models have been developed.

The recognition of a certain degree of violent behavior on all levels in all cultures is one of the recent "truths" in anthropological writings. The fact that anthropologists have for a long time explained away this reality has been highlighted recently by Elizabeth Colson (1989) and John Davis (1992). In Colson's analysis, anthropologists have "downplayed the violence, cruelty and unhappiness" because of our "belief that such actions were momentary departures from cultural norms that generated long-term harmony" (1989:3). Taking the argument one step further, Davis argues that wars, violence, and famines are indeed normal features of the cultures that anthropologists study. His own proposal to deal with the methodological gap that has allowed for the entrenchment of two types of anthropology— the anthropology of maintenance and the anthropology of repair—provides a unified picture of anthropology that he calls the "anthropology of suffering" (Harrell-Bond and Voutira 1992).

On a different level, a similar quest for a unified approach on the level of policy and implementation rather than theory has been voiced by Robert Chambers (1986). In Chambers's latest work on refugees, the focus of criticism becomes the refugee-centric approach of researchers, which has led to the neglect of an important dimension of the political economy of aid, namely, the impact of refugee aid programs on the "poorer" host populations.

On a more personal and self-critical tone, one can use the above insights to assess progress in the field of forced migration. Most of us have tended to be concerned primarily with the "anthropology of repair" and the need to interfere, rather than with developing theoretical models of explanations of the situations we study. Thus we find ourselves guilty of a similar type of refugee-centrism that construcs refugees as the passive victims in need of our help. Drawing from the above diagnosis, the aim of this chapter is to suggest a tentative outline for such a theory in which refugees are present but are neither glorified nor explained away.

THE SOCIAL STRUCTURE OF REFUGEE CAMPS

We began by challenging the notion of trust as an unambiguous concept, as well as the implied assumption that all normal human relationships are predicated on trust. We did this by drawing from anthropological experience that documents the variable contexts within which trust is both assumed through its absence and acknowledged as important. As Marjorie A. Muecke's account (this volume) of the Cambodian women who survived the Khmer Rouge invasions in 1979 shows, trust, though universally experienced, varies in its signification according to culture. Her case is instructive because of its striking contrast with Western understandings. Buddhism radically divorces "truth" from "trust." Trust is identified with secular human attachments, themselves undermined by the refugee experience. This chapter differs greatly from this type of analysis, characteristic of most of the other contributions in this book, in that it does not deal with cultural constructions of trust. The substantive issue it addresses is, where is the locus of trust in the refugee situation?

Daniel and Knudsen identify the restorative process of trust as the main aim of humanitarian interference. Evidently then, to test this proposition, it is necessary to examine a situation in which refugees and their helpers interact. The ideal candidate is the refugee camp. The camp is a unique social enclave in which refugees interact and are forced to come to terms with the humanitarian aid regime. It is in this sense that survival in the camps becomes the test case for cultural adaptation. The fact that refugee camps are designed to be temporary should not be seen as weakening our argument. As Muhammad Siddiq documents in this volume, the Palestinian people perceive their cultural predicament as being a "refugee nation in camps."

The usual picture of the refugee camp organization identifies all forms of intergroup behavior in terms of a simple polarity between "us" and "them"; the former identified with the aid regime, the "helpers," and the latter with the "needy." In fact, the whole institution of the refugee camp, its raison d'être, is predicated on the existence of a population that has been defined as requiring assistance. The refugee camp tradition was invented as the most efficient method of distributing aid to a constituency that had been labeled as requiring it.

The reality, we submit, is in fact far more complicated. The population of refugee camps is essentially multicultural. This multicultural dimension exists on all levels of the organization of authority, for example, dominated-dominating/ givers-recipients. To capture the complexities, a map of the variety of actors and activities is in order. For the present purposes, this map of actors is partial. It does not include those in the host country or the country of origin who may either *refoul* or attack from across the border. Such threats in many refugee situations are actual rather than imagined, as the proliferation of media reports in 1993–1994 from Kenya and the former Yugoslavia has demonstrated (see also Harrell-Bond 1986:173–175).

AN "IDEAL TYPE" REFUGEE CAMP

In an ideal type refugee camp, one can identify the following hierarchy of authority and division of labor as regards the responsibilities of law and order and the administration of aid. Starting from the top down, a refugee camp is administered by officials assigned by the host government whose power is enforced by the presence of armed police or paramilitary personnel. Although rarely benefiting from access to the host government's legal system, most camps have a place for extrajudicial detention of refugees who have committed some act deemed by the camp authorities to be an offense.

The management and distribution of material assistance is carried out by international nongovernmental (NGO) humanitarian agencies as implementing partners of the office of the United Nations High Commissioner for Refugees (UNHCR) in contractual agreements that include the host government. These agencies are assigned responsibilities for different sectors—food, health, education, agriculture, "vulnerable groups," and so on—and are all identifiable through their respective offices and their insignia on buildings, radios for communicating to their offices in the capital, and vehicles and by the differing standards of living staff members enjoy. One of these agencies is designated as the "lead" agency, responsible for coordinating the work of all the others. This is a key variable that allows for innumerable variations in the structure of possible power relations. Adding to the cultural complexity, another set of parameters of the camp includes the nations of origin; sources of funding; varieties of actual and hidden agendas of these agencies that have led them to the camp; and, finally, the contingently defined motivations of their staff.

On the receiving end are the refugees. For the majority, their residence in the camp is the result of coercion rather than choice. Not necessarily mirroring the extreme cultural variety of the administrative structure, the refugee population is nevertheless usually highly heterogeneous in terms of religion, status, class, ethnic background, and political allegiance. Refugees also differ widely in terms of the nature of the experience that led to their forced displacement and uprootment.

We have identified, even at this level of abstraction, the challenge to any unified and coherent system of communication on the inter- and intragroup level. The situation on the ground is infinitely more complex. For example, a refugee population usually includes one-parent families that may be headed by a father, mother, grandparent, or older sibling (any of which may be "fictive") and may include unaccompanied minors, guerrilla fighters, "political" activists, the handicapped, the elderly, and the mentally ill. Evidently, the only way out of this complex situation is to resort to the common link that binds the different actors together, which is the aid itself.

Although aid is the unifying principle that brings these diverse groups together, the administration of aid requires a whole machinery of power, the struggle and exercise of which defines the social reality of each refugee camp. For example, who holds the aid to be allocated and administered? Who distributes the aid? (The two do not necessarily converge.) Who owns the aid? If the aid is for the refugees, then theoretically it is their property (Harrell-Bond, Voutira, and Leopold 1992).

POWER GRIDS IN THE DISTRIBUTION OF AID

Such considerations necessarily require that one focus on the social organization of the administration of assistance, which entails a system of actors, roles, rules, and goals, the most important activities being the allocation, distribution, and acquisition of the material resources.

Ever since Marcel Mauss (1925a, 1925b) and Bronislaw Malinowski (1922), anthropologists have focused on the cultural universe of giving and receiving and the complexity of power involved in any transfer of commodities (Appadurai 1986). More recently, Annette Weiner (1992) has undertaken to explore more fully the universal principle of reciprocity. Her work shows that reciprocity as a principle of exchange is not only "giving while receiving" but a series of disguised strategies of power relations that she describes as "keeping while giving."

In the refugee camp (see Harrell-Bond, Voutira, and Leopold 1992), borrowing from Mauss's idea of the gift, the transfer of goods from the donors to the recipients creates a whole chain of hands and networks of power. The point we wish to emphasize here is that refugees are bound to their helpers in terms of the existence of these lateral and vertical chains of hands that "handle" the aid, which originates from afar. The overall pattern of distribution of aid to refugees constitutes an inverse relationship, specifically, between distance and power.

Distance becomes a factor in the accumulation of power. That is, the closer the material assistance moves toward its recipients, the greater the power of the handler over its allocation. For example, the ultimate authority in the chain of distribution lies with the person, whether a foreign aid worker or a refugee, who performs the penultimate act in the chain of handlers, "tipping" the grain into the sack of the kneeling beneficiary. This inverse relationship, which holds for givers and recipients, embodied in the act of kneeling to receive the grain, is dramatically represented in the fund-raising literature of many humanitarian agencies. It does not, however, exhaust the power structures relevant in the administration of assistance.

DONORS AND GIVERS—PATRONS AND CLIENTS

As the ideal type of the refugee camp that we have described shows, the multicultural nature of the aid regime leaves a wide space for competition as regards the administration of the allocation of resources. Resources have to be given away. The question is not simply who gets it, but who gets to give it away? The two issues are normally confounded. Introducing this dimension of conflict among the helpers themselves enables us to understand the sense in which the notion of trust is highly problematic. The sources of this problem, the role and seat of trust, may be identified analytically on at least seven levels:

1. Donors and host governments;
2. Donors and intermediaries (UNHCR and NGOs);
3. Relationships among the intermediaries (UNHCR and its nongovernmental implementing partners);
4. Relationships between the intermediaries (international agencies) and the host government in the camp;
5. Relationships between the intermediaries and the recipients in the camp situation;
6. Host population and refugees; and
7. Inter- and intragroup relationships among the refugees themselves.

In each one of these visible "segmentary groups," one can identify different sets of interests and sources of competition and conflict. Unlike the segmentary system of the Nuer, described by E. E. Evans-Pritchard (1940), the aid regime lacks an overall principle of "fusion" and "fission" that could provide the framework of cohesion on which different layers of trust could be built.

Donors and Host Governments: Competition for Sovereignty

Happy is the host government that is able to stretch its resources to accommodate the material needs of refugees and, in the process, to engage its own people in actively supporting the incorporation of refugees into its social and economic life. Such governments have the luxury of mobilizing public opinion, planning, deciding priorities, and implementing their own policies. However, most refugee situations today occur in the poorest parts of the world, where it is assumed by both the host government and the international humanitarian regime that the local infrastructure cannot cope without external aid. (Even where such absolute poverty cannot be claimed as justification for soliciting international assistance, some governments still use the presence of refugees as leverage.)

In Africa, up to the late 1970s, it was normal donor practice to channel aid bilaterally so as to support programs implemented by host governments as well as to fund humanitarian activities through multilateral sources, that is, UNHCR. Since that time, most humanitarian aid is channeled through multilateral institutions and nongovernmental agencies. Although probably having more to do with the domestic politics and the foreign relations of the donor, the justification for this change in policy is the lack of trust in host government institutions. Host governments are regularly accused of exaggerating numbers to justify more external aid and of being corrupt (Harrell-Bond 1986:13–15; Harrell-Bond, Voutira, and Leopold 1992).

Once a host government accepts external aid, it is forced into a position of economic dependence that dilutes the exercise of sovereignty in the development of state policy and decisions about priorities. In the day-to-day implementation of programs, host governments and the host populations tend to be marginalized as observers. This, as will be discussed below, undermines relationships among refugees, their host government, and the ordinary local people.[1]

Donors and Intermediaries (UNHCR and NGOs): Competition for Funds

For each new refugee crisis, the office of the UN High Commissioner for Refugees must mount a special fund-raising appeal (UNHCR 1982:16–17). These funds are given to donor governments from funds set aside for humanitarian emergencies. Given the increasing numbers of humanitarian crises around the world, donor governments have been increasing the amounts of funds available for dealing with them at the expense of "development" budgets (Randel and German 1993; Smillie and Helmich 1993). At the same time, depending on foreign policy priorities, donors may be more generous to particular refugee emergencies.

Traditionally, ever since it became involved in assistance programs for refugees, UNHCR was the main conduit for international aid. However, during the early 1980s, many donor governments began to express their lack of confidence in UN organizations by diverting funds to support the activities of their own national NGOs. Consequently, in any refugee emergency, UNHCR must also rely on NGOs for resources. Thus, at the international level in competition for funding and at the field level in the exercise of authority, UNHCR and NGOs find themselves competing.

NGOs, which depend on government sources for the majority of their funding, may compromise their independent "nongovernmental" status (Smillie and Helmich 1993:27). (Could one say the same for NGOs that rely for funding on the European Union?) Others seek to maintain their independence by only implementing projects for which the majority of the funds come from private sector donations.

Relationships Among the Intermediaries (UNHCR and Its Nongovernmental Implementing Partners): Competition for Power

Although UNHCR's mandate was initially restricted to the protection of refugees, over the past three decades it has assumed the major responsibility for coordinating material assistance to refugees. For the *implementation* of aid programs, with the exception of its programs in Bosnia in the early 1990s, it relies on nongovernmental agencies, usually northern based. Although theoretically UNHCR has the mandate to "coordinate," at the field level it usually designates one NGO as the lead agency. The use of the common term "NGO," referring to all nongovernmental organizations, conceals an enormous variety of agents, structures, distinct agendas (religious, secular, political), and levels of competence.

Tripartite contracts are drawn up between UNHCR, the host government, and the NGO. (On occasion, a special office of the host government or a local NGO may be included as an implementing partner.) UNHCR's funding sources include donor governments (and the European Community), who may earmark monies for specific projects and/or agencies; these may be supplemented by the funds obtained by the NGOs directly from their own governments (and the EC) or raised from the public. Normally, the NGOs that sign tripartite contracts as implementing partners with UNHCR are also dependent on it for the majority of their funding.

As noted, the degree to which NGOs are successful in raising their own funds determines the level of autonomy vis-à-vis UNHCR with which they can operate in the field situation. However, the relative autonomy of both UNHCR and NGOs may be limited by the host government, which has veto power over who may operate within its borders. But because most host governments view themselves as dependent on international aid as a matter of course (India being a major exception), UNHCR maintains enormous leverage over governments in the development of their refugee assistance policy (Harrell-Bond 1986:chap. 2; Karadawi 1983).[2] Thus the deck is stacked against any NGO wishing to continue operating in a country while not conforming to UNHCR policy.

Occasionally similar limitations run in the other direction as well: UNHCR's power over an NGO may be undermined if that NGO stands in a privileged position with respect to its own government if the latter is a major donor. In that event, this government's donations to UNHCR would be earmarked for exclusive use by that NGO. To make matters worse, some northern-based NGOs, funded by their governments, are able to establish an office in a host country and act as local donors to other NGOs and even to UNHCR. The factional scenarios that can be visualized in this cooperative and competitive administrative structure, where it is evident that each member has a different interest in the refugees, do not require any further elaboration. What needs to be stressed, however, is that every negotiation among and between these organizations entails different possibilities of conflict, and even when some type of resolution is achieved, there are still legitimate reasons for the actors to distrust rather than to trust each other.

Relationships between the Intermediaries (International Agencies) and the Host Government in the Camps: Competition for Authority

If we recall our ideal type of the refugee camp, the symbolic representation of the different insignia allows us to discern another set of levels of struggle for power over the refugees. In principle, the camp is administered by a representative of the host government that has established its own office. In many cases, some of the costs for maintaining this office are borne by UNHCR.[3]

The role of such offices in the camps often turns out to be primarily decorative since most of the executive powers are held by the lead agency. In symbolic, representational terms, this division of labor is often exemplified by the different "uniforms" encountered within the distinct spatial arrangement of each camp. At the gate, refugees usually meet armed, uniformed police or paramilitary personnel, representing the maintenance of the government's sovereignty, often more in word than in deed. Registration of the refugees takes place in the government's administrative office—the navel of the camp, given the priority that both the UNHCR and the host government assign to statistical records and accurate numerical representation.[4]

Yet the real centers for the exercise of authority within the camp may be isolated in the agencies' offices where the decisions concerning the modes of distribution and the final allocation of aid are executed. Again, this picture is partial because it does not expose the actual arenas of the decision-making processes, which are neither exclusively "Geneva," the offices in the host or donor government capitals, nor the region of the camp itself. In each one of these places, a different set of negotiations occurs and different, often hidden, agendas are being promoted. The resulting complexity of agencies and agents pursuing their individual private as well as relevant political interests that result from specific collaborations among the relevant parties defies any tragic denouement.[5] Again, in this context, issues of *mistrust* become highly relevant given that deliberation on an individual and group level is structured in terms of competition and suspicion concerning the hidden agendas and underlying motives of the interlocutors.

Relationships between the Intermediaries and the Recipients in the Camp Situation: Competing Agendas

The next step, which is the actual distribution of aid to the refugees, is then determined by another layer of competition and mistrust. From the point of view of the humanitarians, this presupposes a polarity between "us" and "them," which construes the refugees as individuals who are out to get the most for themselves, given that their behavior finds them not adhering to the principles of fairness and equity to all, which is the norm for the humanitarian regime (Harrell-Bond, Voutira, and Leopold 1992; Harrell-Bond and Wilson 1990; Waldron 1987). Refugees are thus perceived as fundamentally untrustworthy—and with good reason.

When a group of refugees were asked to describe how they behaved when they were hungry, a variety of coping strategies were described. As the quotations (Harrell-Bond 1986:328) below illustrate, all involved some form of deception or manipulation of others.

> The constant starvation led to theft, which I thought by that time was a good activity, but it is not. Anyway, it saved me during that time.
>
> One of the easiest tricks . . . was . . . [to introduce] myself as the son of a famous man. As he [watchman of a hospital] was an old man, he simply accepted my word. After which I was given a great deal of food to eat.
>
> It was [also] high time for girls and women to go for prostitution which helped a lot in feeding us [of course, those (of us who) . . . had sisters . . .]. We very well knew it was wrong, but it was beyond human control.

As one refugee summed it up, "To be a refugee means to learn to lie." Although this situation of mistrust may be taken as characteristic of the different ways in which the "us" and "them" relate, the actual situation is far more complicated as regards the relevant interests of the two groups that are at stake.

Earlier in this chapter, we identified the common kernel of interest that brings helpers and refugees into contact. Yet this does not in itself explain the actual interests that become established. As with most bureaucratic structures, the latent functions quite often diverge from the manifest aims. Indeed, the whole purpose of the bureaucracy is to maintain and perpetuate itself independently of resolving the contingent crisis situation that necessitated its formation.

Seen from the perspective of the refugees, the disparity between manifest and latent ends of the bureaucracy becomes evident and influences their behavior toward the camp authorities. From their standpoint, they have legitimate claims as regards the promotion of their interests, which include becoming sufficiently independent so as not to need the camp. Such realizations are seldom articulated because they would threaten the fragile (paternalistic) relationship on which the refugees are forced to depend (Harrell-Bond 1986:6). The familiar response from the refugee quarter often takes the form of songs sung in praise of the agencies, or metaphorical references, in a familial idiom, to describe UNHCR's relationship to them. In striking contrast to such positive reinforcement of the image of selfless humanitarian sacrifice, one woman who was being denied her rightful ration at a food distribution exercise in Malawi cried out, "Remember, you have your job because we are here."

To be sure, such utterances are primarily elicited in extreme situations and quite possibly our own presence as witnesses made it worth the risk. Yet one may still be allowed a minimal generalization as regards the competition over incompatible resources. Put differently, we can say that the helpers and the recipients are not competing over the same resources. Rather, they are competing for resources that become contingently incompatible.

For the helpers, the ultimate "good" is the maintenance of their exercise of authority; for the refugees, it is the acquisition of material goods. In the woman's terms, what legitimizes the helpers' authority is not merely the presence of the refugees but the maintenance of the exercise of their allotted function. Such maintenance is itself quite independent of the actual needs of the refugees, who could quite capably administer and distribute the aid among themselves (Harrell-Bond, Voutira, and Leopold 1992).

Host Population and Refugees: Competing Perceptions

Who really assists refugees? International aid is always late on the scene. In fact, the local people are the ones who bear the brunt of the needs of refugees in an emergency. In most cases the majority of people who have found refuge in the poorest host countries of the world are living (spontaneously settled, as UNHCR describes them) among the host population; only a minority of refugees receive official assistance. In Africa, it is estimated that not more than 25 percent are under the international "aid umbrella" (Kibreab 1989).

Once aid arrives, those refugees who become the recipients of this highly visible assistance program are confined within the circumference of the camp. From then on, a different set of relationships develops between themselves and the host population. From the local people's point of view, their meager resources and modest hospitality have been rejected in favor of the outsiders' help. In terms of their access to scarce resources, the refugee camp appears as an island of privilege. Lorries move in and out carrying food, blankets, and clothes. Foreign visitors arrive in new four-wheel-drive cars to take charge, wells are dug, schools, clinics, and office buildings are being erected, and medical services are offered.

From the point of view of the refugees, most of whom may actually be unwilling residents of the camps, their security is no longer dependent on good relations with the host but on maintaining and manipulating the existing paternalism of the aid regime. Part of this manipulation includes investing their trust in the foreign aid workers and organizations. Such identification of their security and future with the foreigners alienates them from the local population, which does not enjoy such privileges. This becomes the basis for the formulation of a series of negative stereotypes between refugees and their hosts. Later on, when anything goes wrong in the aid pipeline, and, as so often happens, food rations do not arrive on time, invariably refugees blame their hosts, especially the government. How could "Geneva" be wrong?

More recently in Europe, similar processes are at work. In the Czech Republic, for example, where the entire burden for hosting refugees falls on the state, no refugee could be found who believed that his or her standard of living was not the result of corruption in the government. In Greece, the new refugees from Abhazia have organized themselves to sue the government for embezzling European Community funds earmarked for them. In both cases, refugees are construed as living at a higher standard of living than a citizen on welfare would have been able to afford (Voutira 1994).

Inter- and Intragroup Relationships among the Refugees

We have already noted the heterogenity of the refugee camp populations. Such heterogenity is not exhausted in the diversity of ethnic, class, and status backgrounds and political allegiances. An important parameter of this diversity also includes the contingent conditions that lead people to avoid or to seek inclusion in the camp. Families often strategically divide their members, allocating them so as to maximize access to different resources so as to increase the survival possibilities of the family as a whole. This finds camp populations made up of many vulnerable individuals, for example, orphans, widows, elderly, the ill, and women-headed households, alongside complete families or competent individual adults.

Despite the apparent commonality of their experience vis-à-vis their country of origin, one seldom finds a sense of political solidarity among refugee populations. More often than not, refugee populations are highly factionalized in relation to their different strategies for resolving the causes that led to their flight.

The power of the humanitarian regime over limited supplies generates inter- and intragroup conflict, as individuals seek to ingratiate themselves with the authorities in competition with their fellows. For example, from the point of view of the less well educated Ugandan refugees in southern Sudan, being able to speak English (usually the language of the aid givers) was described as "bribing" the authorities (Harrell-Bond 1986:Addendum, chap. 2). Speaking the same language (or practicing the same religion) as the foreign helpers puts individuals in a structural advantage over their fellows who do not possess such skills. As powerful middlemen, they play the role of informant for both "us" and "them." These privileges often include paid employment, or, more likely, individuals may be assigned unpaid positions in which they may act as spokespersons for sections of the camp and be invested with authority over other refugees on behalf of the aid regime. Such conditions seriously undermine any potential for unity and solidarity of the population as a whole while at the same time introducing new grounds for cleavages and factions.

Under these conditions, it would be difficult to discern any space in which trust could be fostered either in the psychological sense of reliability and meeting of mutual expectations or the sociological sense of a fully functioning normative system.[6]

CONCLUSION

We hold, first, that trust is an ambiguous term that characterizes human relations; second, that trust is not a necessary desideratum in all forms of healthy (nonpathological) interpersonal relations; and, third, that the concept of trust as methodologically relevant in the context of a refugee crisis is questionable. Our analysis has focused on the "deconstruction" of the refugee camp as the paradigmatic case of humanitarian intervention.

The aim of the exercise has been to avoid the pitfalls of the usual monolithic research approach in refugee studies that tends to focus exclusively on the category "refugee." The analysis of the social world of refugees and their helpers in camps has challenged the notion that the encounter between refugees and their helpers has potential for the restoration of trust in any simple sense. In examining the relations between actors, situations, and established humanitarian practices, we have seen that there is no locus for nurturing "trust." What we have shown is that the whole structure of the humanitarian regime is predicated on the exercise of a type of authority, which is itself maintained and legitimized by the absence of trust between the givers and the recipients. In fact, the whole structure of the humanitarian regime is fraught with competition, suspicion, and mistrust.

In Malawi, attempts to prevent cheating include the requirement that refugees build their own houses before they are formally registered in the camp's master register and issued a ration card (Dzimbiri 1992). At each registration, the ration card holder must personally appear, whether old, handicapped, or otherwise unfit to travel the long distances required. "Collecting for two rationees, even if one card-owner is too weak to walk the distance, much less to carry the load back home, is absolutely not allowed" (Harrell-Bond 1992:32).

From the standpoint of the givers, the overall atmosphere of mutual distrust is most dramatically illustrated in OXFAM's ABC on refugee registration (Mitchell and Slim 1990). Among the techniques for managing assistance, it advises nighttime invasions for accurate census taking and daubing refugees with gentian violet so as to avoid anyone getting double rations. The authors warn their fellow humanitarians that the dye is only effective for "about 48 hours and can be removed by the determined cheater." The handbook includes a special annex entitled "Cheating," which is meant to prepare agency staff for what they will encounter in the emergency situation. Far from describing conditions directed toward engendering trust in individuals or environments, the handbook suggests and reinforces the commonly held belief that refugees are inherently untrustworthy.

One possible interpretation of such a mind-set may be the projection of the Western categories of cognition on other cultures. In our own society, the category of trust figures prominently as a value term. We choose our friends, spouses, and colleagues on its basis, taking them in "trust." If we accept the principle that a society values and promotes the things it needs most, then trust becomes a value because the conditions needed to establish social success do not guarantee the maintenance of trust. Hence a different type of leverage is required. Trust enters into human deliberations as a safety valve against risk, unpredictability, and the recalcitrance of human nature. On the institutional level, one can think of the whole political and educational system that tends to promote models of artful persuasion and successful hypocrisy rather than the pursuit of truth. In this context, the notion of trust is identified with the efficiency of the result (trusting in one's abilities), while the moral category of trustworthiness becomes an elusive concept to be pursued through art and literature (Voutira 1990).

On the societal level, the relevant interpersonal notion of trust is evident in the context of guarantees against its mistrust. Signatures are required to validate transactions and, where contractual agreements are ensured, by recourse to law. Such guarantees are meant to preserve the efficiency of the system and the rule of law and to guard against any regress to irrelevant criteria such as status and origins. Whatever the ostensible reason and justificatory processes, the crux of the matter remains that such institutions are predicated on the absence of trust; they exist to guard against interpersonal mistrust.

These insights into our society may give us a clue as to why the humanitarian regime seeks to impose ab initio similar guarantees to guard against refugee untrustworthy behavior. They also point to an interesting hypothesis as to why the aid authorities are so averse to what would appear to be the most efficient method of distributing aid, namely, the community itself. Such a solution would entail the application of the traditional criteria of allocation and distribution of goods according to "native" categories of value, which are often incommensurate with our Western criteria of equity and allocation of trust as a moral human prerogative (Harrell-Bond, Voutira, and Leopold 1992).

Taking trust in this sense on a par with our normative system of values entails a different notion from the one that informs Daniel and Knudsen (1991). Our initial example of the Sierra Leonean notion of trust and trustworthiness demonstrates the conceptual gap and the degree of cultural dissonance that defines the challenge of the encounter between refugees and their helpers. Unless this challenge is taken seriously, any assistance provided by the humanitarian regime is likely to fail in its aims.

NOTES

1. Similar tensions exist between northern and southern academics. In his report of a meeting concerning research on forced migration, G. Loescher (1994:4–5) writes, "Many participants felt that most international refugee policy . . . is formulated in the North. . . . [I]t is frequently the case that researchers in the South are not included in the research done by northern refugee research organizations and are even often unaware of research taking place in their own part of the world. In most instances, northerners are the ones who initiate and control the research agenda, attract donor and foundation funds for research projects, enjoy ready access to current literature, claim privileged access to information from both governments and international organizations, and publish and disseminate the research findings, even those written by southern researchers."

2. Host governments were formerly part of this international competition. The issue was whether donors would provide aid through bilateral arrangements with host governments or through multilateral aid to inter- and nongovernmental agencies, the latter being deemed more "trustworthy." See Harrell-Bond 1986:chap. 2 and Harrell-Bond and Karadawi 1984 for a discussion of the struggle between UNHCR and the Sudanese government for control over international aid for refugees.

3. Concerning the extent to which UNHCR bears the costs of maintaining the host

governments' offices, there are great variations. In some cases, salaries are topped up and vehicles and other equipment are provided; in others, the government receives no direct support from UNHCR. Where the host government insists on expanding its involvement in a program, the numbers of nationals employed may expand dramatically, as in Pakistan and Malawi. However, these people are employed on temporary contracts with funding from UNHCR. They do not receive the normal benefits provided other civil servants. The effects of their insecurity on policy and their relations with the better-paid international agency staff introduces another level of competition and conflict in the camps (Dzimbiri 1992; Harrell-Bond 1986). Government officials from five southern African countries who met together for the first time in September 1991 were extremely interested in exchanging information on these variations (Refugee Studies Programme 1991).

4. The rationale and implications of this point of congruence is further explored in Harrell-Bond, Voutira, and Leopold 1992.

5. While holding for Africa, our model of the typology of conflict and competition between host governments and international agencies will require further expansion, elaboration, and additional refinement to apply to other situations in the world. The balance of power between UNHCR and the host government differs from place to place and depends very much on the resources of the host to assert its sovereignty claims over its need for external assistance. Sierra Leone, for example, did not allow UNHCR to establish an office and did not receive international aid to support the Fula refugees from Sekou Toure's Guinea. Similarly, Guinea did not receive international aid or allow an office of UNHCR to be established in response to the refugees from the anticolonial war against the Portuguese in Guinea Bissau. Even where a host government is highly dependent on international aid, for example, Thailand and Pakistan, the host government may be able to assert its policy over that of UNHCR because it knows that the foreign interests of donors assures funding, whatever its policy. Hong Kong may be seen as a situation where there is the least conflict and competition between the actors.

There are instances where, at the expense of diplomatic relations with the host and donor governments, an individual UNHCR representative may openly oppose a host government policy in order to protect refugees. This occurred, for example, in one country where the government was using military force to move refugees at the border into camps. The balance of power was restored through a horse trade: that host government agreed to remove a member of its staff and UNHCR withdrew its representative, who was openly objecting to the host's policy.

Where the balance of power totally favors the host government, as in the Sierra Leone and Guinea cases, refugees receive no international assistance and, at least in Sierra Leone, were completely free to move into the local economy. In Pakistan, where the donors and the host government were aligned with the overall objectives of the Mujahidin, competition and conflict over access to aid in the camps were affected by the cleavages and structure of power relations among Afghan groups.

6. Many camp situations do not fit our model, as they have existed for as long as three decades and are no longer a place where refugees and their helpers interact. For example, see Malkki's (1990) study of refugee camps in Tanzania where she found conditions favorable to the formation of a particular type of historical and political consciousness. Elsewhere we wrote, "Thus, far from contributing towards the intended policy goal of de-politicization and control, the context of camp life provides people with the opportunity to engage in the

creative activity of interpreting their flight and articulating and constructing a collective narrative concerning common past" (Harrell-Bond, Voutira, and Leopold 1992). The invasion of Rwanda by refugees from Uganda, which relied on recruitment from the camps, is an example.

REFERENCES

Appadurai, Arjun, ed.
  1986   *The Social Life of Things: Commodities in Cultural Perspective.* Cambridge: Cambridge University Press.
Chambers, Robert
  1986   "Hidden losers? The Impact of Rural Refugees in Refugee Programmes on the Poor Hosts." *International Migration Review,* Special issue, Current Status and Directors for the Future.
Colson, Elizabeth
  1989   "Overview." *Annual Review of Anthropology* 18:1–16.
Daniel, E. Valentine, and John Chr. Knudsen
  1991   "Trust and the Refugee Experience: A Proposal for a Workshop at the United Nations University, World Institute for Development Economics Research." Helsinki.
Davis, John
  1992   "The Anthropology of Suffering." Elizabeth Colson Lecture, *Journal of Refugee Studies* 5(3):149–163.
Dzimbiri, Lewis
  1992   "Managing Refugees in Malawi: An Overview." Manuscript.
Erikson, Erik
  1963   *Childhood and Society.* New York: W. W. Norton.
Evans-Pritchard, E. E.
  1940   *The Nuer: A Description of the Modes of Livelihood and Political Institutions of a Nilotic People.* Oxford: Oxford University Press.
Harrell-Bond, Barbara E.
  1975   *Marriage Among the Professional Group in Sierra Leone.* Leiden: Mouton.
  1978   "The Fear of Poisoning and the Management of Urban Social Relations among the Professional Group in Freetown, Sierra Leone." *Urban Anthropology* 7(3): 229–241.
  1986   *Imposing Aid: Emergency Assistance to Refugees.* Oxford: Oxford University Press.
  1991   "Pan Licking." *Africa Events* (October/November):37–38.
  1992   "Anthropology and the Study of Refugees." *Anthropology Today* 8(4):6–10.
Harrell-Bond, Barbara E., and Ahmad Karadawi
  1984   "But Will It Be Just Another Ripple in the Pool?" Special Report on the Oxford Refugee Conference. *Disasters* 8(4):254–262.
Harrell-Bond, Barbara E., and Eftihia Voutira
  1992   "Anthropology and the Study of Refugees." *Anthropology Today* 8(4):6–10.
Harrell-Bond, Barbara E., Eftihia Voutira, and Mark Leopold
  1992   "Counting the Refugees: Gifts, Givers, Patrons, Clients." *Journal of Refugee Studies* 5(3/4):205–225.

Harrell-Bond, Barbara E., and K. Wilson
    1990   "Dealing with Dying: Some Anthropological Reflections on the Need for
                Assistance by Refugee Relief Programmes for Bereavement and Burial."
                Journal of Refugee Studies 3(3):228–243.
Hirschon, Renee
    1989   "Presents, Promises and Punctuality: Expressions of Freedom in Greek
                Social Life." Manuscript.
    1992   "Greek Adults' Verbal Play, or, How to Train for Caution." *Journal of Mod-
                ern Greek Studies* 10(1):35–56.
Karadawi, Ahmad
    1983   "Contraints on Assistance to Refugees: Some Observations from the
                Sudan." *World Development* 11(6):537–547.
Kibreab, Gaim
    1989   "Local Settlements in Africa: A Misconceived Option?" *Journal of Refugee
                Studies* 2(4):486–490.
Loescher, Gil
    1994   "Summary of Meeting Refugee Research in the 1990s: Need for Institution
                Building and Greater Collaboration." Report of Ford Grantees meeting,
                12–14 November 1993. Unpublished.
Marsella, J. Anthony, George DeVos, and Francis L. K. Hsu
    1985   *Culture and Self: Asian and Western Perspectives.* New York: Tavistock.
Malinowski, Bronislaw
    1922   *Argonauts of the Western Pacific.* London: Routledge and Kegan Paul.
Marx, Emanuel
    1990   "The Social World of Refugees: A Conceptual Problem." *Journal of Refugee
                Studies* 3(3):189–204.
Malkki, Liisa
    1990   "Context and Consciousness: Local Conditions for the Production of His-
                torical and National Thought among Hutu Refugees in Tanzania." In
                National Ideologies and the Production of National Cultures, ed. Richard G. Fox.
                American Ethnological Society Monograph Series, no. 2.
Mauss, Marcel
    1925*a*   *The Gift.* Trans. Ian Cunnison. New York: Free Press.
    1925*b*   "Essai sur le don: Forme et raison de l'exchange dans les societies
                archaiques." *L'Anne Sociologique,* n.s. 1:30–186.
Mitchell, John, and Hugo Slim
    1990   *Registration in Emergencies: OXFAM Practical Health Guide,* no. 6. Oxford:
                OXFAM.
Randel, Judith, and Tony German, eds.
    1993   *The Reality of Aid.* ICVA, Europestep. Produced by Actionaid, June. Lon-
                don: Actionaid.
Smillie, Ian, and Henry Helmich, eds.
    1993   *Non-Governmental Organisations and Governments: Stakeholders for Development.*
                Paris: OECD.
Refugee Studies Programme
    1991   *Refugees as Resources for Development: Opportunities and Constraints.* Report of the

Southern Africa Regional Workshop on Refugee Policy, sponsored by RSP, September.

UNHCR

1982   *Handbook for Emergencies: Part One: field Operations.* Geneva: UNHCR.

Voutira, Eftihia

1990   "Scientific and Literary Narratives in the Explanation of Emotions: Doesn't Shakespeare Do It Much Better?" *Hughs Hall Journal* (Winter). Cambridge University.

1994   "International Aid, Government, and the Development of the Balkan Periphery: The Case of the Soviet Greek Refugees in Thrace." Paper presented at the Forum Against Ethnic Violence, University of London, February.

Waldron, Sidney

1987   "Blaming the Refugees." RSP/BRC *Refugee Issues* 3, no. 3 (April).

Weiner, Annette

1992   *Inalienable Possessions: The Paradox of Keeping-While-Giving.* Berkeley, Los Angeles, and Oxford: University of California Press.

TWELVE

Forms, Formations, and Transformations of the Tamil Refugee

E. Valentine Daniel and Yuvaraj Thangaraj

In its details, this chapter is about Sri Lankan Tamil refugees. But the details chosen are intended to have a bearing on our understanding of the refugee experience more generally. Our main focus will be on the formation of refugees in a relatively underreported area of that island nation, the eastern province of Batticaloa, and their and other Tamils' attempt to resettle as refugees in Great Britain. We have chosen to enter our case studies, however, by way of a brief theoretical prolegomenon.

SOME PRELIMINARIES

Trust and the Individual

Trust, as is claimed in the introduction, is an integral part of the will and the capacity to tame chance. Obviously, the formulation needs refinement. Untamed, chance lets in surprises that can be either pleasant or unpleasant. Trust, in the context of refugee experience, has more to do with experiences that are pleasant than with those that are unpleasant. Thus an assertion such as "I trust him to hurt me" does not quite fit our understanding of trust.

Holding this in mind, let us begin somewhat abstractly. In what must have been a very enigmatic definition of a "human being" for someone in the nineteenth century (let alone the late twentieth century), the logician-philosopher Charles Sanders Peirce defined man [*sic*] as a sign (5.313).[1] What he intended to convey by this was the fact that a human being was not a thing in itself but a representation of something other than itself. Peirce might have done well to have defined (wo)man, not as a sign (in the singular) but, borrowing an expression from his friend, William James, as a "buzzing and booming" constellation of signs. Because each individual is constituted of a multitude of signs representing a multitude of objects, undermining thereby the strict sense of the term "individual"—"that which cannot be divided." To put it differently, human beings are loci of intense sign activity. The technical word for sign activity is semiosis.[2] We could describe ourselves as embodiments of semiosis; but that would give one the idea of an unwarranted compactness or even an image of a container (of signs). This would not do, unless we imagined the contents of this container to be radioactive and the container quite leaky at that. For the curious thing about signs is that they are not signs unless they are interpreted as such, and a large measure of such interpretations is carried out in loci and by agents that are outside this "box of flesh and blood" we call the individual (C. S. Peirce 7.591). Thus we arrive at a definition of a sign that calls for three components, or three irreducible correlates: a *representation* that stands for something, an *object* that that representation stands for, and an *interpretant* to whom or which the representation stands in some respect or capacity. The interpretant is best understood as the significant effect of the relationship between the first two on a third. All three correlates need to be set into play for a sign to be a sign in the full sense of that term and, by extension, for a (wo)man to be a (wo)man in the full sense of that term. Anything short of this can only be a virtual sign, not an actual one. Peirce gave us a technical word in Latin for such a virtual sign. He called it a *representamen*. A representamen is a sign sans an interpretant. Thus a woman who appears at the border of a country that is not her own, wounded, hungry and in rags, seeking asylum, may be a bearer of representamena of a human-made or natural disaster; but she does not become a "refugee" in the strict sense, unless she is recognized as such by significant members or institutions of the new country. In this case, it is this recognition that serves as the interpretant, triangulating and completing her significance as a "refugee." But the activity of signs does not stop with the completion of a sign or set of signs, for every interpretant in its turn becomes a further representamen for the same or a more elaborate object to yet another interpretant, and so on, ad infinitum. Thus continuity and openness are fundamental in semiosis. It is equally fundamental in human life. As a social and cultural being a human must be able to open up to the world. She or he cannot remain closed in on herself or himself.

What is it that gives a human being his or her integrity if all she or he is, is this generative locus of sign activity? To be sure, not all signs generated in a person, whether they are physical, biological, chemical, or mental, find their completion as signs outside the person. There are myriad signs that are "triangulated" in a person's private world, inside "this box of flesh and blood." Yet what does make us human qua human is that we are both meaning-taking (representations of) and meaning-making (representations to) creatures. And meanings are largely about signs of convention. Conventions require, if not public validation, at least public controversy. Private meanings[3] are possible and do exist, but if carried to the extreme and deprived of other human interpretants, these meanings can become indicators of pathology. For example, the extreme introversion characteristic of some torture victims, reaching the point of comatosity, may provide a tenuous state of hyperintegration, but such a state amounts to a state of pathology.[4] Smoke and fire, as signs of nature, coexist as representamen and object, whether or not an interpretant exists. By contrast, conventions are highly dependent on human agreement and disagreement, understanding and misunderstanding. Take away the interpretant and the link between a convention and its object dissolves. This is why we hold that a large part of human semiosis is fundamentally directed outward, toward other conventional interpretants. However, to swing caution in the other direction once more, a human being whose private world of sign activities is torn asunder, shredded by torture, strewn before a "public" that may choose to do with it whatever it wills, is as robbed of his or her humanness as is the one who is forced to retreat into a private and hyperintegrated world. In fact, both phenomena often occur simultaneously. In the formation of a refugee, the wide thoroughfare of cultural life of give-and-take having been narrowed to as much as the width of a high-wire, we often see the individual balancing his or her way in between these two possibilities. A fall in either direction could end up being a fall into the same abyss. In Seattle, Daniel acted as a translator for a Sri Lankan who was intercepted on his way to Canada where he planned to request asylum. The lawyer had secondhand evidence that this boy had seen his home burned to the ground, that his father and brother were taken by the army and never returned, that his sister was raped and then shot to death by Indian soldiers before his eyes, and that he himself was tortured. But the lawyer could not get him to speak. He was terrorized by the whole idea of yet another interrogation and shrank into the corner of the room. Bereft of home, family, possessions, and then, under torture, extorted of information he did and did not have, what more could be left to be revealed? Had he not been emptied? In that tight ball of silence, in the corner, he had chosen to conceal from public glare whatever little was left of his integrated core. Another way of preserving the integrity of an internal core from further shredding is to keep external signs from entering. This is powerfully illustrated by Marjorie A. Muecke (this volume) in her discussion of the number of Cambodian women suffering from psychosomatic blindness. "It makes sense," she says, "that a response to having witnessed and experienced such totalizing brutalities over a prolonged period of time might include a person's closing out the possibility of continued witness through the loss of the capacity to see."

What does all this fuss about signs have to do with trust, the theme of this volume? Trust has to do with that area of life where signs generated by a person and intended for interpretive completion by significant others are interpreted in a manner that does not brutally deviate from that person's expectations so as to cause him or her pain; or to state it differently, where the outward flow of semiosis is not interrupted or shockingly redirected toward ends that were unexpected by the person generating these signs. For instance, in a nation-state, an ethnic group that is attacked by another group takes the signs of such an attack to the police, expecting the police to interpret these signs as deserving of help, protection, and justice. In Sri Lanka in July 1983, when victims of anti-Tamil riots turned to the police and the armed forces expecting protection, many policemen and soldiers either joined the rioters and attacked the victims or stood by to watch or encourage the mob on its rampage. These victims were shocked and felt their trust betrayed. Evidently, the signs[5] of trauma that they evinced were not interpreted as expected. Many then turned to the courts with the same evidence. Sometimes they got the expected results; more often they did not. In the immediate aftermath of the riots, the republic's president and the minister of National Security expressed sympathy and understanding, not for the victims of the riots, but for the Sinhalese majority from among whom the rioters came. The very institutions to whose charge had been committed a large share of the task of taming chance had turned chancy.

In Sri Lanka the initial response to this breach of trust was to withdraw into one's group and even into one's self. Those Tamils who had openly lived as Tamils in the predominantly Sinhalese south of the country now tried their best to conceal their Tamilness. They worked hardest to suppress all exterior signs of their identity. Their women stopped wearing gold jewelry, silk saris, and the vermilion mark, or *pottu*, on their foreheads. Men and women desisted donning sacred ash on their foreheads (a custom of Shivite Hindus), many ceased going to Hindu temples or did so only secretly, and they avoided speaking the Tamil language within earshot of a Sinhalese person or a stranger.

With time these signs of trauma found new expressions in new interpretants, spawning new significant effects. Some among the affected Tamils turned to international opinion, which was capable of visiting chastisement on the Sri Lankan government, some to foreign states for recognition of Tamils as refugees, and some to Tamil militant groups that were committed to defend the Tamil people with counterviolence. If these redirections of sign activity introduced new sources of trust, new interpretants that could "read" the signs of trauma as expected, they also ushered in unexpected uncertainties.

To Trust Where the "Norm" Is to Mistrust

In the third paragraph of the introduction to this volume, the editors left us with the following claim: "The capacity to trust needs to be underwritten by the capacity to tame chance, especially the chance of being hurt. This capacity is not an individual matter but a gift that a cultured society gives an individual." Here, the three phenomena of trust, the capacity to tame chance, and culture appear to be inseparably yoked together. The important point is that their contraries, whatever they may be, are not complementary opposites of equal value as much as necessary concomitants of lesser value; they are backgrounds that enable the foregrounding of trust, culture, and the capacity for taming chance, respectively. Let us set aside, for the moment, what has been called the capacity to tame chance and analyze the relationship between the other two, trust and culture, or rather, trust in culture. Is "mistrust" the mere concomitant of trust, the necessary but lesser complement in a hierarchy, even in societies in which it is normatively valued more than is trust? Barbara E. Harrell-Bond and Eftihia Voutira (this volume) seem to have their doubts; even though the editors, in their introduction, are at pains to emphasize that the reign of mistrust is of an extraordinary degree in refugee life as opposed to "ordinary" life. "In the life of a refugee," they say, "trust is overwhelmed by mistrust, besieged by suspicion, and relentlessly undermined by caprice." But Harrell-Bond and Voutira would insist that in West Africa "relationships that people admit to trust are very much the exception." On the face of it, the South Asian societies studied by Daniel and Thangaraj would appear to be similar with respect to the place and privilege of mistrust to the West African societies studied by Harrell-Bond and Voutira. Must we concede to an impasse here, or find an escape clause in the editors' claim to the "extraordinary degree of mistrust" referred to above? We believe that there is a third, more productive way out of this apparent conundrum.

Among the Tamils and the Sinhalese of Sri Lanka, to be trustworthy is normatively esteemed; to trust, however, is not held up as possessing similarly unambiguous value. A trusting soul is often seen as a gullible one. Proverbs and tales abound which caution people against trusting too easily. But we need to make a distinction between this normative, prescriptive level, and what David M. Schneider (1976:192-203) called the cultural domain. In this we follow Schneider, who said this about the normative and the cultural: "Culture contrasts with norms in that norms are oriented to patterns *for action*. . . . Whereas norms tell the actor how to play the scene, culture tells the actor how the scene is set and what it all means" (ibid., 202–203). While we may differ with Schneider on several details,[6] we agree with him on one crucial point: the cultural is not to be equated with the normative. No matter how many rules and axioms for behavior one learns, no matter how well one masters a society's norms, that alone does not make one a part of a culture. Moreover, where "norms" of mistrust are recited, practiced, and even celebrated, they are embedded in a cultural matrix of trust. This cultural domain wherein we locate trust is as deep as it is wide and, for the most part, unconscious. Trust at the deepest level is as ingrained as are habits: the habit of getting up in the morning and finding the roof of your house still over your head, the habit of walking into your kitchen and not finding a burglar scrambling eggs, the habit of wishing your neighbor a good morning and not having him take a swing at you. Unlike a norm, the bedrock of trust does not depend for its existence on conscious recitations of axioms or even on self-consciously putting such axioms to practice. If one is to belong to a culture one must, at a profound level, be able to trust the symbolic constitutedness of the cultural process of which one is a part.

During the 1983 anti-Tamil riots, hundreds of Sinhalese sheltered their Tamil friends and neighbors from marauding mobs. Despite the normative admonishments in the culture about not trusting, Tamils trusted their Sinhalese friends and neighbors to give them shelter. When their expectations were met, they were grateful though not surprised. It was in those instances when friends refused to protect their Tamil friends that the breach of trust was shocking. Because of these breaches, the mistrust that ensued was no longer a normative mistrust or a mere "paper mistrust"—to adapt Peirce's phrase—but one that pervaded the entire Tamil community and its cultural interstices.[7]

In the absence of trust, or an awareness of what it is to trust, mistrust would be a meaningless category. Another way to state this is to say that absolute mistrust is so meaningless as to be self-negating. This does not mean that when thus negated, it is replaced by its putative opposite, trust. What is left is meaninglessness. The closest we have come in our study of refugee formation to witnessing absolute mistrust is in our encounters with torture survivors and with children who have witnessed events too horrifying for words. Such individuals usually lose all or much of their capacity for speech or even language and have, in their friends' and neighbors' lay characterization, "gone mad." They either stare blankly with no reaction to their environment or react to stimulation in unpredictable ways. Here is an example.

A man in his forties, a witness to "an atrocity" committed by soldiers in the north of Sri Lanka, was interviewed by Daniel in a refugee camp in South India. This man goes in and out of a vegetative state of total silence, abstinence from food, and a disinterest in his environment to the point of not even reacting to danger. His niece, who took care of him, reported an incident of a burning ember falling off the hearth and setting fire to a chopping block. The flames from the burning wood ignited a line of clothes hung up to dry in the kitchen. As for her uncle, she said, "There he was near the door, where we had left him. He hadn't moved. He was looking straight at the fire, but hadn't moved." She describes another occasion as follows:

> Once I asked my husband to carry this heavy pot of rice to the back, outside, to strain the water from it. I couldn't lift it then. I was nine months pregnant. My husband drops it right on my uncle's lap. We make the biggest fuss you have heard. Bring cold water! Bring some oil! Bring this! Bring that! All the time trying to make him stand up or move so that we could dust the rice off his lap. From him, not a twitch. His eyes are set where they had been set all morning. On the wall.

Her uncle suffered third-degree burns from this accident.

Daniel asked this man, during one of his "normal" days, if there was anything he could recall from his vegetative state. He replied that he knew everything that was going on when he was in that state but that the most important thing he was able to recover was his *disbelief* in everything. (The Tamil word for belief, *nambikkai*, encompasses the notion of trust as well.) During the course of the same interview this onetime teacher of Tamil literature had this to say (pointing to his nephew walking toward him on the beach):

> Now that child is walking and I know he is walking. Then [i.e., when in his "vegetative state"]: That which walks doesn't walk, that which doesn't walk walks, that which doesn't walk doesn't walk, that which walks walks.

Since the Tamil word for "walk" *(natai)* also means "happen," the "quatrain" could be read as: "What happens won't happen, what won't will, what will will, and what won't won't." By covering all possibilities, he has chosen none. The reign of caprice is total. To the extent that he talks about this ineffable state, we may say that he (we) are caught in a contradiction. Not so. To the extent that his knowledge is positively about something, even if that something is only the possibility of everything and the actuality of nothing, he has identified something that he "believes" in. The point is that it is from a state of "the possibility of belief" that he is able to talk about, intimate, or point toward that state of self-negating mistrust, from whence he could not have identified anything positively.

Fortunately, such states of absolute and, therefore, self-negating mistrust are rare or perhaps, more correctly, rarely knowable or known. But the experiences of refugees—of which, to be sure, there are as many experiences as there are refugees—tend to move them more toward the eddy of absolute mistrust than toward the shores of trust.

TAMILS IN EASTERN SRI LANKA

Background

For centuries the Eastern Province[8] of Sri Lanka had been home to Portuguese Burghers.[9] In the civil war that began in 1983 in that part of the island, this was the only ethnic group that escaped armed attacks. Until as recently as three and a half decades ago, all four ethnic groups had found a niche for themselves in the social and ecological order that enabled predictable and conflict-free interethnic relationships. This is not to say that this area was an idyllic garden of harmony. Rather, it is to underscore the fact that the lines of conflict and the lines demarcating ethnic groups were, neither by definition nor fact, co-incidental. The Tamils practiced Hinduism and spoke Tamil, the Muslims followed Islam but also spoke Tamil, the Sinhalese were Buddhists and spoke Sinhalese, the Burghers spoke an archaic dialect of Portuguese and practiced Catholicism. Members of all four groups spoke Tamil in addition to their primary language; and there were Christians among the Tamils and Sinhalese. The matrilineal-matrilocal kinship structure distinguished this area from the rest of the island (McGilvray 1982; Yalman 1967). The Hindu Tamils and Buddhist Sinhalese were not very discriminating as to where and how they worshiped. Their rituals overlapped. As far as the ritual officiate was concerned, the *kapurala,* or exorcist-priest, was more significant for the Sinhalese than was the Buddhist monk. Hindu Tamils turned to him as well for help. In the more recent years prior to the beginning of active state nationalism, most Sinhalese were itinerant traders, migrant fishermen, businessmen, or government officials. These Sinhalese married among the Tamils and vice versa, losing and gaining identities as easily as chameleons. Many of the schools had both

Tamila and Sinhalese streams of instruction. Where Sinhalese migrant fishing communities lived in sequestered areas along the coast, they did so not to assert their ethnicity but to conform to local conventions pertaining to divisions of fishing areas.

The Beginnings of the Tamil-Sinhalese Split

Since independence in 1948, however, each one of Ceylon's and (later) Sri Lanka's national governments embarked on a nation-building program that was based on an exclusively Sinhalese-Buddhist nationalism. This had adverse consequences for the island's Tamil minority. The literature that covers the development, enactment, and consequences of this nationalism is extensive.[10] This nationalism was to become indistinguishable from a new, virulent form of Sinhalese-Buddhist chauvinism that sparked off an equally pernicious form of nationalist chauvinism on the Tamil side. In the section that deals with Tamils in Britain, we shall encounter some of these effects on Tamils generally. Here our focus is limited to the Eastern Province of Sri Lanka.

The one hundred fifty years of British colonial rule was also the period in which Sri Lankan nationalism swelled. Sometime, somewhere, in the early stirrings of Sri Lanka's nationalist imagination, the idea of an agricultural paradise took hold. That an island as lush and verdant as theirs with relics of an ancient hydraulic system scattered over the land should be an importer of grain was seen as a national tragedy. Long before independence from Britain, the new nationalists were determined to restore the country to its "lost national glory." The twist to the design, however, was that first only its true nationals were to draw from the benefits of such a restoration; the others had to wait their turn downstream, in more than the literal sense of this expression. These true nationals were the Sinhalese. It was not coincidental, then, that the Gal Oya river irrigation project in the Batticaloa district,[11] begun in the early 1950s, was the first wedge in what was to become a great divide between Tamils and Sinhalese of the Eastern Province. The rate at which Sinhalese colonists were brought in from the south and settled here so far exceeded the number of landless Tamils settled from the local districts that within a decade it dramatically changed the ethnic composition of the area (Manogaran 1987: chap. 3). The colonists, who were primarily peasants from the south, were settled upstream, in the newly developed areas, thereby further reducing these Tamils' already limited supply of water.

The settlements were planned so as to give them a characteristic that was to be distinctively Sinhalese and Buddhist. Along with each settlement of colonists by the government came the building of a local Buddhist temple and the presence of a Buddhist priest. With the latter also came a form of Buddhism that was committed to purge folk elements of worship from local Buddhist practices. The monk's importance, backed by state power and ideology, rose so as to overshadow the importance of the *kapurala*. The local Tamils, who had hitherto partaken in what they thought and knew as common Buddhist-Hindu practices, were struck by the exclusivist self-definition of the new state Buddhism and reacted to it by withdrawing into an exclusive Hindu-Tamil self-definition of their own. The local Sinhalese, briefly caught in the middle, found the pressures of settler ridicule, on the one hand, and allures of state patronage, on the other, too much to resist, and their submission to and incorporation into a state-fabricated Sinhalese national culture was to be completed in short order. The breach between the Tamils and the Sinhalese had extended. State Buddhism, at least in its rhetoric, discouraged cultural miscegenation for fear that that would have compromised the state's attempt to undermine the Tamils' claim that this was their homeland, because the government's own design to establish unequivocal Sinhalese claims could not be supported as strongly by a culturally hybrid population as it could be by "pure" Sinhalese Buddhists. Tamil hostility toward the state grew in proportion to the number of Sinhalese settlers. The Sinhalese were seen as agents of this hostile state. This perception was encouraged not only with the arrival of an increasing number of civil servants but also by the policing, even of predominantly Tamil areas, by an increasing number of Sinhalese policemen. These policemen embarked on a campaign of selective harassment of Tamils of the area. Colonization by settlers was compounded by village expansion schemes in which crown land in the vicinity of border Sinhalese villages was given to local and nonlocal Sinhalese. These expanding border areas pushed deeper in toward the center of predominantly Tamil country. Near Kanthalai, parts of unused land that had been taken away from Tamil and Muslim peasants for the development of sugarcane plantations were later redistributed among Sinhalese settlers. Ancient sacred Buddhist sites, such as Digavapiya, were identified, and land along these sites was alienated from their Tamil and Muslim owners and gradually redistributed among the Sinhalese. By the early 1980s, the heat of Tamil antagonism toward the state had been so liberally fueled by state policies and antistate Tamil rhetoric that all it needed for conflagration was a match. And the match was the islandwide, state-backed, anti-Tamil riots of July 1983.

The Rise of Armed Tamil Militancy

The center of Tamil militancy was of course not the Eastern Province but the northern peninsula of Jaffna. In the early 1970s, in response to the increasing discrimination against them by the state and harrassment by the armed forces, a section of the Tamil youth began to spurn the nonviolent tactics of their elders. Of this, a tiny group of no more than a dozen Tamil youth embarked on a campaign of selective assassinations. Between 1970 and 1983, twelve people had been killed, all but one of them Tamils, all linked to the state machinery and considered by the Tamil militants self-interested colluders in state oppression. Try as they might, this band of ragtag militants barely added to their numbers. By the end of the decade this small group—an original cohort of friends—had split up into four smaller ones, each continuing to claim a membership of less than ten. Conservative Jaffna was not ready to turn to violence.

The July 1983 riots radically undermined this status quo. In the wake of the riots the four major militant groups already in place began recruiting new members with astounding success. Young men and women started signing up by the hundreds. That same summer, India got involved in Sri Lanka's difficulties. Initially its involvement was indirect. Providing both arms and training, it allowed the setting up of training camps for Sri Lankan Tamil militants in South India in an effort to control as much as to assist them. The South Indian state of Tamil Nadu, its people, and its government all lent their support to the militants. Three years later, India got directly involved in the island's conflict, which began with her sending a peace-keeping force to the island's north and east. But in the summer of 1983, the recruitment of volunteers to militancy spread like wildfire throughout the Tamil-dominated areas of the island, including Batticaloa. And there as elsewhere, the campaign for a Tamil homeland took a violent turn.

The government countered by settling even larger numbers of Sinhalese in the border regions, most of whom were landless peasants from the deep south. The Tamil militants saw these settlers as agents provocateurs of the state, sent to change the demographic character of the area in favor of the Sinhalese. They thus became legitimate targets of militant activity. When these initially surprised settlers fled to refugee camps, they were denied provisions by the government, thereby forcing them to return to their settlements. Furthermore, on condition of their willingness to return, they were promised various benefits. They were promised military protection and were also encouraged to defend themselves, in some instances with state-supplied arms and in others, without. Military camps scattered around these settlements were intended to protect the settlers, transforming, in short order, the settlements and the camps into one defensive space.

The Tamil-Muslim Rift

The state's strategy was to transform the conflict into one of Tamil militants versus the rest. To accomplish this, the state had to subvert the signs of trust, whose traffic among Tamils, Sinhalese, and Muslims had held the three groups together in a shared flow of common understandings. By August 1983, the Sinhalese, including the local Sinhalese, had become total victims of state design. The Tamil militants, with their own mistrust of every Sinhalese, had become accomplices of the state in this regard.[12] The next crack in the community to be levered apart was the one that had taken form between the Tamils and Muslims. The pry was two-pronged.

With the rise of Tamil militancy and its clamor for a homeland, bona fide national parties of the past had become (ir)relevant, and so had the politicians elected under those party labels. In the Batticaloa area the party of such (ir)relevance was the ruling United National party, under the name of which several Muslim leaders had been elected. Being a minority within a minority, the Muslim community's imagined future in a Tamil homeland was an anxious and ambivalent one, and the Muslims who were the most anxious were the leadership. They wanted restored the freedom of expression of the Muslims in general and their own political relevance to their people in particular. But in the climate of militant Tamil nationalism, anyone with nonhostile links to the national parties was considered treacherous, and any expressions of such ambivalent and anxious sentiments were not possible without armed protection. The request for armed protection by elected officials was what the state wanted and soon received. Thus was inserted the first prong in the interethnic crack.

This, however, was not sufficient. After all, the Tamil-speaking Muslims of the Eastern Province were also victims of the state's discriminatory policies, especially with respect to the colonization and alienation of lands. Furthermore, many young Muslims had already joined various Tamil militant groups. Despite calls from the Muslim leadership to identify with the "state protectors," the Muslims who lived in settlements that were scattered among the Tamils realized that such an alliance would only isolate them in fortified pockets. But at least the leadership managed to stem the flow of Muslim youth joining militant groups. This was done by invoking the safety of the Muslim community. For the army's campaigns of terror that were summoned on entire villages and settlements suspected of harboring "terrorists" were known only too well. A few Muslims who had joined the militants were also convinced to return to their communities to prevent the attack of the army on their families and neighbors. But to split up Batticaloa's multiethnic community further, the military had to find informants. This is where the second prong was put to work.

In its campaign of "counterinsurgency," the information-starved military's first recruits were former policemen. They were to recultivate old networks and penetrate the community to locate sources of information, communities and sources that were essentially unknown to the more recent police forces who had come to serve in the area after antistate hostilities limited their movement to the vicinity of their stations. The brutal punishments meted out by Tamil militants to traitors, whether imagined or real, were so horrifying that the military, even with the recalled policemen's help, found it extremely difficult to open lines of communication with the citizenry, let alone recruit them for its ends. Hence the armed forces worked in stages. They began by choreographing a realm of traitors. It is in this task that the demothballed policemen were of help. They were able to map the sociopolitical landscape of the area better than anyone else.[13] The army's goal was achieved in the following manner.

The army would raid certain houses or arrest some "suspects." The victims tended to be non-Muslim Tamils. When family and friends of the victims would go to the authorities to inquire about the release of their kinsmen or friends, the officer in charge would respond by saying that they had been arrested on information supplied by "your people." (This term covered Tamils as well as Muslims but was intended, in these early days, to point more toward the Muslims.) They would express their displeasure in having to make such raids and arrests but declare that they were duty-bound to act on any information received. The Muslims, especially those who had renounced militancy, would become the first suspects of the non-Muslim Tamils. Divisions among Tamils were to follow much later, with their own internecine feuds among the various militant groups being exploited in a similar manner. But the first order of business was to ensure the Muslim-Tamil rift.

The state also used Muslim officers to infiltrate the Muslim trade network, a network that had deep and widespread roots in time and space among the Tamils. Once the first case of "treachery" (real or imagined) became known, every itinerant trader who sold anything from sewing needles to pieces of textile became a target of suspicion. In addition to itinerant traders, there were many Muslims among the landless agricultural wage laborers who moved back and forth between Tamil and Muslim villages and fields. They were the next to be suspected of being informants. In addition to the mistreatment these traders and laborers suffered at the hands of Tamil militants, their traditional means of making a living was abruptly placed in serious jeopardy. The Muslim community as a whole began to identify with their party members' demands for military protection of the itinerant Muslims. The state got what it had wanted. The Muslims' demands for the army's protection was seen as a clear and undeniable act of betrayal of the Tamils by the Muslims. Assaults by individuals on individuals that in the past would have been sorted out by both communities within a few days now invited military intervention and Tamil militant counterintervention. Individual fights turned into group conflicts. Muslims led assaults of revenge against Tamil villages under the protection, assistance, and encouragement of the armed forces. Tamil militant groups massacred innocent Muslims in their homes, in their fields, and at prayer. All the while the attacks of the armed forces and the Home Guard (an armed militia of Sinhalese and Muslims) continued to fall on Tamil civilians, all of whom were suspected of protecting Tamil militants. The Special Task Force, which was deployed in May 1985, continued its ruthless work of arrest and torture, spawning informants and traitors by the hundreds, real and fabricated, throughout the province.

The Tamil-Tamil Fissures

The fracturing of the Tamil community is too complex a story to be told in this brief space and therefore must be sketchy. To begin with, the Tamils of Sri Lanka do not constitute a monolithic bloc. There are the Tamils of the highlands who were brought by the British in the nineteenth and early twentieth century to work on the coffee and tea plantations. These Tamils of relatively recent Indian origin are distinguished from the rest of the Tamils whose claim to the island of Sri Lanka is as ancient as that of the Sinhalese. The latter group of Tamils is split up into at least three further groups: the Northern Tamils (who are also called Jaffna Tamils, after the name of the northernmost peninsula where most of them come from), the Tamils of the northwest coast (who also go by the name of the major town in their region and are known as Mannar Tamils), and the east coast Tamils centered around the port towns of Batticaloa and Trincomalee. The only Tamils who have not resorted to armed militancy as a group are the Tamils of recent Indian origin who still live in the south and south central regions of the island. Even though the leadership of all the Tamil militant movements came from Jaffna, young Tamil men and women from all three of the other groups joined the various militant groups to battle their oppressor, the Sri Lankan army.

At one count there were as many as sixteen militant groups. As the civil war dragged on and expanded, this number dropped to four. Many young men and women in the early years found themselves in one group as opposed to another, not because they knew what group they were joining, but because in the fever pitch of post–July riot recruitment, they signed up with the first solicitor who came their way. In the very early months, most recruits were volunteers; subsequently, they were to become victims of coercion and threats. All four groups competed among themselves for supremacy and sole leadership of the Tamil cause. The civilian population was accordingly split. In time, neutrality was the hardest, if not the most dangerous, of all political stances. Friends, neighbors, and families were split along lines of actual or purported group allegiances. Within families cousin was pitted against cousin, in-law against in-law, brother against sister, and, in some instances, brother against brother. Intergroup rivalry turned nasty and bloody. Material and financial support for the groups was both solicited and extorted. An individual who donated to one group under threat and intimidation would find himself on the hit list of another group for being a supporter of a rival group. The leadership of the various groups were as paranoid as they were ambitious. The search for informers and spies preoccupied them as much as their plans to liberate their people. New recruits who wished to prove themselves and their loyalty hankered for the chance to carry out the orders of their leaders, especially if it entailed executions. Executions brought one closer to the inner circle. Some young men knowingly misidentified individuals as informers so that they could receive execution orders from the leadership and carry them out, thereby gaining the right to be inducted into the next inner circle, closer to the leader's heart.

Not only did India train and arm these militant groups; it also had its favorites. Different branches of the Indian government were reputed to have had different favorites. The army's favorite might not have been the favorite of the Indian Research and Analysis Wing (RAW, the Indian equivalent of the CIA); the central government's favorite might not have been the Tamil Nadu state government's favorite. In fact, until the assassination of Rajiv Gandhi, two successive state governments and their chief ministers cast their lots with the militant group best known by the name Tamil Tigers. This group was not the Indian army's favorite.

The Indian army landed on the island in June 1987 under the terms of an accord that Indian Prime Minister Rajiv Gandhi and Sri Lankan President J. R. Jayawardena had entered into. From New Delhi's point of view, the persecution and consequent separatism of Sri Lanka Tamils had the potential of igniting similar separatist sentiments among India's 50 million Tamils who lived in that country's southern state of Tamil Nadu. Indeed, South India had already become home to thousands of Sri Lankan Tamil refugees. The majority of the Sinhalese saw the Indian army's presence on their island as Sri Lanka's surrender of its sovereignty to its larger neighbor. As far as they were concerned, the accord was not an accord but the imposition of the will of the stronger neighbor on the weaker one. The Tamil civilian population of Sri Lanka greeted the Indian army with song and garland as their liberator and savior who had stopped the Sri Lankan army's massacre of their people. Before long, hope turned into a nightmare.[14] For the Tamils of the island's north and east, the initials "I.P.K.F." soon came to stand, not for the Indian Peace Keeping Force, but for the Indian People Killing Force.

Very early on during its occupation the Indian army tried to "tame the Tiger," as one official put it. It soon found that it could not do so by itself. During its disastrous peace-keeping mission in the north and east of the island, which lasted almost three years, the Indian army played favorites to the hilt. The Tamil Tigers turned out to be not merely the least favorite of the Indian army but its deadly enemy as well. And so the Indians exploited the internecine rivalry among the Tamil groups, supporting two of the non-Tiger factions in particular with political might, arms, and training. Their mission and the Indian army's mission coincided: bringing the Tigers to heel. The president of the Sri Lankan Republic, Jayawardena, who under pressure from diverse quarters (especially from New Delhi) had invited the Indian army to restore peace, was now facing a campaign of terror from the Sinhalese youth of the south who, among other things, accused him of selling out to the Indians. When his term was up, he slipped into retirement.

Jayawardena's prime minister, who had withheld his support for his government's invitation to the Indian army, now became president of the republic. His intentions were one with that of the Tigers: get the Indians out. The Tigers, who had only a few years earlier been the archenemy of the Sri Lankan army, were now being cheered on by a majority of the Sinhalese of the south in their effort to oust the Indians. The new president, Mr. Premadasa, did everything possible to undermine the peace accord his predecessor had arrived at with India and gave overt and covert support to the Tigers to help him in his mission. Even if the widely held opinion that his support extended to supplying arms to the Tigers remains speculative, confidential and reliable sources have confided in one of the authors that the new government made no attempt to stop the supply of arms reaching them. The Tiger-Premadasa alliance succeeded in its goal. India had met its Vietnam, its Afghanistan. Long before the last Indian soldier left on 24 March 1990, the Tigers turned on their compatriots who belonged to groups that had colluded with the Indians. Without Indian support, these groups were no match for the Tigers. The Sri Lankan army, which had either been lying low in the border areas watching the goings-on in the north and east or been busy quelling the Sinhalese rebellion in the deep south, now returned; first slowly to fill its camps, then more briskly with arms and bombs.

Trust took another ironic turn as the fleeing non-Tiger factions ran to Sri Lankan and even Special Task Force camps for refuge from the Tigers. These camps that had been pitched near the border areas remained there throughout the Indian presence, purportedly to protect the Sinhalese settler population. The non-Tiger groups that had operated freely and powerfully with the support of the Indian army were now abandoned by the departing Indians, outnumbered and outgunned by the Tigers. In their flight for their lives, these Tamils had to steal through Sinhalese settlements and villages to reach the Sri Lankan army camps and in so doing, were, on more than one occasion, caught by the settlers and slaughtered. As far as they were concerned, these were Tamils, they were Tigers, they were killers of innocent women and children, they were enemies of the nation, they were infidels. An exterior and interior landscape on which a cool breeze of trust had once played now broods suspicion, vulturelike, talons bared, and the smell of death covered the fields.

Those who did reach the refuge of the camps were above all valuable sources of information to the Sri Lankan army, which was poised to return to war against the Tigers. These Tamils knew the landscape of the north and the east and the names and addresses of Tiger supporters who could be tortured into betraying the hideouts of the Tigers. After extracting all the information they could from these desperate young men and women, the army resupplied them with arms and sent them out to fight the Tigers until victory or death. Those non-Tiger militants with means and connections escaped to India or to the west. Once all that could be expected was sucked out of the life and will of these fighters, the Sri Lankan armed forces themselves turned in earnest on the Tamil Tigers. The civilian population could only turn from one stunned pose to another, fearing retributions for alliances made or even wondering whether or not and with whom they had made any alliances. There was not a judgment, including their own, they could trust. Before long the Sri Lankan army had subdued Tamil anger in the Eastern Province to a helpless simmer.

Under the heavy bombing of the army and the various militants' attacks a curious relationship developed between space and trust. In normal times, one's home is one's refuge, a place one runs to in times of danger. The war had changed this. Thanguraj has observed a phenomenon whereby when even the faintest rumor of an attack surfaces, people run, not into their houses but out of them: to fields, to temples, or to others' homes, but never to their own. This we may observe as one of the earliest signs of the formation of a refugee.

Those Tamils who could afford it escaped to foreign countries in search of refuge. The world had turned its attention to other matters and events: the Berlin wall, the breakup of the Soviet Union, Iraq, and now Yugoslavia. A troubled and xenophobic Western Europe was collectively trying to devise legal means of blocking the trickle of asylum seekers. Attacks on Tamil refugees in every one of the Western European countries was on the increase, especially in Germany and Great Britain. Even in liberal Netherlands, in quiet little villages, one of us witnessed three occasions, and were told of several more, on which white children were drawn close to their mothers while on a walk when a Tamil refugee was spotted coming toward them on the sidewalk. Interviews with the Dutch revealed a large measure of generosity and gallant kindness but also enough suspicion and fear to make asylum seekers realize that they are not wanted there. In the United States, frustrated expert witnesses and lawyers were told by immigration judges that despite the testimonies they had heard from asylum seekers and experts of repression, torture, and death, because the State Department's position was that there was no persecution in Sri Lanka, in their own last judgment they had to defer to that department's opinion. According to the United States, Sri Lanka's rightist government was still "a friendly government."

By the end of the 1980s, India was supporting its official line that its peace mission had been a success and began repatriating its share of Tamil refugees. Matters had turned desperate, and Tamils who could ill afford it were beginning to escape to the West. Mothers, mostly war widows, began selling all they had to buy a ticket for at least one of their children, as young as five and as old as ten, to put him or her on a plane that flew to Germany. Rumor had it that by German law they could not be deported. The rumor was correct. Newspapers and television quoted some of the children telling the immigration authorities, "Mommy told us to go, that she will come soon." Some Germans snarled, "Economic refugees!" The mothers were accused of long-range planning. The mothers, on their part, had no hope of ever seeing their children again, let alone of migrating to the wealthy West. All they wanted was that at least their child, or "at least this one child," would live.

Even as we compose this paragraph we have received word from Jaffna that the Sri Lankan army is closing in on the Tiger-held peninsula from the sea. Only the old, the poor, and the stubborn are left. It has come to the point that the Tiger army is now made up of children, mostly children. Reports are coming in indicating that most of the dead on the front lines are ten- to thirteen-year-olds. There are many reasons one may give for why these children joined the Tigers. Among these are two undeniable ones: they are too poor to emigrate, and they are too hungry to be able to resist the only source of food they have, the food made available by the Tigers.

TAMILS IN BRITAIN

Phases I and II: Tamil Immigration to Britain

By the time Sri Lankan Tamils were arriving in Britain in the early 1980s seeking asylum, there were Tamils already in Britain who had preceded them under quite different circumstances. These refugees formed but the third phase of Tamil migration to Britain.

The first generation of Sri Lankans who emigrated to Britain were an odd assortment of Sinhalese, Tamils, and Burghers; women and men who came to Britain after the island's independence from its colonial power.[15] What most of them had in common was an upper- or upper-middle-class background, an education in the elite high schools of Sri Lanka, and a cultivated ease with Western ways and tastes. Most of them came to obtain professional degrees in law, medicine, and engineering or to obtain graduate degrees that would ease them into the faculties of the universities and the civil service at home. They cultivated a blend of nostalgia for the colonial days and nationalism. Few had any intention of staying on in Britain, for the comforts of home were too many to be given up. Britain began as a rite of passage. But as time went on, especially after English was displaced from its privileged position and replaced by Sinhalese as the sole official language in 1956, many of this group of immigrants decided to extend their stay and practice their professions in Britain rather than in Sri Lanka. For the Tamils in particular, the first breach of trust committed by their government was in the enactment of the 1956 language bill, which de facto reduced Tamils to second-class citizens. But many more, Sinhalese and Tamils, chose to return. They may not have liked the direction the new government was taking, especially with respect to its language policy, but they had family, estates, and privileges to return to. And above all, they did not wish to raise their children in England, which was seen as culturally decadent. Even those who stayed retained their loyalty for "home" and came to think of their British passport as only a convenience. As is true in all such cases, the children who were born in Britain found their parents' vestige of cultural and national loyalties to Sri Lanka quaint and queer.

What these immigrants deeply held and successfully inculcated in their children was the belief that they, as far as Asians went, were special. They were not Indians. They were certainly not "Pakis." They were Sri Lankans. They favored a high-pedigree dialect of British English, not the kind that was spoken by the Indo-Pakistani immigrants of Southhall and Wembley. They had gone to the best Sri Lankan schools, and their children went to the better ("public," if possible) schools in Britain; they were professionals, as their children ought to be some day. The Sinhalese among this first phase of immigrants came from the upper classes, but not all of them came from the uppermost caste of Sinhalese society. By contrast, the Tamils came largely from the highest Tamil caste in Sri Lanka, the Vellalas. And they made sure that their children knew this.

The second phase of Tamil migration to Britain represented a wider spectrum of class and caste, for in the 1960s and 1970s the universities and schools back home had opened up to and had educated a more diverse population of students. The opening up of the universities, however, made education a more, rather than less, precious commodity. Tamils were bound to face increasing competition from the Sinhalese, whose interest in and access to education was beginning to catch up with the proportion of Sinhalese in the population as a whole. But the competition in and corresponding value of education were further intensified by two policies of the Sri Lankan government. The first was the institution of a quota system that adversely affected the Tamils, and the second was the systematic closing up of the civil services to Tamil candidates.[16] Under these conditions, England became the escape route to many students, and most who migrated in this phase were students.

There were class and caste barriers between the first and the second generation of migrants, but education and the similarities in professional ambitions ameliorated the differences, even though many more were choosing to go to the more recent "polytechnics" rather than to the old British universities. The second generation trusted those who had preceded them and accepted their freely given guidance, advice, contacts, and tips on how to make it in Britain. The second generation was poorer than the first because they came from a poorer class; but even when they did have resources at home, the newly imposed exchange controls in Sri Lanka made it difficult for them to transfer funds out of the country. To top this, Britain increased the fees it charged its foreign students to three times what domestic students were levied. This meant that more of them had to support their studies by working, and most of them chose jobs that were congenial to studying, such as working as night security guards and petrol station attendants. This generation's nostalgia for the home country was qualitatively different from that of the first generation. They had no illusions about belonging to a ruling elite and all the comforts and privileges that went with it. The political climate they had fled from soured them to the Sri Lankan state as well as to most aspects of civil society. Unlike their predecessors, they did not go to school with Sinhalese classmates and study in the English medium but had, as a consequence of the language act of 1956, been schooled in an exclusively Tamil medium of education and had thereby come to consider their Sinhalese compatriots as virtual strangers at best and enemies at worst. Their nostalgia is best described as basic homesickness: the missing of family, temple or church, friends, and home-cooked food. Many in this group who completed their education before the late 1970s found jobs in the United Kingdom or elsewhere in the world and chose not to return to Sri Lanka.

Phase III: Refugees

The Early Phase. The third phase of Tamil emigration to Britain and the West in general began with the Sri Lankan government's imposition of the draconian Prevention of Terrorism Act (PTA) in 1979 in response to a certain section of the Tamil population's campaign for a separate state.[17] To appreciate the scale of the government's excessive and indiscriminate use of force, one can only sadly recite the now well known fact that prior to the 1983 anti-Tamil riots that left thousands of Tamils dead and thousands more homeless, there were no more than a dozen Tamil Tigers, the militant separatist group that was to subsequently grow into one of the most dreaded militant groups in the world. By the late 1970s and early 1980s, for the average Sinhalese soldier every Tamil was not only an anti-Sinhalese but an antinationalist. The PTA fell hardest on the Tamil youth. Every Tamil between the ages of sixteen and forty was considered to be a terrorist whose tactic was to surprise.

They initially came to Britain as students either because that was the only way they knew how to get to Britain or because they were too embarrassed to seek asylum. Once the student route was choked off by Britain's ever-intensifying restrictive policies, they openly sought asylum. For Phase II Tamils, this development was something feared, expected, and understood. So they went to great lengths to assist these fellow Tamils by serving as sponsors, by providing places to stay, and by finding them jobs. Phase II Tamils were also more in touch with the constant changes in immigration laws, their interpretation, and their enforcement—all set up as obstacles to immigration by the British authorities—and the ways of overcoming or circumventing them than were Phase I Tamils. The first generation's advice in these matters was outdated and irrelevant, as indeed the second generation's was to soon become.

Phase III Tamils who arrived at Heathrow Airport knew that they were supposed to walk up to the immigration counter and request political asylum. After being processed, and if they were lucky enough to be spared deportation,[18] they would be asked if there was anybody in London who could care for them. The asylum seeker would have the name and address of a friend or friend's friend ready. Initially these contacts were Phase II Tamils, rarely Phase I types, but subsequently they were fellow asylum seekers who had preceded them. In any event most of their receiving hosts were themselves only temporary residents in Britain. The asylum seeker, or more correctly, the potential asylum seeker, would then be released into the charge of his or her London friend with a Temporary Permit to enter and apply for asylum in the country and to seek permission to work. We make this fine distinction between the potential asylum seeker and the asylum seeker because one does not become an asylum seeker, in the strict sense, until the British Home Office acknowledges the receipt of a Temporary Permit holder's written application for asylum. Currently, the time between the submission of such an application, which the potential asylum seeker does almost as soon as he leaves the airport, and the Home Office's acknowledgment of receipt takes an average of one and a half to two years. Of course, acknowledging an application for asylum is one thing, granting asylum quite another. While awaiting acknowledgment, the potential asylum seeker is legally not permitted to work and receives a dole of thirty-eight pounds a week from the state.

Apart from the fact that all Phase III Tamils are asylum seekers, they are characterized by a continuously changing social and economic profile. The largely politically conservative and socially well-to-do Phase I immigrants found it extremely discomforting to witness the arrival of Tamils among whom there were increasing numbers from the lower ends of caste and class with their poor, even complete lack of, command of English and their off-the-boat dress and demeanor. But they were most aghast by the "ungentlemanly political tactics they employed,"[19] such as stripping themselves down to their underwear at Heathrow to protest deportation. Above all, this group found it difficult to come to terms with the fact that they were seeing "Tamils as refugees."

Once admitted into the country, Phase II and Phase I, especially Phase I,[20] Tamils attempted to fit what they saw into a picture that they knew, remembered, or had heard of. This picture was one of a class/caste-based social order in which the upper castes, when at their best, were helpers and patrons of the lower castes. When advice was extended to these newcomers it was done with ultimately democratic intentions, "to help them become fit for a free and equal society." Initially there was even a sense of urgency in their gestures of help because, among other things, they had the "image of the Tamil in Britain to protect." If nothing more, they had to preserve their identity as "not 'Pakis' and certainly not Afro-Carribean." Before the mid-1980s, much help was given and much received. Phase I Tamils expected the newcomers to conform, to continue to take their advice, to rapidly move up in British society (even as they had done) by turning to education, and above all to keep a low profile until they were fit enough to ensure that the dignity of the Tamil would not be tarnished. It did not take long for matters to sour or require radical reframing. Those of Phase I who refused to reframe their world withdrew from helping the asylum seekers, declaring, at least among their own classes, that these "riffraff" were untrustworthy "tree climbers."[21]

Instead, many of them turned to help those young men and women who never left Sri Lanka but had "chosen" to stay behind and fight the Sri Lankan and Indian armies. Ironically, that these fighters were also predominantly drawn from the lower castes of Tamil Sri Lanka did not matter to Phase I Tamils. Considerable financial and material support from Phase I Tamils went to help the militant "liberation groups" back home. Some of the wealthiest of this class in Britain and in the United States—more in the United States than in Britain—expected their "boys," as these militants were called, to establish a separate nation-state called Eelam in short order, and a few expressed their hope of some day becoming ambassadors of this new nation in some of the leading European and North American capitals. In the meantime they were gallant warriors in a proxy war. While, on the one hand, such fantasies and hopes swelled, on the other, they came to read, witness, and even experience open racism from Britain's whites. Their own trust in the British whom they thought they knew was shaken when they saw Tamils being called "Pakis." Some blamed the asylum seekers for having robbed them of their dignity. "All kinds of riffraff have started coming. They cannot even speak proper English. Some cannot even speak a word," complained one of the first-generation Tamils. But others realized that all the while they had imagined that their white fellow Britons knew the difference, the fact was that these whites neither knew nor cared. A sense of identification with all other nonwhites in Britain had begun among some of them, mainly among the children of this generation.

The only route to dignified settlement that Phase I and II Tamils had known was education. For Phase III Tamils, this was neither their first nor their easiest choice. For one, they were escaping a civil war that had wreaked havoc on their progress in education. Second, they had also spent almost all their family's resources to come to the United Kingdom. This had to be replaced. Third, they had to earn and save up their money to bring their parents, siblings, brides, and spouses out of their strife-torn homeland. Unlike the students who preceded them in Phase II, there were many married men among these asylum seekers. Fourth, given the paucity of the earning potential of their fathers and brothers back home under civil war conditions and their consequent inability to save for their sisters' and daughters' marriages, it fell to these refugees to save money for the dowries. Lucky indeed was she whose prospective groom lived in the West and had permanent residency status. But such a man required a higher dowry. In essence, the times were too urgent for settling for the deferred gratification education had to offer. They needed cash, and they needed it fast.

In the early years of the arrival of Phase III Tamils, the introduction to the means for earning money was prepared for them by Phase II Tamils, most of whom were on student visas. To maintain their residency status in Britain, these Tamils had to be enrolled as full-time students and come up with the high fees levied on nonresident students. They were left with no option but to find remunerative work even though their student visas forbade them to do so. Daytime scholarship was funded by nighttime jobs, and the night shift of a petrol station attendant turned out to be among the most desirable jobs available. These Tamil students had earned for themselves a reputation of being hardworking and reliable. And when their fellow Tamils arrived, they introduced them to the petrol station circuit as well, where they were readily hired, many while they were still only potential asylum seekers. The saying goes, "Today at Heathrow, tomorrow at the petrol station."

Unlike the students, who were prohibited by law from holding full-time jobs, bona fide asylum seekers were allowed to work full-time and overtime if they had to. And this they did. Most of them had no prior experience in retail trading. More than the petrol pumps, the mini-markets attached to them taught them the elements of retail trade. These refugees initially lived together in crowded dwellings, pooled their resources, lived frugally, and at the first opportunity made down payments on new homes. These investments in the late seventies and early eighties turned out to be bonanzas. Those asylum seekers who opted to pursue higher education received special fee waivers due to special provisions made by local governments.

Phase II students began to resent the privileges of the asylum seekers. While the income from their own part-time jobs were siphoned off into exorbitant university fees, the asylum seekers' full-time jobs freed them to save, even invest in real estate, and pay their kinsmen's way out of Sri Lanka. In many cases asylum seekers competed with Phase II immigrants for the same job, in which the asylum seekers had the advantage of official permission and no other constraints on their time. What is more, because of their full-time employment, the asylum seekers were free to move up in rank in their management of the petrol stations. But moving up the ranks was possible only to a certain level, a level short of becoming regional managers. As several Tamil petrol station managers were to tell us, racism from higher levels seemed to kick in at this point. Successful managers were fired, almost always under the flimsiest of excuses, as soon as the inevitability of promotion came up. Sadly, confidential affidavits with accusations of mismanagement were sought by white superiors from Phase II workers against their Phase III compatriots. Subtle and not-so-subtle tactics were employed to extract such affidavits. The growing resentment of some of the students against their Phase III fellow Tamil superiors was exploited by these white superiors. At the price of trust, some students did betray their fellow Tamils.

But those who had been fired from their petrol station jobs left having learned the important skill of retail trade, thanks to the mini-markets they had managed. Some of these individuals leased petrol stations that were not turning a profit and white Britons did not want and turned them into profit-making enterprises of their own. Others leased or bought little "cash and carry" stores from Indians—especially Indians who had come from Uganda a generation earlier—whose Britishized children had no interest in taking over the running of their little "mom and pop stores," which called for hard work and long hours.

After the July riots of 1983, Phase I Tamils realized that they were fighting a losing battle against their shattered illusion of the "dignified Sri Lankan Tamil." For those who were arriving by then were not necessarily young men but older people who were dependents of the post-1979 asylum seekers. In the beginning, renewed attempts were made to cajole the young men and women of Phase III to fall into line with their class/caste-based expectations. This they did by subtle exercises of caste prerogatives, on the one hand, and overt encouragement of old-country gerontocracy, on the other. What they had not realized is that with the rise of the Tamil militant movements in Sri Lanka, gerontocracy had been overthrown by a generalized neocracy. In the wake of the July riots entire families arrived in Britain. Unaccompanied individuals were soon followed by dependents. Marriages were made, and in-laws followed spouses. Some Phase I immigrants saw the "Paki phenomenon"[22] taking shape in the Tamil community before their very eyes. The character of the Tamil immigrant community in Britain was never to be the same.

As Phase III immigrants saw matters, all Phase I types could say was, "Don't do this, *thambi*, don't do that, *thambi*, and be careful, *thambi*."[23] The asylum seekers found both them and their advice largely irrelevant. Unconfirmed rumors abounded that some Phase I immigrants were in collusion with the Home Office, feeding the latter information that could result in their deportation. The following were some of the typical statements gathered from Phase III asylum seekers about their Phase I predecessors: "They want us to go back and fight for *their* Eelam." "They want us to take orders from them; be their bearers." "They are jealous that we can drive cars here. Of course they don't know that we drove cars even in Sri Lanka. They remember the days when the only cars in that country belonged to their grandfathers, and their great-grandfathers sucked up to the colonial white man." "They cheated us then, they'll cheat us now."

Unlike their predecessors, Phase III immigrants were highly politicized to the brute realities of discrimination and were willing to talk about it openly. Phase II immigrants in particular found in this considerable relief. For instance, any Sri Lankan who works in a London petrol station is regularly on the receiving end of racist remarks from white customers. As one informant put it (with only slight exaggeration, I believe), "There isn't a single night, when you work the graveyard shift, that some white punk doesn't call for your attention by shouting, 'Hey you black cunt.' " The students found it difficult to convince Phase I immigrants of the reality of this kind of open racial abuse. The Phase I type "tended to blame the victim while they lived in their suburban homes in Surrey and voted for the Tories," one woman observed.

The Late Phase.   The early arrivals of Phase III had still been those with at least some means: the means to leave before Britain began tightening her laws, before the Immigration Carrier's Liability Act was passed,[24] before racketeers began to facilitate the asylum seeker's escape with false papers at high cost, before the price for getting to Heathrow went from under 400 British pounds to more than 5,000 pounds. The "success stories" with petrol stations and retail stores that we just recounted apply mainly to those who came to Britain before 1985. For the very poor, which was what increasingly became the profile of the average Tamil arriving at Heathrow during the latter part of the 1980s, the new exorbitant passage was bought for only one family member by his or her family going deeply into debt; in some instances, after selling house and possessions. No longer could the one who entered Britain raise enough money to pay back his or her own debt, let alone raise enough to pay the going price for chancy "illegal" exits and entries of other members of the family. And even if and when this was possible, the snares were too many and far too hazardous. There are cases known to the London-based Joint Council for the Welfare of Immigrants in which middlemen—also Tamils—have abandoned groups of Tamils in "transit points" in such faraway places as Bangkok and Nairobi, after these same middlemen absconded with the 5,000-plus pounds "setup money" they received from their charges. Such a middleman takes them to an apartment or a room and tells them to stay put—lest they be caught by the authorities—until he makes arrangements for the next leg of the journey en route to London or some other Western capital. The room or apartment in question is locked from the outside to ensure double protection. The anxious and frightened group waits, at times for days, until hunger and/or suspicion gets the better of them and they break loose or start screaming for help. Some such desperate and penniless escapees are then offered, by yet another set of racketeers, the opportunity of becoming drug couriers as means of buying their way back onto the road to asylum.

Attempts by refugee and humanitarian organizations in Britain to convince the

Home Office of the merits of instituting a family reunion program that would undermine such villainy has been to no avail. As a sop to these organizations, Britain's Home Office declared a policy of allowing family reunion after an individual has been in Britain for over four years and then only after the applicant has convinced the Home Office of "compelling and compassionate circumstances"— the phrase that stipulates the official criterion. In reality it is almost impossible for anyone to qualify for this privilege, as is amply attested by the dossiers of applicants compiled by London's Joint Council for the Welfare of Immigrants and similar organizations that assist refugees. Many of the men who came to Great Britain to escape death after 1985, having left their wives and children, now hold little hope of seeing them. And they live in a state of heightened anxiety as they await the seven-year limit, at which time they will know, by law, whether their application for asylum has been accepted or not. Many are those who, unable to bear the strain, have returned home regardless of the consequences awaiting them. And some have met their death there. Others have gone back after learning that the reason for which they came to Britain in the first place no longer exists; their family has been wiped out by one armed group or another, soldiers or militants. The intransigence of British authorities and the scale of British xenophobia and racism vis-à-vis refugees (as evidenced by the nature of the frequent headlines of London's tabloids) are astounding when one realizes that between 1979 and 1989, Great Britain, with a population of almost 58 million, admitted only 54,935 refugees, a mere .09 percent of the total population. Of these only 7,910 were Sri Lankans.[25] If white Britain's reluctance to give refuge to asylum seekers is astounding, Phase I Tamils' willingness to share in this sentiment is ironic.

By the beginning of the 1990s, further changes were observed in the composition of the more recent asylum seekers. Now, not only did young men and women who had escaped the Sri Lankan and Indian armies seek asylum in Britain but war-hardened and disenchanted militants, escaping tyrannous militant groups of their own, were arriving in London. This group introduced a climate of suspicion so intense that one could seriously say that trust was on trial in the Tamil community of Britain.

Tamils and the British Home Office: Some Further Vicissitudes

Most Sri Lankan Tamil asylum seekers who were admitted to Britain after 1979 were recognized as being granted "exceptional leave to remain." As Stuart Turner (this volume) has observed, "Exceptional leave, unlike refugee status, carries no permanent safety (being subject to annual review) and carries no automatic rights for dependents of the asylum seeker who may have been left behind in the original country. Family separation is common and, although outside the control of the asylum seeker, often constitutes a perfectly understandable source of prolonged fear and guilt."

These leaves are usually given for one year and on appeal may be extended for three more years. On one more appeal the leaves may be extended for a final three years, beyond which extensions are not given. At any time during this process, the British Home Office has the authority to convert an applicant's status from one kind into another. Between the Home Office and the asylum seekers have mushroomed legal advice and aid-dispensing agents and agencies, many of which are Tamil. Tamils seek out Tamil agents and agencies. Some of them are trained lawyers, some are not. But in both groups there are those who are knowledgeable about immigration law and those who know little more than distributing and filling out forms obtained from the Home Office. Many are in it to make a fast buck, especially those who know the least about immigration law. There are also some well-informed agents who dispense good and bad advice selectively. One barrister interviewed by Daniel determined who was and who was not worthy of help based on his evaluation of whether or not the applicant would preserve the dignity of Tamils in Great Britain. Another waited for names of applicants to be cleared by a particular militant organization in Sri Lanka that he supported. Two of the criteria this organization used were whether the applicant in question or members of his or her family had links to rival militant groups and whether or not the applicant had made a suitable contribution to the movement of choice. The Home Office is known to use such ill-trained and prejudicial agents as a means of denying applicants asylum.

There is also evidence that the Home Office attempts to directly sabotage an applicant's chances. The following is a typical strategy the Home Office employs. The typical asylum seeker arrives at Heathrow without a passport. This is a de facto declaration that he does not have the protection of his native country, which in the case of most of these asylum seekers is true. Once having been temporarily admitted, he or she submits, in written form, a detailed application to the Home Office requesting permanent refuge. This application languishes at the Home Office for an average of two years. The applicant is free to seek employment after six months of temporary admission but usually finds a grossly underpaid job immediately to repay the debt of 5,000 pounds paid by either him or her or their family. Under present recession conditions, the available jobs pay only 50 pence per hour. Only when his or her application is accepted by the Home Office, after about two years, does the applicant become an asylum seeker in the technical sense.

In some such instances, the Home Office chooses to break its silence on an application in a very intriguing manner. After months or years pass by, one day the applicant receives a letter from the Home Office informing him that it is willing to give the applicant an extended five years exceptional leave to remain and advises the applicant to go to to the Sri Lankan High Commission, obtain a new passport, and bring it to the Home Office for the appropriate stamp. To many an applicant this letter appears to be like a bonus. The anxious and pleased applicant goes, letter in hand, to the Sri Lankan High Commission in London. In the cases we have tracked down, the Sri Lankan High Commission provided the applicant with a passport without a fuss. It had nothing to lose and something to gain. For in the eyes of the international community and record keepers, Sri Lanka would have garnered one more potential voluntary repatriot, who by the very act of accepting a passport had accepted the protection of his country and thereby acknowledged his country's capacity and willingness to give such protection. From the Home Office's point of view, by accepting the protection of his country, the applicant has undermined his claim to asylumhood.

Tamils and White Britons

The majority of Tamils in Britain are no longer Phase I Tamils who are insulated from "street racism" or even Phase II Tamils who find refuge in their books and university communities but Phase III Tamils for whom attacks from young white men and police harrassment are commonplace. Daniel was doing anthropological field research in May 1992 when the Los Angeles riots broke out after an all-white jury returned a not guilty verdict in favor of four police officers whose brutal assault on Rodney King, an African-American, had been videotaped and shown to both the court and the country on television. This opened up an outpouring of reports to Daniel from Phase III Tamils in London, who maintained that when it came to police harassment and discriminatory brutality, the experience of Tamils in London was no different from African-Americans in Los Angeles. The following two reports were typical.

Case I.   Nathan (a pseudonym), a Phase III Tamil, heard his doorbell ring. At the door, he found a white man who informed him that he had bumped into Nathan's parked car and damaged it. He said that he did so because it had not been parked properly. But he handed Nathan his calling card and told him to get in touch with him if he had any questions. After the man left, Nathan went to check his car and found that it had not been parked improperly and wondered to himself whether anyone had the right to bump into a car even if it had been parked otherwise.

Several days later Nathan went to a park with his wife and their two children. While there Nathan observed that the address on the card he had received a few days earlier was in the vicinity. So he told his wife to wait for him while he tried to locate the man who bumped into his car to get details for his insurance claim.

On his arrival at the address, which turned out to be a car repair shop, the owner of the calling card greeted him by punching him in the nose. Before he had time to react, two of his garage friends joined him with steel bars in their hands. Nathan was a Tamil militant fighter in his day but had sense enough to read the odds and was also aware that his application for asylum was in line for a determination by the Home Office. So, with his shirt covered with blood from a broken nose, he decided to go to the police station and file a complaint instead.

At the police station, with blood still pouring from his nose, he began to relate what had happened to the officer in charge of taking down complaints. The officer seemed amused as he listened and refused to write down anything that was said.

As he turned to leave in exasperation, his assailant walked into the same police station and complained that he had been assaulted by Nathan. At this point the officer wrote down both their complaints and locked them up.

After having waited for hours until sundown, Nathan's wife returned home with her children. Hours later, concerned by her husband's failure to return or call, she telephoned the police and found out that he was in detention. Later, as he was being released on bail, the police officer offered to drop all charges under condition that he withdraw his complaint against his white assailant.

Case II.   Three Tamil men were walking down the sidewalk of a London street when they saw a lone Tamil being beaten up by a group of white teenagers. Two bobbies were watching the incident from across the street. The Tamil boys, who were war-seasoned Phase III immigrants, ran up to the policemen and pleaded for their intervention. The policemen, stroking their truncheons, feigned incomprehension. Recalling the murder of a Tamil man in London under similar circumstances a week earlier, they told the unresponsive policemen that now they knew what kind of protection the police gave Tamils and that if the police did not want to help them they knew how to help themselves. Having said this, they ran across the street. The white youths started to run and the Tamils pursued, caught up with them, and wrestled them to the ground. Within a few seconds, the police were there to issue arrest warrants against the Tamils.

Case III.   Sahitharan Panchatcharam was a twenty-nine-year-old asylum seeker from Sri Lanka. He was waylaid by a group of young whites and bashed to death in London's Eastham. Several of the London-based organizations working for refugees organized a protest march. Over 4,000 people of all ethnic groups joined the march. But there were only 150 Tamils.

The Trustees—all Phase I Tamils—of the Wimbledon Hindu temple refused the organizers of the march the right to hang posters on the temple premises. Their reason? "We do not want to antagonize the white community."

CONCLUSION

To be able to trust, we said, one must have the capacity and the will to tame the kind of caprice that brings pain and suffering. Granted, the taming of chance can never be absolute. And if indeed it were, one could not tell man from machine. In some cultures well-developed religious and ideological systems exist which cultivate a healthy measure of cynicism toward any and all claims to such capacities for taming chance, while others estimate them highly. Consider certain forms of karmic theory or the Buddhist First Noble Truth, "all is suffering," and the Judeo-Christian belief in each "working out one's own salvation." But in the whole range of cultures, everyday life becomes possible and even tolerable because of the fundamental, diffuse, and enduring regnancy of trust. Karma is not the first explanation but the explanation of last resort; it is an explanatory framework that is turned to under the extraordinary conditions that are what most refugees live through. Such a turn to karmic explanations is tellingly illustrated by Marjorie A. Muecke in the case of Cambodian refugees (this volume).

But what of the "culture of terror" that the Jews lived through in World War II, that the Ugandans lived through in the reign of Idi Amin, that the Cambodians lived through in the Pol Pot years, that the Tamils of Sri Lanka have lived through since 1983, and, as Beatriz Manz tells us (this volume), that the Mayan Indians of Guatemala have lived through for over five hundred years? To the extent that we have conjured up a semiotic image of culture wherein there is easy give-and-take in the trafficking of comprehensible symbols and signs, wherein conversation, in the widest sense, is sustained by common understandings and painless expectations, the culture of terror sounds like an oxymoron. But let us make it clear that cultural life is not all a matter of smooth and predictable exchanges. Rather, there is consensus and controversy, custom and craft, calculation and caprice. In all societies humans play with chance and play with trust, sometimes with pleasurable results and at other times not. Some cultures, as Barbara E. Harrell-Bond (this volume) has indicated, have normativized mistrust but—we claim—only against a densely textured background of the possibility of trusting; so much so that to mistrust becomes a privilege afforded by culture.

Our daily lives are filled with contingencies, but these are contingencies we bring under order sooner than later. There are social institutions that are intended to help us do this. The law figures prominently among these institutions, as do constitutions and conventions. But in the life of the refugee, mistrust of countryman, neighbor, friend, and family, even mistrust of the law, shatters his or her cultured world and its expectations and habits that lie at the heart of everyday life. If the laws of Sri Lanka, such as the infamous Prevention of Terrorism Act, are a rationalization of bloody violence, British immigration laws appear to be rationalizations of bloodless bureaucratic violence (La Capra 1990). And as T. Alexander Aleinikoff has so effectively shown in his contribution to this volume, international refugee law itself has the preservation of state rights in mind above that of human rights. Implicit in Aleinikoff's chapter is a call to lawyers, legal scholars, politicians, and judges "not only to state the law but to *judge it*" (Cornell 1992:166). And the judging of the law may entail, not merely breaking it, but breaking *with* it. If justice is to prevail, the law must be perennially on trial.

As violations of trust pursue the refugee from home, through camps, and into countries of asylum, mistrust begins to exchange places with trust in one's cultural life, no longer remaining a surface norm but percolating into cultural depths. Conversely, trust rises up to become an ephemeral affair, opportunistic, hypercontextual, and evaporative. It would appear that in the course of a refugee's life and in that of one who is embedded in a culture of terror, such a person is condemned to mistrust. And yes, the culture of terror is an oxymoron, but no less real for being so. And as we observed in the beginning of this chapter, in individual cases, absolute mistrust results in its own extinction, leaving behind neither trust nor mistrust but absolute helplessness. One cannot help but be moved by the most poignant and powerful testimony to the human spirit, the resilience of human hope and the capacity to trust, shown when a woman like Rigoberta Menchu, despite five hundred years of her people's unspeakable suffering under the white man's terror, can say "we must live together in a pluricultural society, and respect one another, to find room for everyone, and resolve together the problems that bind us" (quoted in Manz, this volume). But we cannot forget that there are many more less resilient souls whose despair, if not alleviated by and into trust, will sooner or later contaminate our common humanity.

NOTES

We would like to thank John Knudsen for reading our essay and offering many valuable suggestions. We, however, take full responsibility for its content.

1. All references to C. S. Peirce are to his *Collected Papers* and employ the convention of citing volume and paragraph number, respectively.

2. From the Greek *sememe*.

3. In a lucid essay on Peirce's account of the self, Vincent Colapietro (1989) makes this point in his contrast of Peirce with his fellow pragmatist, William James: "For the former, the most fundamental feature of personal consciousness is the irreducible fact of privacy whereas, for the latter, its most basic characteristic is the ubiquitous possibility of communication" (78).

4. Such hyperintegrated states are discussed in two papers by Daniel, one manifest in a syndrome called "aloneness" in north central Sri Lanka (1989) and another in the case of torture victims of the Sri Lankan civil war (1992).

5. Henceforth we shall not insist on the finer technical distinction between *representamen* (or virtual sign) and (actual) *sign* but use the latter term to cover both.

6. For example, we hold that culture is a far more dynamic phenomenon than he does, a phenomenon that is constantly creative, emergent, and capable of being apperceived in contexts of significant encounters; and that culture is not constituted of symbolic (conventional) signs alone but also of myriad other kinds of signs, chief among which are indexes and icons (for a more detailed account of our position on culture, see Daniel 1984, 1991).

7. Peirce characterized Descartes's attempt to make doubting a matter of willing as "paper doubt" or "feigned doubt" and contrasted it with "real doubt," which is doubt that at least as long as it lasts, cannot be otherwise (5.514).

8. By "Eastern Province," we intend to refer here only to the districts of Batticaloa and Amparai. The Trincomalee district may, in sociocultural terms, be treated as a transitional area between Batticaloa and northern Sri Lanka.

9. The mixed descendants of Portuguese colonizers of the seventeenth century and Sinhalese and Tamils.

10. See, e.g., De Silva 1986; Manor 1984; Tambiah 1986.

11. This district was subsequently divided into the Batticaloa and Amparai districts,

thereby sequestering the new area, first by name and then by colonization, as a Sinhalese district rather than as part of a larger area in which Tamils had a majority.

12. One of the Tamil militant groups, the Eelam People's Liberation Front, did make an ideological attempt to include the Sinhalese in its imagined, multiethnic nation of the future. Such attempts were feeble ones at best.

13. The Israeli Mossad (the rough equivalent of America's CIA) agents who were housed in the annex of the American embassy, and whose presence and advisory role in Sri Lanka's ethnic conflict is no longer a secret, are believed to have masterminded the choreography.

14. See Hoole et al. 1988.

15. Burghers are the descendants of mixed marriages between Europeans (mainly the Dutch) and the non-Europeans of the island.

16. See De Silva 1979 and Ponnambalam 1983 for a more detailed discussion of facts and figures pertaining to the discrimination against Tamils in these two areas.

17. Among other things, this act provides for arrest without warrant for "unlawful activity" (Arts. 2 and 31), detention in "any place," incommunicado and without trial for 18 months (secs. 6, 7, 11), detention without trial (sec. 15A), the treatment of confessions while in detention as admissible evidence (sec. 16) (Hyndman 1988).

18. There was a period when Sri Lanka asylum seekers were summarily deported, as it subsequently turned out to be, in violation of the law. A newspaper reporter's assiduous tracking of the fate of a couple of these deportees back to Sri Lanka and to their arrest and torture there caused sufficient protest among human rights groups in Britain that the order to deport was rescinded. Even so, less than 5 percent of Sri Lankan asylum seekers have in fact been given asylum. Instead, they are granted an "exceptional leave to remain" for a specified time.

19. This and all other statements within quotation marks that occur in this section are excerpts from interviews with Phase I Tamils obtained during field research in London carried out by either Daniel or Thangaraj.

20. To be sure, there were many among the Phase I immigrants, especially those schooled in the social sciences and some barristers, who were articulate critics of racism, classicism, and casteism; the most prominent figure among them being the current editor of the journal *Race and Class,* A. Sivanandan. Our characterization of Phase I immigrants in this chapter fits best those who chose the professions of medicine, engineering, and the hard sciences.

21. An allusion to a low caste from northern Sri Lanka whose traditional occupation used to be the tapping of toddy from palm trees. Not all Phase III refugees were members of the lower castes. The early ones were of modest means. Though, with the passage of time, each month of the late 1980s and early 1990s brought poorer and more desperate refugees. They truly had nothing to return to. They had sold their last goat or brass pot to buy their passage.

22. "Paki," is a pejorative name by which South Asians in Britain are called. It is intended to conjure up an image of poor South Asian Muslims (presumably from Pakistan) doing menial jobs, speaking a strange language, practicing a strange religion that requires them to prostrate themselves toward Mecca during prayer time wherever they happen to be, and above all, whose women dress in strange clothes.

23. *Thambi* means "younger brother." It can be used as a term of endearment but can also connote paternalism.

24. This act made it the responsibility of air and sea carriers to ensure that its passengers carried valid papers. Failure to do so made the carrier liable to heavy fines.

25. See Turner, this volume.

REFERENCES

Colapietro, Vincent
  1989   *Peirce's Approach to the Self: A Semiotic Perspective on Human Subjectivity.* Albany: State University of New York Press.
Cornell, Drucilla
  1992   *The Philosophy of the Limit.* London: Routledge.
Daniel, E. Valentine
  1984   *Fluid Signs: Being a Person the Tamil Way.* Berkeley, Los Angeles, and London: University of California Press.
  1989   "The Semeiosis of Suicide in Sri Lanka." In *Semiotics, Self, and Society,* ed. Benjamin Lee and Greg Urban, 69–100. Berlin: Mouton de Gruyter.
  1991   *Is There a Counterpoint to Culture?* 2d Wertheim Lecture. Center for Asian Studies, Amsterdam.
  1992   "The Individual in Terror." In *The Body as Existential Ground: Studies in Culture, Self and Experience,* ed. Tom Csordas, 150–180. Cambridge: Cambridge University Press.
De Silva, C. R.
  1979   "The Impact of Nationalism on Education: The Schools Takeover (1961) and the University Admissions Crisis (1970–1975)." In *Collective Identities, Nationalisms and Protest in Modern Sri Lanka,* ed. Michael Roberts, 474–499. Colombo: Marga Institute.
De Silva, Kingsley M.
  1986   *Managing Ethnic Tensions in Multi-Ethnic Societies: Sri Lanka 1880–1985.* Lanham, Md.: University Press of America.
Hoole, Rajan, Daya Somasundaram, K Sritharan, and Rajani Thiranagama, eds.
  1988   *The Broken Palmyra.* Claremont: Sri Lanka Studies Institute.
Hyndman, Patricia
  1988   *Sri Lanka: Serendipity Under Siege.* Nottingham, U.K.: Spokesman.
La Capra, Dominick
  1990   "Violence, Justice, and the Force of Law." *Cardozo Law Review* 11 (5–6): 1065–1078.
McGilvray, Dennis
  1982   "Mukkuvar Vannimai: Tamils' Caste and Matriclan Ideology in Batticaloa, Sri Lanka." In *Caste Ideology and Interaction,* ed. Dennis B. McGilvray, 34–97. Cambridge: Cambridge University Press.
Manogaran, Chelvadurai
  1987   *Ethnic Conflict and Reconciliation in Sri Lanka.* Honolulu: University of Hawaii Press.
Manor, James
  1984   *Sri Lanka in Change and Crisis.* New York: St. Martin's Press.

Peirce, Charles Sanders

1934–1935   *Collected Papers*. Vol. 5. Edited by Charles Hartshorne and Paul Weiss. Cambridge: Belknap Press of Harvard University Press.

1958   *Collected Papers*. Vol. 7. Edited by Arthur W. Burks. Cambridge: Belknap Press of Harvard University Press.

Ponnambalam, Satchi

1983   *Sri Lanka: The National Question and the Tamil Liberation Struggle*. London: Zed Books.

Schneider, David M.

1976   "Notes Toward a Theory of Culture." In *Meaning in Anthropology*, ed. Keith H. Basso and Henry Selby, 197–220. Albuquerque: University of New Mexico Press.

Tambiah, Stanley

1986   *Sri Lanka: Ethnic Fratricide and the Dismantling of Democracy*. Chicago: University of Chicago Press.

Yalman, Nur

1967   *Under the Bo Tree: Studies in Caste, Kinship and Marriage in the Interior of Ceylon*. Berkeley and Los Angeles: University of California Press.

THIRTEEN

State-centered Refugee Law: From Resettlement to Containment

T. Alexander Aleinikoff

In a world that abhors the presence of unadministered spaces or people, the presence of forced migrants must be treated as abnormal. Government authorities invariably react to refugee situations by trying first to contain them and later to eliminate them.

—LEON GORDENKER (1987)

Refugee law as it exists today is fundamentally concerned with the protection of powerful states.

—JAMES C. HATHAWAY (1990)

The concept of "refugee" both reflects and problematizes the modern construction of an international system of states. That system is premised on an understanding of the world as divided into legally equal, sovereign states, where sovereignty is taken to mean the legal right to govern demarcated portions of the globe. In such a world, individuals need to belong to a state both to ensure their protection and acquisition and to permit the system of states to ascertain which particular state has responsibility for (or control over) which persons (Arendt, 1951: 287–298). In short, the modern world operates under the motto of a state for everyone and everyone in a state.[1]

The idea of a system of states does not entail closed borders or immutable memberships. States may work out rules for the transnational movement of persons, the protection of citizens of one state in another state, and even the transfer of loyalties from one state to another. Indeed, these kinds of practices—issues of immigration and naturalization—reinforce the notion of state control over membership decisions.

Refugees, however, represent a failure of the state system, a "problem" to be "solved." As "involuntary migrants,"[2] refugees evidence a breach of the state of origin/citizen relationship, calling into question the legitimacy of a system that, in practice, relegates people to the largely unfettered exercise of sovereignty of a state over its citizens (Carens 1991). The acts of the country of origin, then, constitute an injury to both the refugee and other states. The existence of refugees, and the weight of their moral claim to protection, also puts pressure on a basic premise of international law, that state sovereignty entails plenary power to determine admissions policies. Yet affirmation of the authority of states to exclude refugees may well leave the refugee virtually stateless, unable to enter a country of asylum and unable or unwilling to return to the country of origin. The result appears to be a logical contradiction: "solution" of the "refugee problem" within the existing system of states threatens a first principle (state control over admissions) of that system.

This chapter explores the international regime of refugee law, seeking to show how legal solutions to the refugee problem are profoundly state centered. I argue that discussions of "solutions" in refugee law and policy have taken a dramatic turn in recent years, replacing an "exilic bias" with a "source control bias." This new orientation focuses attention on countries of origin, supporting repatriation and human rights monitoring before and after return. I suggest that the shift in emphasis, albeit grounded in part by humanitarian concerns, presents real risks when realized within a system committed to the protection of human rights in theory more than in practice. Ultimately, source control measures may end up being more about "containment" of migration than about improved protection of refugees. I also argue that the state-centeredness of legal discourse has shown disturbingly little concern with the actual experiences and desires of refugees themselves. Concluding with a discussion of a case study of a Salvadoran refugee family, I hope to demonstrate how the dominant state/membership discourse of refugee law may misdescribe and distort the refugee experience and the issues of trust implicit within it.

STATES AND REFUGEES

From a sociological perspective, refugees are most broadly conceptualized as involuntary migrants—persons forced to leave their habitual place of residence because of conditions that make life there intolerable. The causes of flight may be human-made (persecution, civil disorder, economic crisis) or acts of nature (floods and droughts). Narrower definitions have been suggested,[3] but what is significant about the social science conceptualizations is that notions of statehood, sovereignty, and boundaries play subsidiary roles in defining persons in need of assistance (although any complete analysis of causes and solutions could not be wholly indifferent to the forms and structures of political power).

The legal concept of refugee, in contrast, is closely related to understandings of the state, state sovereignty, and membership. The earliest notions of "sanctuary" and "asylum" followed directly from the idea of a polity having exclusive sovereignty over specified territory: when an individual fled from his or her native land to another country, presence in the receiving state offered "protection" because the country of origin could make no claim that its laws could control within the territory of another state (Kennedy 1986).

The situation of hundreds of thousands of displaced persons after both world wars, coupled with a new emphasis on human rights protection, supplied a humanitarian basis for emerging international refugee law norms, but the legal thinking remained state centered. Refugee status was predicated on the requirement that a person be outside his or her country of origin and that he or she be without the "protection" afforded by state membership (where "protection" was understood to refer, not to assistance, but rather to the acquisition of a legal status).[4] Clearly, persons who had been denationalized and were therefore stateless so qualified. But postwar humanitarianism expanded the circle to include the "de facto" stateless as well: persons for whom the bonds between them and their societies had been so disrupted, such as victims of persecution, that they had been effectively denied protection by their home countries.

The legal concept of refugee was rendered concrete in the 1951 Geneva Convention relating to the Status of Refugees.[5] The convention was drafted to deal with the situation of post–World War II Europe, where millions of persons found themselves outside their countries of origin and unable or unwilling to return. It defined "refugee" as a person who

> as a result of events occuring before 1 January 1951 and owing to a well-founded fear of being persecuted for reasons of race, religion, nationality, membership in a particular social group or political opinion, is outside the country of his nationality and is unable or, owing to such fear, is unwilling to avail himself of the protection of that country; or who, not having a nationality and being outside the country of his former habitual residence as a result of such events, is unable or, owing to such fear, is unwilling to return to it. (Art. 1 [A][2])[6]

The definition is quite clearly based on the idea that a refugee is someone who has lost the protection of his or her state, is now located outside that state, and is in need of a new guarantee of protection. That is, the "problem" to be solved is the de jure or de facto loss of membership, as measured by the likelihood of persecution on the specified grounds. Atle Grahl-Madsen, in his classic treatise, explains the convention's concept of refugee this way:

> It is characteristic of the situation of political refugees that the normal mutual bond of trust, loyalty, protection, and assistance between an individual and the government of his home country has been broken (or simply does not exist) in their case, and that they are afraid of returning to that country lest they shall have to make a complete political submission to a government which they consider repugnant and maybe also "illegal." (Grahl-Madsen 1966:79)

Similarly, James C. Hathaway (1991*b*:135) argues that the status of refugee is based on "a notion of disfranchisement or breakdown of basic membership rights." Refugees are distinguishable from other persons "at risk of serious harm" because "their position within the home community is not just precarious" but also accompanied by "an element of fundamental marginalization."[7]

Although refugee status is grounded in the idea of loss of membership, refugee law does not guarantee attainment of membership elsewhere. Recognizing the fundamental international law norm that states have complete control over the entrance of aliens into their territory,[8] the convention carefully fails to establish any duty on states to admit refugees.[9] Its central protection is the guarantee of *non-refoulement*—the right of refugees not to be returned to a country in which they would suffer persecution (Art. 33).[10] Subsequent attempts to conclude an international treaty on territorial asylum have failed (Grahl-Madsen 1980).

Furthermore, the convention neither mandates procedures for refugee status determinations nor creates an international body to make such decisions. It also fails to establish any formal reporting requirements or monitoring devices for investigating state compliance. Thus the adjudication of who is a refugee—on which all the protections of the convention turn—is left entirely to state authorities.

In a deep way, therefore, the convention fails to solve the problem that refugee status poses for the state system. The premise of state control of its borders blocks recognition of a right to asylum, yet the humanitarian norm of nonrefoulement bars return of a refugee to a place where he or she would suffer persecution. It should hardly be surprising, then, to find literally millions of refugees around the world languishing in "temporary" arrangements, not forced to return to their countries of origin but denied permanent resettlement in countries of asylum.[11]

STATE-CENTERED "SOLUTIONS": FROM EXILIC BIAS TO SOURCE CONTROL BIAS

It is commonly said that there are three "durable solutions" for refugees: voluntary return to their countries of origin, settlement in the country of asylum, and resettlement in a third country (Stein 1988:50). The underlying reasoning here is straightforward. If refugee status constitutes dissolution of "social bonds," then unmaking refugees demands the creation or reestablishment of "social bonds"— either in the country of origin or elsewhere.[12] In short, a "durable solution" repairs the tear in the state system fabric by ensuring that no individual goes without membership in some state.

For roughly three decades following adoption of the convention, it was generally assumed that external settlement of refugees was the durable solution of choice. This view—which Gervase Coles (1988:109) labels the "exilic bias" of refugee law—reflected geopolitical realities (World War II refugees would not be asked to return home), cold war doctrine (the West scored ideological points by welcoming refugees from the East), and Eurocentric humanitarianism (surely refugees were better off if they could settle in the civilized, developed West). As long as the numbers of refugees remained small, governments could proclaim generous policies of asylum. Legal advocates for refugees, too, contributed to the exilic bias, urging expansive programs of resettlement and broad interpretations of the convention's definition. The idea that refugees would seek return to their native lands—at least any time soon—seemed almost inconceivable.

In the past decade or so, we have witnessed the breakdown of the exilic approach to refugee law. A legal regime constructed to handle the problems of European refugees already settled in European countries of asylum (and individual East bloc "defectors") began to witness mass flows of refugees in the third world and the movement of third world asylum seekers to the Western developed nations. Short-term assistance to refugees in countries of first asylum began to look more long-term, as few refugees received offers of permanent resettlement from the developed world.[13] Moreover, because it was believed that many of those displaced over national boundaries were not "true" refugees (i.e., did not meet the rather narrow criteria of the convention), the need for permanent resettlement seemed less clear; once the political violence ceased, innocent victims who had not been targeted before flight could return to pick up their lives where they had left off. And as recent events in Eastern Europe and Afghanistan demonstrate, even targeted individuals may be able to return following a change in regime.

Resettlement was challenged on consequentialist grounds as well. The exilic bias was said to unjustifiably relieve countries of origin of responsibility to their citizens and other states burdened by refugee flows, to undermine a refugee's right to seek the support of the international community in obtaining safe return, and to institutionalize exile at the expense of the fundamental right to return to one's home country (Coles 1989:391).[14]

These pragmatically based considerations were supported by theoretical developments, as arguments grounded in both liberal and communitarian perspectives began to challenge the traditional case for resettlement. From a liberal, human rights approach, it was argued that the fundamental wrong done to refugees was a denial of their right to live freely in their home countries. Furthermore, forced exile violated the internationally recognized right of citizens to return to their countries of origin. From this perspective, resettlement can never be the primary remedy because it does not restore the right; rather, the "basic solution" must solve the problem of the denial of freedoms attending exile, either by preventing the conditions that compel flight or by remedying those conditions after flight (Coles 1988:201).[15] Preference for resettlement, it may also be argued, fails to appreciate the importance of ties of persons to the organic communities in which they resided prior to flight. Lawyers may be able to conceive of membership as a legal status that may be easily shed and acquired. But human beings do not so effortlessly cast off or take on a sense of belonging, roots, and ties to the land of one's ancestors (a sociological conception of membership). These communitarian considerations would favor a solution of repatriation, so that refugees can reestablish themselves within the social setting that is constitutive of their sense of self.[16]

Shrinking hopes of resettlement, combined with these theoretical considerations, have produced a fundamental rethinking of "solutions" to the refugee problem, with voluntary repatriation now considered the preferred durable solution.[17] Thus, in 1980, the Executive Committee of the UNHCR Program adopted a resolution stating that "voluntary repatriation constitutes generally . . . the most appropriate solution for refugee problems"—a conclusion it reaffirmed five years later, noting "the basic rights of persons to return voluntarily to the country of origin" and urging that "international co-operation be aimed at achieving this solution and should be further developed." The 1980s have witnessed massive returns of refugees; large numbers of Mozambicans, Afghans, Ugandans, Salvadorans, Kurds, Ethiopians, and Nicaraguans have gone home (under varying kinds of arrangements with varying degrees of coercion). In 1991, High Commissioner Sadako Ogata could proclaim that 1992 would be "the year for voluntary repatriation."[18]

The real-world conditions that precipitated the new thinking about durable solutions also led the international community to focus attention on ways to prevent mass refugee flows from occurring. The reasoning here is that an ounce of prevention is worth a pound of remedy. One obvious solution—simply closing borders—was rejected as an impermissible abridgment of the principle of nonrefoulement (although the U.S. interdiction and return of Haitian boat people is an example of a flagrant violation of international law).[19] But refugee flows could be staunched, it was argued, by undertaking efforts to ameliorate the "root causes" of mass flight across borders. In 1981, the UN General Assembly, expressing "grave concern" over the "continuing massive flows of refugees in many parts of the world," established the Group of Governmental Experts charged with producing a report, "International Co-Operation to Avert New Flows of Refugees."[20] The report, issued in 1986, identifies a number of political, socioeconomic, and natural causes of mass flows. It not unsensibly recommends that states "refrain from creating or contributing by their policies" to causes of such flows by respecting human rights, nondiscrimination norms, and international law.[21] Efforts at removing "root causes," it was suggested, could also be aided by the establishment of "early warning" monitoring mechanisms that could identify for the source country and the international community conditions likely to produce flows of refugees in the near future (Gordenker 1987).

So far, the discussion has concerned theoretical developments at the international level. But it should be apparent that the exilic bias has also lost its appeal to most of the governments of the developed West. The reasons are complicated and varied but surely include (1) a sharp rise in the number of asylum seekers (estimates for Germany this year top 350,000), which has produced virulent antialien movements in Europe and elsewhere; (2) cultural differences between refugees and their host countries; (3) large increases in outlays for refugee support programs and adjudication procedures;[22] and (4) an end to the cold war, which removed the ideological attractiveness of liberal resettlement policies (Martin 1988). These developments have led Western states to view the "refugee problem" as triggering not humanitarian concern but rather policies of control and deterrence. States, as matters of domestic law, have adopted narrow readings of the convention's definition of refugee, established policies of detention of asylum seekers, instituted new visa controls, and sought to impose sanctions on carriers who transport asylum seekers. Serious proposals have been made to amend the German Constitution, which alone among Western constitutions guarantees a right of asylum. And measures are currently being drafted which seek a united European approach to adjudicating asylum claims (Guest 1991; Martin 1992). Refugee law has become immigration law, emphasizing protection of borders rather than protection of persons.

The international preference for voluntary repatriation and concern with root causes, coupled with deterrent measures adopted by states, has produced a dramatic shift in the focus of refugee law and policy. As resettlement possibilities become more remote and "temporary" arrangements become depressingly long-term, primary attention is now being directed to the countries of origin of refugee flows. In short, in the past decade the "exilic bias" has been superseded by a "source control bias."

A RECONCEPTUALIZATION OF THE PREMISES OF REFUGEE LAW?

Does the move from an exilic bias to a source control strategy indicate a fundamental shift in the premises of refugee law? From one view, the new bias remains profoundly state centered. The deterrent policies of the West are quite clearly attempts to stop the kinds of movements of people that create practical and theoretical problems for the state system. And a preference for repatriation—whether or not conceptualized in human rights terms—is grounded in restoring the citizen to his or her state.[23] Facilitating the return of refugees removes the challenge to the sovereignty of the receiving states that the humanitarian claims of refugees inevitably pose. Indeed, once states invoke their sovereign right not to resettle refugees—an exercise of power, it should be recalled, not condemned by the convention—then repatriation becomes the only viable durable solution.[24]

Interventionist strategies in countries of origin aimed at ameliorating root causes of flight or guaranteeing safe return may be more difficult to place within the conventional model. Traditionally, refugee law has left the sending states as it found them: refugees were persons outside their countries of origin, and receiving states chose either to admit them or to send them to a third country. Only persons who could not meet the standards for establishing refugee status were returned home; and because returnees did not come within the protection of the convention, refugee law stopped at the border of the home country.

With a little ingenuity, a source control model can be explained as consistent with a state-centered approach premised on the notion of equal and independent states. First, as noted by the Group of Governmental Experts convened to report on averting large-scale flows of refugees, mass flight "may affect the political and social stability, as well as the economic development, of the receiving States, and also carry adverse consequences for the economies of the countries of origin and entire regions, thus endangering international peace and security." On this account, the creation of refugees may be characterized as an offense against the system of states warranting remedial measures by the international community (Report at 16; see Garvey 1985). State abuse of its citizens also produces problems for the state system as a whole because it threatens to undermine the legitimacy of the state system by calling into question the justness of the principle that assigns citizens to states and states to citizens (Carens 1991; Hathaway 1991*a*). In other words, the recognition of a state's sovereignty by the community of states could be deemed to be predicated on the humane treatment of the citizens assigned to the state by the state system. Thus interventionist efforts to protect human rights or civil order would be a permissible infringement on state sovereignty if it could be reasonably justified in system maintenance terms.

By contrast, "source control" strategies might be viewed as a dramatic reformulation of refugee law, replacing an emphasis on states and membership with a humanitarianism concerned with persons, not borders. The theoretical groundwork for a paradigm shift has begun. Hathaway (1991*a*) has proposed conceptualizing the definition of "refugee" in human rights terms; and Coles (1988, 1989) has suggested a human rights approach to "solutions." Demands that states respect the human rights of their citizens to prevent refugee flows may more easily be characterized as concerned with the welfare of human beings than with maintenance of the state system.

International practice may also be interpreted as moving in such a direction. Under recent repatriation arrangements, UNHCR has agreed to accompany the refugees to their home country and monitor their protection after return (certainly a role unanticipated by the drafters of the convention) (Guest 1991).[25] The creation of a safety zone for Kurds in Iraq following the Gulf War represents the zenith of intrusions into the sovereignty of refugee-producing nations and has reinvigorated the debate on humanitarian intervention (Adelman 1992; Nafziger 1991).

The implications of a paradigm shift would be considerable. Replacing state-centeredness with a robust humanitarianism would call into question the convention's definition of refugee, which covers only a small portion of involuntary migrants. Refugee law, under such an account, would be grounded on a "principle of refuge"[26] that seeks to ameliorate the suffering of all those forced to leave their home countries. The new paradigm would also put significant pressure on the requirement that a person be "outside the country of his [or her] nationality" to qualify as a refugee. From a human rights perspective, the internally displaced are at least as needy (and perhaps more vulnerable) as those who have managed to flee across national borders (Aga Khan 1990). Indeed, it may be those who are unable to flee who are most in need of assistance; at this point, refugee law would collapse into human rights law, and the shift would be complete. The possibility that refugee law could do serious human rights work in countries of origin helps account for the current political strength of the preference for repatriation. Both human rights advocates and governments of countries of asylum—for very different reasons—can support policies of return (see Chimni 1991; Coles 1988).[27]

Whether the new emphasis on source control strategies represents a corollary of a state-centered approach or instead constitutes movement toward a new paradigm may ultimately be a moot question if practical politics in the real world block serious efforts at breaching the borders of the states of origin. I fear this is likely to be the case. The work of legal scholars to the contrary notwithstanding, state authorities charged with interpreting and implementing the convention hardly appear interested in expanding the convention's definition of refugee. As to the willingness of states to take measures in states of origins to prevent refugee flows, consider the significance of the conclusion in the report of the Group of Experts cited above that "the task of averting massive flows of refugees requires improved international co-operation at all levels . . . *in full observance of the principle of non-intervention in the internal affairs of sovereign states"* (16; emphasis added).

In this respect, the unwillingness of European nations to intervene in the conflict in the former Yugoslavia, which has created more than two million refugees, may represent the norm to which the interaction in Iraq on behalf of the Kurds is the rare exception. Furthermore, the empirical evidence on repatriations is decidedly mixed. As Fred Cuny and Barry Stein (1989:293) note, "In the literature on voluntary repatriation the assertion that voluntary repatriation is the 'most desirable' durable solution is often closely followed by pessimistic evaluations of its prospects." While some repatriations have been successful, these are usually in states in which the refugee-creating conflicts have ended, either by way of a regime change or a cease-fire. Most recent repatriations, however, have occurred within the context of continuing civil disorder; and the ability of international organizations to ensure the security of the returnees has been sorely tested (Stein 1992; UNHCR Report 1991). Certainly, the early news from Cambodia is cause for considerable concern. It appears that state sovereignty is more easily transcended in theory than in practice.

Rather than a paradigm shift, then, we may well be witnessing the troubling use of a humanitarian discourse to mask a reaffirmation of state-centeredness.[28] That is, the emphasis on repatriation and root causes will help developed states justify the new strategies adopted to "solve" their asylum "crises," yet deeply entrenched practices of nonintervention will prevent serious measures to improve human rights situations in countries of origin. If this analysis is correct, then the story of change is not about the melding of refugee law into human rights law; rather, it is the exchange of an exilic bias for policies of *containment*—detention of asylum seekers, visa requirements, closing opportunities for resettlement, pushbacks, and return. These policies are grounded less in a desire to breach the walls of state sovereignty than in an attempt to keep third world refugee problems from inconveniencing the developed states. The significant risk here is that a politics of containment will have the ugly result of abandoning refugees to the very states from which they fled in search of assistance and protection. If this is so, then refugee advocates who see recent repatriation efforts as vehicles for doing human rights work within the sending countries may be unwitting allies in reinforcing the state-centered paradigm they seek to overthrow.

ALTERNATIVES AND THE VOICES OF REFUGEES

If the preceding analysis is correct, then refugee scholars and advocates would do well to stay off the repatriation bandwagon until there are far stronger reasons to believe that the international regime stands ready and able to keep its human rights commitments to returnees and other victims of persecution.

Other proposals worth investigating include nonsource control strategies that both avoid the current problems plaguing resettlement efforts and appeal to the self-interest of states. For example, Jack I. Garvey (1985) suggests that norms of state responsibility be invoked to hold sending states liable to countries of asylum.[29] And Hathaway (1991a:114) has proposed an internationalized burden-sharing scheme that would strike "a reasonable accommodation between the inevitability of special claims [of refugees] and the sovereignty of states." Another alternative that neither concedes the field to unbridled state power nor simply appeals to pie-in-the-sky humanitarianism might focus on developing strategies at the intraregional level through collaboration of countries of origin and countries of asylum.[30] Such efforts include expanded definitions of "refugee" (under the OAU Convention and the Cartagena Declaration) and multilateral security and repatriation arrangements (CIREFCA) (Arboleda 1991; Cuellar et al. 1991). Regional approaches, based on shared cultural and historical perspectives, may be able to tolerate a kind of flexibility in approach and ambiguity in status not usually deemed appropriate for universal instruments and arrangements.[31] Interventionist strategies may also appear less threatening when carried out in the name of intraregional norms rather than universal principles enforced by powerful states outside the region.

Finally, it would be wise to bring the knowledge, experience, and goals of refugees to bear on the search for alternatives. Legal scholars have generally written from a state-centered perspective, betraying a preoccupation with questions of membership that may or may not be in the best interest of refugees. Lawyers, like states, have difficulty with persons unattached to political communities because such membership is believed to be the only basis for secure possession and protection of rights. Thus legal academics in the developed states have primarily focused their attention on obtaining some form of membership for refugees who have made their way to the West. Temporary protection devices (such as the European "B" status or the U.S. "temporary protected status") are seen as acceptable only when domestic politics makes full membership impossible or when it is clear that those sought to be protected do not come within the convention definition.

Yet what is so curious about the membership bias is that it has been developed (and, in fact, imposed) by the lawyers and the legal system with little consultation with the refugees themselves. In the United States, for example, forced migrants may seek an official status only after they have been thrust into the immigration process because they have been apprehended or because they seek employment authorization. Lawyers seem to view membership as a coat that can be taken off and replaced rather than as a constitutive part of identity;[32] and the law's unexamined preference for membership rarely considers the serious consequences it poses for refugees—frequently to make return far more difficult and therefore to officially break ties with family and community in their countries of origin. The law, in this fashion, forces refugees to (re)construct their identities to gain the status that the law determines is most appropriate for them.[33] It is at least plausible that refugees might prefer an ambiguity and flexibility that does not compel an immediate consideration of identity questions and that keeps options open for future return or resettlement.

While I am fairly confident of my characterization of lawyers, I am quite unsure of my representation of the experiences and objectives of refugees. To say this is to identify a basic problem with the existing state-centered model: it has been developed by and for states and lawyers. Speaking the language of sovereignty and membership, it has viewed refugees as helpless objects of pity who must be assigned to some political community in order to have an identity at all (even the word "protection" suggests a paternalistic relationship between the powerful protector and the needy protected).[34] Few Western legal academics have any deep appreciation for, or knowledge of, the refugee experience; yet in an area where they ought to feel ill at ease imposing categories and perspectives, they have made themselves the "insiders" by adopting a discourse that keeps the discussions on their home turf.[35]

A shift to a humanitarian approach, it should be clear, does not automatically put the refugees' voices front and center. Indeed, the power of the humanitarian appeal is precisely that such refugees are stateless, helpless, and voiceless.[36] I am suggesting, therefore, that refugee issues might be considered from the bottom up, with participation by refugees in the definition of both "the problem" and acceptable "solutions." For instance, it has been suggested that the tripartite repatriation commissions consisting of the countries of origin and asylum and the UNHCR be expanded to include representatives of the repatriating refugees (Goodwin-Gill 1989*b*:384).[37] Interestingly, the vast majority of refugees who repatriate do so not as a part of an internationally sponsored effort; rather, they do so on their own. As Stein (1992:8) notes,

> The refugees are the main actors in the contemporary practice of voluntary repatriation. They are the main decision-makers and determine the modalities of movement and the conditions of reception. Refugee-induced repatriation is a self-regulating process on the refugees' own terms. The refugees apply their own criteria to their

situation in exile and to conditions in their homeland and will return home if it is safe and better by their standards. Many of the returnees are in desperate circumstances—in part because their return receives woefully inadequate international support, but they do not flee again.

The point here is not that international involvement in repatriation is not necessary but that perhaps the purpose of international assistance should be conceptualized as *facilitative* (focused on aiding refugees in effectuating their choices) instead of *control based* (helping asylum countries contain refugee flows).[38] Such an approach, it should be stressed, would not necessarily adopt a preference for repatriation; thus it would be skeptical of current arguments that a human rights approach entails return as the "basic solution" (cf. Coles 1988). The definition and prioritizing of solutions is exactly what should be left open.

Clearly further research is needed here to inform legal discussions. In the meantime, legal academics might do well to focus more on the worlds refugees construct and inhabit and less on membership and new modalities for international paternalism.

COMMUNITY, TRUST, AND LAW: ONE REFUGEE FAMILY'S STORY

On February 17, 1980, gunmen attacked the home of Mr. and Mrs. G. in San Salvador, killing Mrs. G.'s brother-in-law and a guest in the home and seriously wounding Mrs. G's sister, niece, and another guest. Mrs. G. had been an outspoken leader of her textile workers union, protesting oppressive working conditions, degrading treatment, and union-busting activities by the employer. Mr. G. had helped organize a union in the factory that he serviced as a driver. Elected general secretary, he pressed worker complaints about below minimum wage pay, poor benefits, sexual harassment, and unsafe and unsanitary working conditions. Both Mrs. G. and Mr. G. received anonymous threats, labeling them "Communists" and "subversives" because of their union work.

On the night of the attack by the death squad, Mr. G. and two of Mrs. G.'s brothers were not at home. One brother (Juan) had been arrested several months before and released after eight days of detention and torture. In the hope that the death squads would not attack their home if they were not present, Mr. G. and Mrs. G.'s brothers had stopped returning home. Following the attack, Mr. G. went into hiding and fled El Salvador in the spring of 1981, shortly after Mrs. G's brother Ramon was arrested for his union activities. Attempting to make his way through Mexico, Mr. G. was arrested and detained for fifteen days by Mexican authorities. He was deported to Guatemala but returned to Mexico City a few days later and waited there in illegal status for the rest of his family to join him.

Mrs. G. remained in El Salvador, nursing her sister and niece and caring for Ramon's child while trying to obtain Ramon's release from prison. During this time, she lived in a number of different places and, having left her employment at the factory, undertook odd jobs to support herself and her family. She did not return to her home after the night of the attack. In December 1981, Ramon was released from prison and fled the country. Three months later, Mrs. G. and her five children left El Salvador for Mexico City. In Mexico, the G.'s learned that asylum status was virtually unobtainable for Salvadorans and that the requirements for legal immigrant status were well beyond their means. For three years they remained in a legal limbo, living in seven different places on the outskirts of Mexico City and telling those who asked that they were from Veracruz. They bribed local school officials to enable their youngest children to attend school. In March 1984, Mr. G. learned that his brother had been assassinated when a bomb exploded in the car he was driving.

In 1985, tired of living in constant fear of deportation, the G.'s decided to seek entry to the United States. They were assisted by religious workers who, as part of the "sanctuary movement," helped shelter and support Salvadoran refugees in the United States. The sanctuary movement was based on the conviction that American foreign policy considerations so infected the asylum adjudication process that the cases of Salvadoran applicants were not fairly evaluated. (An extremely low approval rate for Salvadorans—particularly when compared to approval rates for Nicaraguans and Eastern Europeans—gave significant credibility to the sanctuary movement's objections to U.S. asylum procedures.) The U.S. government claimed that the activities of the sanctuary movement constituted illegal smuggling and harboring of undocumented aliens, and several sanctuary workers were prosecuted and convicted in a well-publicized trial in 1985.

The G.'s received sanctuary from a midwestern Quaker congregation. In 1988, they filed applications for political asylum to obtain authorization to work legally in the United States. Almost two years later, a local immigration official notified the G.'s of his intention to deny their applications, giving them time to submit additional documentation. Such information was provided; and, as of this writing, no final determination on their applications has been made. In 1990, Congress enacted legislation granting Salvadorans in the United States "temporary protected status" (TPS) for eighteen months. Salvadorans granted TPS may not be deported and are authorized to work in the United States, but the status grants no long-term right to remain in the United States or to sponsor other close family relatives to the United States. TPS has been administratively extended to June 1993. It is unlikely that the G.'s asylum claims will be adjudicated before the expiration of TPS.

The theme of "trust" runs throughout this disturbing account of human brutality, insensitivity, and perseverance. Indeed, as the narrative clearly demonstrates, the refugee experience is one of breaking and establishing community ties, of losing, gaining, and seeking to maintain relationships in times of great stress. At every point, trust is at stake: in the fellowship of union activity and the breakdown of government-to-citizen trust evidenced by the cruel and calculated act of

unspeakable violence; in the (sometimes clandestine) work of the sanctuary movement and the (frequently mistrusting) relationship between refugees and countries
of asylum; in the professional lawyer-client relationship, where trust is a sine qua
non for the construction of an effective application for political asylum. It is worth
emphasizing that refugee situations may sustain and engender trust (here, among
family, friends, and sanctuary workers) as well as evidence the absence of trust that
gives rise to injury and flight. There is paradox and irony here: the use of illegal
means to attain lawful ends (such as bribing a governmental official to obtain a
passport needed to flee a country of persecution); and perhaps most curious, seeking refuge in a state that has largely sided with one's oppressors back home.

It is not at all clear that the legal concepts of "membership" and "state" are
particularly helpful here. Of course, it is a "state" that sends or tolerates the death
squads and another "state" that rejects or admits persons fleeing persecution. But
this is just another way of saying that the state-centered model dominates Western
legal thinking. For the refugee, the "trust" of the state is something that is rarely
noticed or valued except when it is breached in horrendous ways. And while the
legal concept of "membership" may be important because in this world one must
normally have status to have rights, the G. family did not actively pursue legal status in the United States. They decided to apply for political asylum only as a
means of obtaining work authorization. In fact, had TPS been available at the
time, it would have much been the preferred option: it is a lower-visibility status,
and it does not require the nightmarish reliving of past events triggered by prepar-
ing an asylum application and testifying in court.

The G. family also demonstrates the complexity of membership issues. The
parents and second oldest child are intent on returning to El Salvador if it is ever
safe to do so. The eldest child, who had gone to live with other relatives in the
United States, gained legal status through a 1986 federal law granting amnesty to
undocumented agricultural workers. The third child is engaged to be married to a
U.S. citizen; lawful permanent residence should follow as a matter of course. The
two youngest children, ages fourteen and fifteen at the time of their entry into the
United States, have no desire to return to El Salvador. Again, legal rules both con-
strain and facilitate individual decisions that have enormous consequences for the
family. In this way, refugee law certainly operates on relationships of trust, but the
legal regime—as currently constructed—can hardly be said to be responsive to
the family's needs and desires for community and trust.

We tend to think of refugee law as stepping in when countries of origin have
destroyed trust. But, as we have seen, refugee law imposes rather minimal bur-
dens on receiving states and certainly does not require that refugees be offered
membership in countries of asylum. And refugee advocates who seek to "reform"
refugee law by imposing duties on states to grant membership may not be representing the best interests of refugees. There is, however, a different kind of story to
tell about the relationship of law and trust. Perhaps we should not see law's goal as
re-creating trust but rather as *substituting for it* when all reasonable hope of trust is

gone. That is, the rule of law would condemn death squads and torture, interdiction programs that violate international law, and adjudication procedures that reach decisions based not on the merits of a case but on the foreign policy of the country of asylum. To the extent that law succeeds in restraining states, it may do its most important work on behalf of refugees and trust.

NOTES

This chapter is drawn from a paper prepared for the conference "Trust and the Refugee Experience," sponsored by the UN University/World Institute for Development Economics Research in Bergen, Norway, June 1992. Thanks to the participants for comments. Howard Adelman, Jose Alvarez, Deborah Anker, James Hathaway, David Martin, and Eric Stein also provided careful, critical readings of an earlier draft.

1. This is not to say that the world lives up to its motto, but it is precisely those situations in which the actual deviates from the ideal that present such deep problems for the inter national regime (e.g., the Palestinians, Vietnamese boat people in Hong Kong).

2. See below.

3. E.g., Zolberg, Suhrke, and Aguayo 1989 (focusing on "violence" causing flight).

4. Interestingly, the earliest international measures sought to provide "refugees" with travel documents (in lieu of a national passport, which their situation made unavailable to them).

5. More than one hundred states have ratified the convention, and it is considered the foundation of modern international refugee law today (Jackson 1991).

6. The convention also included in the definition of *refugee* persons who had been considered refugees under earlier international agreements (Art. 1[A][1]).

7. See also Shacknove (1985:277): "[i]t is [the] absence of state protection which constitutes the full and complete negation of society and the basis of refugeehood."

It is intriguing that a concept that appears so directly linked to humanitarian concerns nonetheless gets explained in membership terms. This demonstrates the hold that state-centeredness has on refugee law scholarship. Furthermore, it seems to me that the dominant metaphor said to underlie the notion of refugeehood—a "severed social bond"—is not up to the task. Societies and social relations are far too complex for any easy statement of when a person has experienced the "full and complete negation of society." Refugees usually flee before this point is reached, and recognition as a refugee does not demand such a showing. For example, the *UNHCR Handbook on Procedures and Criteria for Determining Refugee Status* states that discriminatory measures against a person or group may constitute "persecution" if they "lead to consequences of a substantially prejudicial nature for the person concerned, e.g. serious restrictions on his right to earn a livelihood, his right to practise his religion, or his access to normally available educational facilities" (UNHCR Handbook para. 54). Clearly these kinds of deprivations, even if systematic and severe, fall far short of the severing of social bonds; indeed, the phrase sometimes used to describe these measures—"second-class citizenship"—implicitly suggests that some form of tie to the state and society exists. (We could develop measures of deprivation and construct a scale that identifies particularly egregious deprivations as constituting evidence of dissolution of the social bond. But then the "social bond" metaphor provides no explanatory power; it is merely the conclusion we attach to inflictions of injury that are generally considered intolerable.)

8. But see Nafziger 1983. And it should be noted that control over entry does not mean that aliens whom the state chooses to admit are without rights, either under domestic or international law (Lillich 1984).

9. And for those refugees who states admit, the convention imposes no duty to permit their naturalization; rather, in precatory language, it states, "States shall as far as possible facilitate the assimilation and naturalization of refugees" (Art. 34).

10. Even this fundamental principle yields to state interests. Article 33(2) provides that protection against *nonrefoulement* does not extend to "a refugee whom there are reasonable grounds for regarding as a danger to the security of the country in which he is, or who, having been convicted by a final judgment of a particularly serious crime, constitutes a danger to the community of that country." See Hailbronner (1986:866): "The *non-refoulement* provision of the 1951 Refugee Convention indicates that states do not lightly divest themselves of their right to control their borders, a fundamental aspect of state sovereignty."

11. See Martin 1991, which suggested that most forced migrants in developed states end up with de facto asylum because, whether or not they are determined to meet the convention's definition of "refugee," few are ever returned.

12. The goal of reestablishment of the social bond is not usually stated in "membership" terms. To so characterize the goal would be a move toward recognition of a "right to asylum," which would undermine the premise that states have unfettered authority to determine admissions policies. The careful hedging that goes on here is evident in Article 34 of the convention, enjoining contracting states to "as far as possible facilitate the assimilation and naturalization of refugees."

13. The lack of resettlement opportunities is fairly startling. The High Commissioner for Refugees reported last year:

> In 1990, of the then global refugee population of 15 million, UNHCR requested resettlement for just under 150,000 persons or approximately one per cent of the total. [Of these,] the Office registered only 52,000 departures. . . .
>
> The reasons for the shortfall in meeting resettlement requirements in 1990 are attributable to several interdependent factors which over the past years have posed obstacles in achieving this durable solution. The major impediment remains the limited number of countries offering annual refugee admission quotas. *Of the 159 member states of the United Nations only 10 governments establish and announce annual refugee resettlement quotas* (emphasis added). *(Resettlement as an Instrument of Protection,* EP/SCP/65)

Also, for numbers and diversity, see Bach 1989: 317–322.

14. There are counterarguments here, however, that must be taken seriously: in today's world, most returns are to areas still involved in civil strife or serious rights abuses; policies of host countries often make returns less than fully voluntary. UNHCR and nongovernmental organizations (NGOs) lack resources and access to effectively monitor human rights protections for returnees; focusing on repatriation undercuts assistance efforts and may lead to a watering down of the refugee definition (Harrell-Bond 1989; Stein 1992).

15. According to Coles (1988), "external settlement" can constitute a permissible solution only when (1) the basic solution is not possible and (2) the refugee freely acquires the nationality of another country and enjoys the protection of that country.

16. Goodwin-Gill (1989*b*:270): "Return is the objective to which international law

aspires; it derives from the conception of nationality in international law, being coterminous with the notions of attachment and belonging." But see Bach (1989:314), who argues that repatriation is not a return home but rather "a process of creating a new home" in a changed society.

17. New focus has also been placed on making settlement in countries of first asylum more secure and permanent through policies of development-oriented assistance that seek to help refugees become self-sufficient in host communities (Cuénod 1989; Stein 1991). For a searching critique, see Harrell-Bond 1986.

18. See also 1991 Report of the High Commissioner: "Voluntary repatriation is the most desirable of all durable solutions to the refugee problem, and remains a priority for UNHCR within the context of the limited resources available to the Office."(10).

The headlong rush toward repatriation needs some careful scrutiny. As has been recently argued by Barry Stein (1992:1–2), "The conventional wisdom regarding repatriation is wrong and activities based upon it are likely to be irrelevant at best or harmful and wasteful at worst. . . . A new 'conventional wisdom' regarding voluntary repatriation needs to recognize that most repatriation is refugee-induced and occurs under conditions of conflict. In many situations 'repatriation' is the wrong term, because there has been no restoration of the bond between citizen and fatherland. . . . Similarly, 'voluntary' is suspect, because far too many refugees go home under pressure or threat or to flee attacks by host elements in their country of asylum."

19. The case for policies of "pushback," "interdiction," and (the Orwellian sounding) "humanitarian deterrence" can be made only on the (unrealistic) assumption that all persons so deterred do not come within the convention's definition of refugee or that processing in the country of origin is a viable alternative (perhaps true in the former Soviet Union, but not in Haiti).

20. G.A. Res. 36/148, Dec. 16, 1981. See also the report by Sadruddin Aga Khan, written for the UN Commission on Human Rights, "Study on Human Rights and Massive Exoduses." UN Doc. E/CN.4/1503 (1981).

21. The report, which is short on specific recommendations, clearly reflects a compromise between developed and developing nations: states are called on to refrain from domestic policies that create refugees and to abide by principles of nonintervention whose violation is "particularly prone" to cause new massive flows of refugees (Lee 1986).

22. Hathaway (1991a:129) reports that developed states currently spend between 5 and 8 billion dollars a year on refugee determinations schemes, more than ten times the annual budget of UNHCR.

23. "Development-oriented assistance" also seeks to further community attachment.

24. Other suggestions by commentators, while innovative, likewise reaffirm state-centeredness: Garvey 1985 (state responsibility); Hathaway 1990 (international efforts to achieve resettlement by appealing to self-interest of states).

25. Development assistance for returnees also aids the local population.

26. The phrase is Goodwin-Gill's:

The "principle of refuge" is used here to signify the multifaceted duty to accord aid to those in distress, varied though its content may be. In the present context it covers, in particular, refugees in both [a] broad and narrow [sense] . . . ; those in danger of torture if returned; or those who face serious discrimination; or cruel, inhuman or degrading treatment. But the principle is potentially much wider; *a priori*, it does not exclude the shipwrecked, the victim of natural disaster, the conscientious objector or the deserter. What the law has yet to do is to contribute to the next generation of answers. (1989*a*:15, n. 43)

27. This is not to say that refugee advocates approve of deterrent measures adopted by receiving states. They clearly do not, given the serious risk that such measures deter bona fide asylum seekers and make no attempt to guarantee protection in the country of origin.

28. Or, as Eric Stein has suggested to me, a use of humanitarian talk to mask the pursuit of an interventionist foreign policy.

29. As Hathaway (1991*a*:119) notes, Garvey's solution might lead to an increase in human rights abuses if states of origin take efforts to prevent escape of the persecuted in order to reduce liability to countries of asylum.

30. Cf. Hathaway 1990:183.

31. Contrast the willingness of Western European states to provide temporary safe haven to hundreds of thousands of persons fleeing warfare in the former Yugoslavia with the deterrent measures imposed by the same states on asylum seekers from the third world.

32. Perhaps the assumption is that since refugees have no membership, they will eagerly accept membership in a country of resettlement. But this ignores that refugees are *involuntary* migrants who may want to maintain membership in their home communities. They are not immigrants who have chosen to replace one home with another. Rather, they are people who have been evicted and who are in immediate need of shelter. Whether or not they want to move their official residence must remain an open question.

33. The asylum application process compels forced migrants to construct themselves to fit domestic law categories. The process of legal definition seeks a coherent, unambiguous story that resonates with domestic policy objectives (consider the different treatment that the United States has accorded asylum seekers from El Salvador and Nicaragua).

34. See Harrell-Bond 1985.

35. Cf. Harrell-Bond (1986:25), who as a thoughtful and empathic observer of refugee situations nonetheless concedes, "However serious were my efforts to explore a social process from the insiders' point of view, I was always a spectator and as such I was limited by my own categories of thought in what I could see."

Consider, in this regard, the Declaration written at the close of a colloquium of lawyers and refugee advocates from 25 countries held to mark the 40th anniversary of the convention. While the document urges "facilitating the involvement of refugees in the resolution of their problems," it makes no specific recommendations on how this might be done. With the lawyers' attention focused on states, international law, and UNHCR, the refugee is virtually absent from the document.

36. Consider the telling response of one refugee, invited to participate in an international conference in England on refugee issues, when asked how refugees would like to be portrayed in the media: "Why not publicize our energy and our power to help ourselves?" (Harrell-Bond 1985:4).

37. Cf. Helton (1991). In an otherwise admirable examination of humanitarian aspects of the Kampuchean repatriation effort, he suggests adding nongovernmental organizations to the tripartite commission. He notes that currently "there is no systematic involvement of non-governmental organizations (or refugees) in such arrangements" (562). The use of parentheticals, I argue, is a telling indication of the international lawyer's perspective.

38. The Salvadoran *masivas* provide an example of refugee-led, UNHCR assisted,

return programs (Weiss Fagen and Eldridge 1991). See also Cuny and Stein 1989:306: "Spontaneous repatriation restores a refugee's sense of his own effectiveness and importance, while organized repatriation excludes refugees from tripartite commissions and gives them little voice in the modalities and conditions of their return."

REFERENCES

Adelman, Howard
    1992   "Humanitarian Intervention: The Case of the Kurds." *International Journal of Refugee Law* 4: 4–38.

Aga Khan, Sadruddin
    1981   "Study on Human Rights and Massive Exoduses." United Nations Document E/CN.4/1503.
    1990   "Looking into the 1990s: Afghanistan and Other Refugee Crises." *International Journal of Refugee Law* (Special Issue): 14–28.

Arboleda, Eduardo
    1991   "Refugee Definition in Africa and Latin America: The Lessons of Pragmatism." *International Journal of Refugee Law* 3: 185–207.

Arendt, Hannah
    1951   *The Origins of Totalitarianism.* New York: Harcourt Brace.

Bach, Robert
    1989   "Third Country Resettlement." In *Refugees and International Relations,* ed. Gil Loescher and Laila Monahan, 313–332. Oxford: Oxford University Press.

Carens, Joseph H.
    1991   "States and Refugees: A Normative Analysis." In *Refugee Policy: Canada and the United States,* ed. Howard Adelman, 18–29. Toronto: York Lanes Press

Chimni, B. S.
    1991   "Perspectives on Voluntary Repatriation: A Critical Note." *International Journal of Refugee Law* 3: 541–546.

Coles, Gervase
    1988   "The Human Rights Approach to the Solution of the Refugee Problem: A Theoretical and Practical Enquiry." In *Human Rights and the Protection of Refugees under International Law,* ed. Alan E. Nash, 195–222. Halifax, N.S.: Institute for Research on Public Policy.
    1989   "Approaching the Refugee Problem Today." In *Refugees and International Relations,* ed. Gil Loescher and Laila Monahan, 373–410. Oxford: Oxford University Press.

Cuéllar, Roberto, Diego Garcia-Sayán, Jorge Montano, Margarita Diegues, and Leo Valladares Lanza
    1991   "Refugee and Related Developments in Latin America: Challenges Ahead." *International Journal of Refugee Law* 3: 482–498.

Cuénod, Jacques
    1989   "Refugees: Development or Relief?" In *Refugees and International Relations,* ed. Gil Loescher and Laila Mohanan, 219–254. Oxford: Oxford University Press.

Cuny, Fred, and Barry Stein
  1989   "Prospects for and Promotion of Spontaneous Repatration." In *Refugees and International Relations,* ed. Gil Loescher and Laila Monahan, 293–312. Oxford: Oxford University Press.
Garvey, Jack I.
  1985   "Toward a Reformulation of International Refugee Law." *Harvard International Law Journal* 26:483–500.
Goodwin-Gill, Guy
  1989*a*   "The Language of Protection." *International Journal of Refugee Law* 1:6–19.
  1989*b*   "Voluntary Repatriation: Legal and Policy Issues." In *Refugees and International Relations,* ed. Gil Loescher and Laila Monahan, 255–292. Oxford: Oxford University Press.
Gordenker, Leon
  1987   *Refugees in International Politics.* London: Croom Helms.
Grahl-Madsen, Atle
  1966   *The Status of Refugees in International Law.* Vol. 1. Leyden: A. W. Sijthoft.
  1980   *Territorial Asylum.* New York: Oceana Publications.
  1986   "Protection of Refugees by Their Country of Origin." *Yale Journal of International Law* 1:362–395.
Guest, Iain
  1991   "The UNHCR and Refugee Protection: A Non-Specialist Analysis." *International Journal of Refugee Law* 3: 586–605.
Hailbronner, Kay
  1986   "Non-Refoulement and 'Humanitarian' Refugees: Customary International Law or Wishful Legal Thinking?" *Virginia Journal of International Law* 26: 857–896.
Harrell-Bond, Barbara E.
  1985   "Humanitarianism in a Straightjacket." *African Affairs* 84: 3–13.
  1986   *Imposing Aid: Emergency Assistance to Refugees.* Oxford: Oxford University Press.
  1989   "Repatriation: Under What Conditions Is It the Most Desirable Solution for Refugees? An Agenda for Research." *African Studies Review* 32: 41–69.
Hathaway, James C.
  1990   "A Reconsideration of the Underlying Premise of Refugee Law." *Harvard International Law Journal* 31: 129–183.
  1991*a*   "Reconceiving Refugee Law as Human Rights Protection." *Journal of Refugee Studies* 2:113–131.
  1991*b*   *The Law of Refugee Status.* Toronto; Austin, Texas: Butterworths.
Helton, Arthur C.
  1991   "The Role of Refugee, Humanitarian and Human Rights Law in Planning for the Repatriation of Kampuchean Asylum Seekers in Thailand." *International Journal of Refugee Law* 3: 547–563.
Jackson, Ivor C.
  1991   "The 1951 Convention Relating to the Status of Refugees: A Universal Basis for Protection." *International Journal of Refugee Law* 3: 403–413.
Kennedy, David
  1986   "International Refugee Protection." *Human Rights Quarterly* 8:1–69.

Kerll, Horst-Wolfram
   1990   "New Dimensions of the Global Refugee Problem and the Need for a Comprehensive Human Rights and Development-oriented Refugee Policy." *International Journal of Refugee Law* (Special Issue): 237–251.

Krenz, Frank E.
   1966   "The Refugee as a Subject of International Law." *International and Comparative Law Quarterly* 15: 90–116.

Lee, Luke T.
   1986   "The Right to Compensation: Refugees and Countries of Asylum." *American Journal of International Law* 80: 532–567.
   1987   "Toward a World without Refugees: The United Nations Group of Governmental Experts on International Co-Operation to Avert New Flows of Refugees." *British Yearbook of International Law* 57: 317–336.

Lillich, Richard B.
   1984   *The Human Rights of Aliens in Contemporary International Law.* Manchester: Manchester University Press.

Martin, David A.
   1988   "The New Asylum Seekers." In *The New Asylum Seekers: Refugee Law in the 1980s,* ed. David A. Martin, 1 20. Boston: Martinus Nijhoff.
   1991   "The Refugee Concept: On Definitions, Politics and the Careful Use of a Scarce Resource." In *Refugee Policy: Canada and the United States,* ed. Howard Adelman, 30–51. Toronto: York Lanes Press.
   1992   "Restrictive Practices Affecting Asylum Seekers: A Preliminary Report." Manuscript prepared for the Committee on the Legal Status of Refugees of the International Law Association.

Nafziger, James A. R.
   1983   "The General Admission of Aliens under International Law." *American Journal of International Law* 77: 804–847.
   1991   "Self-Determination and Humanitarian Intervention in a Community of Power." *Denver Journal of International Law and Policy* 20: 9–39.

Shacknove, Andrew E.
   1985   "Who Is a Refugee?" *Ethics* 95: 274–284.

Stein, Barry
   1988   "The Nature of the Refugee Problem." In *Human Rights and the Protection of Refugees under International Law,* ed. Alan E. Nash, 47–72. Halifax, N.S.: Institute for Research on Public Policy.
   1991   "Refugee Aid and Development: Slow Progress Since ICARA II." In *Refugee Policy: Canada and the United States,* ed. Howard Adelman, 143–170. Toronto: York Lanes Press.
   1992   "Policy Challenges Regarding Repatriation in the 1990s: Is 1992 the Year for Voluntary Repatriation?" Manuscript.

Suhrke, Astri
   1983   "Global Refugee Movements and Strategies of Response." In *U.S. Immigration and Refugee Policy: Global and Domestic Issues,* ed. Mary Kritz, 157–173. Lexington, Mass.: Lexington Books.

UNHCR

1979   *UNHCR Handbook on Procedures and Criteria for Determining Refugee Status.* Geneva: UNHCR.

1980   Executive Committee of the UNHCR Program, Conclusion 18, 31st sess. (Voluntary Repatriation). Geneva.

1985   Executive Committee of the UNHCR Program, Conclusion 40, 36th sess. (Voluntary Repatriation). Geneva.

1986   Report of the Group of Governmental Experts on International Co-Operation to Avert New Flows of Refugees. A/41/324. Geneva.

1991a   Note on International Protection. A/AC.96/777. Geneva.

1991b   Report E. Geneva.

1991c   Report 65. Geneva.

Weiss Fagan, Patricia, and Joseph T. Eldridge

1991   "Salvadoran Repatriation from Honduras." In *Repatriation under Conflict in Central America,* ed. Mary Ann Larkin, Fred Cuny, and Barry Stein, 117–184. Washington, D.C.: Hemispheric Migration Project, Center for Immigration Policy and Refugee Assistance, Georgetown University; Dallas: Intertect Institute.

Zohlberg, Aristide R., Astri Suhrke, and Sergio Aguayo

1989   *Escape from Violence: Conflict and the Refugee Crisis in the Developing World.* Oxford: Oxford University Press.

CONTRIBUTORS

T. Alexander Aleinikoff is Professor of Law at the University of Michigan, Ann Arbor.

Barbara E. Harrell-Bond is a social anthropologist. She is the Director of the Refugee Studies Programme, Queen Elizabeth House, Oxford University.

E. Valentine Daniel is Professor of Anthropology at the University of Michigan, Ann Arbor.

Michael M. J. Fischer is Professor of Anthropology at the Massachusetts Institute of Technology.

John Chr. Knudsen is Professor of Anthropology at the University of Bergen.

Mary N. Layoun is Associate Professor of Comparative Literature at the University of Wisconsin, Madison.

Beatriz Manz is Professor of Geography at the University of California, Berkeley.

Marjorie A. Muecke is Professor in Anthropology and Nursing and teaches at the School of Nursing at the University of Washington.

Jeffrey M. Peck is Associate Professor of Germanic Studies at Georgetown University.

Julie M. Peteet is Assistant Professor of Anthropology at the University of Louisville.

M. Nazif Shahrani is Associate Professor in the Department of Anthropology and Uralic and Altaic Studies at Indiana University, Bloomington.

Muhammad Siddiq is Professor of Arabic Literature in the Department of Near Eastern Studies at the University of California, Berkeley.

Yuvaraj Thangaraj is a doctoral student in anthropology at the University of Rochester.

Stuart Turner is a Senior Clinical Lecturer in Psychiatry and Co-Director of the Traumatic Stress Clinic, University College, and Middlesex School of Medicine, London.

Eftihia Voutira is Research Associate of the Refugee Studies Programme. She is a philosopher and an anthropologist.

INDEX

Abortions, 44–45
Abu-Lughod, J., 173
Accad, Evelyn, 139–140
Adnan, Etel, 139, 140
Afghan refugees, 187–206; community of, within camps, 196–199, 200, 201; demographics of, 193–194; internal, 202 n.1; in Iran, 187, 188, 192, 193, 200, 202 n.10; mistrust aid organizations, 189, 199–200, 201; mistrust government, 195–196, 201; in Pakistan, 10, 178–179, 187–188, 192–202; resistance among, 198, 199, 200; self-identity of, 189–190, 192 193; in Western countries, 195; women, 198
Aguayo, Sergio, 2, 189
Aid, to refugees, 174, 179, 180; in camps, 197–198, 210–218; cheating in, 216, 218, 219; host government's role in, 209, 212–213, 214, 215, 217; mistrust in, 189, 199–200, 201; by nongovernmental agencies, 210, 212, 213, 214; power hierarchy in distribution of, 211–218, 219; refugee-worker relationship in, 4–5, 21, 22–24, 29, 209–211, 215–217, 218, 219; trust among agencies of, 211–217; UN coordinates, 210, 212
Alamehzadeh, Reza, 133
Aleinikoff, T. Alexander, 6, 11, 252
Alienation, 66–67, 90, 91
Amnesty International, 58
Ansari, Zafar Ishaq, 189–190
Antonovsky, Aaron, 37
Arab refugees. See Palestinian refugees

Argueta, Manlio, 156–157
Asia Minor, 74, 76, 78, 173
Asian refugees, 111, 117. See also Cambodian women refugees; Vietnamese refugees
Assimilation, 28–29, 173, 174, 175; in Germany, 106–107, 108–109, 111, 112–116, 118–119; resistance to, 170, 171, 177–178, 184
Asturias, Miguel Angel, 155–156
Asylum, 26, 27, 258; assimilation after, 28–29; in Germany, 102– 103, 104, 105, 107, 109, 263; in Great Britain, 61–62, 248–249; persecution after, 56, 102, 103; temporary, 260, 261, 263, 266. See also Resettlement
Avoidance, 43–44, 64–65
'Azzām, Samīra, 93, 95

Bakhtin, Mikhail, 2
Bataan, 20
Baudrillard, Jean, 8
Bettelheim, Bruno, 4
Borders, 89–91; state controls, 260, 264
Bourdieu, Pierre, 1
Brecht, Bertolt, 75, 77, 81
Buddhism: Cambodian Theravada, 36–37, 38, 39–41, 46–48; karma in, 37, 39–40, 47; Sinhalese, 231, 232–234, 238; on suffering, 36, 37, 39–40; on trust, 36–37, 39, 209; on truth, 209; on women, 37

Cacoyannis, Michael, 82
Cairo Accords, 169

Cambodian women refugees, 7, 36–55; abortions by, 44–45; avoidance symptoms of, 43–44; as Buddhist, 36–37, 39–41, 46–48; in camps, 44, 45–46, 47, 48; identity of, 41; kinship traditions of, 45; not trusted, 42–43, 44, 49, 59; psychological support for, 43–44, 46, 47, 48; repatriated, 265; resettled, 47, 48; separated from children, 44–46; suicide by, 42; survival strategies of, 38–39, 44–45, 49; trauma of, 43, 48, 59; trust by, 37; trust regenerated for, 46–47; virtue of, 41–44

Camps, refugee, 13, 207–224; for Afghans, 196–199, 200, 201; aid given in, 21, 22–24, 197–198, 210–218; for Cambodians, 44, 45–46, 47, 48; community maintained in, 196–199, 200, 201; as heterogeneous or multicultural, 210–211, 218; identity maintained in, 174; in Lebanon, 168, 169, 172, 173, 174–177, 178–179, 180–181, 182; as limbo, 18–19, 19–21; in Pakistan, 197–198, 201; for Palestinians, 95–96, 97–98, 99, 174–177, 182–184; socialization in, 20–21; social structure of, 209–211; trust/solidarity in, 174–177, 182–184; UN-run, 169, 174, 179, 180; for Vietnamese, 20; women restricted in, 176

Catholic Church, 156–157
Cavafis, C. P., 73–74, 77
Centlivres, Pierre, 178
Centlivres-Dumont, Michline, 178
Chambers, Robert, 208–209
Chandler, David, 40–41
Chedid, Andree, 139, 140
Children: assimilate, 28–29; mistrust/trust of, 207, 208; socialization of, 17–18, 27; terror affects, 159, 160–161
Chile, 67
Coles, Gervase, 260, 264
Colson, Elizabeth, 208
Constantine, King of Greece, 76
Cooke, Miriam, 139, 140
Culture: as process, 2–3; trust as construct of, 209, 228–229; violence as norm in, 208
Cuny, Fred, 265
Cyprus, 73–74, 80, 82–83, 84 n.4

Daniel, E. Valentine, 6, 10, 11, 117–118, 170, 181, 207, 209, 220, 227, 229, 230, 249, 250
Danieli, Yael, 43–44
Darwīsh, Maḥmūd, 92–93, 99 n.4
Davis, John, 208
Davis, Mike, 129

Dehlavi, Jamil, 142
Denial, 49
Depression, among refugees, 62, 65, 131
DeVos, George, 207
Disappeared, the, 154
Displaced persons. *See* Refugeeism/refugees, internal
Dorfman, Ariel, 154, 163
Drawe, Mathias, 143
Duncan, Dr. Julianne, 48
Duras, Marguerite, 139
Durkheim, Emile, 207

Ebrahamian, Ghassem, 132
Egoyan, Atom, 138, 141, 142
El Salvador, 57, 158–159, 160–161, 268–269
Erikson, Erik, 37, 207
Evans-Pritchard, E. E., 212
Exile, 23–24; Iranian refugees in, 130–134; migration compared to, 133–134; Palestinians in, 168, 170, 171–175, 177–179, 180, 181; resistance to, 170, 171, 172–173, 174–175, 177, 178–179, 180, 181; trust lacking in, 130–131

Family: Cambodian, 41, 42; destroyed, 16, 57, 58–59, 161; identity based on, 17–18, 24–25, 26–27, 41; torture/terror affects, 57, 58–59, 69, 161; trust in, 57, 58–59, 169, 172, 182, 183, 208; Vietnamese, 17–18, 24–25, 26–27
Fanon, Franz, 143
Farr, Grant, 188
Fassbinder, Rainer Werner, 143
Fear. *See* Terror
Ferguson, James, 173
Films, refugee, 127–128, 129–133, 143–144; on Holocaust, 143; Indian, 141–143; Iranian, 132–134, 139; Palestinian, 138, 139–141; as therapy, 145–146; Vietnamese, 134–138
Fischer, Michael M. J., 8–9, 117
Forrest, David, 17
Freire, Paulo, 162
Frey, Gerhard, 102–103

Gambetta, Diego, 24
Gandhi, Rajiv, 237
García Márquez, Gabriel, 164–165 n.3
Garvey, Jack I., 266
Geertz, Clifford, 36, 38, 190
Geneva Convention (1951), 259–260, 264, 265, 271 n.5

Germany, 102–125; Asian refugees in, 111, 117; asylum policy in, 102–103, 104, 105, 107, 109, 263; citizenship based on blood in, 112, 118; differentiation of foreigners in, 109–116, 117–120; guest workers in, 103, 104, 105, 110, 114–115, 117; "Heimat" concept in, 103, 109, 112–113, 115, 116, 118, 119–120; hostility to refugees in, 102, 103; identity in, 105, 106–107; immigration to, 104, 105, 106, 114; integration into, 106–107, 108–109, 111, 112–116, 118–119; internal refugees in, 103, 105, 110, 111, 117; nationalism in, 105–106, 115; numbers of refugees in, 104, 108; racism in, 103, 104–105, 106, 107, 108, 110–111, 114–115, 119; Tamil refugees in, 239, 240; Turks in, 110, 111, 113, 143–144; "volk" concept in, 115–116; xenophobia in, 8, 103, 104, 105, 106 107, 108, 109, 114–115, 119

Ghatak, Ritwik, 142

Ghosananda, Maha, 50 n.5

Goodwin-Gill, Guy, 273–274 n.26

Gordenker, Leon, 257

Grahl Madsen, Atle, 37, 259

Great Britain, 59 62, 65; asylum policy in, 61–62, 248–249; racism in, 247, 248, 250–251; Tamil refugees in, 225, 232, 240–251

Greeks: invade Asia Minor, 74, 76, 78, 173; as refugees, 74, 76, 80, 81

Guatemala, 9, 151–167; community in, 162–163; the disappeared in, 154; internal refugees in, 152; ladino-Indian relationship in, 153, 155, 163; mistrust in, 162; Spanish treatment of Indians in, 152 153, 155; repatriation in, 161, 163; resettlement from, 152, 164 n.1; terror/violence in, 152–164

Gupta, Akhil, 173

Habibi, Imil, 91–92

Harrell-Bond, Barbara, 2, 10, 229, 252

Hathaway, James C., 257, 259, 264, 266

Hawkins, Latasha, 129

Heder, Stephen, 40

Heidegger, Martin, 1

Hijrah, 190–192, 193, 197, 200

Hirschon, Renee, 208

Hitler, Adolf, 115

Holocaust, 143

Hong Kong, 19, 20

Hsu, Francis L. K., 207

Hussain, Syed S., 197

Identity, 5, 13, 22; Afghan, 189–190, 192–193; based on family, 17–18, 24–25, 26–27, 41; based on past, 24–26, 88; based on place, 170, 171, 173–174, 175, 178, 180, 183; female, 119; as fluid or ambivalent, 6, 38; German, 105, 106–107; loss of, 38, 94, 168; maintenance of, 174; Palestinian, 88, 170, 171, 173–174, 175, 178, 180, 183; as refugee, 78, 83, 162–163; Vietnamese, 17–18, 24–25, 26–27

Immigration control, 60–61, 260, 264

India: involved in Sri Lanka, 234, 237–238, 239, 240; refugees from, 141–143

Iran: Afghan refugees in, 187, 188, 192, 193, 200, 202 n.10; refugees from, 130–134, 139

Iraq, 264, 265

Jabra, Jabra Ibrahim, 97

Jalben, Felipe Ixcot, 155

James, William, 225

Janata, Alfred, 187–188

Jayawardena, J. R., 237, 238

Jeyepalan, V. I. S., 118

Jihad, 191, 192, 193, 197, 200

Jiménez, Bernardo, 162

Kanafani, Ghassan, 93–94, 95–96, 97–98, 99 n.4, 139

Kapoor, Raj, 134

Karma, 37, 39–40, 45, 47, 251 252

Ka Sunbaunat, M. D., 47

Keller, Stephen L., 126, 127, 143, 145, 146

Kheleifi, Michel, 138, 139, 146

Khmer. See Cambodian women refugees

Khmer Rouge, 38–40, 41, 43, 44

Kinzer, Stephen, 102

Knudsen, John Chr., 5, 6–7, 117–118, 181, 207, 209, 220

Koppel, Ted, 129

Krystal, Henry, 38, 43

Kurd refugees, 61, 264, 265

Kureishi, Hanif, 143

Kuwait, 181

Las Casas, Bartolomé de, 152–153

Lamorisee, Albert, 131

Layoun, Mary N., 7–8

Lebanon: films of, 139; refugee camps in, 168, 169, 172, 173, 174–177, 178–179, 180–181, 182

Lenin, V. I., 187, 190

Levi, Primo, 3, 4, 5, 31–32 n.21, 66

Levinas, Emanuel, 128

Lévi-Strauss, Claude, 21
Literature, refugee, 117–118, 129, 144–145; on
    border, 89–91; on homeland, 89, 90, 91–93;
    mistrusted, 76–80; narrative time v. story
    time in, 76–77, 85 n.9; Palestinian, 87–88,
    89–99, 139–140; on refugee as revolutionary,
    89, 93, 96–98; on returning to homeland,
    89, 96, 98–99; trust in, 128; written as wit-
    ness, 155–156
Loescher, G., 220 n.1
Lowenthal, David, 109
Lyotard, Jean-François, 128

Mai Thu Van, 135, 137–138
Malawi, 219
Malinowski, Bronislaw, 211
Malkki, Liisa, 6
Man, as sign, 225–226
Manz, Beatriz, 9, 252
Maronites, 168–169
Marsella, J. Anthony, 207
Martín-Baró, Ignacio, 57, 154, 158–159,
    160–161
Masud, Muhammad K., 191
Mauss, Marcel, 211
Memory, 76; filtered, 31–32 n.1; terror affects,
    161; of trust, 75, 81
Menchú, Rigoberta, 155, 163–164, 253
Mexico, as refuge, 152, 164 n.1, 268–269
Migrants, 133–134; involuntary, 257, 258,
    274 n.32
Minh-ha, Trinh T., 135–138, 139
Mistrust, 4, 73–86; by Afghans, of aid groups,
    189, 199–200, 201; by children, 208; as cul-
    tural value, 2; faithlessness as, 74; of govern-
    ment, 38, 195–196, 201; in Guatemala, 162;
    as reaction to torture, 230; of refugee narra-
    tive, 76–80; v. trust, 76, 77–78, 80, 82; trust
    overwhelmed by, 228–229
Mollica, Richard, 43, 44, 46, 48, 67
Montesinas, Antonio, 153
Muecke, Marjorie A., 2, 7, 209, 227, 252
Muhajirin, 10, 189–192. *See also* Afghan refugees
Muhammad, 187, 190, 191
Mukherjee, Bharati, 144, 145
Muslim refugees. *See* Afghan refugees; Palestin-
    ian refugees; Tamil refugees

Naficy, Hamid, 131, 132
Newland, K., 190
Nguyen Du, 135, 136

Nguyen Hue, 136
Nieh, Hualing, 144–145
Norway, refuge in, 14, 20, 23, 27–28
Nostalgia, 180–181

Ogata, Sadako, vii, 262
Ören, Aras, 113

Pacheco, Gerardo, 162
Pakistan, Afghan refugees in, 10, 178–179,
    187–188, 192–202
Palestine Liberation Organization, 171, 180
Palestinian refugees, 8, 9, 87–101, 168–186, 189;
    alienation of, 90, 91; on borders, 89–91;
    camps for, 95–96, 97–98, 99, 174–177,
    182–184; diaspora, 88–89; as exiles/stateless,
    168, 170, 171–175, 176, 177–179, 180, 181; feel
    betrayed by other Arabs, 172, 181–182; films
    by, 138, 139–141; on homeland, 89, 90,
    91–93; identity of, 88, 170, 171, 173–174, 175,
    178, 180, 183; internal, 92; in Kuwait, 181; in
    Lebanon, 168–186; literature of, 87–88,
    89–99, 139–140; nationalism of, 92, 171;
    numbers of, 168; oral culture of, 88–89; on
    repatriation, 89, 96, 98–99, 170, 171, 177–178,
    184; on resettlement, 177–178; as revolution-
    aries, 89, 93, 96–98; seen as terrorists, 96,
    99; survival techniques of, 175–176; trust/
    solidarity of, 174–177, 182–184; trust lacking
    in, 172, 182; women, 176
Pandey, Gyanendra, 141–142
Peck, Jeffrey M., 8
Peirce, Charles Sanders, 225, 226, 230
Peteet, Julie M., 9
Plato, 73
Poirier, Richard, 8, 89
Posttraumatic stress disorder, 62, 64, 65

Qur'an, 190, 191, 192, 193

Racism: in Germany, 103, 104–105, 106, 107,
    108, 110–111, 114–115, 119; in Great Britain,
    247, 248, 250–251
Ramsay, Rosalind, 43
Rasmussen, O. V., 44
Räthzel, Nora, 105, 106
Reciprocity, 211
Refoulement, 260, 262
Refugeeism/refugees: causes of, viii, 262, 263,
    265; control by, 4, 21, 26; defined (legal sta-
    tus of), 20, 38, 59, 170, 178–179, 180,

188–189, 259–260, 264, 265, 266, 271 n.7; as
destabilizing, 81, 82, 168–169, 257–258, 264,
265; economic, 61; internal, vii, 59, 92, 103,
105, 110, 111, 117, 152, 202 n.1, 264; marginalized, 96; massive flows of, 262, 263–264, 265;
media attention on, 126, 127–128; numbers
of, vii, 59–60, 187, 193–194; politicized,
96–98; prevention of, 262, 263, 264, 265;
reception of/reaction to, vii–viii, 61, 102–104,
217, 262; screened, 19, 20, 21, 22, 61; as sociological category, 126–127; stereotyped, 60,
102–103, 115, 116; uncertainty in, 113,
116–117, 177; as victims, 106
Refugee law, 11, 252, 257–278; as exilic, 258,
260–261, 262, 265; Geneva Convention as
basis of, 271 n.5; as humanitarian, 258, 259,
260, 262, 263, 264–265, 266, 267; as source
control, 258, 263 265, 266; as state-centered,
258, 259–260, 262–263, 264, 265, 266, 267,
270, 271 n.7
Reitz, Edgar, 123 n.26
Relief. See Aid
Renais, Alain, 139
Repatriation, 20, 258, 263, 266, 267 268; to
Cambodia, 265; forced, 260, 262; to
Guatemala, 161, 163; Palestinians on, 89,
96, 98–99, 170, 171, 177 178, 184; trust in,
151; UNHCR on, 261–262, 264
Resettlement, 47, 48, 81, 260, 261, 263, 267;
resisted, 177–178
Rushdie, Salman, 142–143, 144

Saderi, Dadi, 113
Sa'edi, Gholem Hossein, 133, 134
Said, Edward, 8, 89, 184
Samayoa, Joaquin, 160
Santer, Eric, 143
Sayyad, Parviz, 133
Schneider, David M., 229
Seyhan, Azade, 113
Shahrani, M. Nazif, 10, 170–171
al-Shaykh, Hanan, 139, 140
Siddiq, Muhammad, 8, 209
Sidwa, Bapsy, 142
Sierra Leone, 208, 220
Signs, 225–227
Silence, 20–21, 22, 25, 26, 43–44, 46, 151
Singh, Kushwant, 142
Sliwinski, Marek, 195
Slote, Walter, 17, 18
Smith-Hefner, Nancy, 42

Sobrino, Jon, 157
Socialization: in refugee camp, 20–21; in Viet
Nam, 17–18, 27
Söllner, Alphons, 114–115
Soteriou, Dido, 7, 76, 77, 78–79, 81
Soviets, in Afghanistan, 187–202
Sri Lanka, 11, 225–256; ethnic hostility in,
227–228, 229, 231, 232–240; India involved
in, 234, 237 238, 239, 240; nationalism in,
231, 232–233, 234, 235; Tamils in (see Tamil
refugees); trust betrayed in, 227–228,
229–230, 241
Stein, Barry, 265, 267–268
Suhrke, Astri, 2, 189
Suicide, 42, 61
Survival strategies, 19–24, 29, 38–39, 44 45,
175–176; denial as, 49; silence as, 20–21, 22,
25, 26

Talib, Abu, 191
Tamil refugees, 11, 225–256; in Germany, 239,
240; in Great Britain, 225, 232, 240–251; in
India, 238, 240; separate state for, 242, 244;
split among, 236–240
Terror (fear): children affected by, 159, 160–161;
community destroyed by, 154; as debilitating, 157; family destroyed by, 161; in
Guatemala, 152–164; hope within, 157; to
maintain control, 156, 158; secrecy in, 154;
silence in, 151; therapy after, 163; trust
eroded by, 157 158
Thangaraj, Yuvaraj, 8, 10, 11, 229, 239
Therapy: film production as, 145–146; psychological, 43–44, 46, 47, 48; after terror or torture, 67–70, 160–161, 163; testimony as,
67–68, 69–70, 163
Thränhardt, Dieter, 110, 111
Tichy, Roland, 116
Timerman, Jacobo, 57, 58, 160, 161
Torture, 7, 56–72, 151; covert, 58; defined, 56,
57; in El Salvador, 57; physical reaction to,
62, 63, 65, 227; psychological reaction to,
62–67, 69, 230–231; purpose of, 58, 59, 63,
68, 69; sexual, 63, 64–65; survivors' guilt
after, 66, 67, 68, 69; therapy for, 67–70,
160–161, 163; in Turkey, 61; witnesses
affected by, 159, 160
Trauma, 43, 227–228, 230–231; avoidance to
deal with, 64–65; flashbacks after, 48; silence
after, 43–44, 46; stress after, 62, 64, 65. See
also Terror; Torture

Trust: among aid agencies, 211–217; associated with pleasant experiences, 225; betrayed/breached, 74, 75, 77, 80, 81, 93–94, 227–228, 229–230, 241; breakdown of, 269–270; Buddhism, 36, 37, 39, 209; in camps, 4–5, 174–177, 182–184; in children's development, 207; as cultural construct, 2–6, 7, 13, 36, 209, 228–229; defined, 169; family-based, 57, 58–59, 169, 172, 182, 183, 208; gullibility linked to, 229; inability to, 207, 208; inner-directed, 172–173, 182; lacking or lost in refugees, 42–43, 44, 49, 59, 74, 118, 130–131, 172, 182; memory of, 75, 81; misplaced, 66; mistrust compared to, 76, 77–78, 80, 82; mistrust overwhelms, 228–229; past and homeland linked to, 76, 77–78, 80, 82, 181; in refugee narrative, 128; relationships linked to, 37, 56, 65, 169, 172; in repatriation, 151; restoration of, 46–47, 209, 219; in Sierra Leone, 208, 220; torture and terror erode, 57, 58–59, 63, 69, 157–158; value of, 229
Tuneay, Ragit, 143–144
Tuqān, Fadwā, 90, 91, 93
Turkey, 61, 74, 82–83; refugees from, 110, 111, 113, 143–144
Turkistan, 189
Turner, Stuart, 7, 248
Tyler, Stephen, 128, 134

United Nations, 59; on Cyprus problem, 82–83
United Nations High Commissioner for Refugees (UNHCR), vii, viii, 198, 199, 213, 214, 215, 216; and agencies, 210, 212; refugee defined by, 38, 271 n.7; on repatriation, 261–262, 264
United Nations Relief and Works Agency (UNRWA), 169, 174, 179, 180
United States, refugees in, 20, 47, 48, 152, 164 n.1, 195, 269

Vargas Llosa, Mario, 164–165 n.3
Vietnamese refugees, 13–35, 134–138; boat people, 6–7, 14, 19; family-based identity of, 17–18, 24–25, 26–27; films by, 134–138; internal (north to south flow), 14–15; resettled, 14, 19, 20, 23, 27–28; socialization of, 16, 17–18, 27
Voutira, Eftihia, 2, 10, 229

Wallenrod, Konrad, 137
Weber, Max, 2
Wiener, Annette, 211
Witte, Karsten, 116, 118
World Food Program, 199

Xenophobia, German, 8, 103, 104, 105, 106–107, 108, 109, 114–115, 119

Yassin, Nessié, 75, 76, 81
Yehoshua, A. B., 145
Yugoslavian refugees, vii, 265, 274 n.31
Yusuf, Muhammad, 194

Zolberg, Aristide R., 2, 189, 201

Designer: U. C. Press Staff
Compositor: ComCom, Inc.
Text: 10/12 Baskerville
Display: Baskerville
Printer: Haddon Craftsmen, Inc.
Binder: Haddon Craftsmen, Inc.

HV 640 .M57 1995

Mistrusting refugees